Basic Techniques of
PSYCHODYNAMIC
PSYCHOTHERAPY

Basic Techniques of
PSYCHODYNAMIC PSYCHOTHERAPY
Foundations of Clinical Practice

Edited by MICHAEL P. NICHOLS, Ph.D.
and THOMAS J. PAOLINO, Jr., M.D.

Foreword by GEORGE STRICKER, Ph.D.

GARDNER PRESS, INC.
New York & London

GARDNER PRESS, INC.
19 Union Square West
New York 10003

All foreign orders except Canada and South America to:
Afterhurst Limited
Chancery House
319 City Road
London N1, United Kingdom

Library of Congress Cataloging-in-Publication Data

Main entry under title:

Basic techniques of psychodynamic psychotherapy.

   Includes bibliographies and index.
   1. Psychotherapy—Technique. I. Nichols, Michael P.
II. Paolino, Thomas J., 1940-   . [DNLM: 1. Psych-
therapy—methods. WM 420 B311]
RC480.5.B374 1986   616.89′14   85-15849
ISBN 0-89876-111-5

Book Design by Raymond Solomon

PRINTED IN THE UNITES STATES OF AMERICA

To
Lee B. Macht, M.D.
1937-1981
Friend and Mentor

Contributors

George Ainslie, M.D.
Jefferson Medical College at
Coatesville
Coatesville, Pennsylvania

William A. Binstock, M.D.
Deceased
Harold N. Boris
Cambridge Hospital
Cambridge, Massachusetts

Herbert N. Brown, M.D.
Cambridge Hospital
Cambridge, Massachusetts

Charles P. Ducey, M.D.
Cambridge Hospital
Cambridge, Massachusetts

Ronald J. Karpf, Ph.D.
Northeastern Neuropsychiatric
Institute
Center Square, Pennsylvania

Jonathan E. Kolb, M.D.
McLean Hospital
Belmont, Massachusetts

Lawrence C. Kolb, M.D.
Veterans Administration Hospital
Albany, New York

Zvi Lothane, M.D.
Mount Sinai Hospital
MedicalSchool
New York, New York

Joseph M. Natterson, M.D.
U.C.L.A. School of Medicine
Los Angeles, California

Michael P. Nichols, Ph.D.
Albany Medical College
Albany, New York

Thomas J. Paolino, M.D.
Butler and the Miriam Hospitals
Providence, Rhode Island

Reuben J. Silver, Ph.D.
Albany Medical College
Albany, New York

Contents

Foreword

It is rare for patients to enter psychotherapy with the ability to deal with their internal and external worlds in a comfortable and efficient manner, and unusual for them to enter with a clearly demarcated formulation of their problems and goals. It is the therapist's initial task, and one that may be repeated continuously throughout treatment, to assist the patient in arriving at such a problem formulation, and then reaching the established goals. Most therapists will agree that such movement is not simply a natural process of unfolding, and therapists are more than just observers who function best when they interfere least with this natural process. It is incumbent upon the therapist "not just to sit there, but to do something," although it often is the case that, in an educated way, the best stance is "not just to do something, but to sit there" in an empathic and responsive manner. Recognizing that the appearance of doing nothing is often doing something, it is the task in this volume to examine what it is that therapists do.

Depending upon the level of abstraction at which we function, there may be three or four major approaches to psychotherapy, or there may be literally hundreds. The umbrella chosen by the authors is a broad one, embracing all of the various psychodynamic approaches. As such it should be of relevance to the Freudians and the neo-Freudians, the ego psychologists and the object relations theorists, therapists for adults and for adolescents (and, to only a lesser extent, for children). Psychoanalysis as we know it began with Freud, but there have been at least dozens of significant revisionists, from Jung and Adler to Kohut and Kernberg, each of whom presents crucial changes in perspective, while remaining within the basic framework that defines a psychodynamic approach.

To belong within the psychodynamic framework a number of assumptions must be accepted. All behavior must be seen as determined, with behavior defined generically to include thoughts and feelings as well as actions. Unconscious processes exist, so that the determinants are multiple and often out of the immediate awareness of the individual. The contents of the unconscious are historically cumulative, so that early experiences give shape to later ones. There are acrimonious debates about how early the experiences are, how current they can be, and at which point(s) the most important formative experiences occur, but there is agreement that the person does not act freely in a historical vacuum. And, finally, the psychodynamic approach is marked by a conviction that a key element in the process of change is understanding, and that it is crucial to understand the resistance to change that will occur, with transference being one of the key forms that such resistance will assume.

The varieties within this simple framework are myriad, and in many cases contradictory, so that agreement can only be achieved at a high level of abstraction. The psychodynamic literature has become so voluminous that no scholar can possibly be familiar with it all, and many retain a sense of being current by excluding large portions of that literature, often with the disdainful attitude that what they omit is not really psychoanalysis.

As one might expect, given the orientation toward understanding of psychodynamic approaches, the overwhelming preponderance of the writings in the field is concerned with "why" questions, and all too little of it with "what to do" questions. Fledgling psychodynamic psychotherapists can develop an impressive ability to explain patients' problems, but often are much less well versed in how to intervene in an effective and helpful manner. If they look to the literature, authors such as Greenson, Menninger, Langs, Wolberg, and Bibring will prove to be helpful, but the list is a limited one. Further, most of these technical volumes deal with psychoanalysis, which is the best known of the psychodynamic approaches, but hardly the most widely practiced.

Psychodynamic psychotherapy is not simply the adulterated practice of psychoanalysis. The introduction of parameters such as reduced weekly frequency, face-to-face sessions, and shorter extension in time necessitate alterations in technique and goals. To expand on a metaphor coined by Freud and woven throughout this volume, we begin with the pure gold of psychoanalysis and create a variety of alloys by adding not only the copper of suggestion, but a variety of other substances, and in a variety of proportions. The crucial step beyond the metaphor is the recognition that gold is not always the best material, and that some alloys are better suited for some purposes.

Building upon a framework initially established by Bibring, Nichols and Paolino have set for themselves the task of explicating what it is that psychodynamic psychotherapists do and, true to the orientation, placing what is done in a historical context so the reader can also appreciate why it is done. Depending on one's preferences, it would have been possible to combine some of the categories, or to subdivide them further, or even to select somewhat different ones, but however the organization occurs, these are the interventions that the psychodynamic psychotherapist has available.

The volume provides a rare combination of the scholarly and the practical. The historical–theoretical chapters furnish the context for understanding, while the technical chapters illustrate the applications of the intervention. It is important to note that the more scholarly approaches do not neglect the clinical, and incorporate some appreciation of the implications for application, while the more practical approaches do not take the form of an atheoretical cookbook, but retain a recognition of the overreaching theoretical framework within which applications occur.

Because of the comprehensive approach taken, it is likely that different parts will be valued differently by various readers, but there is something of value in this book for all psychodynamic psychotherapists. The more experienced practitioners are likely to find the technical chapters interesting, but to discover in the historical chapters a fascinating source of information that adds a new dimension of understanding to interventions already well within their grasp. Beginning therapists will appreciate the scholarly context, but are likely to place the greatest value on the extremely practical and clinically sophisticated guides to interventions, replete with clinical examples that illustrate the points being made. Whatever individual alloys are constructed from the elements that are provided, the clinician should be richer for having this material available, and the editors are to be thanked for bringing it together in an imaginative and thoughtful organizational schema.

GEORGE STRICKER, PH.D.

GARDEN CITY, NEW YORK

Preface

Psychodynamic psychotherapy is being rediscovered by a new generation of clinicians. Competing approaches—behavioral, experiential, and family systems—have not lost their grip on the imagination, but time has proved them useful adjuncts rather than replacements for psychodynamic psychotherapy. For a quick fix of troubling symptoms, these alternative methodologies have demonstrated their worth. But none of them offers the same hope of deep and lasting personality change as psychodynamic psychotherapy.

At the same time that psychodynamic ideas are once again commanding interest, there is considerable vagueness and disagreement about the fundamentals of technique. Most recent writing in this field falls into one of three categories: discussions of abstract concepts, such as transference and countertransference; exploration of pathological syndromes, especially narcissistic and borderline conditions; or specialized approaches to treatment, such as those of Heinz Kohut, Otto Kernberg, Merton Gill, and Robert Langs. Missing from this valuable array, however, is a single comprehensive analysis of basic techniques.

It is important—no, essential—that clinicians understand transference and resistance, and know something about how they are manifest in various groups of patients. No matter how much they understand, however, clinicians must translate their understanding into action. They act first to create the necessary conditions for therapy, and second to bring about new insight and understanding.

Contrary to the misunderstanding of many novices who try to practice psychodynamic psychotherapy, the patient does not come in and start opening up the secrets of the unconscious mind to a therapist, who then applies the appropriate technique. Nor does the patient "just start talking." This is a common fallacy, and it is a common error in technique to tell the patient no more than, "Speak freely." Free association, which is the sine qua non of what the patient must do to uncover the unconscious, is so unusual that it requires more careful explanation than is usually given. The patient must be taught, at the outset, to enter a dreamlike state, to let his or her thoughts drift where they will, and to report everything that comes to mind. What happens next—when the therapist intervenes to shape new understandings—is a complex art.

Our purpose here is to examine this complex art in more depth than is done in most texts. For that reason we contacted a group of experienced clinical practitioners and teachers, and asked each one to explore at length the implications and applications of a particular technique.

Our target audience is those who seek the broadest possible understanding of psychodynamic practice. For students in training, many of the issues addressed in these pages will be new. They will find, in one place, discussions of historical and contemporary perspectives on every aspect of psychodynamic technique. Experienced professionals will find classic themes discussed in the light of the latest thinking in our field. Every effort was made to ensure that each chapter presents the most thorough and comprehensive discussion possible of its subject matter. For that reason this book should serve as an invaluable resource for anyone wishing to learn more about any or all of the basic techniques of psychodynamic psychotherapy.

For purposes of analysis, we have divided psychodynamic psychotherapy into six techniques: suggestion, catharsis, manipulation, confrontation, clarification, and interpretation. Breaking down what is in fact a complex amalgam of technique into six specific types of interventions enabled us to examine the details of the therapeutic art in the maximum depth. Of course any subdivision of a complicated enterprise is necessarily artificial. We thus begin with an introduction, describing how the separate pieces fit together. Furthermore, you will see that each of the individual authors has been careful to explain how every technique relates in context with the others.

The organization of this book permits it to be used in one of two ways. Because of its comprehensive outline, it can be utilized as a basic text on technique. Alternatively, because each chapter stands alone as a sophisticated analysis of a particular technique, it can be employed as a supplemental text for students, or as a sourcebook for anyone looking for a complete discussion of any of the basic techniques.

The editors wish to thank the authors for devoting so much energy to this writing. All are busy professionals with many competing demands, yet they managed to find the time to do an enormous amount of research and writing—and rewriting. Thank you all.

We would also like to thank the staff at Gardner Press for bringing this project into print. Thank you, Gardner, Lance, and Marsha for your thoroughgoing professionalism and for the personal warmth you have shown us.

Basic Techniques of
PSYCHODYNAMIC
PSYCHOTHERAPY

1
Introduction

MICHAEL P. NICHOLS, Ph.D.

Today there is such a bewildering variety of psychoanalytic theories that it often seems impossible to stay informed. New syndromes stimulate new conceptual models, spawning an ever-increasing number of theoretical positions, each with its own specialized approach to treatment. The fact that competing approaches are usually practiced and taught in isolation from one another further magnifies this sectarianism. Just to keep up with the latest developments in treatment of the borderline syndrome or narcissistic personality disorder would be a full-time job. In response to this complex heterogeneity, students and practitioners alike are tempted to ignore the foundations of psychodynamic therapy, in favor of mastering the intricacies of specialized approaches. This unfortunate and premature concentration gives the illusion of competence, but it is built on a weak foundation.

The innovators of specialized systems are usually well-trained experts, thoroughly grounded in the basics of their profession. Kohut and Kernberg, for example, mastered classical psychoanalytic theory and technique long before they developed their unique modifications. Those who come later, drawn to the latest developments, often take shortcuts that result in their knowing about "transmuting internalizations" or "splitting," but being unable to recognize transference and resistance—or know how to respond to them.

Theory and technique are reciprocally related in such a way that it is impossible to understand one without the other. Still, one of the ironies of current practice is that there is greater continuity in technique than theory. Early in this century, Freud defined basic conditions for psychoanalysis that have been changed little since. Elaborations and modifications

1

of psychoanalytic theory have affected the *content* of our understanding far more than the *form* in which we convey it to our patients.

As we move from psychoanalysis to psychodynamic psychotherapy, things become a bit more complex. In classical psychoanalysis interpretation remains the principal and definitive technique (Strachey, 1934; Greenson, 1967). Modifications are available, in the form of "parameters" (Eissler, 1953), but these are reserved for special circumstances. The parameters of psychoanalysis are the legitimate techniques of psychodynamic psychotherapy.

Here we pause briefly to define "psychodynamic" in order to place our ideas in context. The literature is filled with descriptive labels for psychoanalytic treatment—psychoanalysis, psychoanalytic psychotherapy, psychodynamic psychotherapy, insight-oriented psychotherapy, uncovering psychotherapy, exploratory psychotherapy, and so on. We do not propose to evaluate these terms, or to offer exhaustive distinctions among them. This is a book about technique, intended to be more practical than Talmudic.

"Psychodynamic" is an ambiguous term, used to describe a variety of approaches based on psychoanalytic principles, but including supportive methods as well. Often this usage extends to approaches that are not analytic, in which "interpretations" may be primarily emotive, educational, or manipulative. "Psychodynamic psychotherapy," as we use it, means understanding and explaining based on the broad principles of psychoanalytic theory. This type of therapy is designed to uncover and illuminate, linking the present to the past, and behavior to motivation. Psychodynamic is not, however, a synonym for psychoanalytic (Paolino, 1981); it is a more encompassing viewpoint, according to which psychopathology is a product of repression and ignorance of one's own mind, and therapy is designed to bring insight primarily through understanding of resistance and transference. Various psychodynamic perspectives differ on *what* is repressed, *how* the mind works, and *how to* bring about insight; psychoanalytic refers specifically to Freudian principles and techniques.

Thirty years ago, in what is now considered a classic paper, Bibring (1954) defined the basic techniques of psychodynamic psychotherapy. He listed five—suggestion, catharsis, manipulation, clarification, and interpretation—and elaborated their technical application and curative effects. Although there are numerous alternative classifications (e.g., Greenson, 1967; Langs, 1973), we believe that Bibring's inventory is a good one, with one exception. We have added confrontation to the catalog because we believe that it is basic and useful.

Like any list of techniques, this one is somewhat arbitrary. Different labels could be attached to any of the six, and the number could be changed by condensing two categories (say suggestion and manipulation) into one, or by further subdividing the basic six. Our answer to possible criticism on these grounds is simple: the number we chose is useful and the categories widely acknowledged. A more serious shortcoming would be leaving out major categories of intervention. Regardless of how long we make the list or what names we choose, it is essential that we not omit fundamental procedures. What about analyzing transference, or overcoming resistance, for example? To look (in vain) for chapters in this volume on these and many other essential operations would be to commit a category mistake. Analyzing transference and overcoming resistance are complex operations, including attributions of meaning and many activities. Once the attributions are made—say, that a patient is projecting archaic feelings onto the therapist—then the clinician must intervene. And there are only a limited number of ways in which psychodynamic therapists actually intervene. The techniques described in this book are those basic activities of psychodynamic psychotherapy, not the theoretical –diagnostic–intervention complexes that are often referred to in the literature.

Bibring's purpose was not simply to list the basic techniques, but to describe how to apply them and explain how they cure. He succeeded brilliantly, and his article remains an important guide to practice. Our purpose, in this volume, is to expand on Bibring's seminal ideas and to bring them up to date with current developments in the field. Our aim is to equip the reader with enough knowledge of basic techniques to know how to intervene and enough understanding of their purpose to know when to intervene. The complete clinician will continue to read and reread theories of personal development and maldevelopment. Sufficient grasp of theory enables one to master the literature and shine in academic discussions. But those who would help real people must discover how those theories apply to unique individuals, not to a set of abstract generalizations.

The six techniques described in this book are the fundamental instruments for psychodynamic investigation of the human mind and for the alleviation of unhappiness. Take special note of the second clause, the alleviation of unhappiness. It is this goal that motivated modifications in classical psychoanalysis and that is responsible for the technical considerations that distinguish psychodynamic psychotherapy from psychoanalysis. Freud was committed to truth. Knowledge, not health, was for him the highest value. Elevating understanding to the paramount psychoanalytic value made interpretation supreme. As long as clinicians limit themselves to expanding their patients' knowledge, there is little need to be anything but an oracle.

In some circles psychoanalysis is a religion, with its own dogma and holy quest for truth. This is understandable—life is complex and it is comforting to give over uncertainty to a higher power—but it has had a stifling effect on the field. Viewed from the perspective of classical psychoanalysis, some of the techniques in this book are unorthodox, even heretical. They were introduced by compassionate healers, who went beyond thinking and knowing to feeling and acting, in order to treat the whole human personality. In many texts these other techniques are not emphasized; they are considered "copper that alloys the pure gold of psychoanalysis." But they are used by intuitive therapists, including psychoanalysts. It is not possible to remain pure and limit oneself exclusively to interpretation and also be an effective agent of cure. These modifications should neither be shunned nor used uncritically. It is this conviction that made us decide to include two chapters on every technique: first examining the history and theory of the intervention, and then exploring its application.

Each of the six basic interventions is designed for a specific purpose and is appropriate to particular circumstances in treatment. However, they are unified by a common purpose: psychodynamic understanding and cure. Before considering the techniques separately, we will briefly discuss how, taken together, they achieve their curative effect.

Freud first defined the goal of analytic treatment as making the unconscious conscious (Breuer & Freud, 1895). Later, when he developed the structural theory, he revised the formulation to emphasize achieving rational control over the dark forces of the mind: "Where id was, there shall ego be" (Freud, 1923). Recently Brenner (1976) stated that the goal of analytic treatment is to alter the patient's psychic conflicts in such a way as to eliminate or alleviate their adverse effects. This statement has the advantage of covering both symptomatic and characterological change, and of avoiding the false dichotomy of cure *or* self-knowledge. Psychodynamic psychotherapy offers both, cure *through* self-knowledge.

These formulations are valid, but abstract. Since this is a practical manual, our concern is not so much with defining metapsychological goals as with explaining, in concrete terms, how to achieve therapeutic effects. We are not concerned here with subtle processes that may be going on covertly—desensitization, reinforcement, and so on—but rather with the major vehicles of cure, the processes we deliberately aim for. The two major vehicles of cure in psychodynamic psychotherapy are insight and emotional experience.

The primary goal of psychodynamic psychotherapy is insight. When the therapist intervenes, the ultimate purpose should always be to foster understanding. That interpretations are designed for this purpose is fairly obvious. But the other techniques must also be organized with this goal in mind. Other, mediating processes, such as tension reduction through catharsis, ultimately will foster understanding. Even when nonanalytic interventions are deemed necessary, as expedients or in emergencies, they should do as little as possible to interfere with learning, and they should eventually be subject to analysis.

As important as insight is, we believe that emotional experience is equally vital. By emotional experience we do not mean expressing feelings. Rather we mean experiencing, with emotion, hidden and private aspects of the self, in the context of a significant relationship. This may sound like a "corrective emotional experience" (Alexander & French, 1946), which cures through the power of the relationship. But this is not what we mean either. Advocates of a corrective emotional experience generally work in an active fashion, placing themselves at center stage and joining the patient as one of the principal actors in the therapeutic drama. Most patients welcome this active participation. In their confusion and uncertainty, struggling adults redouble their dependency on experts, hoping at last to find an idealized parent figure. For their part most experts are equally willing to accept the status that this dependency conveys upon them, and consequently exaggerate their own role. Most of us have illusions of therapist as hero, zapping patients with lightning bolts of wisdom.

Self-exploration in the patient is not something that the therapist can actively bring about. Rather it is something that the therapist allows to happen; being present but standing out of the way and allowing the patient to unfold, to open up, and to experience inadmissible interior realities. This is a courageous act on the part of the patient (facing the self as it is), but this more complete openness to experience is requisite to self-knowledge and prerequisite to fundamental personality reorganization.

Only by gradually experiencing deeper layers of the archaic personality can patients know the truth about themselves. Some of what they find is frightening, reason enough to turn away. But entwined with destructive instinctual forces are hidden potentials for growth and development—the roots of a more passionate life and deeper interpersonal relationships.

The foundations and applications of psychodynamic interventions are examined in the following chapters. Each intervention is considered thoroughly, so that by studying the chapters, the reader should be equipped to understand how and when to apply the basic techniques. The authors chosen to write these chapters are all well-trained, thoroughly experienced clinicians. They are also known as clear and sensitive teachers, who are highly sought after as clinical supervisors. All of the authors have been exposed to a wide variety of influences, though most can be described as practicing within the mainstream of psychodynamic therapy. In addition each author brings a little something extra to the analysis of a particular technique. This special sensitivity is a product of having studied and written about that technique, and having something worthwhile to say about it.

Only by reading both chapters on each of the basic techniques will the reader be able to achieve the fullest understanding of its application. We thought it would be useful, however, to introduce the material with a brief summary and analysis, to prepare the mind and whet the appetite for what follows.

OVERVIEW OF THE BASIC TECHNIQUES

Suggestion

Suggestion is one of those ubiquitous features of helping relationships that operate, often out of awareness, no matter what is going on officially. Various critics, notably Jerome Frank (1961) and Arthur Shapiro (Shapiro & Morris, 1978), have impishly delighted in pointing out that psychotherapists of all persuasions achieve their results through suggestive influence far more than they realize. Suggestion is, in fact, precisely the kind of direct and homey procedure that psychodynamic practitioners normally eschew. Whatever short-term gain is achieved through suggestion is thought to be canceled out by contaminating and forever precluding resolution of the transference. Psychodynamic therapy is aimed at rendering human events intelligible and therefore amenable to rational control—so is not suggestion out of bounds? Yes, and no.

First, since suggestions may be a universal feature of influencing relationships, therapists must be aware of their subtle and covert tendencies to make suggestions. This awareness enables the therapist to decide when and how to use suggestion, rather than to continue to do so blindly. Second, we must distinguish between *non*analytic and *anti*analytic procedures. The former are ways of influencing patients that are not based on rational interpretation. They may bring about valued behavior changes *and* they do not interfere with subsequent understanding. Antianalytic procedures, on the other hand, are interventions that obscure and block understanding. Rather than simply declare ourselves on the side of the angels—"Whenever *we* deviate, it is nonanalytic"—we urge the reader to keep this distinction in mind when reading the chapters on suggestion. Kolb's chapter in particular raises many objections to even the well-intentioned use of suggestion, and it is thus one of the most provocative chapters ever written on the subject.

Suggestion takes place when the therapist takes advantage of an authoritative relationship by inducing in the patient various ideas, feelings, or behaviors that are relatively uninfluenced by the patient's logical or realistic thinking. It is a phenomenon that occurs between a therapist in an authoritative role and the patient in a dependent role (Bibring, 1954). The consequences of suggestion range from the patient's slight tendency to believe and obey to the patient's almost unlimited credulous obedience.

Freud's definition of suggestion (Freud, 1888–89, p. 82) is as valid today as it was during his time.

> I should like to put forward the view that what distinguishes a suggestion from other kinds of psychical influence, such as a command or the giving of a piece of information or instruction, is that in the case of suggestion an idea is aroused in another person's brain which is not examined in regard to its origin but is accepted just as though it had arisen spontaneously in that brain.

Direct suggestions are explicit and unambiguous verbal attempts to induce in the patient a specific idea, feeling, or behavior. Direct suggestion might take the form of a command or a directive, such as "take this medication," or "stop acting that way." Or the direct suggestion might be in the form of advice, such as, "If you continue not sleeping, you will injure your health." Whether the suggestion is a command or advice, the message is explicitly stated. As Charles Ducey points out, direct suggestion has a limited range of application in modern psychotherapy.

Indirect suggestion uses the same forces as direct suggestion but the ideas the therapist wants to induce in the patient are less explicit, and might even be imperceptible to a third party observing the interaction. Indirect suggestion is nonverbal, not because words are not used, but because the therapist's verbalizations are only indirectly connected through a series of associations to a message that the therapist wants to implant in the patient's mind. However, even though the intervention is implicit and indirect, the therapist should be conscious of the idea he or she is trying to communicate and should have a specific goal in mind.

Direct suggestions are commonplace and easily identified. Perhaps an illustration of indirect suggestion would be helpful. Let us take the case of a 21-year-old college senior who has delusions that he is terminally ill. Upon hearing about this for several sessions, the therapist switches the subject to ask the patient about his applications to graduate school. By focusing on the future, the therapist is indirectly communicating to the patient that he is in fact not about to die. Another example is the patient who feels inferior and unable to do a specific job. The therapist tells the patient about available job openings, indirectly suggesting that the patient is capable of doing those jobs. Another example of indirect suggestion is the placing of a box of tissues beside the chair of a patient. By putting them there, the therapist indirectly communicates the message, "You need not fear crying in here; it's okay to cry." (Recognizing that leaving tissues out may also convey undesirable messages—I expect you to be dependent; I will provide for your needs; you may take something of mine with you—highlights the issue.)

In his splendid chapter on history and theory, Ducey points out that theorists have tended to ignore suggestion in favor of more exotic types of influence. Once Mesmer's dramatic cures were judged to result from suggestion, and not animal magnetism, he was discredited. Freud first used, and then discarded, suggestive hypnotherapy; but according to Ducey, he retained a healthy respect for the value of indirect suggestion in psychotherapy.

Freud discovered what was only hinted at in mesmerism, namely, that love, *Eros*, lies behind the screen of suggestion. Ducey writes, "Like the person in love, the compliant and suggestive subject replaced his or her own ego-ideal with the object." As elsewhere Freud was able to illuminate the role of suggestion by going beyond the obvious and the surface to the subtle and unconscious heart of the matter. Ducey traces Freud's thinking and subsequent modifications, using the topic of suggestion to provide a *tour de force* examination of the development of psychoanalysis. He also brings in diverse ideas from related disciplines, including social learning theory, cognitive theory, and social psychology. Although his chapter is rich in theory, it is also eminently practical, as Ducey takes time to offer a number of practical clinical applications of his ideas.

Ducey argues convincingly that suggestion is all the more pervasive in nondirective psychodynamic therapy because patient and therapist are unaware of their subtle, and mutual, suggestive influences. He also uses the research literature to explain some anomolous clinical findings—for example, some of the reasons why people who seek psychotherapy may *not* be particularly susceptible to suggestion, and what the implications of this fact are for practice. One other example will illustrate the wide range of practical implications in Ducey's analysis. Delinquents, he points out, seem not to be suggestible only as long as they stay on the level of consciousness. In fact, "with most pathetic slavishness, they act out the unconscious desires of their parents, to whom they only *appear* intransigently opposed."

Catharsis

Catharsis is not, strictly speaking, a technique, but an outcome. One does not do catharsis, one promotes it. Still we have chosen to use the word in this form to maintain balance with the other techniques, which are described by single words.

Catharsis is derived from the Greek word *katharsis*, meaning to cleanse, purge, and purify (Laplanche & Pontalis, 1973). In psychotherapy it means to remember with strong feeling. The dual emphasis is on memory and affect, not on action. Hitting someone may make you feel better; more likely it will make both of you feel worse. But in either case, it is not catharsis. The reason that some people make this mistake is that "catharsis" has been freighted with the surplus meaning of getting rid of something, originally feelings, but later impulses as well. Freud, himself, used the idea of catharsis in this way. For him the value of catharsis was tied to his (early) hydraulic model of emotions—the human mind as a vessel that can fill up with emotions, and so must periodically be drained. Nonsense! As Nichols makes clear in his chapter on the history of catharsis, it does not get rid of anything. On the contrary, remembering with feeling helps recover experience, and, perhaps even more important, it helps people become more feelingful and more alive.

Catharsis played a pivotal role in Freud's development of psychoanalysis, and the success of the cathartic method helped confirm that neurotic patients were suffering from pathogenic emotional influences from the past. When Freud subsequently shifted his emphasis to understanding, rather than purging, traumatic memories, catharsis fell out of favor. Today catharsis is described by analytic writers in terms of subtle condescension usually reserved for prodigal children—lively, but not very grown up.

The role of catharsis in contemporary psychodynamic psychotherapy is further diminished by a reaction against the emotional excesses of the human potential movement. If "they" use catharsis, it must not be entirely kosher. In the chapters on catharsis in this book, these facile assumptions are challenged and some novel recommendations for intervention are offered. Nichols and Kolb describe how to focus feelings, counter defenses, and facilitate the expression of unconscious thoughts and feelings. These chapters emphasize that some of the controversy about catharsis is fanned, not only by confusion about what the term means, but also by the discomfort many of us experience in the face of strong and painful emotion.

Manipulation

The word "manipulation" is toxic and conjures up distasteful images that blind us to sober evaluation of this aspect of psychotherapy. This point was driven home to us when one analyst, well known for manipulating his patients' social environments, was outraged that we asked him to write a chapter on manipulation

Manipulation is not exploitation. Rather, as George Ainslie explains, it is a means of influencing motivation by altering the balance of ambivalence. Manipulation can be defined as seeking therapeutic change in the patient by purposely changing the external environment in an attempt to mobilize dormant mental processes of adaptation. It is important to keep in mind that the external environment is not limited to concrete objects. The critical concept is that the therapist changes what is perceived by the patient. This might be words, people, or attitudes. An example of manipulation is arranging for a phobic patient to be exposed to the dreaded object. Or a therapist might purposefully probe painful themes, thereby engendering anxiety to motivate change.

Manipulation is distinguishable from suggestion in that it does not influence the patient to adopt a desired conviction as a result of the therapist's persuasive powers. Instead the therapist's manipulation causes a redirection of psychical forces within the patient, taking advantage of the patient's susceptibility to authority, so that psychical processes take over in a way that facilitates the progress of psychotherapy. Suggestion uses persuasion; manipulation uses artful influence.

Suppose a patient comes to therapy, not to change, but to please his father. Recognizing this, the therapist informs the patient that she expects him to act of his own free will and to be responsible for his own therapy. The patient, still eager to please parental figures, gradually assumes more autonomy toward his therapy, paradoxically trying to be independent in order to please the therapist. The example just given demonstrates more than suggestion, since the manipulation was not directed at getting the patient to adopt a desired conviction because of the therapist's persuasive power. Instead the therapist redirected psychical forces within the patient by manipulating the patient's desire to please.

Manipulation of the environment promotes learning by subjecting the patient to experiences habitually avoided. This produces direct benefits through desensitization, and indirect benefits by stirring up dormant feelings—grist for the analytic mill. Used in this way manipulation is more common early in psychodynamic psychotherapy. Later, as patients gain more autonomy, interpretation replaces the need for manipulation.

Manipulation is also prominent in arranging the basic conditions of treatment. Whether they are designed to facilitate self-exploration, or merely for the therapist's convenience, the ground rules themselves are manipulative. Leasing the hour, for example, is to the therapist's financial advantage, *and* it serves the useful function of making the patient responsible for treatment. Still to some people the idea of charging patients even for sessions that they miss seems unduly harsh. Critics often respond to the rigid rules of therapy—the sharp eye we keep on the clock, absolute avoidance of extra-therapeutic contact, and so on—as though these were nothing but manipulations. Many analytic clinicians only exacerbate this reaction by behaving as though these rules were somehow made in heaven. The truth is that using (or not using) the couch, setting fees, and structuring the time are manipulations. Our job is not to defend self-righteously what are in fact manipulations, but to understand them. As Reuben Silver points out in his chapter on technique, the question is not whether we should use manipulation, but when and how.

Dr. Silver describes six "technical" (to enhance the process of therapy) manipulations, in a masterful exposition of creating a therapeutic alliance. Not all of Silver's suggestions are new, but his treatment is so lucid that, as we read, we realize the purpose, and the pitfalls, of many arrangements that we often take for granted. By carefully explaining the reason for various therapeutic manipulations, Dr. Silver helps us to get maximum mileage out of them. Moreover, by making explicit operations that many clinicians use unwittingly, this chapter clarifies the dangers of common therapeutic manipulations.

Dr. Silver's position is reminiscent of Frieda Fromm-Reichman, who counseled humane and personal treatment of severely disturbed patients, rather than strict analytic neutrality. When ego functions are missing, the therapist may have to lend them. Manipulations of this kind can be compassionate and therapeutic in the hands of a Frieda Fromm-Reichman, but it can also be a power play in an effort to control patients. The therapist's conscious intentions alone are not a sufficient guide, because, as Silver points out, manipulation is often the product of countertransference. The impact of this chapter is not to recommend more or less manipulation, but to shed light on this usually murky part of our work. Silver's recommended standard for evaluating manipulation is to ask: Is it for the therapist's or the patient's needs?

Dr. Silver goes outside the analytic arena to describe techniques from today's masters of manipulation, the strategic family therapists. He finds much in this literature that is useful for importation to analytic work, and he offers sensitive guidelines for using strategies such as reframing—without abusing patients or robbing them of the insightful self-mastery, which is the ultimate goal of psychodynamic treatment.

Confrontation

In ordinary language "confrontation" carries the image of combat; it is a bellicose and brave word, meaning to stand up to and oppose someone boldly. Antagonistic confrontation occurs in therapy, but it is not therapeutic. Most of the time when a therapist "confronts" a patient as an antagonist, it is a sign of countertransference at work.

In psychodynamic psychotherapy "confrontation" means forcefully to direct the patient's attention to something previously overlooked. As such it is similar to interpretation, which is also a form of pointing something out. The difference between them is that confrontation calls attention to something whereas interpretation explains it. Consider the ubiquitous example of a patient who comes late. Like anything else, we assume that such behavior is motivated, and we are interested in explaining it. Before we can do so, however, we must agree that it is worth explaining. If the patient does not agree (does not notice the lateness or considers it insignificant), then we confront the issue. To put the matter another way, confrontation is used to make what was ego syntonic, ego alien.

As Ronald Karpf points out, it is the therapist's motivation that differentiates a confrontation from a countertransference-based attack. The goal is an immediate reaction, but the desired response is engaging the patient's ego in the therapeutic task, rather than dumping the therapist's problem onto the patient. In practice the line between the two is sometimes difficult to draw.

Confrontation, and how we use it, is intimately related to resistance and how we view it. When Freud thought of resistance as nothing but an impediment to recollection, he blasted away at it, using confrontation and manipulation. Later, when resistance itself became an important focus of understanding, confrontation was designed not to do away with resistance, but to draw attention to it. The form of confrontation may vary from a forceful and blunt statement to a hesitant question, but in both cases the aim is to draw the patient's attention to experience—felt, acted on, or avoided.

Dr. Karpf writes that when a therapist confronts, there is an inevitable feeling of struggle. The struggle should not, however, make combatants of the paticipants; rather the struggle is with the patient's resistance, and both parties to treatment can be allies. With this in mind, the therapist can gauge the patient's reaction to determine whether a confrontation has cemented the alliance or disrupted it. Karpf urges tact and offers several useful examples to demonstrate how confrontations can be used to further the task of understanding.

Karpf also describes a special role for confrontation when a negative therapeutic reaction leads to self-destructive acting out. He says that acting out involves major denial, and, therefore, "a shock to the patient's psychic equilibrium is needed to block this behavior and make him or her amenable to insight. Often the best shock is a confrontation."

Zvi Lothane's clinical chapter illuminates not only the use of confrontation, but also the whole clinical enterprise. Lothane distinguishes three distinct models in Freudian theory, based on memory, dreams, and transference, and explains the practical consequences of each. The transference model is, according to Lothane, a model of love, and psychotherapy, done well, is an act of love.

Love—real love—means respect for the full humanness of the other person; respect does not, however, mean passive acceptance of troubled and troubling behavior. As Lothane explains, love often necessitates honest confrontation. The difference between confrontation and nagging is that the therapist does not criticize the character of the patient, but speaks only for himself or herself—stating his or her perceptions and attitudes, while inviting the patient to examine his or her own moral choices.

Clarification

Clarification was introduced to psychotherapy by Carl Rogers. In Rogerian therapy (and its humanistic offshoots), clarification is aimed at conscious material, notably feelings. In psychodynamic therapy clarification goes deeper, to the preconscious, and wider, to the full range of thinking, feeling, and acting. Herbert Brown's chapter on theory begins with an interesting consideration of the relative values of experiencing and insight in dynamic psychotherapy. Clarification, he says, is the natural bridge between the two, because it is the gentle beginning of interpretation.

Clarification, which in the hands of Carl Rogers started the humanistic trend away from insight toward emotional experiencing, is now being revisited in the work of Heinz Kohut and the self psychologists. Brown's position is clear: empathy is useful, but understanding is essential.

Tunneling through the darkness of ignorance, the therapist leads the way with clarification. Interpretations are reserved until later, when the explorers together come close enough to see the light of a decisive breakthrough. Dr. Binstock's chapter on the clinical application of clarification begins with a section defining the concept. Normally this material would be restricted to the chapter on history and theory, but Binstock's definition is so thoughtful and clinically relevant that it provides a splendid introduction to his remarks on technique. Clarification makes the preconscious conscious—in contrast to interpretation, which makes the unconscious conscious. Conceptually the two techniques are closely related, but, as Binstock demonstrates, there are important practical distinctions in their application.

Interpreting the unconscious is more dramatic than clarifying the preconscious. Not surprisingly, therefore, Hollywood psychoanalysts speak only in brilliant, if obscure, interpretations. Workaday therapists, more concerned with helping than impressing, devote far more time to making clarifications. In Binstock's image they often get more mileage out of reminding patients that two and two are four, than from introducing some obscure new equation.

Clarifications may be delivered in a variety of forms, and Binstock describes how to use this technique to the best effect. His strongest advice is, however, not about tactics, but strategy. The therapist who understands not only the value of insight, but also the tenacity of defense, will approach the psyche from the surface—consistently clarifying before making interpretations. There may be bigger fish in the psychic depths, but the therapist who first spreads a net wide across the surface eventually will catch more of them.

Binstock suggests that clarification can usefully elucidate transference by connecting conscious perceptions of the therapist to remembered conscious perceptions of the parents. Even Strachey (1934), he points out, when speaking of "mutative interpretations," emphasizes the innumerable small steps for getting to them. Binstock, in a long and interesting case study, illustrates how to take these small steps, demonstrating not only how a skillful clinician forms conjectures, but also how to impart them most effectively to the patient. One of the most useful aspects of Binstock's treatise is his explanation of the partnership between clarification and interpretation. Other writers have described how clarifications prepare the way for interpretations; Binstock covers this, but also shows how clarification is essential to the working-through process—clarification as interpretation's successor.

Interpretation

"Interpretation" is an everyday word and so it may seem that we do not need to define it. The problem is that interpreting is a special activity in psychodynamic psychotherapy, one that is often misunderstood. In this technical arena, interpretation means to make the unconscious conscious. Alert readers will notice that this definition carries some extra baggage, namely, the metaphysical concept of the unconscious. A more accurate, careful definition might be limited to the action involved: drawing the patient's attention to something. The trouble is that the nature of that "something" is a critical part of the definition.

What we interpret are activities—thoughts and feelings, as well as behavior—that had previously gone unnoticed or were ignored. In this way we help make our patients' lives intelligible, bringing meaning and purpose where none was thought to exist. This is what we mean when we say "making the unconscious conscious." We could be more specific and mention the manifestations of the unconscious that are the subject of most interpretations (parapraxes, dreams, symptoms, transference, and resistance), but this leads to the complication that psychodynamic clinicians have different opinions about which of these aspects of experience should be interpreted, and so we will not develop this further.

Before leaving the matter of definition, however, we should point out that the concept of interpretation is often misused, or at least used loosely. Nonanalytic clinicians sometimes scoff at the use of interpretation, and claim that it does little good. When interpretation is used to mean giving opinions, advice, and rationalizations, they are probably right. Telling patients that they are doing the right thing or the wrong thing is not useful—and it is not interpretation. Analytic clinicians sometimes misuse "interpretation" to mean blaming patients, attributing to their understandable reactions devious or pathological roots. We do this when we fail to treat patients with dignity and respect, and when we are totally blind to our own contributions to their reactions. Robert Langs had done a good job of pointing this out, though he exaggerates the therapist's responsibility. Interpretation means pointing out; it should not be confused with criticizing or disqualifying the validity of patients' experience.

In his chapter on the history and theory of interpretation, Harold Boris says that interpretation cuts away the self-deceit that patients use to protect themselves against the truth of their experience. Some truths about ourselves and our experience are so painful we cannot bear to face them. So we transform painful reality into a more palatable cover story, and, through repression, we seek comfort in not knowing. In the act of interpreting, the therapist brings back these truths. As Boris puts it, "Psychodynamic psychotherapy introduces a person to him or herself."

Freud discovered that his patients' lives were predicated on certain key fictions. These he uncovered and exposed through interpretation. Freud was both a methodologist and a theoretician. He began with the observed facts—symptoms, and later dreams, transference, and resistance—and he speculated about what was behind them. Boris traces the development of Freud's procedure from reconstruction of the past to decoding the meaning of behavior in the therapeutic relationship, always emphasizing interpretation as an instrument of knowledge.

Dr. Boris argues that interpretation is not a cool scientific process, for the patient or the therapist. The therapist must listen not only for the meaning of what the patient is saying, but also to the use to which it is being put ("patients speak for effect"). But the therapist is not a dispassionate technologist. Instead, as Boris vividly demonstrates, the therapist must unleash his or her "sympathetic imagination." Moreover, both parties to the treatment must join to become "two minds hard at work, to get to the raw material of experience."

Interpretation begins as a cognitive process, conveying information, but it quickly involves the patient's experience—it hurts to be exposed. This, too, becomes an important arena of experience for interpretation.

Boris cautions therapists to be wary of going beyond interpretation in order to induce patients to change. This, he says, is countertransference at work. He gives due credit to the noninterpretive techniques, but says that their ultimate purpose is to smooth the way for interpretation. "Psychodynamic psychotherapy is interpretive psychotherapy."

If interpretation is the decisive technique in psychodynamic psychotherapy, then Joseph Natterson's chapter on its clinical application is the culminating contribution of this volume. Natterson weaves his exposition through vividly detailed case material, so that the reader gets to peek through the door of the consulting room. Just as the art of interpretation requires softening the message with support, so this style of presentation conveys hard-won truths about clinical technique in a form that makes them easy to absorb. As Natterson himself emphasizes, interpretation is a cognitive device, but one that cannot be isolated from the total, living reality of the therapeutic relationship.

Memorable interpretations are often flashy statements of penetrating conjecture. When his patient commented on a grandfather clock, Theodor

Reik demanded: "Why didn't you tell me you were pregnant?" This marvelous piece of psychoanalytic theater was a dazzling display of keen deduction, and it is part of the reason why some people think of psychoanalysts as Sherlock Holmes with a couch. There is some truth to this but, I regret to say, not much. Forming the conjecture that may later be stated as an interpretation is a creative act. It requires a similar free-floating use of the imagination that, in patients, we call free association. Natterson's examples illustrate the kind of playful, experimental attitude that generates the freedom of thought necessary to penetrate the unconscious mind. Still, when a conjecture is translated into an interpretation, when the therapist's private thoughts are finally offered to the patient, tact and patience are more important than drama.

In contrast to the showy interpretations that light up the imagination, Dr. Natterson demonstrates a mixture of warmth and frankness, and stresses the need for working through—the slow, steady process by which an interpretation spoken becomes an interpretation experienced. This process is richly illustrated with examples from the practice of a master clinician.

Natterson gives us an exceptional discussion of the interpretation of transference. Transference, he says, is a gold mine of understanding because it is part of the only interaction that both parties participate in directly. It is, therefore, an immediate and reliable source of information. But here Natterson issues two strong cautions. First, do not force transference interpretations. Second, beware of obscuring the reality of the relationship by blaming the patient for any and all reactions to what is going on. This is not just a matter of admitting errors, but of recognizing that the therapist's real actions stimulate the patient's reactions—conscious and unconscious. Interpretations should link symptoms or signs of disturbance to issues in the patient's life *and* in the therapeutic relationship, not exclusively one or the other.

Natterson mentions the important issue of validation (how we know when we are on target), and he urges therapists to overcome the need for flattery and gratitude. If that is what you want, the best way to get it is by being friendly and helping people shore up their defenses. Ours is not an easy business.

Dr. Natterson begins his conclusion by underscoring the primacy of insight, but he goes on to say that interpretations must enhance experiencing of repressed parts of the self. This dual emphasis could serve as the theme of this volume. In the chapters that follow, the authors give close attention to how to achieve insight and enhanced experience of the self. Before turning to that material, however, there is one issue so important that we have chosen to highlight it in a special section of its own.

ESTABLISHING THE ANALYTIC ATMOSPHERE

In our preview of the chapters on technique, we have consistently emphasized the process of uncovering—getting to deeper and hidden layers of personality—to make possible new understanding and enriched experiencing. Each of the basic techniques plays a role in this process. But the techniques themselves are nothing without the proper setting.

Much of what is written about psychodynamic psychotherapy presumes that the therapist is neutral, a blank screen, and that the therapeutic relationship is a *tabula rasa* upon which the patient writes the text of his or her pathology. This naive view is based on habits of linear thinking, according to which whatever one person (the therapist) does is *because* of what the other one (the patient) does. Wrong! Much of what patients respond to are the actions of the therapist, which serve as the exciting cause for the patients' responses. It works the other way too. Both parties are intensely involved in a spiraling process of mutual influence. Ignoring this fact leads to falsely attributing responsibility to the patient for everything that goes on (we call it "transference"), but that is not all.

People do not readily reveal hidden parts of themselves. Before you even get to the unconscious, there are vast reservoirs of experience that are kept private to avoid shame and embarrassment. Nonanalytic therapists encourage disclosure by their warmth, and they cajole it with active interventions. They get plenty of material to keep them busy (a lot can be accomplished without disturbing the sleeping unconscious), but they do not get the raw material of psychodynamic psychotherapy. Hot pursuit of dynamic material only chases it away. People's private fears and wishes emerge slowly. It takes time, and it takes the presence of a sympathetic listener willing to wait, willing not to take control, and willing not to intrude. This is the hardest part of being a dynamic therapist: remaining in the background and allowing the patient's associations to unfold. Only the therapist's muted responsiveness allows the patient's inner life to emerge—not as a projection on a blank screen, but as a voice that cannot be heard and will not be raised in a noisy room. The most important activity of the psychodynamic psychotherapist is listening.

Listening is a strenuous but silent activity, rare in our culture. Silence minimizes interference and makes it clear that the therapist does not take responsibility for solving the patient's problems. Silence creates a pressure for the patient to search, associate, and communicate. There are no iron-clad rules to determine the optimal mix of listening and intervening, but most therapists talk too much.

There are many reasons, and twice as many rationalizations, for excessive activity, but they have a common result: the therapist becomes overly central. Even well-intentioned interventions may do more harm than good. Questions, for example, keep the patient close to the surface. They promote conscious communication and direct the patient to what the therapist thinks is important. Only a relatively silent therapist will be able to follow the patient's *free* associations to unsuspected avenues of meaning. When something is missing from a person's experience of himself or herself, direct questioning will not tease it out of hiding. Psychotherapy may be "a collaborative inquiry" (Greenberg & Mitchell, 1983), but only the patient can provide the right material. The therapist helps find crucial dimensions of meaning, but must be forebearing to let the material emerge.

Silence, when it is encountered in everyday life, usually means uncomprehension or disinterest. Some patients thus may experience a therapist's silence as unempathic, or even as outright rejection; most, however, will perceive it as a gift of understanding and compassion. The listening attitude that we give our patients allows them room to explore and to open themselves to inner experience. This responsibility is also a terrible burden because it exposes them to feelings of helplessness and the dread of primitive conflicts. Patients, anxious and eager to be relieved of this burden, induce many therapists to be more active than necessary. Therapists are prone by nature to accept this projected responsibility; in addition to the conscious desire to be helpful, most of us have unconscious motives for taking over—seductive, aggressive, narcissistic, controlling, manipulative—and many learn to avoid painful unconscious material by hugging the shores of the surface.

In addition to silent listening, there are other basic conditions of a sound, therapeutic holding environment (Bion, 1977); these may seem obvious, but are too important to take for granted. Compassion and tact are necessary to make people feel safe enough to expose preconscious secrets of which they are ashamed, and to sustain them through a process devoted to questioning the validity of their very way of being.

There is room for legitimate disagreement between those who emphasize warmth and tact (Stone, 1961; Kohut, 1971) and those who counsel silence and technical correctness (Brenner, 1976; Langs, 1982). The variations in practice, however, are relatively slight among experienced therapists. Incidentally compassion is better conveyed by attitude and manner than by "supportive" comments.

The techniques described in this volume are the essential tools of our trade. Mastering them will equip you to be a thoroughly competent technician; applying them, however, requires an ambiance in which patients can relax their defenses and curtail conscious selectivity. Opposition to or disruption of this basic therapeutic holding environment can come from the patient or therapist. The initial job of therapy is to counter the one and avoid the other. Psychodynamic therapy begins with a quiet show of strength; the therapist resists pressure to direct or reassure; initial activity is limited to establishing the ground rules of treatment and interpreting early resistances. Then the therapist sits back, conveying empathy primarily by listening with interest, and responding with sensitivity and tact.

REFERENCES

Alexander, F.G., and French, T.M. *Psychoanalytic therapy, principles and application.* New York: Ronald Press, 1946.

Bibring, E. Psychoanalysis and the dynamic psychotherapies. *Journal of the American Psychoanalytic Association,* 1954, *2,* 745–770.

Bion, W. *Seven servants.* New York: Jason Aronson, 1977.

Brenner, C. *Psychoanalytic technique and psychic conflict.* New York: International Universities Press, 1976.

Breuer, J., and Freud, S. (1895) Studies on hysteria. *Standard edition.* Vol. 2. London: Hogarth Press, 1955, pp. 1–310.

Eissler, K.R. The effect of the structure of the ego on psychoanalytic technique. *Journal of the American Psychoanalytic Association,* 1953, *1,* 104–143.

Frank, J.D. *Persuasion and healing.* Baltimore: Johns Hopkins Press, 1961.

Freud, S. (1888–89) Preface to the translation of Bernheim's *Suggestion. Standard edition.* Vol. 1. London: Hogarth Press, 1966, pp. 77–86.

Freud, S. (1923) The ego and the id. *Standard edition,* Vol. 19. London: Hogarth Press, 1961, pp. 1–60.

Greenberg, J.R., and Mitchell, S.A. *Object relations in psychoanalytic theory.* Cambridge, Mass.: Harvard University Press, 1983.

Greenson, R.R. *The theory and technique of psychoanalysis.* New York: International Universities Press, 1967.

Kohut, H. *The analysis of the self.* New York: International Universities Press, 1971.

Langs, R. *The technique of psychoanalytic psychotherapy,* Vol. I. New York: Jason Aronson, 1973.

Langs, R. *Psychotherapy: A basic text.* New York: Jason Aronson, 1982.

Laplanche, J., and Pontalis, J.B. *The language of psychoanalysis.* New York: Norton, 1973.

Paolino, T.J. *Psychoanalytic psychotherapy: Theory, technique, therapeutic relationship and treatability.* New York: Brunner/Mazel, 1981.

Shapiro, A.K., and Morris, L.A. The placebo effect in medical and psychological therapies. In S.L. Garfield and A.E. Bergin (Eds.), *Handbook of psychotherapy and behavior change: An empirical analysis.* 2nd ed. New York: Wiley, 1978.

Stone, L. *The psychoanalytic situation.* New York: International Universities Press, 1961.

Strachey, J. The nature of the therapeutic action of psychoanalysis. *International Journal of Psycho-Analysis,* 1934, *15,* 127–159.

2
Suggestion: History and Theory

CHARLES P. DUCEY, Ph.D.

Suggestion is the most ancient and ubiquitous of all psychotherapeutic techniques, and one of the fundamental bases of all human social interaction. It undoubtedly has evolutionary biological roots, for "social and physical influenceability, the plasticity for adapting to changing conditions, extreme conditions, and conditions continuously being newly created by human beings, is precisely what has been naturally selected for" (Pepitone, 1981, p. 983). Indeed, it is the very ubiquity and generality of suggestion in everyday social intercourse that has led countless critics of psychotherapy to dismiss the evident effects of the process as attributable to "nothing but mere suggestion." In response to such criticisms, Freud (1909, p. 102), with characteristic acerbity, observes that

> It has been discovered how great an economy of thought can be affected by the use of the catchword "suggestion." Nobody knows and nobody cares what suggestion is, where it comes from, or when it arises,—it is enough that anything awkward in the region of psychology can be labelled "suggestion."

A serviceable nonspecific definition of suggestion is "the process of inducing thought or action without resorting to techniques of persuasion or giving rise to reflection in such a way as to produce an uncritical response" (Urdang, 1968, p. 1314). Psychoanalytic specifications tend to emphasize the irrational, authoritarian–submissive elements of this process; Bibring's (1954) seminal article emphasizes the therapist's taking advantage of an authoritative role and the patient's credulity to induce ideas, emotions, or actions independently of the patient's rational, critical, and realistic thinking. As we shall see, this emphasis was made partly for tendentious purposes, to differentiate psychoanalysis from "suggestive" psychotherapies. This review broadens the concept to embrace both ordinary usage and Freud's early proposal (Freud, 1888 p. 82) that "an idea is aroused in another person's brain which is not examined in regard to its origin but is accepted just as though it had arisen spontaneously in that brain." In other words, we shall employ the word in its modern general sense and in its ancient Latin sense (*suggestio*), which implies the *process of verbally supplying what is needed or furnishing what is missing*, as exemplified in ancient rhetoric when the orator provides the answer to the question the orator has just posed.

The following summarizes what is known of this mysterious, yet taken-for-granted, mode of interpersonal influence as applied to psychodynamic psychotherapy. I begin with an overview of psychoanalytic theories of suggestion; review relevant psychological research; present some original formulations regarding its psychopathology, based on ethnopsychoanalytic and clinical perspectives; and conclude with a discussion of psychotherapeutic uses of suggestion.

THEORIES OF SUGGESTION

The roots of contemporary psychoanalytic theories of suggestion can be traced back to the notion of "magnetism" in Parcelsus; Mesmer and his disciples, and Charcot and Bernheim, among others, set the stage for Freud's contributions, which provided a dynamic theory and extended the therapeutic application of the theory of suggestion. Since, in the history of human knowledge, the exotic rather than the commonplace initially calls for an explanation, the literature on the exotic state of hypnotism and other altered states of consciousness is as vast as the literature on everyday suggestion is scant. The focus here is suggestion itself; hypnosis is treated only insofar as it relates to the main topic.

Prepsychoanalytic Theories

Prior to the 19th century, there seems to have been, at least in the "mainstream" of Western thought, little distinction between interpersonal influence and other forms of influence. Renaissance theories of human behavior tended not to distinguish physical, psychological, and spiritual influences. Nonetheless, especially in the work of thinkers who have had lasting impact on modern knowledge, such as Shakespeare, Montaigne, and Burton, we find remarkably penetrating analyses of what might now be regarded as interpersonal suggestion and autosuggestion, particularly in the appreciation of the power of the imagination (the sensory experience of realms not immediately present to perception) to engender contagious or influential passions and emotions (Ducey, 1980a).

Under the influence of Paracelsus (1443–1541), the theory of suggestion was incorporated into the broader schemes of the universe and temporarily banished from the world of human interaction. The curative properties attributed to iron and other minerals by Paracelsus were transformed two centuries later into Mesmer's influential theory of animal magnetism. The now quaint-sounding theory, which postulated the flow of universal and invisible magnetic fluid from the magnetizer to the subject in such a way as to revitalize the subject's nerves, was part and parcel of the Enlightenment's scientific and political revolutions (Darnton, 1968). Ironically, closer investigation of mesmerism opened the way back to a less exotic and more human view of the topic of interpersonal influence.

Mesmer seems to have been the first to label the unusual influence of magnetizer upon subject as *rapport*. He conceptualized it within the framework of his "physical" theory of magnetic field, although disciples such as Puységur and Bertholet recognized primarily the psychological dimensions of imagination and imitation. Indeed, a Royal Commission appointed in 1784 in Paris to evaluate the theory of animal magnetism not only upheld by controlled experiments a psychological causation theory of the dramatic effects of mesmeric suggestion as against the magnetic theory, but also appended a secret report to the King warning of the erotic connotations of the process of being "magnetized." A proliferation of artistic, philosophical, and scientific works that received public attention in the last years of the century and the early 19th century associated magnetic rapport with erotic attachment and cure of illness through love. Mozart's great opera *Così Fan Tutte* (1791), which includes a bogus magnetizer and his—actually her—patients, could easily be called "The Cure of Love through Love." Magnetic rapport was even recognized as reciprocal and compared to the absolute unity of the pregnant woman and her unborn fetus (Hufeland, 1811; Ellenberger, 1970, p. 152). Such are the roots of the concepts of transference and symbiotic relations.

As often happens in the history of ideas, the baby of Mesmer's valuable observations and theories was thrown out along with the bathwater of his spiritualist–physiologic fantasies of mysterious influence. Yet others offered naturalistic theories of such phenomena. In 1823 Bertrand grounded "artificial somnambulism" in the normal process of imagination, expectant attention, and desire (Sarbin & Coe, 1972), and Braid (1843) employed psychological as well as physiological concepts to explain what he coined as hypnosis: fixed attention, monoideism (leading to concentration and trance), hypnotizability as a personality trait, and even "double consciousness," later to appear in Janet and Freud.

The next major step in this history was the acrimonious debate between Charcot and the Nancy school, represented by Liébeault and Bernheim. Charcot, perhaps for the first time, sharply dissociated normal suggestion from "pathological" hypnosis. He regarded hypnosis as an artificially produced hysteria in a neuropathological patient, and offered only physiological explanations.

Bernheim, by contrast, claimed that suggestibility, the "aptitude to transform an idea into an act," was an ordinary trait of all human beings, and that nearly everyone was, therefore, hypnotizable to some degree. He elaborated a purely psychological theory of suggestion: There is a natural tendency for ideas, derived from sensory impressions, to activate behavior, and also an inhibitory influence that permits the person to check his or her perceptions by logic and reason and to evaluate the consequences of actions. Under hypnosis the inhibitory influence is diminished, and the person is more accessible to suggestive influences. Freud was obviously influenced by both Charcot and Bernheim; but while he rejected Charcot's physiological bias, he noted (Freud, 1888) that Bernheim could only fall back on an undefined term such as suggestion.

Another major 19th-century European theory of suggestion focuses the dilemmas raised by all the scientific theories reviewed. Wilhelm Wundt, founder of experimental psychology, offered a sophisticated associationist theory of hypnosis and suggestion based on the principle of functional compensation, which emphasized the complementary relationship in the brain between the increased reactivity to stimuli associated with suggested ideas and the reduced sensitivity to all other impressions (Wundt, 1892; Sarbin & Coe, 1972). Wundt's explicit denigration of the importance of rapport observed by Mesmer has unfortunately been perpetuated through his heirs, even into the late 20th century. The mechanistic explanation of processes of *interpersonal influence* (suggestion and hypnosis) by physiological or merely behavioral concepts dramatize the absurdity of discounting human experience in psychological theories; Wundt's and his descendants' theories of interpersonal influence resemble Paracelsus's mechanistic–spiritualistic fantasies more closely than they do Freud's theories, the findings of modern psychological research, or human subjective experience.

The final pre-Freudian thread to be traced in the history of the theory of suggestion originated with Pierre Janet's nondynamic concept of dissociation and culminates with his U.S. descendants' work on suggestive therapeutics. Morton Prince and Boris Sidis proposed the existence of a set of subconscious selves that ordinarily act in unison (and therefore invisibly) but become dissociated in illness. Sidis (1898) further postulated that "suggestibility varies as the amount of disaggregation, and inversely as the unification of consciousness"; the implication is that influenceability is pathological per se, which is a theory like Charcot's, but in psychological dress. Prince (1927) posited that consciousness was reintegrated through a process of "suggestive repersonalization." The conversion of the eminent neuropathologist James Jackson Putnam from therapeutic suggestion to psychoanalysis, however, left the Janet–Prince–Sidis axis without progeny in the United States and ushered in the widespread acceptance of the psychoanalytic theory and approach (Hale, 1971; Vasile, 1977).

Psychoanalytic Theory

Freud's so-called "papers on hypnosis and suggestion" (1888–1892) did not so much advance a theory of suggestion as extend its therapeutic application; it was Freud's translations of Bernheim's books that played a major role in reintroducing therapeutic hypnosis to Vienna from its French "exile," a century and a quarter after Mesmer's momentous transplantation of magnetism from Vienna to Paris. To be sure, Freud provided some material for the scaffolding of a theory that contradicted both scientific and popular prejudices and anticipated his own later theories of attention cathexis and the Pcpt.-Cs. (perceptual conscious) system. Most notably, he sharply distinguished direct suggestion, an interpersonal influence that has an impact only in so far as the subject's will permits, from indirect suggestion, which, as an unconscious physiological process, gives rise to hysterical phenomena as well as their spontaneous or suggested removal (Freud, 1888). The physician does not cure hysteria by suggestion, as Bernheim contended; but can only offer to redirect the willing patient's attention to internal processes—which are ony descriptively, not dynamically unconscious (i.e., potentially conscious through attention, not repressed) at this stage of Freud's theory (Andersson, 1962)—and thereby stimulate the patient to an autosuggestive removal of the hysterical symptom. The independent operation of the subject's will and the distinction of suggestion from autosuggestion have been clearly upheld in scientific research on hypnosis (Fromm et al., 1981). But in spite of his criticisms of Bernheim's ubiquitous appeal to suggestion as explanatory, Freud himself could still offer no theory of the interpersonal process and continued to ignore Mesmer's *rapport*.

Ironically, it is one of Freud's least known papers (1890)—so obscure as initially to be inaccurately dated by a decade and a half in the otherwise meticulous *Standard Edition* (Strachey, 1966)—that constitutes what is perhaps Freud's most important contribution to the theory of psychotherapeutic suggestion apart from his "Group Psychology" (1921). In fact "Physical Treatment" may be the best brief analysis of the efficacy of therapeutic suggestion across historical epochs and cultures—in spite of the fact that it preceded the very invention of modern psychoanalytic technique by several years, modern social psychological studies by several decades, and our current understanding by nearly a century!

Freud makes plausible to his readers the seemingly magical therapeutic effects of words by offering numerous examples of the impact of the mind upon the body through strong emotion, focusing of attention, and volition, particularly in influencing physical and mental illness and recovery. He analyzes the role of expectation—what Merton (1957) later called the "self-fulfilling prophecy"—in effecting both illness and so-called miraculous cures, and isolates numerous suggestive components of such cures. These include pious belief; magnification of the individual's emotions by the enthusiasm of a group (or its psychological substitute, reputation); rituals that serve as contrivances to enhance the difficulty, and therefore the value, of the cure (Festinger's [1957] reduction of cognitive dissonance); and, last but not least, personal ambition and competitiveness with other sufferers for divine favor. "Where so many powerful forces converge, we need feel no surprise if the goal is sometimes really reached" (Freud, 1890, p. 290). Similar forces apply to fashionable popular treatments and "nature healers," except that in these cases the attribution of power by the patient to the healer and his or her "purely human liking" for the healer plays a significant role in the cure. The patient's confidence in and affection for the secular healer is the counterpart to attribution of divine power to the healer of the sacred ages.

Freud thus reintroduces the lost intersubjective (as distinct from interpersonal) dimension, particularly independent internal psychological experiences (affect, attention, volition), into a literature that had shown either a heavy physiological (Charcot) or a simplistic social (Bernheim) bias. The person is no longer a pawn, subject only to the whims of either an authoritarian hypnotist or his or her own neurophysiological constitution. Moreover, Freud reemphasizes the significance of rapport, which greatly increases the subject's influenceability; indeed he anticipates his later work on transference by comparing hypnotic rapport (with all focus of attention upon the hypnotist) to a nursing mother's infant-focused sleep, a loving child's credulity, and a lover's extreme devotion and exclusive attachment to the beloved. Another foreshadowing contained here is the concept of resistance to the cure of illness: the "autocratic" (autonomous) nature of personality limits the therapeutic effectiveness of suggestion.

Although Freud maintained a lively lifelong interest in the therapeutic use of suggestion, he devoted only one other major work to the theory of suggestion (Freud, 1921). Without any reference to his own earlier work (Freud, 1890), Freud "rediscovered" in Le Bon (1895) the similarity between hypnotic influence and emotional contagion in a group: both hypnotized subjects and group members are credulous, suggestible, lacking in critical faculties, and bound by a mysterious and irresistible power arising from fascination with the "magnetic" hypnotist/leader. Freud's crucial contribution lies in his assertion that love relationships, the binding power of Eros, hold together all groups and lie "concealed behind the shelter, the screen, of suggestion" (Freud, 1921, p. 91). The theoretical advance is completed, and brought into the therapeutic framework, by Freud's definition of an interpersonal relationship (e.g., between hypnotist and subject) as a "group of two" and his elegant intrapsychic analysis of this relationship. Like the person in love, the compliant and suggestible subject replaces his or her own "ego ideal" with the object: the subject permits the hypnotist temporarily to assume the functions of reality-testing and direction that the ego ideal customarily performs for the individual. The "unlimited devotion" of the subject is predicated upon the generation of erotic desire that remains unsatisfied.

Freud's analysis of suggestion transcended simplistic uses of the term that earlier theorists had accepted as an unexplained "given" of interpersonal relationships. Yet he was not satisfied with this analysis; he regarded it as incomplete, as it does not explain the apparent paralysis and subjective sense of helplessness in relation to a superior power that characterizes hypnotic suggestion. Relying upon his theory (Freud 1919b) that the sense of the uncanny is based upon familiar but repressed experiences, Freud connects the subject's surrender of will to the hypnotist's mysterious power with the subject's "archaic heritage": he or she assumes toward the hypnotist the same attitude of helplessness and awe as the individual member of the primal horde did toward the terrifying primal father. Freud makes only passing reference to the subject's relations with his or her actual parents, as he apparently believed that such relations do not explain the universal and profound dimensions of the experience. Later psychoanalysts have been more fainthearted in approaching the supraindividual realm; it is perhaps only a Freud (1921, p. 91) who can say, "I like to avoid concessions to faintheartedness." At the same time, he reminds us that the subject retains his or her will in relation to suggestions, for he or she recognizes that hypnosis is in fact "only a game, an untrue reproduction of another situation of far more importance to life" (Freud 1921, p. 116).

Most early psychoanalytic contributions to the theory of suggestion are either based upon this theory or derived from other Freudian ideas. It was Ferenczi (1909) who first connected suggestibility with the transference to the hypnotist of unconscious infantile erotic desires toward and fears of the parents. He distinguished love and dread as the two most powerful motives of hypnotic suggestibility, and posited that these different attitudes were generally mobilized according to the subject's transference of feelings, respectively, toward the mother and the father. He also noted, without adequately explaining, the fact that this transference aspect led to both heightened suggestibility and resistance to suggestion.

Other early contributions tended to elaborate the developmental dimension of suggestion. In his analysis of Coué's system of self-mastery through autosuggestion, Abraham (1925) emphasized that the temporary effectiveness of autosuggestion derived from its narcissistic elements. The patient identifies with the power of the idealized father and thereby permits the operation of the omnipotence of thoughts. As a regression from differentiated object relations to infantile narcissism, autosuggestion permits an overemphasis on the power motive at the expense of threatening sexual ties to real others. Similarly, Ernest Jones (1923) pointed out the suspension of the critical ego ideal in autosuggestion and suggestion alike: insofar as ego and superego are reconciled, the subject experiences an ego-syntonic regression to primary process thinking and the omnipotence of thoughts. In this work Jones anticipates Kohut (1971) in distinguishing the "grandiose self" and the idealized object as the relevant intrapsychic variables for, respectively, autosuggestion and suggestion. Both these states of mind have a narcissistic basis.

Later psychoanalytic theorists, notably Glover (1931) and Fisher (1953b), elucidated the unconscious id-related or primary-process significance of suggestions in psychoanalysis as good or bad, friendly or persecuting, erotic or sadistic substances (milk, urine, feces, phallus, baby).

Ego psychologists (Gill & Brenman, 1959) reopened the opportunity to fashion a more broadly based theory of suggestion, although, like many other psychoanalytic theorists, they focused their attention upon altered states of consciousness, such as hypnosis. Their theory involves the complex dynamic, genetic, structural, and adaptive intrapsychic conditions that underlie all processes of internal and interpersonal influence, including suggestion. They show that influenceability and suggestibility are heavily dependent upon shifts in an individual's relative ego autonomy from his or her drive experience and from the environment (Hartmann, 1939; Rapaport, 1951, 1958). The ego is a slave to neither the id nor the environment, but is relatively autonomous of both. This relative autonomy can be altered, however, by deautomatization; that is, by interferences with the automatic functioning of the apparatuses of perception, motility, and thinking through diminished input, increased drive urges, or strong environmental pressure. In such "suggestive" situations as hypnosis, the relative autonomy of the ego from the environment is reduced, with an accompanying decrease of autonomy from the drives, since the hypnotist offers the possibility of gratification of desire in regressive ways. But this loss of autonomy is only partial and provisional, as the subject is capable of overruling the hypnotic suggestions; hence only a subsystem of the ego is said to be regressed. This theory provides a comprehensive intrapsychic formulation of the process of suggestion, particularly the fluctuations both within and across subjects of environmental, and particularly interpersonal, responsiveness and influenceability.

Modern Psychological Research

The topic of therapeutic suggestion opens the door to a vast amount of relevant psychological literature on human operant conditioning, attitude change, and interpersonal influence. This work could be summarized by the simple observation that a remarkable number and complexity of variables must be invoked to explain the pervasive effects of interpersonal influence. Since comprehensive reviews of interpersonal persuasion and psychotherapy are available (Goldstein, et al., 1966; Frank, 1974; Beutler, 1978), I shall focus upon the reseach most directly relevant to psychodynamic suggestion, which involves variables from the social learning paradigm (outcome control, experimenter expectations), cognitive theory (cue control, knowledge of a subject's past history), and the social–psychological literature on persuasion and attitude change (influential characteristics of the persuader, the communication, and the recipient).

The social learning paradigm has generated extensive psychological research on interpersonal influences. Attitude and behavior changes result from the reinforcement of desired responses through positive or negative incentives. Hence the operator of influence (experimenter, psychotherapist, communicator) is believed to manipulate rewards and punishments to maintain "outcome control" over the recipient (subject, patient, audience) and thereby enhance the probability of desired behavior. This influence extends even to minimal signals of approval and disapproval: simple affirmative or discouraging grunts have been shown to shape some responders' verbal behaviors in the expected directions (reviewed by Bandura, 1969), although subjects are of course differentially responsive. Hence such "nondirective" forms of psychotherapy as the psychodynamic can hardly be regarded as free of suggestive influence; indeed, such influence is likely to be all the more pervasive to the extent that therapist and patient are not fully aware of the subtlety and power of seemingly insignificant mutually reinforcing interactions. Even in the absence of apparent conditioning influences, an experimenter's very unspoken and even unconscious expectations influence subjects' performances extensively (Rosenthal, 1969). Such subtle influence is so powerful and ubiquitous as to be transmissible through a third person, with no contact between investigator and subject (Frank, 1974, pp. 122–123).

The most important development in psychology over the past three decades, the refinement of cognitive theories of behavior, has had an enriching effect upon the simplistic social learning paradigm in the understanding of interpersonal influence. A "neglected source of interpersonal power" is cue control (as distinct from outcome control), which involves the arousal and activation of specific dispositions in the subject by the provision of appropriate cues or useful information (Jones & Gerard, 1967). Thus even when the operator (e.g., the psychotherapist) has minimal direct control over the subject's outcomes, he or she may influence the subject by supplying information that provides greater meaning and structure to the subject's experience. Schachter's (1965) classic experiment was an elegant demonstration of the determining power of cognitive cues provided by another person in the experience of affect: the same state of physiological arousal was interpreted as anger, levity, or no emotion according only to available external cues. Moreover, the more the operator knows about the subject's past history, the greater influence he or she wields, because of the diversity of stimulus-habit contingencies that can be mobilized.

The implications of this research for psychotherapy are clear. The therapist's aid in specifying affect is curative, in part, merely through the suggestive influence of substituting a clear feeling for a vague, amorphous, or undefined one (e.g., anxiety, depression). The very act of labeling an overwhelming emotional experience makes it feel to the patient more comprehensible and controllable. In addition, knowledge of the patient's past history permits the therapist to influence the patient merely through the suggestive mobilization of expectable traits and habits.

A further relevant social–psychological area of research concerns persuasion and attitude change, apart from the psychotherapy situation. The findings from this extensive research may be organized conveniently according to (1) persuader attributes, (2) characteristics of the communication, and (3) the recipient's qualities, in determining the effectiveness of the persuasive attempt (Jones & Gerard, 1967; Beutler, 1978).

1. With regard to influential characteristics of the *persuader*, early work on hypnosis regularly emphasized the prestige of the hypnotist in inducing compliance (Hull, 1933). The persuasion literature has upheld the finding of the effectiveness of expert status in persuasion; other things being equal, the greater the discrepancy between a highly credible persuader and the recipient, the greater will be the recipient's attitude change (Bergin, 1962). but the "other things" in this case are crucial mediating variables. For instance, a low-credibility source may have a "sleeper effect" just as powerful over time as the highly credible persuader (Hovland & Weiss, 1951), or even more powerful if believed not to have ulterior motives (Walster et. al., 1966). The credibility of the persuader has more persuasive effects on altering beliefs, whereas general similarity in values between persuader and recipient has a stronger effect in changing the recipient's values (Jones & Gerard, 1967). Yet in general such compatibility, as indicated by interpersonal similarity and attractiveness, exerts an influence on persuasiveness only when directly relevant to the issues at hand (Berscheid, 1966), and in fact only establishes a potentially persuasive relationship, instead of effecting persuasion per se (Beutler, 1978).

2. The various characteristics of the *persuasive communication* may

be analyzed according to (a) cognitive, (b) affective, and (c) behavioral dimensions.

a. In the cognitive domain, the persuasive potency of the message is enhanced by rhetorical questions (instead of factual or imperative statements), repetitiveness, one-sidedness of presentation for already convinced or less sophisticated subjects, and presentation of a two-sided (alternative-offering) argument to initially disagreeing or more sophisticated subjects. The two-sided approach also enhances resistance to further change of opinion (Jones & Gerard, 1967).

b. In terms of affective quality of the communication, the available evidence suggests that moderate affect arousal has a more persuasive influence than either excessive (defense-generating) of insufficient (affectively indifferent) arousal (Janis & Feshbach, 1953).

c. Two complementary aspects of the behavioral component of the communication are thoroughly documented. First, the greater the subject's active participation in improvising persuasive arguments in favor of the communicator's suggestions, the stronger and more persistent will be the attitude change (Hovland et al., 1953). Second, coercive persuasion generally generates "reactance" and reduces persuasibility (Brehm, 1966; Brehm & Cole, 1966). These findings could be summarized by the proposition that suggestion alone, without further rationale or auxiliary techniques, has persuasive effects only insofar as the subject (i) is made moderately anxious by the suggestion; (ii) is already prone to agree with the pyschotherapist; (iii) experiences no infringement of his/her freedom in accepting the suggestion; and (iv) provides the justification for it himself/herself.

3. The characteristics of the *recipient* of a message that affects persuasibility may be either situation-specific or characterologic in nature. For instance, high evaluation apprehension, whether a personality trait or an artificially (experimentally) manipulated experience, increases susceptibility to persuasive influence and to experimenter bias (Rosenberg, 1969). The most extensive relevant research involves perceived locus of control (Rotter, 1966). In general those who preferentially perceive and expect external control—as distinct from those who are internally motivated or are subjected to actual coercion—are susceptible to overt and subtle persuasive influence, particularly by persuaders viewed as competent, independent, and internally controlled (reviewed in Beutler, 1978).

The psychopathological dimensions of suggestibility and the role of suggestion in psychodynamic psychotherapy are yet to be explicated. But modern psychological research has shown numerous ways in which any interpersonal relationship has powerful suggestive components.

PSYCHOPATHOLOGY OF SUGGESTION

Cultural–Historical Dimension

Ethnopsychoanalytic studies suggest the value of distinguishing between the pathologists of suggestion and the pathologies of autonomy. Western cultures enshrine independence as a cultural value. Since psychopathological syndromes tend to be extreme and at times absurd caricatures of dominant cultural values (Devereux, 1980), the West is particularly plagued with the pathologies of autonomy and rigid character, such as the obsessional and paranoid disorders (Shapiro, 1981). The cultural or "meta-individual" conflict that the rigid, uninfluenceable individual is attempting to solve through his or her symptomatology derives from the paradoxical communication surrounding the cultural value of autonomy: an absolute submission to a controlling authority is perpetuated in the individual's rigid treatment of himself or herself, and this rigid "superego" must serve as the supposed guarantor of independence.

By contrast, numerous preindustrial and preliterate cultures, which fell outside the influence of more complex cultures of the Eurasian land mass until the last half-millenium (or even the last century), show evidence of "pathology of suggestion." Five categories of this variety of pathology are surveyed with a view abstracting their common features: (1) culture-bound "echo" syndromes; (2) symbiotic childhood disorders; (3) projective and symbiotic adult disorders; (4) mass movements; and (5) counter-suggestive disorders.

1. The most obvious examples of the psychopathology of suggestion are the culture-bound but fairly common echolalic and echopraxic syndromes (Malay *latah*, Ainu *imu*, Siberian *myriachit* or *ämirjacenie)*, the uncontrolled repetition of the words and actions of another person, triggered by a frightening or sexually arousing stimulus and manifested as a startle reaction and apparent seizure. The helpless sufferer, ordinarily a woman referred to as the "plaything of men," can be systematically conditioned to the point of mechanical obedience to command or imitation of the instigator's behavior (Ducey, 1976; Devereux, 1980). The attack ceases only when the instigator stops goading a sufferer, who is helpless to halt the seizure of her own will.

2. A second "hypersuggestible" group in the ethnopsychoanalytic literature are children who maintain symbiotic bonds to emotionally unresponsive and traumatizing parents. For example, in Anyi culture the trancelike and depressed state of the latency-age child seems to derive from early violation of body boundaries (by force feeding and enemas) in an extended symbiotic relationship with the mother, and to result in highly influenceable and pessimistic adults (Parin et al., 1971; Ducey & Teschke, 1979).

3. A third common class of the suggestive pathologies are the symbiotic and projective disorders of adulthood that characterize numerous preliterate cultures. These disorders, which involve "influenceability at a distance" through sorcery, spirit possession, and soul loss associated with preoedipal experience (Ducey, 1976), should not be classified as "paranoid" psychopathology, as they are heavily dependent upon primary-process (magical) explanations of illness provided by the culture itself (i.e., are not idiosyncratically delusional), and are not characterized by a paranoid focus on a plot or a persecuting agent. True paranoid psychoses seem to arise predominantly in anal-restrictive autonomy-promoting cultures (Parin et al., 1971; Shapiro, 1981).

This analysis suggests that the "pathologies of suggestion" arise predominantly in cultures in which early symbiotic relationships are not interrupted through the separation-individuation process, and external agencies remain the major guiding and restraining forces in personality structure (Muensterberger, 1969). In place of the "relatively autonomous" (from drives and environment) ego and "internalized" superego (involving individualized moral responsibility), many preliterate cultures show evidence of a "group ego" and a "clan conscience" as major constituents of personality structure (Parin et al., 1971). Hence the pathologies of suggestion are caricatures of the cultural value of the maintenance of group cohesion through submission of the individual will. But precisely who is susceptible to suggestive psychopathology in such a group-focused culture? Two further classes of the pathologies of suggestion provide an important lead.

4. The hypersuggestibility of members of crowds and mass movements is the subject of innumerable philosophical (Le Bon, 1895; Canetti, 1960), social–psychological (Festinger et al., 1956), anthropological (Lewis, 1971), historical–sociological (Rosen, 1968), and psychoanalytic (Simon, 1978) works. Their overall drift is clear. Socially and economically disenfranchised individuals are disproportionately represented in crowds and mass movements. The greater the threat of the group's disintegration from within or attack from without, the more authoritarian influence the group exerts over in its members.

5. A final class of disorders of suggestion appears at first glance to be the pathology of countersuggestion. For instance, the picturesquely termed "Crazy Dog Wishes to Die" among the Crow Indians and *berdache* of other formerly warrior Indian tribes do the opposite of what is expected of them. But this apparent "autonomy" is, of course, a manifestation of the surrender of will rather than self-direction; their behavior is entirely controllable by another's ordering them to do the opposite of what he wants them to do (Devereux, 1980). The assumption of the social role of the *berdache*, a "womanly man," is the only way to "opt out" of the warrior role predetermined for men in warrior cultures; this dispossessed

individual *must* behave in a negativistic or "mirror-image" way, to differentiate himself from the "real" men, the warriors. That similar social outcast and "womanly man," the Siberian shaman, is expected to behave in a deviant, countersuggestible fashion, to differrentiate himself from the male hunters, on the one hand, and the hypersuggestible, mostly female, "playthings of the spirits" *(mänärik)* and "playthings of men" *(ömüräk,* sufferers from *ämirjacenie),)* on the other (Ducey, 1976). These examples support Devereux's (1980, p. 210) contention that negativism and countersuggestibility are defenses against excessive suggestibility.

Examination of the five categories of pathology of suggestibility reveals the central common denominator. Those particularly susceptible to suggestion are socially and psychologically powerless. They exist on the fringes of society as outcasts, or else remain firmly under the control of others who exercise an often sadistic influence. Their suggestive pathologies are the "weapons of the weak" against the strong (Binstock, 1975), and often respond quite dramatically to the "psychotherapies of suggestion."

Clinical Dimension

Disorders of suggestibility are somewhat harder to spot at first glance in modern industrialized cultures. In an autonomy-promoting "culture of narcissism" (Lasch, 1979), where the individual recognizes no higher power and little right of others to infringe upon personal freedom, the mental health professional is often impressed by the patient's apparent noninfluenceability. Paradoxically this impression is frequently accompanied by a sympathetic response to the patient's passive victimization (by genes, family, society, and other external forces) rather than his or her active role on the maintenance of psychopathology (Binstock, 1975). A closer look reveals an intimate association in our culture between the pathologies of autonomy and the pathologies of suggestion.

In traditional diagnostic terms, the hysteric has customarily been regarded as suffering from what we have termed a pathology of suggestion; until Freud's (1888–1892) papers on hypnotism and Breuer and Freud's (1895) discussion of Anna O.—an absolutely nonsuggestible hysteric—hysteria, hypnotism, and suggestibility were often treated as inextricably intertwined. Over three-quarters of a century of almost exclusively psychoanalytic investigation has provided a far more intriguing and complex understanding of the role of suggestion in hysteria and, by extension, in other unequal human interactions. In brief, hypersuggestibility, overcompliance, and emotional contagion have been convincingly connected with a variety of unconscious motives: unrecognized sexual excitement under conditions of frustration (Freud, 1921, p. 107); disavowed competitive, envious, and jealous wishes (Freud, 1921, p. 120); subtle defiant violation of the "spirit" of a suggestion "concealed" (i.e., revealed) by exaggerated compliance with its "letter"; a pathetic and self-abasing communication of love for an indifferent or abusing person upon whom one is dependent; and so on. In our culture, and perhaps universally, hypersuggestibility appears to be a manifestation of hostile dependency.

This analysis applies to other clinical conditions as well. The apparent passivity and obedience of the highly suggestible have been linked to unconscious controlling and sadomasochistic maneuvers in works by such outstanding clinical observers as Tausk (1919) for the highly influenceable schizophrenic, Binstock (1975) for the acute and chronic psychotic, Vaillant (1977) for the "suffering" character disorder (such as the hypochondriac and masochist), and Shapiro (1981) for the masochist. The patient may cling to such a passive and vulnerable position for various reasons. The patient, for instance, fails to appreciate through experience the advantages of an autonomous and interdependent relationship with others, preferring unconsciously to "hold out" for the passive gratification and interpersonal acknowledgement of suffering associated with feeling like a helpless, deprived infant.

In brief, the autonomous individual may be more responsive to sensible and realistic suggestions than a hypersuggestible one, because of the greater scope granted to reality-respecting, secondary-process thinking (Binstock, 1978) in the former. The less autonomous person makes hypersuggestibility subserve the aim of continuing enslavement to imaginary external control.

Clinical experience also suggests that people who employ predominanatly externalizing defenses (such as projection, denial, and acting out) have more severe psychopathology, and are, therefore, less accessible to psychoanalytic psychotherapy, than those who use internalizing defenses (such as isolation of affect and repression). At the same time, both laboratory and clinical research portray individuals with a predominantly external locus of control as less effective in dealing with their environment, more socially maladjusted, and more psychologically disturbed than people with an internal locus of control (reviewed in Beutler, 1978). Yet it appears that such subjects with external expectation of control are more susceptible to directive, suggestive, and even coercive therapies. Research on persuasibility as a personality trait is consistent with this portrayal: excessive susceptibility to suggestive influence has been associated with low threshold for anxiety, lack of self-confidence, low self-esteem, submissiveness, a sense of external rather than internal control, and a tendency toward "sensitization" (perceptual vigilance toward threatening stimuli) rather than "repressiveness" (perceptual defensiveness) (reviewed in Frank, 1974).

Although some of these characteristics have been found in general in people who seek psychotherapy, the preponderance of evidence does not associate the seeking of psychotherapy per se with persuasibility (Hovland et al., 1953). Nonetheless, in individuals who do seek psychotherapy, the most persuasible tend to show a coherent set of situational and symptomatic variables: they seek help primarily because of social inhibitions and feelings of personal inadequacy, are emotionally highly responsive, manifest overt distress, and express their difficulties primarily in interpersonal terms and in reaction to interpersonal disruptions and disappointments. By contrast, the least persuasible show more circumscribed and fixed symptoms that are less clearly associated with interpersonal relations and less attributable to current environmental stress (e.g., hypochondriacal complaints, insomnia, work inhibitions, somatic symptoms), and they are less likely to acknowledge conscious distress (reviewed in Frank, 1973). In contrast to the findings for hypersuggestibility, these findings for everyday persuasibility imply that true susceptibility to suggestive influence in psychotherapy, as opposed to hypersuggestibility, is a subset of broader interpersonal and emotional responsiveness, which in turn provides the foundation of all accessibility (not only suggestive) to psychotherapeutic influence.

A synthesis of these diverse findings is made possible by reference to the psychoanalytic theory of ego autonomy, which should be sharply separated in this case from the cultural value of independence. Insofar as one has attained ego autonomy, one has demonstrated a preference for "reality-respecting" (largely internalizing) defenses and has the capacity for relationships with real people who are clearly differentiated from oneself (Binstock, 1973, 1978). The inverse of this proposition has similar clinical validity. Insofar as one has failed to achieve ego autonomy, one is prone to use "reality-distorting" (largely externalizing and immature) defenses and to become involved in symbiotic, sadomasochistic, and unequal or imbalanced relationships with fantasied "objects" not clearly differentiated from primitive aspects of the self or one's "imagoes." According to this analysis, the hypersuggestible person, who is actually not very accessible to interpersonal or psychotherapeutic influence from a real other person, feels helplessly at the mercy of superior external forces against which he or she is powerless, for the simple reason that these "forces" are magically influential components of the self projected onto, or at least attributed to, other people.

This theory helps to explain some anomalous clinical findings. Time and again the adolescent delinquent has been mistakenly portrayed as nonsuggestible (Hull, 1933; Beutler, 1979), and so independent and autonomous. This conception embraces the obviously observable and conscious while elminating the subtly observable and the unconscious. More astute psychotherapeutic observation (Johnson & Szurek, 1952; Devereux,

1980) has shown the heavy unconscious suggestibility of adolescent delinquents. With an almost pathetic slavishness, they act out the unconscious desires of their parents, to whom they only *appear* intransigently opposed. Hence, while parading their independence and absolute uninfluenceability by any adult, they subtly manifest their utter lack of ego autonomy from their parents and their own superego. As Devereux (1980) has shown, they are "superego-ridden," not "impulse-ridden," and not easily accessible to psychotherapeutic suggestion for that reason: compliance would constitute a betrayal of loyalty to parental imagoes. There is, moreover, strong evidence that a high proportion of these delinquent adolescents were subjected to incestuous and violent abuse as children (Fliess, 1956; Silber, 1979); their "defiance" is a pathetic, unacknowledged appeal for the recognition of a family "secret."

In sum, in our culture the psychopathology of suggestion tends to be a manifestation of self-proclaimed, and even self-willed, helplessness and powerlessness resulting from the failure of ego autonomy and the sense of hostile dependency upon others. Such pathology may inevitably accompany situations of actual dependency when the "caretaker" behaves in a controlling and sadistic, or in a helpless and masochistic, fashion. The child, for instance, enters a self-hypnotic and hypersuggestible state in response to parental sexual abuse (Fliess, 1956; Silber, 1979), or alternatively the institutionalized patient increases "helpless" disruptiveness in response to staff members whose ego ideal is founded upon limitless reserves of tolerance and patience (Binstock, 1975). Thus, to determine the patient's susceptibility to suggestive and other psychotherapeutic influence, it is necessary for the therapist to specify the level of the patient's ego autonomy and the motives for his or her apparent suggestibility or countersuggestibility. The dimensions of ego autonomy and accessibility to suggestive influence may be largely independent of one another, but the pathological exaggerations of both dimensions may be closely aligned, or even largely indistinguishable.

PSYCHOTHERAPIES OF SUGGESTION

Cultural—Historical Context

The foundation of all premodern psychotherapy is suggestion, according to the classic works on the subject (Freud, 1890; Kiev, 1964; Frank, 1974). The healer employs both direct and indirect suggestion. The basic technique employed for a minor ailment is direct suggestion, and may be appropriately administered by either a healer or a layperson.

This form of supportive psychotherapy consists of everyday common-sense techniques for making a distressed person feel better: moral, support, appeal to reason, "good advice" from the standpoint of experience and sympathy, allying oneself with the person's view of the situation, and so on. A good verbatim example is provided by Devereux (1961, pp. 97). This form of treatment is so universal and unexotic that it is either contemned or ignored in both psychiatric and anthropological literature.

The varieties of indirect suggestion that enter into any psychotherapeutic treatment are too numerous to list, but this technical dimension is the true sine qua non of psychotherapy, and so pervasive as to be taken for granted or else entirely overlooked. This category includes the tacit or explicit methods that arouse the patient's hope and confidence, bolster self-esteem, generate "mutative" emotions, assure him or her of the meaningfulness of the illness, and strengthen his or her ties with and reintegration into the group. The elaborate ceremonies, great expense, group participation, and charisma of the healer are constant suggestive techniques employed the world over to ensure maximal impact of the treatment on a serious emotional disturbance or physical illness. Confusion over his or her mysterious illness makes a sufferer's accessible to therapeutic influence, and this susceptibility is frequently reinforced and augmented by inducing an altered state of consciousness by rhythmical stimuli, emotional exhaustion, hypnotic suggestion, and so on (Frank, 1974; Ducey, 1976).

Close ethnopsychiatric investigation of specific cultures shows the intimate association between a culture's theory of disease, its diagnostic methods, and its curative techniques (Whiting & Child, 1953; Muensterberger et al., 1960–1981, passim; Kiev, 1964, passim; Bahr et al., 1974; Simon, 1978). In preliterate cultures that promote the pathologies of suggestion, it stands to reason that cure relies heavily upon suggestion as well. Hence the proper treatment for possession by malevolent spirits is their dramatized expulsion; for soul loss, an other worldly journey to recover it; for bewitchment, the exposure and punishment of the offending sorcerer. The culture's conceptual scheme of illness and cure has been perpetuated and individualized in accordance with the patient's "assumptive world"; by making comprehensible the chaotic feelings associated with illness, and particularly by enlisting the aid of supernatural forces to counteract the mysterious forces of illness, the healer through suggestion alone increases the patient's sense of mastery and sets in motion the natural forces of recovery that play an indispensable part in health (Frank, 1974).

Another crucial feature of premodern health techniques is the reaffirmation of a disrupted group solidarity and the reintegration of the patient into the community. The diagnosis by the healer applies not only to the individual patient's malady, but also to hidden sources of tension within the group to which the afflicted person belongs (Turner, 1967, 1968, 1969; Simon, 1978). The sensitivity of the healer to these sources of group tension and appropriateness of the prescriptions and punishments meted out to patient and group members exert a crucial "suggestive" influence in persuading the patient to give up his or her illness and in inducing the group to cease using the patient as its scapegoat. Indeed, one cannot help, noticing that the effective healer is here using not only suggestion, but also an unspoken form of psychotherapeutic interpretation in the accurate assessment of and intervention in a conflict-generating situation. These elements of group tension do not necessarily detract from the positive suggestive effects of group support. When one Navaho informant reflected upon the beneficial influence of a ceremony, he singled out the thought that "all of my friends are close to me" (Kaplan & Johnson, 1964). This curative influence is all the more significiant in group-focused cultures.

While the evidence is extensive that suggestion lies at the base of all premodern psychotherapy, this assertion is no justification for an ethnocentric derogation of its subtlety or effectiveness. At least two centuries of the scholarly investigation of the most thoroughly studied of premodern cultures, the cultures of European classical antiquity, have demonstrated the ancients' remarkably detailed and sensitive understanding of the complexities of human interaction. The most penetrating analyses of ancient Greek poetic, philosophical, and oratorical works that bear upon the subject of psychotherapeutic suggestion may be found in Lain Entralgo (1958) and Simon (1978); here we can survey only a few high points.

Even the most ancient Greek literature, the Homeric epics, contains powerful and moving instances of psychotherapy. The *Iliad* beautifully portrays the resolution of the implacable grief of the enemies Achilles and Priam, in which the acceptance of a common humanity and a common mortality is effected through the culturally syntonic suggestive devices of reintegration within the group of warriors and ancestors through the narration of an exemplary tale, restoration of the social and cosmic equilibrium, and appeal to socially available precedent for ways of handling despair (Simon, 1978, p. 72). (It is perhaps not insignificant that Achilles backs up his psychotherapeutic suggestions, that Priam should eat and thereby choose to live, with a death threat!) Such "psychotherapy scenes" as appear in the tragedies (e.g., Euripides' *Bacchae* and *Heracles*) show a sensitive attunement of therapists to delusional "patient" and a flexible and responsive intermingling of suggestion and clarification (Devereux, 1970; Simon, 1978).

Plato was opposed to the magical and irrational effects of suggestion and the seductive ones of persuasion. He held that the philosopher could help a "patient" attain true *sōphrosynē* (an untranslatable word with overtones of temperance, serenity, and a harmonious balance among conflicting beliefs, desires, and virtues) by supplying the *logos* (word, reason), properly accommodated to the passions, character, and state of mind of the patient, that could cure the disorder of the latter's psyche, just as a physician supplies the proper medicine for the body (Lain Entralgo, 1958, p. 114). Indeed, Plato went beyond the "supportive psychotherapy" of the soothing bard, as his dialectic is designed to produce discomfort in the always disconcerting search for truth (Simon, 1978, p. 180). In this respect Plato is rightly regarded as the forerunner of Freud in his devotion to unwelcome and unpleasant truths.

In his *Rhetoric*, Aristotle offered a tripartite analysis of the effects of persuasive communication remarkably similar to our modern psychological analysis. In brief, the persuasiveness of the communication is based upon the interaction of the characteristics of the speaker, the message, and the hearer. The speaker's persuasive capacity arises from a combination of prestige, natural talents (eloquence), moral qualities, and developed skills and techniques. The influence of the message depends upon its propriety, orderliness, and adequacy or responsiveness to the hearer's needs. Finally, the hearer contributes character, present condition (illness or state of ignorance), responsiveness to current environmental circumstances, and a certain "self-presentation" (i.e., transference) of soul to the speaker. In Aristotle's conception the speaker purposely stirs up certain passions and challenges beliefs in order to excite confusion and emotional tension, the better to resolve it by suitable and timely verbal expressions that encourage a more refined, differentiated, and integrated experience of reexamined passions and beliefs," Lain Entralgo (1958, p. 245) and Simon (1978, p. 144) thus expand the meaning of "catharsis." This is truly a psychotherapeutic process, since the person without *sōphrosynē* is sick in both mind and body; like most pre-Cartesians, the Greeks believed in a psychosomatic unity. In addition, these processes are suggestive ones, in the emphasis upon supplying what is needed or called for. Not only is this the meaning of *suggestio* in later Roman rhetoric, but it is also, I propose, the best psychotherapeutic definition of the term.

The ancient Greek "therapy of the word" had no immediate offspring, as far as the historical sources suggest. This does not mean, however, that sugestive therapy disappeared, but rather that is was shifted onto a supernatural plane. We note the continuing presence of suggestive cures of suffering, mainly in relation to the spiritual realm. A remarkable example is recorded in the *Sacred Tale* of Aelius Aristides, the hypochondriac orator of the second century of our era. His extreme suffering was counteracted only by miraculous cure by the god Asclepius, a process that resulted in narcissistic self-inflation through identification with the god, as recorded in Aristides' dreams (Ducey, 1980b). The cycle of torturing illness and miraculous cure, eternally repeated, is a commonly remarked feature of suggestive disorders and therapies (Kaplan & Johnson, 1964; Ducey, 1976).

The Christian offshoot of the suggestive therapies was embodied in the sacrament of confession, which also permitted the sinner reintegration into the imaginary community of the blessed, and had cathartic, abreactive effects. But the premodern era of the West has also seen evidence of numerous chiliastic and reformatory movements, which, in their root-edness in despair of the powerless, their histrionic nature, and their trans-formative effects, bear striking resemblances to the psychotherapies of suggestion (Cohn, 1957; Rosen, 1968). Even some treatments for witch-craft and demonic possession, such as ceremonies of exorcism, were founded on suggestive therapeutics, in a way remarkably similar to the treatment of spirit possession in preliterate cultures.

As Western thought became more secularized in the Renaissance, psychotherapies of suggestion that form the foundation of modern psy-chotherapeutic movements began to appear, and culminated in the practice of animal magnetism by Mesmer and the hypnosis of his descendants (Ellenberger, 1970). In general, suggestion in the premodern era—as well as in several modern forms of psychotherapy—was employed primarily for direct symptom removal in individuals who had circumscribed ego-dystonic maladies with otherwise intact functioning, as is apparent in Bernheim's, Liébeault's, Prince's, and Sidis' suggestive therapeutics. Sug-gestion was also employed in the treatment of severe mental disturbances by Janet, not to remove an intractable symptom so much as to make it bearable. For instance, he would suggest the substitution of a hallucination with a positive affective tone for a frightening or threatening hallucination. It was, of course, Freud's disaffection with suggestion as the primary therapeutic tool that ushered in the subordination of suggestion and the modern era of psychotherapy.

Developments in the Modern Era

In his major technical and historical works on psychoanalysis Freud (1905, 1910, 1911–1915, 1914, 1916–1917, 1919a, 1925, 1926, 1937a, 1937b, 1940), alludes to several reasons for abandoning hypnosis and its associated therapeutic technique, suggestion.

1. Suggestion produces often dramatic, but ultimately unstable, ther-apeutic results. Even if a patient is suggestible, symptom recurrence is inevitable. Moreover, as Bernheim himself confided to Freud (1925, p. 18), his own success involved only his (public) hospital patients, not private ones; as we might understand this observation, suggestion is more likely to be effective with patients prone to a pathology of suggestion, that is, those who have less social and economic power, less education, and fewer psychological and social resources to effect a cure on the basis of active mastery over passively experienced suffering (Freud, 1920). The capri-

ciousness of the procedure and unreliability of results make suggestion by itself a palliative rather than a therapeutic measure.

2. Suggestion superimposes a nonexistent construction on the patient, while analysis makes what is already present emerge. The suggestive therapist assumes an unwarranted authoritarian power over the patient, which is objectionable not only on moral grounds ("an evident injustice and an act of violence" [Freud, 1921, p. 89]), but also on practical ones, since it repeats the parents' mistake of crushing the patient's independence and, by stimulating resistance, makes the neurosis hard to influence or banish. Suggestion is designed more to flatter the suggestionist and bolster his or her sense of power than to cure the patient.

3. The temporary gratification derived by the suggestive therapist from being considered a miracle worker provides insufficient recompense for the incapacity of suggestion to stimulate and satisfy scientific curiosity and understanding; "for it cleared away the psychical resistances in a certain area while building them up into an unscalable wall at its frontiers" (Freud, 1910, p. 51). Hence, the suggestive removal of symptoms, apart from being unreliable and unstable, is a cosmetic approach that ultimately strengthens the forces of repression and thereby perpetuates the neurosis.

Freud's early disciples added their voices to the chorus of criticism of the apparently widespread suggestive psychotherapies (Dubois, Prince, Coué) derived from Bernheim and Janet. Such therapies are an "education in blindness," self-deceit, and concealment (Ferenczi, 1912); by making the patient's credulity the precondition of success, they destroy a person's capacity for the recognition of truth (Ferenczi, 1913). Psychoanalysis, by contrast, encourages the patient's utmost skepticism and complete honesty in airing doubts and criticisms of the analyst. Abraham (1925, p. 326) similarly contends that a suggestive cure "spares the patient a laborious adjustment to reality" and encourages ignorance. Ernest Jones (1910, 1923) contrasts psychoanalysis, in which the transference is made conscious and examined, with suggestive therapies, in which transference feelings become destructive by being unexamined and thereby remain primitive and totalistic. He also points out the the suggestive cure is dependent upon continued contact with the therapist. His final, rather intriguing, argument is that the patient "cured" by suggestion buys temporary peace of mind at the expense of impeding object love; where psychoanalysis urges a reconciliation or tolerance of the conflicting demands of the ego ideal and the "repressed alloerotism," suggestion perpetuates the "stultifying effects" of autoerotism and narcissistic self-absorption.

Another sharp-sighted early critic of suggestion, Edward Glover (1924), pointed out that the therapist who actually does advise, persuade, convert, or command a patient inhibits the free development and recognition of the "imaginary," fantasy-inspired transference neurosis and thus deprives the treatment of its central technical device for inducing recognition of the neurotic repetition compulsion. In his classic influential article, Glover (1931) proposes that inexact or incomplete psychoanalytic interpretations function in precisely the same way as nonanalytic suggestions. All these technical maneuvers serve to create an iatrogenic and ego-syntonic symptom substitution that deflects therapist and patient from the psychological truth. The patient is relieved to accommodate to the therapist's superego-induced pleas for ignorance and self-deception; the sidetracking of honest inquiry in the service of ethical or rationalistic prohibition serves not only to reinforce the patient's self-satisfaction by obsessional canceling of unconscious sadistic desires, but even to justify continued sadistic behavior. The outcome of a successful suggestive treatment, or an unsuccessful psychoanalytic one, may be an obsessional inhibition or expiatory ceremonial, an ego-syntonic phobia, or a "friendly paranoia" involving dependence on magical drugs.

Does suggestion, then, play any role in the properly conducted psychoanalysis or psychodynamic psychotherapy? In spite of his severe criticisms of suggestive treatment, and his constant aim to distinguish psychoanalysis from it, Freud is quite explicit in according suggestion a place in psychodynamic psychotherapy. Suggestion promotes treatment in the beginning stages (Freud, 1926), carries forward the curative process by countering resistances (Freud, 1923a), provides a "new superego" for analytic after-education to compensate for parental mistakes (Freud, 1940), and promotes the patient's final independence by encouraging him or her to accomplish the psychical work necessary for permanent improvement (Freud, 1912). Indeed "the results of psychoanalysis rest upon suggestion" (Freud, 1912, p. 106), insofar as suggestion means the nonerotic positive transference, the proper handling of which makes the patient accessible to influence and promotes the cure (Freud, 1916–1917, p. 451). Even the "copper of direct suggestion" can be alloyed with the "pure gold of analysis" in the treatment of traumatic psychopathology (Freud, 1919a). Similarly, in his controversial "active technique," which forced or suggested fantasies designed to unblock the free associations, Ferenczi (1920, 1924) argued that suggestion could promote the analysis by stimulating the patient's inhibited active strivings (Balint, 1967).

As in so many other areas, Freud turns out to appear more flexible than his systematizing followers. In sharp disagreement with Glover (1931) and also with numerous critics of psychoanalysis, Freud (1937b, p. 262) asserted that the danger of leading the patient astray by suggestion had been enormously exaggerated; an analyst who had committed such a misdeed "would have to blame himself with not allowing his patients to have their say." In perhaps his most penetrating discussion of the subject, he freely acknowledges the fact—experimentally confirmed by Pötzl (1917) and Fisher (1953a)—that both the manifest and latent contents of dreams are influenced by suggestion. The analyst need not be concerned about misleading the patient through suggestion; not only are the patient's resistances (negative transference) too effective in averting excessive influence, but also the analysis succeeds only through the accurate fitting together of a "confused heap of fragments," as with a jigsaw puzzle with no alternative solution (Freud, 1923b). Only a suggestion that tallies with what is real in the patient will have a curative effect (Freud, 1916–1917, p. 452). In a view diametrically opposed to Glover's, Freud (1937b) even claims that a false construction may net an accurate interpretation.

Psychoanalysts after Freud have generally derogated the importance of suggestion in psychoanalysis, confining its use either to such a slightly devalued aims as strengthening the ego through the uninterpreted transference in psychotherapy (Bibring, 1954; Gill, 1954), or to such adjunctive nontherapeutic goals as the initial establishment of a narcissistic alliance (Paolino, 1981) or the encouragement of the endurance of pain or frustration (Greenson, 1967). But a long-established, though renegade, psychoanalytic tradition associates the psychotherapeutic use of suggestion with the replacement of once inadequately fulfilled parental functions.

This movement may be traced ultimately to Ferenczi's (1930) later technique of relaxation and neocatharsis, in which the analyst made a positive and, it was hoped, corrective response to the regressed patient's longings so as to avoid a retraumatization due to the analyst's frustrating responses. Ferenczi did not doubt the power of suggestion in this situation. The analyst's supportive suggestion, as the figurative counterpart of mother's locomotive support, provides a reparation for a former authoritarian suggestion that demanded only obedience. The analyst's suggestion, by contrast, "bestows a power of individuality," self-esteem, and renewed will power (Ferenczi, 1932, p. 255). In his last major book, Freud (1940) himself took up this theme of correcting parental errors and respecting the patient's individuality.

The best-known development of these principles is the "corrective emotional experience" of Alexander and French (1946). They encouraged the therapist to play a role opposite to the behavior of the initial traumatizing figure, and aimed to counteract the development of a regressive transference neurosis and dependency. This therapeutic stance clearly derives from a theory of psychopathology that emphasizes actual deprivation or faulty behavior on the part of the parents, and can be traced back through Ferenczi (1933) to Freud's early seduction theory of neurosis. It is highly probable that this shift to literal experience (rather than fantasy) as etiologic and to the rediscovery of therapeutic suggestion can be ascribed to the widening scope of problems addressed by psychodynamic therapy (Stone, 1954).

Another stream of influence in this revival of suggestion in psychodynamic therapy derives from the English object-relations school, as represented by Balint (1965), Winnicott (1958, 1965), and Guntrip (1968).

Although these writers tend to avoid the term suggestion, they clearly imply that psychodynamic psychotherapy has curative effects not so much because of insight gained through interpretation, a view strongly represented in the American version of classical psychoanalysis (e.g., Blum, 1979; Kernberg, 1979), but because of the suggestive effects of the analyst's actual replacement of the inadequate maternal care the patient received as a child. Even some classical American analysts have regarded the "diatrophic" or fostering influences of the analyst as curative per se, or at least as the precondition for promoting the patient's autonomy and capacity for insight (e.g., Spitz, Gitelson, Zetzel, Paolino).

The work of Kohut (1971, 1979, 1984) is clearly the culmination of these Hungarian and British traditions, both of which may be traced to Ferenczi (1930). The analyst is expected to play the corrective role of an empathic self-object to the patient who has suffered faulty or incomplete development as a result of unempathic handling by the parental self-objects. Kohut implies that cure is effected by "transmuting internalizations" of the analyst's empathic responsiveness rather than by insight into drive-defense patterns gained through interpretation. Like most other post-Freudian technical theorists, Kohut avoids a conception of this process as therapeutic suggestion, since this term has received such bad press in psychoanalytic writing. A psychoanalytically informed rehabilitation of suggestion must take this element of empathic responsiveness into account.

Psychotherapy Outcome Research

Before closing this overview with such an attempt, I shall glance briefly at the extensive research on the outcome of psychotherapy, with special reference to the role of suggestion. In a remarkable statistical meta-analysis of all psychotherapy outcome studies through the mid-1970s, Smith, Glass, and Miller (1980) demonstrated the positive, powerful effectiveness of nearly *all* forms of psychotherapy studied, including those that rely predominantly upon suggestion (such as hypnotherapy, rational-emotive therapy, and behavioral therapies). Even placebo treatment, the whipping boy of psychotherapy outcome studies, has documented effects. As might be predicted, outcome measures that showed greater improvement than others under the impact of any form of psychotherapy may be reasonably regarded as highly susceptible to suggestive influence (e.g., fear and anxiety, patient and therapist ratings of improvement, emotional or somatic complaints, and vocational or personal development); conversely, outcome measures resistant to suggestive influence (e.g., objective life indicators of adjustment, personality traits, and sociopathic behavior) showed the greatest resistance to change, although all were positively influenced by psychotherapy. These findings may be interpreted as empirical support for many of the premises of this overview, particularly that suggestion has general therapeutic effects on a wide range of psychological problems, especially on nonspecific, subjective indicators of psychopathology.

A second relevant area of research involves the differential suggestive effects of characteristics of the therapist. A series of studies by Beutler and others (reviewed in Beutler, 1978) has resulted in a number of important distinctions. The therapist's consistency increases credibility and therefore the patient's trust, while the therapist's warmth and empathic interest increase the patient's attraction and are thus instrumental for alliance building, but not for effective therapeutic influence per se. (Recall the parallel finding from the persuasion literature: interpersonal attractiveness sets the stage for persuasion, but does not accomplish it.) The most intriguing finding for suggestive therapeutic influence is that initial discrepancy, not similarity, of values between patient and therapist is associated with proportional changes in the patient's expressed beliefs toward those of the therapist; to have an impact upon the patient, the therapist's values should be divergent but acceptable to the patient. High personality similarity between the two may actually decrease the therapist's attractiveness and impede therapeutic progress.

A final line of research that helps define the role of suggestion compares psychodynamic therapy with directive therapies (especially cognitive modification and systematic desensitization) when the patient groups are varied according to type of defenses used or locus of perceived control. The results of the studies of highest quality (in ratings by Beutler, 1979) are remarkably consistent. Psychodynamic psychotherapy, and other nondirective therapies that rely predominantly upon techniques other than suggestion, are more effective than directive therapies with patients who have complex symptoms (McReynolds, 1970), employ internalizing modes of defense (Sloane, et al., 1975), and experience themselves as the center of control of their lives or have an internal locus of control (Friedman & Dies, 1974; Abramowitz et al., 1974). Conversely, the available literature suggests that directive and suggestive therapies are more effective with patients who have simple or circumscribed symptoms, employ externalizing defenses, and experiene an external locus of control for their actions (Beutler, 1979). Analogous findings show the greatest therapeutic effects produced by pairing independent, dominant therapists with submissive, dependent patients (Beutler, 1978).

Suggestion in Psychodynamic Psychotherapy

These findings imply that what is distinctive about psychodynamic psychotherapy are nonsuggestive techniques such as interpretation. Yet suggestive elements still play their part as the backdrop of even this specialized form of psychotherapy. Apart from the general suggestive components of all psychotherapies, psychodynamic therapy has its own specific suggestive aspects, beautifully summarized by Frank (1974, p. 233) as follows:

> The therapist is a model with whom the patient can identify. His refusal to offer overt guidance leads the patient to become increasingly dependent on him on the one hand and, on the other, to attribute progress to his own efforts, thereby increasing his sense of mastery. The detailed review of the patient's past life mobilizes guilt feelings with confession and implicit forgiveness, conveyed by the therapist's steady interest. It also helps the patient to reconstruct his history in order to support a better self-image. Interpretations implicitly convey approval or disapproval and reduce the patient's cognitive confusion by naming his inchoate feelings and ordering them within a conceptual framework. They may stir the patient up by confronting him with disowned aspects of himself or alleviate distressing emotions by changing his perception of their causes. Interpretations of symptoms as oblique efforts to control others may lead to beneficial changes in behavior. Finally, they implicitly convey the therapist's theory of human nature and philosophy of existence, which may help the patient to bear his suffering or actually reduce it by placing it in a broader context that gives it significance.

Promotion of self-cure is perhaps the most important suggestive aspect of psychodynamic psychotherapy, and the research supports its impact. Long-lasting therapeutic change is enhanced by treatments that encourage the patient to interpret change as due to internal rather than external forces (Davison & Valins, 1969). (Recall the similar findings regarding the resistance to later change of attitudes for which the person has provided the evidence and argument.) Hence, apart from the actual content of the therapist's interventions (such as interpretations), the very context and style of conveying those interventions have powerful implicit suggestive influence; and thus, as Freud (1912, p. 106) said, psychoanalytic results "rest upon suggestion."

The overall drift of my argument leads to clear conclusions regarding the role of suggestion in psychodynamic psychotherapy. Modern theorists have created too narrow a role for suggestion based upon a rigid and tendentious definition and an intransigent opposition to the explicit exertion of interpersonal influence. As seminal as has been Bibring's paper (1954), its focus upon technique at the expense of intersubjective human relationships has encouraged psychodynamic psychotherapists to overlook the forest for the trees. What makes the difference in any psychotherapy is the therapist's responsive action to what the patient actually needs (Grotjahn, 1967).

Accurate and empathic responsiveness is not the privileged preserve of any one school, but is the very precondition for all curative effects in psychotherapy. The more aware the therapist is of different levels and conflicting aspects within the patient, and the more spontaneous and flexible in tailoring the intervention to the patient's complex self-presentation, the more effective he or she will be as a therapist. If this point of view is formulated with sufficient clarity, debates such as those between Kohut (1979) and Kernberg (1979) about whether empathy per se or interpretation per se is curative should wither on the vine. Both are predicated upon the therapist's accurate, tactful, and multileveled responsiveness to the patient's actual needs.

In short, it is not so much what technique the therapist uses as the empathic responsiveness to diverse aspects of the human condition that makes for effective psychotherapy. The talents called for in being a good parent are similar to those called for in being a good psychotherapist, talents that Erikson (1980) has summarized by the term *generativity,* or the capacity to promote the maturation of dependent individuals. Careful study of human behavior, particularly its unconscious dimension, is the sine qua non of high-quality psychodynamic psychotherapy. But without a natural human empathic responsiveness and a generative personality structure, no accumulation of knowledge will make a person a responsive psychotherapist; for that matter, the lack of such personal qualities may make appreciation of psychoanalytic findings impossible.

Such empathic responsiveness in psychotherapy must include the tactful and judicious use of suggestion. The effectiveness of suggestion alone is beautifully illustrated in one of Freud's (1892) earliest case histories. As penetratingly analyzed by Blum (1979), Freud's remarkable cure of a mother who could not feed her newborn infant is predicated upon the use of suggestion in an entirely new and nontraditional way. Freud did not employ suggestion to banish, deny, or suppress the symptoms, as this technique only generates the patient's "counterwill" (later termed resistance) and regressive tendencies (not yet so labeled). Instead he gave forceful and directive suggestions that presented to the patient an awareness of her unconscious internal conflicts. Not only is his technique here the immediate precursor to psychodynamic psychotherapy, but it in fact represents Freud's penetrating intuitive insights into psychopathology, years before his formal psychoanalytic investigations. For instance, in his effective suggestion that the mother should rail angrily at her family for failing to feed her, Freud recognized the mother's own infantile wish to be fed, her envious identification with her infant, her oral-aggressive demandingness, and her regressive sense of helpless dependency lying at the root of postpartum depression. Freud needed no textbook of the unconscious to make this suggestion, only his responsiveness to the complexity of human behavior.

Suggestion in this case was no less effective—and possibly more so—than interpretation would have been, for he conveyed his empathic understanding directly to the patient with an accurate and responsive assessment of her unconscious conflict.

It is fitting to close with this clinical specimen of psychodynamic suggestion. Freud's therapeutic responsiveness, flexibility, and unconventional activity may remind us that psychotherapeutic techniques are only as curative as the psychotherapist who employs them. Like any other technique, direct psychotherapeutic suggestion has a limited range of applications. But since indirect suggestion is ubiquitous in all psychotherapies, and indeed in all interpersonal relationships, psychodynamic psychotherapists ignore this powerful technique at their patients' expense, and at their own peril.

REFERENCES

Abraham, K. (1925) Psychoanalytical notes on Coué's system of self-mastery. In: *Clinical papers and essays on psycho-analysis*. New York: Basic Books, 1955.

Abramowitz, C.V., Abramowitz, S.I., Roback, H.B., and Jackson, C. Differential effectiveness of directive and nondirective group therapies as a function of client internal-external control. *Journal of Consulting and Clinical Psychology*, 1974, *42*, 849–853.

Alexander, F.G. and French, T.M. *Psychoanalytic therapy: Principle and applications*. New York: Ronald Press, 1946.

Andersson, O. *Studies in the prehistory of psychoanalysis*. Stockholm: Svenska Bokförlaget/Norstedts-Bonniers, 1962.

Bahr, D.M., Gregorio, J, Lopez, D.I., & Alvarez, A. *Piman shamanism and staying sickness*. Tucson: University of Arizona Press, 1974.

Balint, M. *Primary love and psycho-analytic technique*. New York: Liveright, 1965.

Balint, M. Sandor Ferenczi's technical experiments. In: B.B. Wolman (Ed.), *Psychoanalytic techniques*. New York: Basic Books, 1967.

Badura, A. *Principles of behavior modification*. New York: Holt, Rinehart, & Winston, 1969.

Bergin, A.E. The effect of dissonant persuasive communications upon changes in self-referring attitudes. *Journal of Personality*, 1962, *30*, 423–438.

Berscheid, E. Opinion change and communicator-communicatee similarity and dissimilarity. *Journal of Personality and Social Psychology*, 1966, *4*, 670–680.

Beutler, L.E. Psychotherapy and persuasion. In: L.E. Beutler & R. Greene (Eds.), *Special problems in child and adolescent behavior: A social ecological and psychological behavioral approach*. Westport, Conn.: Technomic Publishing, 1978.

Beutler, L.E. Toward specific psychological therapies for specific conditions. *Journal of Consulting and Clinical Psychology*, 1979, *47*, 882–897.

Bibring, E. Psychoanalysis and the dynamic psychotherapies. *Journal of the American Psychoanalytic Association*, 1954, *2*, 745–770.

Binstock, W. On the two forms of intimacy. *Journal of the American Psychoanalytic Association,* 1973, *21,* 93–107.

Binstock, W. *The weapons of the weak.* Unpublished manuscript, 1975.

Binstock, W. The psychodynamic approach. In: A. Lazare (Ed.), *Outpatient psychiatry: Diagnosis and treatment.* Baltimore: Williams & Wilkins, 1978.

Blum, H.P. The curative and creative aspects of insight. In: *Psychoanalytic technique and theory of therapy. Journal of the American Psychoanalytic Association,* 1979, *27* (suppl.), 41–69.

Braid, J. *Neurypnology.* London: Churchill, 1843.

Brehm, J.W. *A theory of psychological reactance.* New York: Academic Press, 1966.

Brehm, J.W., & Cole, A.H. Effect of a favor which reduces freedom. *Journal of Personality and Social Psychology,* 1966, *3,* 420–426.

Breuer, J., and Freud, S. (1895) Studies on hysteria. *Standard edition,* vol. 2., London: Hogarth Press, 1955.

Canetti, E. *Crowds and power.* New York: Seabury Press, 1960.

Cohn, N. (1957) The pursuit of the millennium., 2nd ed. New York: Harper & Row, 1961.

Darnton, R. *Mesmerism and the end of Enlightenment in France.* Cambridge, Mass.: Harvard University Press, 1968.

Davison, G.C., and Valins, S. Maintenance of self-attributed and drug-attributed behavior change. *Journal of Personality and Social Psychology,* 1969, *11,* 25–33.

Devereux, G. (1961) *Mohave ethnopsychiatry: The psychic disturbances of an Indian tribe.* Bureau of American Ethnology, Bulletin 175. Washington, D.C.: Smithsonian Institution, 1969.

Devereux, G. The psychotherapy scene in Euripides' *Bacchae. Journal of Hellenic Studies,* 1970, *90,* 35–48.

Devereux, G. *Basic problems of ethnopsychiatry.* Chicago: University of Chicago Press, 1980.

Ducey, C.P. The personality and creative psychopathology of the shaman: Ethnopsychoanalytic perspectives. *The Psychoanalytic Study of Society,* 1976, *7,* 173–230.

Ducey, C. Melancholy and epidemic frenzy, 1600–1800. First Lecture Series on the History of Psychiatry, Harvard Medical School, 1980a.

Ducey, C. Dread of transformation and the search for solace in the early Roman empire. Second Lecture Series on the History of Psychiatry, Harvard Medical School, 1980b.

Ducey, C.P., and Teschke, G.I. Review of Parin, P., Morgenthaler, F., and Parin-Matthey, G. *Fürchte deinen Nächsten wie dich selbst: Psychoanalyse and Gesellschaft am Modell der Agni in Westafrika. Journal of the American Psychoanalytic Assoication,* 1979, *27,* 247–258.

Ellenberger, H. *The discovery of the unconscious: The history and evolution of dynamic psychiatry.* New York: Basic Books, 1970.

Erikson, E.H. Elements of a psychoanalytic theory of psychosocial development. In: S.I. Greenspan and G.H. Pollock (Eds.), *The course of life: Psychoanalytic contributions toward understanding personality development, Vol. I: Infancy and early childhood.* Washington, D.C.: National Institute of Mental Health, 1980.

Ferenczi, S. (1909) Introjection and transference. In: *Sex in Psychoanalysis.* New York: Dover, 1958.

Ferenczi S. (1912) Suggestion and psycho-analysis. In: *Further contributions to the theory and technique of psycho-analysis.* London: Hogarth Press, 1960.

Ferenczi, S. (1913) Belief, disbelief, and conviction. In: *Further contributions to the theory and technique and psycho-analysis.* London: Hogarth Press, 1960.

Ferenczi, S. (1920) The further development of an active therapy in psycho-analysis. In: *Further contributions to the theory and technique of psychoanalysis.* London: Hogarth Press, 1960.

Ferenczi, S. (1924) On forced fantasies: Activity in the association technique. In: *Further contributions to the theory and technique of psycho-analysis.* London: Hogarth Press, 1960.

Ferenczi, S. (1930) The principles of relaxation and neocatharis. In: *Final contributions to the problems and methods of psycho-analysis.* London: Hogarth Press, 1955.

Ferenczi, S. (1932) Suggestion = action without one's will. In: *Final contributions to the problems and methods of psycho-analysis.* London: Hogarth Press, 1955.

Ferenczi, S. (1933) Confusion of tongues between adults and the child: The language of tenderness and passion. In: *Final contributions to the problems and methods of psycho-analysis.* London: Hogarth Press, 1955.

Festinger, L. *A Theory of cognitive dissonance.* Evanston, Ill.: Row, Peterson, 1957.

Festinger, L., Riecken, H.W. and Schachter, S. *When prophecy fails.* New York: Harper & Row, 1956.

Fisher, C. Studies on the nature of suggestion. I: Experimental induction of dreams by direct suggestion. *Journal of the American Psychoanalytic Association,* 1953a, *1,* 222–225.

Fisher, C. Studies on the nature of suggestion. II: The transference meaning of giving suggestions. *Journal of the American Psychoanalytic Association,* 1953b, *1,* 406–437.

Fliess, R. *Erogeneity and libido: Some addenda to the theory of the psychosexual development of the human.* New York: International Universities Press, 1956.

Frank, J.D., *Persuasion and healing: A comparative study of psychotherapy.* Rev. ed. New York: Schocken, 1974.

Freud, S. (1888) Preface to the translation of Bernheim's *Suggestion. Standard edition,* Vol. 1, 75–85. London: Hogarth Press, 1966, pp. 75–85.

Freud, S. (1888–1892) Papers on hypnotism and suggestion. *Standard edition,* vol. 1. London: Hogarth Press, 1966, pp. 61–128.

Freud, S. (1890) Psychical (or mental) treatment. *Standard edition,* vol. 7. London: Hogarth Press, 1953, pp. 283–302.

Freud, s. (1892) A case of successful treatment by hypnotism with some remarks on the origin of hysterical symptoms through "counterwill." *Standard edition.* vol. 1 London: Hogarth Press, 1966, pp. 117–128.

Freud, S. (1905) On psychotherapy. *Standard edition,* vol. 7. London: Hogarth Press, 1953, pp. 257–268.

Freud, S. (1909) Analysis of a phobia in a five-year-old boy. *Standard edition,* vol. 10, London: Hogarth Press, 1955, pp. 5–149.

Freud, S. (1910) Five lectures on psycho-analysis. *Standard edition,* vol. 11, London: Hogarth Press, 1957, pp. 9–55.

Freud, S. (1911–1915) Papers on technique. *Standard edition,* vol. 12. London: Hogarth Press, 1958, pp. 83–173.

Freud, S. (1912) The dynamics of transference. *Standard edition,* vol. 12. London: Hogarth Press, 1958, pp. 99–108.

Freud, S. (1914) On the history of the psycho-analytic movement. *Standard edition*, vol. 14. London: Hogarth Press, 1957, pp. 7–66.
Freud, S. (1916–1917) Introductory lectures on psycho-analysis. *Standard edition*, vols. 15 and 16. London: Hogarth Press, 1961, 1963.
Freud, S. (1919a) Lines of advance in psycho-analytic therapy. *Standard edition*, vol. 17. London: Hogarth Press, 1955, pp. 159–168.
Freud, S. (1919b) The "uncanny". *Standard edition* vol. 17. London: Hogarth Press, 1955, pp. 219–256.
Freud, S. (1920) Beyond the pleasure principle. *Standard edition*, vol. 18. London: Hogarth Press, 1955, pp. 7–64.
Freud, S. (1921) Group psychology and the analysis of the ego. *Standard edition*, vol. 18. London: Hogarth Press, 1955, pp. 69–143.
Freud, S. (1923a) Two encyclopedia articles. *Standard edition*, vol. 18. London: Hogarth Press, 1955, pp. 235–259.
Freud, S. (1923b) Remarks on the theory and practice of dream interpretation. *Standard edition* vol. 19. London: Hogarth Press, 1961, pp. 109–121.
Freud, S. (1925) An autobiographical study. *Standard edition*, vol. 20. London: Hogarth Press, 1959, pp. 7–74.
Freud, S. (1926) The question of lay analysis. *Standard edition*, vol. 20. London: Hogarth Press, 1959, pp. 183–258.
Freud, S. (1937a) Analysis terminable and interminable. *Standard edition*, vol. 23. London: Hogarth Press, 1964, pp. 216–253.
Freud, S. (1937b) Constructions in analysis. *Standard edition*, vol. 23. London: Hogarth Press, 1964, pp. 257–269.
Freud, S. (1940) An outline of psycho-analysis. *Standard edition*, vol. 23. London: Hogarth Press, 1964, pp. 144–207.
Friedman, M.L., and Dies, R.R. Reactions of internal and external test-anxious students to counseling and behavior therapies. *Journal of Consulting and Clinical Psychology*, 1974, *42*, 921.
Fromm, E., Brown, D.P., Hurt, S.W., Oberlander, J.Z., Boxer, A.M., and Pfeifer, G. The phenomena and characteristics of self-hypnosis. *International Journal of Clinical and Experimental Hypnosis*, 1981, *29*, 189–246.
Gill, M.M. Psychoanalysis and exploratory psychotherapy. *Journal of the American Psychoanalytic Association*, 1954, *2*, 771–797.
Gill, M.M. and Brenman, M. *Hypnosis and related states: Psychoanalytic studies in regression.* New York: International Universities Press, 1959.
Glover, E. Active therapy and psycho-analysis: A critical review. *International Journal of Psycho-Analysis*, 1924, *5*, 269–311.
Glover, E. (1931) The therapeutic effect of inexact interpretation: A contribution to the theory of suggestion. In: M.S. Bergmann and F.R. Hartman (Eds.), *The evolution of psychoanalytic technique.* New York: Basic Books, 1976.
Goldstein, A.P., Heller, K. and Sechrest, L.B. *Psychotherapy and the psychology of behavior change.* New York: Wiley, 1966.
Greenson, R. *The theory and practice of psychoanalysis.* New York: International Universities Press, 1967.
Grotjahn, M. Responsive action in psychoanalysis. In: B.B. Wolman (Ed.), *Psychoanalytic techniques.* New York: Basic Books, 1967.
Guntrip, H. *Schizoid phenomena, object relations, and the self.* New York: International Universities Press, 1968.
Hale, N.G. *Freud and the Americans: The beginnings of psychoanalysis in the United States, 1876–1917.* New York: Oxford University Press, 1971.
Hartmann, H. (1939) *Ego psychology and the problem of adaptation.* New York: International Universities Press, 1958.

Hovland, E.I., Janis, I.L. and Kelley, H.H. *Communication and persuasion: Psychosocial studies of opinion change.* New Haven, Conn.: Yale University Press, 1953.

Hovland, C.I., and Weiss, W. The influence of source credibility on communication effectiveness. *Public Opinion Quarterly,* 1951, *15,* 635–650.

Hufeland, F. *Über Sympathie.* Weimar: Verlag des Landes-Industrie-Comptoir, 1811.

Hull, C.L. (1933) *Hypnosis and suggestibility: An experimental approach.* New York: Appleton-Century-Crofts, 1968.

Janis, I.L. and Feshbach, S. *Effects of fear-arousing communcations. Journal of Abnormal and Social Psychology,* 1953, *48,* 78–92.

Johnson, A.M., and Szurek, S.A. The genesis of antisocial acting out in children and adults. *Psychoanalytic Quarterly,* 1952, *21,* 323–343.

Jones, E. (1910) The action of suggestion in psychotherapy. In: *Papers on psychoanalysis.* 4th ed. Baltimore: William Wood & Co., 1938.

Jones, E. (1923) The nature of auto-suggestion. In: *Papers on psychoanalysis.* 5th ed. Boston: Beacon Press, 1948.

Jones, E.E. and Gerard, H.B. *Foundations of social psychology.* New York: John Wiley & Sons, 1967.

Kaplan, B., and Johnson, D. The social meaning of Navaho psychopathology and psychotherapy. In: A Kiev (Ed.), *Magic, faith, and healing: Studies in primitive psychiatry today.* New York: Free Press, 1964.

Kernberg, O.F. Some implications of object relations theory for psychoanalytic technique. In: *Psychoanalytic technique and theory of therapy. Journal of the American Psychoanalytic Association,* 1979, *27* (suppl.), 207–239.

Kiev, A. (Ed.), *Magic, faith, and healing: Studies in primitive psychiatry today.* New York: Free Press, 1964.

Kohut, H. *The analysis of the self.* New York: International Universities Press, 1971.

Kohut, H. The two analyses of Mr. Z. *International Journal of Psycho-Analysis,* 1979, *60,* 3–27.

Kohut, H. *How does analysis cure?* Chicago: University of Chicago Press, 1984.

Lain Entralgo, P. (1958) *Therapy of the word in classical antiquity,* New Haven, Conn.: Yale University Press, 1970.

Lasch, C. *The culture of narcissism.* New York: Popular Library, 1979.

Le Bon, G. *The crowd* (1895). New York: Ballantine, 1969.

Lewis, I.M. *Ecstatic religion: An anthropological study of spirit possession and shamanism.* Harmondsworth: Penquin, 1971.

Lichtenstein, H. (1961) Identity and sexuality. In: *The dilemma of human identity.* New York: Jason Aronson, 1977.

McReynolds, W.T. Systematic desensitization, insight-oriented psychotherapy and relaxation therapy in a psychiatric population. *Dissertation Abstracts International,* 1970, *30,* 12B.

Merton, R. *Social theory and social structure.* Glencoe, Ill.: Free Press, 1957.

Muensterberger, W. Psyche and environment: Sociocultural variations in separation and individuation. *Psychoanalytic Quarterly,* 1969, *38,* 191–216.

Muensterberger, W., Axelrad, S., Esman, A, and Boyer, L.B. *The psychoanalytic study of society, 1–9* (1960–1918). New York: International Universities Press, 1960, 1962, 1964, 1967, 1972, 1975. New Haven, Conn.: Yale University Press, 1976, 1979. New York: Psychohistory Press, 1981.

Paolino, T. *Psychoanalytic psychotherapy: Theory, technique, therapeutic relationship, and treatability.* New York: Brunner/Mazel, 1981.

Parin, P, Morgenthaler, F, and Parin-Matthey, G. *Fürchte deinen Nächsten wie dich selbst: Psychoanalyse und Gesellschaft am Modell der Agni in Westafrika.* Frankfurt am Main: Suhrkamp Verlag, 1971. English trans., *Fear Thy Neighbor as Thyself: Psychoanalysis and Society among the Anyi of West Africa.* Chicago: University of Chicago Press, 1980.

Pepitone, A. Lessons from the history of social psychology. *American Psychologist,* 1981, *36,* 972–985.

Pötzl, O. (1917) The relationship between experimentally induced dream images and indirect vision. *Psychological Issues, 2* (Monograph 7), 1960.

Prince, M. (1927) Suggestive repersonalization: The psychophysiology of hypnotism. In N.G. Hale (Ed.), *Psychotherapy and multiple personality: selected essays.* Cambridge, Mass.: Harvard University Press, 1975.

Rapaport, D. (1951) The autonomy of the ego. In: M.M. Gill (Ed.), *The collected papers of David Rapaport.* New York: Basic Books, 1967.

Rapaport, D. (1957) The theory of ego autonomy: A generalization. In M.M. Gill (Ed.), *The collected papers of David Rapaport.* New York: Basic Books, 1967.

Rosen, G. *Madness and society.* New York: Harper & Row, 1968.

Rosenberg, M.J. The conditions and consequences of evaluation apprehension. In: R. Rosenthal and R.L. Rosnow (Eds.), *Artifact in behavioral research.* New York: Academic Press, 1969.

Rosenthal, R. Interpersonal expectations: Effects of the experimenter's hypothesis. In: R. Rosenthal and R.L. Rosnow (Eds.), *Artifact in behavioral research.* New York: Academic Press, 1969.

Rotter, J.B. Generalized expectations for internal vs. external control of reinforcement. *Psychological Monographs,* 1966, *80,* (whole no. 609).

Sarbin, T.R., and Coe, W.C. *Hypnosis: A social psychological analysis of influence communication.* New York: Hold, Rinehart, & Winston, 1972.

Schachter, S. The interaction of cognitive and physiological determinants of emotional state. In: P.H. Leiderman and D. Shapiro (Eds.), *Psychobiological approaches to social behavior.* London: Tavistock, 1965.

Shapiro, D. *Autonomy and rigid character.* New York: Basic Books, 1981.

Sidis, B. *The psychology of suggestion.* New York: Appleton, 1898.

Silber, A. Childhood seduction, parental pathology, and hysterical symptomatology: The genesis of an altered state of consciousness. *International Journal of Psycho-Analysis,* 1979, *60,* 109–116.

Simon, B. *Mind and madness in ancient Greece: The classical roots of modern psychiatry.* Ithaca, N.Y.: Cornell University Press, 1978.

Simon, B. Hysteria—the Greek disease. *The psychoanalytic study and society,* vol. 8. New Haven, Conn.: Yale University Press, 1979, pp. 175–216.

Sloane, R.B., Staples, F.R., Cristol, A.H., Yorkston, N.J., and Whipple, K. *Psychotherapy versus behavior therapy.* Cambridge, Mass.: Harvard University Press, 1975.

Smith, M.L., Glass, G.V., and Miller, T.I. *The benefits of psychotherapy.* Baltimore: Johns Hopkins Press, 1980.

Stone, L. The widening scope of indications of psychoanalysis. *Journal of the American Psychoanalytic Association,* 1954, *2,* 567–594.

Strachey, J. Editor's introduction to Freud (1888–1892). *Standard edition,* vol. 1. London: Hogarth Press, 1966, pp. 63–69.

Tausk, J. (1919) On the origin of the "influencing machine" in schizophrenia. In: R. Fliess (Ed.), *The Psychoanalytic reader.* New York: International Universities Press, 1948, pp. 31–64.

Turner, V. *The forest of symbols: Aspects of Ndembu ritual.* Ithaca, N.Y.: Cornell University Press, 1967.

Turner, V. *The drums of affliction.* New York: Oxford University Press, 1968.

Turner, V. *The ritual process: Structure and anti-structure.* Chicago: University of Chicago Press, 1969.

Urdang, L. (Ed.) *The Random House dictionary of the English language, college edition.* New York: Random House, 1968.

Vaillant, G.E. *Adaptation to life.* Boston: Little-Brown, 1977.

Vasile, R. *James Jackson Putnam: From neurology to psychoanalysis.* Oceanside, N.Y.: Dabor Science Publications, 1977.

Walster, E., Aronson, J., and Abrahams, D. On increasing the persuasiveness of a low-prestige communicator. *Journal of Experimental Social Psychology,* 1966, *2*, 325–342.

Whiting, J.W.M., and Child, I.L. *Child training and personality.* New Haven, Conn.: Yale University Press, 1953.

Winnicott, D.W. *Collected papers: Through paediatrics to psycho-analysis.* London: Tavistock, 1958.

Winnicott, D.W. *The maturational processes and the facilitating environment.* New York: International Universities Press, 1965.

Wundt, W. *Hypnotismus and suggestion.* Leipzig: Engelmann, 1892.

3
Suggestion: Clinical Application

JONATHAN E. KOLB, M.D.

In his often quoted remarks about briefer forms of treatment, Freud (1918) spoke of alloying the pure gold of analysis with the copper of suggestion. Not all pairs of substances can be alloyed, however. In this chapter I consider whether or not there is a role for suggestion in psychodynamic psychotherapy, and if there is, spell out a plan for such an alloy that keeps something of the essential character of each ingredient. I will not resort to the alchemy of declaring that all therapy, psychodynamic or not, works by suggestion.

As noted in the previous chapter, the concept of suggestion describes a good many of the effects one person can have on another. Suggestion has been used as a term of opprobrium in psychoanalytic writings since Freud's ambivalence about it was succeeded by Glover's (1931) total rejection of it. Yet, as outlined in the previous chapter, suggestion forms the basis for a good many psychodynamic therapies. Even if it is not a decisive technique in psychoanalysis and psychodynamic psychotherapy, suggestion as a kind of influence certainly contributes to the therapeutic process and result.

In this chapter I consider suggestion as a techique, consciously or unconsciously employed by the therapist to enchance or achieve his or her goals. This is a more restricted effort than documenting the ways in which suggestion as a process operates in therapy. After some definitions I address the direct use of suggestion to bring about change, focusing on some of the problems that make this rarely advisable in psychodynamic psychotherapy. Next I consider whether suggestion has more value when used to promote a treatment that cures by other means.

There are some clinical situations in which frustration of the therapist's ambitions can provide a powerful stimulus for the use of suggestion, and a few of those also are described. Finally, I attempt an overall assessment of how to deal with the potent force of suggestion in therapy.

DEFINITIONS

Suggestion has been defined by Bibring (1954) as, "the induction of ideas, impulses, emotions, actions, etc., in brief, various mental processes by the therapist (an individual in authoritative position) in the patient (an individual in dependent position) independent of, or to the exclusion of, the latter's rational or critical (realistic) thinking." Crucial to this definition of suggestion is the use of interpersonal influence (an authoritative therapist, a dependent patient) to substitute for or overcome critical, rational thought. By its nature suggestion relies on asymmetrical aspects of the therapeutic relationship.

Psychodynamic psychotherapy refers to a "talking cure" that is based on psychoanalytic *principles,* but is not necessarily confined to the kinds of practices normally used in psychoanalysis. In this definition "psychodynamic" refers to a way of thinking, based on the principles of psychic determinism, the existence and importance of unconscious mental life, the persistence of infantile conflict in adult life (the genetic point of view), and the ubiquity of resistance and transference in the therapeutic interaction. This definition of psychodynamic psychotherapy is silent about whether the therapy is "supportive" or not. A useful aspect of all psychotherapy, psychodynamic or not, is that it is as supportive as it needs to be. The judgments about which aspects of the therapy are supportive, and what they are designed to support (the patient, the status quo, his or her defenses, and which defenses) can be made according to a variety of criteria. When the thinking that informs these judgments is based on these principles, then the therapy may be called psychodynamic.

Of these principles resistance and transference merit further elaboration here, because they are most likely to conflict with the use of suggestion. Resistance is the operation of defense within the context of the therapy, and refers to the unconscious tendency of patients to act in opposition to their own and the therapist's avowed aims and procedures. Concern with analyzing resistance derives from Freud's abandonment of simple notions of cure by suggestion and abreaction (catharsis). Resistance, rather than being the problematic and irrelevant obstacle to progress that its name suggests, has been recognized not only as an inevitability, but also as the dynamic that provides the therapist and patient with an opportunity to work in a meaningful way on those aspects of the patient's pathology that have become structuralized as symptom, character, and habitual defense. One special form of resistance is transference, the patient's tendency to replay within the therapeutic relationship aspects of crucial past relationships. In "The Dynamics of Transference," Freud (1912) described the centrality of the tranference resistance to the progress of analysis as the way in which the infantile neurosis is brought into the analysis in a "real" way. To the extent that talking freely is the agreed-upon *modus operandi* of therapy, resistance refers to whatever impedes the patient's talking freely, and transference emerges as resistance when it is experienced as centering on the therapist. ("I can't tell you that, because it would hurt your feelings.") Resistance and transference make their appearance in other forms of therapy besides psychoanalysis and psychodynamic therapy. Again what distinguishes psychodynamic psychotherapy from other types is not the presence or absence of these phenomena, but their recognition by the therapist and the systematic attempt to interpret them to promote healing.

To complete a discussion of the components of our proposed alloy, one more definition is needed. Edward Bibring (1954), in his seminal paper on technique that forms the theroretical scaffolding for this book, distinguishes between the technical and the curative uses of interventions in psychotherapy. An intervention is used in a *curative* sense when it is used to produce the desired change in the patient directly. For example, Breuer and Freud (1895) attempted to use hypnosis directly to produce remembering of traumatic events, which they hoped would result in a cathartic cure. On the other hand, an intervention is used in a technical sense if it is used to promote the treatment; for example, Freud's (Breuer & Freud, 1895) use of the suggestion that something would come to the patient's mind when he pressed on her temple. Freud's intention in this act was not to cure, but to further the treatment by producing a positive attitude in the patient, which would encourage her to produce more material. Often the technical use of an intervention has as its root the twofold goal of producing more material and inducing a positive attitude, both of which are essential conditions if the more curative effects of other factors are to operate. In practice, distinctions between technical and curative uses of a technique are difficult to make. For example, with a depressed patient whose hopelessness is a central part of the symptom complex, the production and maintenance of a hopeful attitude by whatever technical route might be curative, not merely a way station on the road to a cure via insight.

In summary, suggestion is a technique that takes advantage of specific, asymmetrical aspects of the therapeutic relationship. Psychodynamic psychotherapy is therapy based on psychoanalytic principles, in particular where therapist and patient attend to and analyze transference. It is this principle that seems likely to conflict with suggestion's use of the tranference as a vehicle for persuasion. Finally, as a therapeutic technique, suggestion may be used in a curative or technical sense. In the next section I explore the uses of suggestion in both these senses and under certain special circumstances, to see if the conflict between the use of the transference and its analysis can be resolved.

THE CURATIVE USE OF SUGGESTION

When suggestion is used as a curative technique, its aim is to alter some psychic feature (attitude, memory, habit, fear) in a single step.

There are many reports in the literature of therapy that works in this way, often dramatically and quickly. Freud's (1892) case of a cure by hypnosis is a good example. He cured a woman suffering from a postpartum refusal to nurse her baby with the suggestion that she angrily demand food for herself. Blum (1979) has explicated the psychological sophistication that underlay such a powerful effect. Freud did not merely overpower the woman's symptoms with the force of his personality; he stressed movement along an important dynamic avenue, the expression of oral aggression.

There are more commonplace examples of suggestive influence in the direction of cure as well. The therapist treats the patient with respect, as though the patient (no matter what his or her circumstances) is an adult whose uniqueness is valuable. This is by itself a powerful suggestion operating in the direction of improvement. When a patient is hospitalized, the institution and treaters anticipate the date the patient will be discharged. This tends to convey the expectation that, whatever the problem, it can be solved, or at least ameliorated, in 60 days (or however long insurance coverage lasts). Of course, once the patient has responded to such a suggestion, disappointment is also possible. To consider the advantages and disadvantages of this direct use of suggestion in more detail, I will explore a clincial example. As with any intervention, we look to the subsequent flow of the patient's associations (whether deepened, quickened, clearer, more affective, etc.) to see the immediate effects of the suggestion.

> The patient, a 23-year-old engineering graduate student, came to a psychiatric outpatient clinic anxious and depressed about his failure to develop intimacy with women. He had been preoccupied with fantasies about a particular woman, with whom he had a friendly but casual relationship.

Ambivalence characterized his thought processes, and his rendition of events was full of worries, doubts, second thoughts, and obsessive calculations of danger.

His history included a traumatic experience that seemed to link up powerfully with his current life experiences and his dominant preoccupations. When he was 4 years old, his mother had been burned in an explosion in the basement of their house. She came running up the stairs with her clothes aflame, but he felt paralyzed and incompetent. He blamed himself afterward for the extent of her injuries, which he linked to his failure to react well in the crisis. In the first three months of what was to be a brief treatment, he demonstrated not merely the obsessional features evident in his presenting history and symptoms, but also some capacity for his thinking to regress to a primitive, wish-fulfillment level, especially in interpreting a casual interaction as an overt seduction by a woman. He used the therapist to "reality-test" some of his inclinations to respond inappropriately (e.g., his plan to fly to another city because a woman friend had said it would be "nice" to see him sometime).

He began the session by discussing (ambivalently) his plans for relocating to another city. The arrangements were "coming along," but he felt "backed into a corner." Then he described "trouble on the road." He had dented his car running over a "rod" in the middle of the highway. He was having trouble getting it fixed. He had a "moral obligation to keep the car safe and not run into anything." He then discussed a party he attended at which others used nitrous oxide and other drugs "like a sponge." He had watched others get into drugs for a year, but refused to indulge because it could be too incapacitating.

Therapist: You want to maintain control?
Patient: Yes, but not all situations can be controlled. I'm not good in emergencies—that situation on the road, the time my mother was burned, my father's death, the time my bicycle was stolen.
Therapist: How could you have avoided the bar in the road?
Patient: I panicked. I was unable to turn the wheel. Maybe I could've turned it faster, but there might've have been a blowout. It would be a complex equation to figure how fast you could turn it at that speed.
Therapist: You did the best you could.

Here the therapist is engaged in a rational, seemingly helpful, attempt to do battle with the patient's punitive superego via the technique of suggestion. He attempts to implant the idea that the patient is not at fault, and that he blames himself, perhaps in an overdetermined way. This kind of intervention ought to be helpful, but is it?

Patient: Well, I don't think I was paying attention. All the other cars ahead of me were swerving. I should've known better; I should've been able to read the signals. I didn't process the information.

Here the patient explicitly contradicts the suggestion, which he (in this way) identifies as a premature and inaccurate assessment of the current reality. He goes on immediately to recall a dream.

I had a dream about Lara the cat; she belongs to Mike and Betty. We were in G. (his hometown) and mother was selling the house. I saw Lara on the street. She jumped into my lap. I carried her into the house. I said to my mother, "I'd like you to meet my friend." Mother was upset that I was treating Lara like a person.

Some associations followed: "I like Lara. I have no delusions about her being a person though. I wanted to call Mike and Betty and ask to visit them. They'd be annoyed because I'd be just going to visit the cat. If a cat jumps in my lap, there's nothing I can do about it."

If we look at the dream, as it demonstates the patient's response to the therapist's intervention, what is apparent is that the dream describes an intervention that is perceived as not helpful. The mother is upset at the patient's attempt to "introduce" something to her. The cat seems to be a vehicle for externalizing instinctual urges, like the "rod" in the story of the accident, where a "failure to process information" has been presented as an unavoidable danger situation that had just "come up." In his zeal to move the patient in a particular direction, the therapist, like the mother in the dream, failed to hear what was being presented. The result in the session and the dream was that the patient's difficulty with managing his impulses and prohibitions was not addressed.

This example illustrates some basic problems with suggestion when it is used as a curative technique.

1. *Suggestion is unreliable.* To return to the example, it is clear from the patient's immediate response and subsequent associations that he does not accept the suggestion. The notion that the asymmetrical relationship provides a likely setting for effective suggestion is not always (or often) borne out in practice. As those who study hypnosis have documented, not everyone is suggestible to a significant (useful) degree. It may be as fruitful to rely on a kind of opposition to suggestion as to rely on sug-gestibility. The practioners of paradoxical family therapy seem to un-derstand this when they prescribe a symptom or an action they fully expect the family to oppose. The positive relationship between therapist and patient is neither simple nor univalent. From a theoretical point of view, it seems likely that suggestion as it is commonly used does not really introduce a new idea into the mind of the patient; it is more correctly viewed as a form of manipulation, reinforcing an idea already present, but ineffective, repressed, or inoperative. Moreover, the matter of chang-ing the balance between opposing or alternative ideas ("I am always to blame" versus "I am not always to blame") is not a simple one. If suggestion could be counted on to work reliably, especially with firmly held ideas such as those connected with self-blame, therapy would hardly be a long and difficult process, and could indeed be practiced by parents, spouses, self-help authors, and other would-be agents of change. Many forms of cure by suggestion achieve some successes, but we demand more of a technique than haphazard results. To use suggestion effectively, we need some way of choosing when and with whom to use it, and of predicting responsiveness.

Even though suggestion does not always work, it would still be reasonable to try it occasionally under desperate or special circumstances,
or at the outset of the treatment, or on some sort of schedule, were it not
for the fact that its use can have negative consequences. In fact, it is
because of the inherent negative effects of suggestion that is has such a
limited role in psychodynamic psychotherapy.

2. *Suggestion contaminates the analysis of the transference.* This is
the most obvious disadvantage of suggestion as a curative technique, and
one that accounts for its virtual disappearance as a subject of serious
psychoanalytic inquiry in the past 30 years. It is awkward to rely on
tranference during one phase of therapy and attempt to minimize it during
the next. It is not easy for the therapist to insist that a dependent attitude
is distortion, a product of the patient's neurosis and inappropriate to the
actual experience of the therapist, if he or she fosters such dependence
by pronouncements, subtle and not-so-subtle attempts to influence, and
other suggestive pressures.

Even in treatments not specifically oriented toward interpretation,
where one intends to deal with conscious and preconscious experience
only, the use of suggestion can foster a transference that precludes termination. Perhaps the most renowned example of this effect was the case
of Anna O., Breuer's patient, with whom he pioneered the talking cure
(Breuer & Freud, 1895). Breuer relied on suggestion as the sole curative
agent by having the patient expose each symptom and its antecedent
memory, and then suggesting its removal. When Breuer announced his
intention to terminate their successful treatment, Anna O. responded with
news that she was pregnant, complete with abdominal swelling and labor
pains. Breuer was to be the father of this imaginary child, and Anna O.
expected him to leave his wife for her. As Jones (1953) reported, Anna
O. fared badly for some time after the abrupt termination of treatment.
This was the trauma that drove Breuer to abandon the talking cure, while
Freud chose to pursue it.

3. *Suggestion distorts the material produced by the patient.* A further
difficulty inherernt in the curative use of suggestion is its capacity to
create a change in the patient's associations. This distortion can occur
whenever suggestion is employed, regardless of the intent of the therapist.
In the case example of the engineering student cited earlier, the suggestive
intervention is followed by the patient's shift away from the theme he had
been pursuing ("I fail under instinctual pressure") to the dream and subsequent associations centering on his search for love objects (the cat). A
prominent, affectively charged current has been introduced: that of not
being understood by the caretaker (mother). As noted, in this way the
patient comments on his experiencing of the therapist's listening qualities
at the moment. Complaints about mothers who do not understand, den-
tists who drill without anesthesia, and medical students who experiment

on people are familiar indicators that the patient is becoming uncomfortable with the therapeutic situation, and as such point the way to some sort of therapeutic remedy—clarifying or rectifying a distorted framework (Langs, 1976). Such a process does not necessarily bring the therapy any closer to the dynamic and genetic underpinning of the patient's disturbance, however. It is often the case that the interactions that follow attempts at suggestion relate more clearly to the act of suggestion than to the specific dynamics of the patient.

4. *Suggestion substitutes one form of neurosis for another.* To the extent that suggestion is effective, it replaces one kind of belief with another. In the case cited, the therapist's intention was to modify a primitive superego, substituting a more temperate view of the self for a harsh one. In such a formulation, the essential nature of the psychological problem becomes distorted. The patient does not suffer from a primitive superego in the way he might suffer from a physical disease. He judges himself harshly because of specific "crimes" that he feels he committed. We can be fairly sure that the screen memory of mother's being on fire was traumatic not just as an event, but as a symbol for a kind of psychological situation that involved some mixture of reality and fantasy. It is more accurate to say that the patient's belief about his own culpability ("I always react badly in a crisis") is not wrong, but out of context, disconnected from other memories that would make it understandable. The use of suggestion, then, works against the therapeutic effort to discover repressed connections, and interferes with the patient's ability to forge his or her own unique understanding.

THE TECHNICAL USE OF SUGGESTION

The technical use of suggestion attempts to further a treatment whose curative elements are considered more substantial ones, that is, ones that foster insight or personal growth. Freud's pressure technique (Breuer & Freud, 1895), with the direct suggestion that memories will come, is the prototype of the technical use of suggestion. It is of note, however, that this suggestion works not because it is accepted uncritically, but rather because it conveys an atmosphere of hopeful expectation. In this regard the technique is consonant with Frank's (1961) notion of the generally persuasive power of the therapist or healer, which is a necessary, but not sufficient, component of any therapy. Although we no longer press on the temples, contemporary psychotherapists employ many "pressure techniques" of their own to foster the process of the treatment. The basic conditions of treatment (regular appointments, fees, the office and its furnishings) all carry implications as to what will happen, and how the treatment is expected to work. It is suggested that regular patient attention in the form of listening and talking will help. The box of tissues suggests tears may be appropriate, and the absence of a punching bag discourages the expression of other affects in too raw a form.

It is easy to go on from these structures, unacknowledged pressures to more tailored ones. The therapist may speak slowly and quietly to a patient who seems too often excited or in a hurry; he or she may use colorful language or exaggerations with a constricted patient, precision with a hysterical patient, and cogent rational thinking with a psychotic, all designed to suggest another way to speak, to think, or to be. For every kind of patient, it is possible to formulate a therapeutic style or stance that exerts pressure for movement in a direction the therapist decides is useful. This kind of suggestion basically makes treatment flow more easily, allowing the more substantial and longer lasting curative principles of treatment a chance to work.

The results of technical suggestion were studied systematically by Fisher (1953). He gave the suggestion "You are going to have a dream," or "You are going to have a dream about me [the therapist or teacher]," to both patients in psychoanalysis and nonpatient research subjects, and he studied their subsequent dreams and associations. The majority responded by dreaming, often with the analyst or teacher appearing undisguised in the manifest dream. An analysis of the latent content of the dreams revealed a striking preponderance of themes of pregnancy and childbirth, experienced in pregenital terms: oral incorporative pregnancies and anal expulsive births. Breuer's patient Anna O., whose pseudocyesis we noted above, was not alone in her tendency to respond to suggestion by elaborating the fantasy that, with her doctor's intimate help, she could produce something greatly valued by him. The foregoing highlights the most problematic aspect of suggestion in psychodynamic psychotherapy: it can lead to material of great interest, but of questionable significance in relation to the patient's current concerns. What Breuer produced in an extended treatment, Fisher stimulated with a single suggestion. From a scientific point of view, such a powerful stimulus distorts the therapeutic process immeasurably. If Fisher had merely used the technique to elicit dreams and then reported on the dreams, he would have concluded that most people, whether in treatment or not, dream about having babies for their analysts or teachers. Similarly, when one uses suggestion to further a therapy, one is no longer sure whether it has furthered therapy in a direction the therapy was meant to go, or one has contaminated the field, filling the "blank screen" of the traditional analysis with a movie whose theme was supplied by the projectionist.

Ingenuous Suggestion

From the discussion to this point it seems that, Freud's (1918) notion of an alloy notwithstanding, the intentional use of suggestion detracts from treatment more than it enhances it. Yet, as the previous chapter argued, suggestion is a feature of all forms of successful healing. Further, it plays a pivotal role in the psychodynamic psychotherapy encounter. Bibring (1954, p. 762) articulated this role:

> Suggestion in the technical sense is at work right from the beginning. When the patient has confidence in the analyst from the start, when he expects to be cured or markedly improved, though one does not guarantee anything and promises very little, this is due to suggestion.

In contrast to the intentional uses of suggestion for curative or technical purposes, the suggestion Bibring seems here to be referring to is ingenuous or unconscious, exerted by the therapist without specific intent. In fact it may be important that such suggestion is transmitted unconsciously, or at least without guile. As an analogy we need only to consider the difference between a high-pressure salesperson, who insists that one cannot live without some new acquisition, and the committed person who believes in something and communicates genuine excitement to the buyer. The hopeful expectation that is usefully communicated by a committed, expectant therapist cannot be feigned. Indeed, the depressed or burnt-out therapist who tries to suggest hopefulness communicates not only his or her true affective state, but also the need to deny and cover up such feelings. Thus it is in the rich and powerful matrix of unconscious communications that suggestion acts to influence the patient in the ways of the therapist.

Psychoanalysis uses the language of physical metaphors of taking in (incorporation, internalization), or borrows from descriptions of children learning (imitation, identification), to label the mechanisms that underlie these effects. While the precise nature of these mechanisms and the distinctions between them may be obscure, as a class of phenomena they are easily recognized in practice.

> The schizophrenic patient, after spending three months in the ward in the relative isolation of his ongoing psychosis, stops shaving. In a few weeks, as his psyche is coming together, the scraggly growth on his face begins to resemble the beard of his resident therapist.

Examples such as this primitive identification, as evidence of the influence of the therapist on the patient, are no doubt familar to all clinicians. Although the forces of status and role tend to operate in the patient–therapist dyad primarily in one direction, there is always some degree of mutual influence. The interest in the professional literature on various forms of countertransference reflects an awareness of the fluidity of unconscious aspects of communication in therapy (Searles, 1965; Langs, 1976; McLaughlin, 1981). The following vignette, from an hour of therapy early in a treatment and early in the career of the therapist, illustrates such mutual influencing.

> A young, attractive female patient with a hysterical paralysis and a prom-iscuous, masochistic pattern of relationships with men has just begun ther-apy with a young, attractive, unmarried male therapist. In the fourth session, she begins to describe a weekend during which her boyfriend became jealous. When he called, she didn't answer the telephone. Later she explained that she couldn't get to the phone "because we were fixing the car." As she gives all signs of abandoning this line of discussion in favor of a new theme, the therapist asks her who she had been referring to with the provocative "we." She answers that she was with a former boyfriend who had chanced to come by; then she pursues the theme of the current boyfriend's irrational jealousy. She likes to stop at a bar on the way home from work but always loses track of the time. She thinks someone in the bar will turn out to be her dream man; no one does, but she often sleeps with someone, and anyone she gets involved with soon tires of her combined unfaithfulness and dependency. The therapist follows this with a judg-mental comment about her promiscuity.

It seems clear that the therapist is responding with the same affect and behavior that the patient had sought to provoke in her boyfriend; he asks her the jealous question she expected her boyfriend to ask. She responds to this enactment of her *femme fatale* theme by further elaboration, in-cluding a beginning description of the role her fantasies play in her be-havior. But the therapist seems stuck in an aggrieved, moralistic stance and chastises her. It is unclear from this excerpt whose story of prom-iscuity and discipline is being enacted here; the interactive nature of the dialog suggests that each participant contributes some form and content to the overall outcome. We cannot tell whether we are hearing the patient's fantasies ("The doctor, like all men I meet, begins by promising to fulfill my wishes for a nurturant father, but will end up more interested in sex and in controlling and punishing me") or the therapist's fantasies ("This patient will try to control and manipulate me through her sexuality, and she needs a strong man to resist this temptation and set her straight"). We can see the pair engaged in a mutually influencing matrix, where the comments of each seem an unconscious answer to the stimulus of the other. What is demonstrated in this excerpt, then, is a therapy that is all suggestion, but unlikely to be therapeutic.

Suggestion in Specific Clinical Situations

Unconscious communication between patient and therapist is a ubiq-uitous feature of therapy. Indeed it is widely accepted that the relationship influences the patient (often for the better), and that suggestion is a part of this influence. There are specific occasions in therapy when suggestion is especially likely to work, and circumstances under which it is practically useless. In the former category are brief encounters and the early phases of therapy, when therapist and patient are highly susceptible to giving and taking suggestions. In the latter category are most encounters with depressed and borderline patients, whose susceptibility to suggestion easily can be overestimated.

Suggestion in Brief Encounters

Although consultation and referral interviews are not typically seen as aspects of psychotherapy, from the patient's perspective they are a part of the overall therapeutic experience. Many patients find their way to a therapist via a one- or two-session consultation with another clinician. In such situations the limited time provides both a freedom from follow-through and a pressure to come to conclusions rapidly, and often both participants can be more open than otherwise might be the case. What results is usually a heightened responsiveness to suggestion on the patient's part, coupled with a greater readiness to suggest on the clinician's.

The patient's susceptibility to suggestion is likely to be enhanced under the special circumstances of an initial venture into the unfamiliar realm of therapy and a visit to a highly recommended authority. A defensive attitude toward the therapy—if the patient anticipates it will be painful, and full of unhappy surprises—also can enhance the patient's suggestibility. Under these circumstances, the patient may hope for a magical first session or consultation that leads to quick change, and obviates the necessity for therapy altogether. In addition it sometimes happens that the consultant has a greater or more specialized reputation than the therapist.

On the consultant's side, the need for a rapid assessment can lead to an active, interventive approach; the wish to offer something helpful can be quite compelling. The result is likely to be a highly charged encounter with an artificial kind of intensity. Indeed patients often remember the consultation interview in great detail. Whether the words of the consultant actually produce positive change and enhance the subsequent treatment is another matter. In one community a popular consultant has a reputation for extreme warmth, directness, and sympathy. Since he often refers patients to therapists who are less experienced, less secure, and perhaps less gifted than himself, the therapists have an uphill battle overcoming the invidious comparison made when the patient discovers the therapist is not able to match the excitement of the consultation. One 45-year-old man who was searching for a therapist recalled his consultation 15 years earlier with the clarity reserved for special peak experiences. He had disliked the therapist to whom he was sent, but this fact in no way diminished his admiration for the consultant. What was important in the patient's recollection was not the failure of the consultant to make a successful referral, but the impression of a moving interview in which "he got me to tears in a few minutes." Here suggestion flourishes, but it may lead nowhere.

The beginning of therapy, for similar reasons, has some of the same charm as the consultation. It is a kind of crisis, and heightened emotions in both participants contribute to a highly charged situation. As usual under such circumstances, it is easier to mobilize than to control suggestive influence. Consider the following example.

> A 22-year-old single female law student sought therapy because of her anxiety and depression, which had snowballed after the end of a four-year relationship. The patient had a marked capacity to idealize others, especially confident, assertive men.
>
> In the period just prior to the initial appointment, after two sleepless nights, she consulted her brother's therapist, who recommended a trip to an emergency facility, where she was given Valium. She was close to panic about the possibility that she was suffering from manic-depressive illness as her grandmother had. In her first interview, she was told she might have an affective illness, and that this might respond to medication, but the therapist felt her primary difficulty at the moment was a response to a series of life events, and that talking would certainly help, and ought to be tried first. She was immediately relieved, and brightened markedly.
>
> In subsequent sessions it soon emerged that this patient had a profound need to idealize men, a need that had been expressed since her childhood in near hero worship of her only sibling, an older brother. It was the telephone call to the brother's therapist that had originally strengthened her self-doubts, associated with the idea of taking medication, and it required a powerful suggestive effort in the opposite direction to reverse her mounting pessimism.
>
> Within a week she had opposed her newly found enthusiasm with reservations about the proposed therapy, and she began to interview several prospective therapists, people who had been recommended in the initial telephone call by the brother's therapist.

In this case the patient's susceptibility to suggestion was enhanced by her state of crisis and her passion for idealizing relationships (such as the one with her brother). Thus the telephone call to the brother's therapist increased the patient's anxiety about the possibility of serious mental illness, and presaged loss of control over the situation and a passive role in her treatment. The therapist's suggestion that talking would help had an immediate effect not only because it was a welcome antidote to the influence of the brother's therapist, but also because it too was taken as authoritative. It is important to note that while this suggestion works, patient and therapist run the risk of relying on an unsustainable idealization. Indeed, in the second session, the patient reported a piece of her history that related to this possibility, a brief seduction by a man she felt was attractive but superficial, whose motives she did not trust because he seemed to be in a hurry to have a girlfriend. She felt he valued the idea of having a successful relationship more than he valued her, a woman he did not really know, and did not try to know better. This vignette alerted the therapist to the possibility that idealized men might be judged superficial and narcissistic on closer examination, and he was cautioned to avoid relying on suggestion in the further course of the therapy.

The beginning of therapy, then, is a time of heightened emotion in both patient and therapist, and, therefore, conducive to attempts at suggestion on the part of one, and susceptibility to it on the part of the other. In the ensuing course of therapy, both may have occasion to abandon their initial enthusiasm, revise their assessment of one another, and even question the apparent progress that was based on an early suggestion. If such changes can be made without undermining the sense of rapport, early suggestions may entail little risk. However, if a pattern has been established for the interaction, it may be difficult to transform a therapy based on suggestion to an exploratory one.

Suggestion with Depressed Patients

When a patient is depressed, unconscious suggestions of hopelessness and helplessness often emanate from patient to therapist. The therapist may respond to these forces with some combination of empathic resonance and resistance. To the extent that the therapist succumbs to the suggestion that "it's all hopeless," the therapy works to depress the therapist, not to help the patient. When the therapist resists feeling these powerful affects, this resistance is often accompanied by hopeful, cheering images that are offered to the patient as alternatives to his or her bleak, empty ones. The following kind of sequence may occur.

Patient: It really seems hopeless. I can't stay at my job, but I can't leave it either. I can see the messes I get myself into much more clearly now, with the therapy, but there is no movement. A friend was talking about his girlfriend's father, who committed suicide. He had an incurable disease, and it seemed sensible to end it. I've been thinking. . . .

Therapist: Your situation doesn't seem so hopeless to me. You *portray* yourself as without alternatives, but you haven't considered. . . .

This kind of intervention inevitably falls flat, for two reasons. First, to the extend that it is a conscious attempt to influence the patient to think positively, its effect will depend on the state of the transference, the patient's disposition to be influenced. A warmly disposed, hysterical patient may try to take such an intervention and use it, but with the underlying issue of self-devaluation not only unresolved but heightened, and made less likely to emerge into consciousness. An oppositional patient, on the other hand, struggling ambivalently with issues of individuation, is likely to be of two minds about such a hopeful and parental offering, wanting both to be influenced and to be independent. A more primitive patient, perhaps a borderline, may well feel abandoned or attacked; for such patients, not to be believed is not to exist. In response such a patient may well counterattack, or feel even more worthless.

There is, however, a second way in which such an intervention can be understood. If the therapeutic enterprise is one of listening and discovering the patient's experience, feelings, and fantasies, and their continuity, the attempt to cheer him/her up is an abandonment of the therapeutic task. Suggestion with a depressed patient always risks being empty reassurance. The unconscious meaning of the therapist's attempt to reassure is likely to be that the therapist is afraid. The patient who reacts with anger or confusion to such an intervention is accurately experiencing the therapist's affects, which contraduct the surface message of the intervention. According to one patient the intervention, "It seems pretty hopeless to me," would be preferable since it would convey the sense that the therapist understands and accepts the patient and is being faithful to the therapeutic method. The interventions that inspire confidence, convey hope, and counteract depression, then, are not those that deny the experience of the depressed patient, but those that convey the therapist's willingness to proceed undaunted in the face of painful affects.

Suggestion with More Seriously Distured Patients

If we separate patients along the traditional lines, that is, neurotic patients (those with analyzable transference neuroses) from more seriously disturbed patients, some differential effects of suggestion can be highlighted. Patients of the first group are more or less autonomous and have intact egos. Freud (1914) distinguished between the transference neuroses and the narcissistic neuroses. He felt that the former may enter into an object relationship and therefore can participate in analysis whereas the latter cannot. Subsequent contributors, however, especially those who report experience treating sicker patients, do not concur that these patients fail to form a transference relationship (e.g., Guntrip, 1971; Searles, 1965). They agree instead that the form of the transference relationship is different; it is more intense because of these patients' more intense need for an object, their incomplete development, and lack of a sense of self. The differences in capacity for relatedness of the two groups of patients leads to a difference in their sensitivity to suggestion.

When a suggestion is offered to the more classically neurotic patients, they can take it or leave it. If we follow Glover's (1931) definition of an inexact interpretation as a form of suggestion, we can look at a common example in the treatment of such a patient. The patient presents a dream and gives a few associations, and the therapist prematurely offers a possible approach to the material. If the suggestion is accurate, no harm is done.

If it is inaccurate, often the patient will politely but firmly disregard it, and pursue his or her course toward the more central meaning of the dream. Even if this suggestion results in a digression, eventually patient and therapist return to their work.

The more seriously impaired patient, by contrast, cannot easily take or leave the therapist's suggestion. A suggestion, like any offering, is too momentous an act for such a patient to disregard. Consider the following case.

> A 22-year-old patient in intensive psychotherapy had repeated troubles with roommates in the hospital, the halfway house, and later in apartments. Several sessions at various times were characterized by her reporting seemingly insoluble conflicts with one of a succession of roommates, who appeared increasingly malevolent to her. She would insist, early in such a session, that the therapist must believe her perception of the current roommate's almost maniacal malevolence, to "validate" her and to agree that she was justified in whatever step she took to extricate herself. She was also terrified of becoming labeled as an impossible roommate, both by peers and by herself. On one occasion the therapist suggested that the sense of insolubility might be an illusion, a consequence of the patient's currently limited view of her own and the roommate's capacity for change. To illustrate the therapist's view that he expected there were solutions to seemingly insoluble problems (even though one couldn't always see them at the time), he used a mathematical analogy to the situation of a two-dimensional being with a problem that was insoluble in the limited world of the plane, but easily solved from a three-dimensional perspective, like looking down on it from above. To illustrate this point more concretely, he drew a diagram of a pair of left-handed gloves on a piece of paper. The patient asked for the diagram, and seemed buoyed by the suggestion. She was totally unhelped by it, however, in the day-to-day struggles with the roommate and in her continued propensity to experience conflict as insoluble.
>
> Conflict in the therapeutic relationship was also experienced as overwhelming. The patient held on to the piece of paper like a talisman, referring to it during a difficult period of separation from the therapist several months later. During a later period of (vacation-related) instability in the therapy, she became preoccupied with bugs in her peripheral visual fields. These frightening illusions or minor hallucinations culminated in a vivid dream, in which the roommate's bedroom separated the patient from her parents; in the dream there were bugs on the ceiling. Her associations led her to connect the bugs on the ceiling to the therapist's prior characterization of his perspective as like being on the ceiling, looking from a different dimension at the problems. In this case she felt he was too removed, unable to accept her perception, and thus unable to help her deal with the roommate's provocation. His remoteness "bugged" her, she said, to the point of being torture for her.
>
> Somewhat later she found a T-shirt decorated by a drawing that resembled the one the therapist had done (the left-handed glove). She wore it, she said, to remind herself of his attempt to be helpful.

The patient in this example is clearly quite vulnerable to the effects of an intervention of any type. An effort at suggestion (that with the therapist's help, she might find the solution to seemingly insoluble problems) has had profound effects. First, it seems to have provided a relic of the moment in the form of the drawing, to aid memory when negatively tinged experience threatens to obliterate any useful remembering of the "good therapist." Second, in spite of its primitive usefulness in this way, the interchange also provided a nidus for the formation of a new symptom of psychotic proportions (the extreme sensitivity to bugs), related to separations in the patient–therapist relationship. Both positive and negative uses of the offering have persisted and changed over time. Finally, it is impossible to foresee an end to the influence of such an action, to predict whether it ultimately will be more helpful or more confusing.

As with Fisher's (1953) report on the suggestion to dream, noted above, the patient in this case responds primarily to the *fact* of the therapist's having offered an idea, not to the content of the idea itself. Uncritical acceptance of the idea is hardly likely. Rather, the patient can be seen to try to take in the suggestion, and the suggesting, and fit them into existing schemes for object relationships. The suggestion may be a sustaining, clarifying gift, to be kept and related to as a concrete entity rather than an idea, in the mode of a child whose difficult period of relatedness predates the development of the capacity to deal with abstract ideas. Alternatively it can be a sham gift from an abandoning parental figure, one who refuses to share the patient's experience. The patient can, at a later stage, exercise her own creativity in generalizing from it, and find a kind of transitional object, the T-shirt, which is more than a mere relic. And so a process comparable to development can occur, with the suggestion serving as an important stimulus to it. In this process, which is a prominent aspect of therapy with more seriously disturbed patients, the suggestion acts as an interpretation, an empathic statement, a self-revelation, or a confrontation—not by virtue of its specific form or content, but as an offering from the therapist to the patient.

Suggestions That Backfire

Although I have expressed considerable doubt that one can reliably use suggestion in psychotherapy, there should be no doubt of its potential power. In fact it is partly because of its power that suggestion is so easily misused. Two examples of suggestion that went awry will illustrate this power.

In the first case, a therapist suffers from suggestion given by a supervisor. The therapist not only had spent several years gaining practical experience in psychotherapy, but had taught it successfully to students. He was particularly noted for his careful attention to issues in the framework of therapy, especially appointment times and fees, and was regarded by students as extremely tough in these matters—uncompromising and critical, but helpful.

> When the therapist began a supervised case with a new and admired supervisor, the two got on famously. The patient was a severely obsessional young man with inhibitions in his sexual functions, work, and social life, and a pronounced tendency to attempt to overcome the inhibitions with futile action; visits to prostitutes and gambling.
>
> Early in the treatment, the patient delayed paying a bill, and procrastinated with his insurance forms. When the therapist and supervisor discussed this harbinger of the struggle to come, the supervisor suggested that in addition to clarifying the nature of the financial obligation, the therapist should exercise some restraint. "A month or two is all right, but I don't want him to be owing you for four months of treatment." The therapist agreed.
>
> As the therapist thought over the supervisory session, he became concerned that his own "rigid" attitude toward money would be seen by this valued superior as self-serving and insufficiently caring. The therapist began to question the conduct of his prior practice and teaching, assuming that the more experienced supervisor had a deeper and less neurotic understanding of financial issues in treatment. He gleaned from the supervisor's remark that a few months of indebtedness by the patient might be tolerable, or even useful, in the search for an alliance. He was, in fact, inordinately susceptible to suggestion, abandoning his own ideas in the face of a guess as to what his supervisor intended.
>
> The treatment ended in a spectacular mess, with four months' fees owed and a decision to interrupt the therapy as temporarily unworkable. (The supervisory relationship survived and moved beyond this inauspicious beginning.)

Suggestion here was based on an authoritative relationship between supervisor and supervisee, fueled by unconscious elements. One might explain the attempt to idealize the supervisor as a camouflage for his aggressive and competitive strivings. An alternative explanation would identify the wish to idealize the supervisor as primary, rather than defensive, and label the aggression embodied in the spectacular mess as a consequence of the therapist's growing discomfort when his supervisor proved to be fallible. We do not have to choose between these hypotheses to recognize a problematic consequence of suggestion in the learning situation. To the extent that patients, like therapists, need to keep their wits about them and value their own ideas (giving them up only as they prove inaccurate), the uncritical acceptance of much of anything is likely to cause discontinuities in thinking. When it does work, it may result in automatic compliance, with the patient resembling the stereotype of the hypnotized subject.

A second example, this one from the psychotherapy of a schizophrenic young woman, will further illustrate how potent suggestion can sometimes be.

The 21-year-old patient had been in therapy for five years, improving markedly from a regressed, deluded, confused state in her midteens to functioning as a competent college student, who, however, had persistent interpersonal difficulties. She was still quite shy and unsuccessful with peers, but at one point entered a period of tentative dating, to which her therapist at one point responded with interest. On one occasion she reported an encounter with a stranger on a bus. The stranger chatted with her, and she accompanied him to a park where they engaged in mutual fondling before she experienced marked confusion and anxiety and she broke off the encounter. When, in a subsequent session, she explored her motivation, the patient sensed some of the therapist's worry about her participation in the experience, and blurted out with genuine confusion, "I thought that's what you wanted me to do."

She pointed out that she had noted the therapist's interest in her forays into the heterosexual world and took this as approval of what she had done, as well as a wish for more, and more daring, participation. No doubt there was an element of suggestion in the therapist's emphasis, perhaps related to impatience in five years' work with a slowly changing patient. The therapist wished she would be more nearly normal, and perhaps if she saw herself that way, it would help. The patient's further associations led to her father and older brothers, and her fantasy that they viewed a woman's role as being subservient to a man. Perhaps she existed to serve a man, she thought, any man who asked her; the therapist and her family had seemed to agree on that. And if they agreed, who was she to refuse? The result was a detached, disconnected enactment of a fantasy of a sexual encounter, experienced as ego alien and not conducive to integration. As a result she did not (at this time) become more aware of her own sexual longings, or address the central issue, her sense of acting as a pawn for others. Rather the suggestion led to an enactment of that issue in her blind compliance.

SUMMARY AND CONCLUSIONS

Although suggestion is ubiquitous in human interaction, in therapy it is most usefully seen as an indirect phenomenon, not as a deliberate technique. As a phenomenon, suggestion is a general term for one of the ways in which therapists and patients influence each other's ideas. The wishes and fantasies therapists have about patients, especially when they are accompanied by strong affect, are powerful influences on the self-perceptions and behavior of patients. Under their sway patients may be influenced to talk about different subjects, act in different ways, feel enhanced, diminished, aroused, turned on, empty, or full—virtually anything they have the capacity to feel on their own. Although suggestion is a powerful force, it is not easily aimed. It is the therapist's beliefs, perceptions, and affects that do the influencing, not his or her intentions or hopes. I have explored how statements made with the conscious intention to be supportive via suggestion, especially in the form of reassurances, can have contrary effects, communicating worry, doubt, or even hopelessness. Suggestive effects can be created by the unconscious communication of a message that is contradictory to the one intended. Where this ambivalence is not a problem, and the suggested message is more uniform and coherent, its acceptance is complicated by the patient's greater reaction to being the recipient of such a communication than to its contents; he or she may discard the gift and save the wrapping. When the message is taken in, it may not be integrated into the mainstream of the patient's experience, but sit (to change the metaphor) like a lump in the psychic insides, causing a dissociated feeling and contributing little or nothing to therapeutic progress.

To be at all effective, suggestion must operate on the level of transference. It rides on the back of the transference, whether it uses a positive (idealizing or erotic) transference to gain acceptance, or, like the paradoxical techniques of the family therapists, relies on a negative relationship to produce its effect of rebellious acting in the opposite direction. The sine qua non of psychodynamic therapy, however, which distinguishes it from other attempts to influence patients for their own good, is its cognizance of the transference and its use of transference as a focus for reexperiencing and understanding. The transference is mobilized to help the patient see his or her own past through it, not to be used to influence the patient in a direction, however laudatory that direction might seem at first. The patient is the one with the answers. Even if we are convinced that he or she cannot see what needs to be seen, and we from our favored vantage point have a much clearer view of the terrain, that view will not help the patient until the patient can connect it with his or her own experience. Suggestion as a technique, then, cannot do much to further the ends of psychodynamic psychotherapy, and can do much to confuse it. As for suggestion as a phenomenon, we need to be clear and perceptive about its effects, so we can understand the many forces that shape the therapeutic interaction.

REFERENCES

Bibring, E. Psychoanalysis and the dynamic psychotherapies. *Journal of The American Psychoanalytic Association*, 1954, *2*, 745–770.

Blum, H., The curative and creative aspects of insight. *Journal of The American Psychoanalytic Association*, 1979, *27*, 41–68.

Breuer, J., and Freud, S. (1895) Studies on hysteria. *Standard edition*, vol. 2, London: Hogarth Press, 1953, pp. 1–310.

Fisher, C., Studies on the nature of suggestion, part II: The transference meaning of giving suggestion. *Journal of The American Psychoanalysis Association*, 1953, *1*, 406–437.

Frank, J.D. *Persuasion and healing.* Baltimore: Johns Hopkins Press, 1961.

Freud, S. (1892) A case of successful treatment by hypnosis. *Standard edition,* vol. 1. London: Hogarth Press, pp. 115–128.

Freud, S. (1912) The dynamics of transference. *Standard edition,* vol. 12. London: Hogarth Press, 1953, pp. 99–105.

Freud, S. (1914) On narcissism: An introduction. *Standard edition,* vol. 14. London: Hogarth Press, 1953, pp. 73–102.

Freud, S. (1918) Lines of advance in psycho-analytic therapy. *Standard edition,* vol. 17. London: Hogarth Press, 1953, p. 168.

Gill, M., and Menninger, K. Hypnoanalysis. *Bulletin of the Menninger Clinic,* 1946, *10,* 110–126.

Glover, E. The therapeutic effect on inexact interpretation: A contribution to the theory of suggestion. *International Journal of Psycho-Analysis,* 1931, *12,* 397–411.

Guntrip, H. *Psychoanalytic theory, therapy, and the self.* New York: Basic Books, 1971.

Jones, E. *The life and work of Sigmund Freud.* New York: Basic Books, 1953.

Langs, R. *The bipersonal field.* New York: Jason Aaronson, 1976.

McLaughlin, V. Transference, psychic reality, and countertransference. *Psychoanalytic Quarterly,* 1981, *50,* 639–664.

Myerson, P. The nature of the transactions that occur in other than classical analysis. *International Review of Psychoanalysis,* 1981, *8,* 173–189.

Searles, H. *Collected papers on schizophrenia and related subjects.* New York: International Universities Press, 1965.

Winnicott, D.W. Transitional objects and phenomena. In: *Collected papers.* New York: Basic Books, 1958.

4
Catharsis:
History Theory

MICHAEL P. NICHOLS, Ph.D.

What role does catharsis play in psychodynamic psychotherapy? Does it foster acting out, does it merely reduce tension, or does it promote significant therapeutic change? The answer to all three questions is Yes, depending upon how catharsis is defined.

Always important, definitions are especially critical where catharsis is concerned, because the widely varying uses of this term have spawned much controversy and misunderstanding. Many apparently conflicting viewpoints arise from differences in definition—differences that could be eliminated by a more precise use of language.

One common usage defines catharsis in behavioral terms as acting on aggressive impulses. In research on the social psychology of aggression, catharsis, typically operationalized by having subjects administer electric shocks to others (e.g., Berkowitz, 1962), often leads to increased hostility and aggressive behavior. These findings are significant, but of questionable relevance to psychotherapy, where angry feelings, linked to specific mental contents (Schafer, 1970), are expressed *verbally*. Although defining catharsis in behavioral rather than expressive terms is more common among those who are not psychoanalytically informed, it does occasionally creep into discussions of psychoanalytic therapy (e.g., Strachey, 1934). To prevent confusion it is suggested that the aggressive behavior cited in these studies be termed retaliation rather than catharsis.

Conversely, a second common usage refers to the patient's speaking freely, and with some feeling, in the service of further reduction in tension.

Consider, for example, the following excerpts from two psychotherapy texts.

> In catharsis, the counselor actively stimulates the client to talk himself out. It is effective only in relatively superficial disturbances it may not even give symptomatic relief, but may reinforce the tension. (Patterson, 1966, p. 86)

> The sheer act of talking can provide an individual with considerable emotional palliation. It furnishes a motor outlet for the release of tension. (Wolberg, 1977, p. 28)

What both texts fail to take into accout is the uncovering of previously repressed or conflictual material, as well as the strong expression of feeling through laughter, shouting, or tears. In the absence of these two elements, what is called catharsis may be little more than aimless rambling, neither emotionally stimulating nor cognitively focused.

For clarity and precision, then, it is proposed that catharsis be defined as *a strong expression of feeling about repressed or conflictual material in the presence of someone other than the object of the original feelings.* It is at once a cognitive and a somatic experience, involving the recall of forgotten or discordant material, along with the physical expression of emotion in laughter, shouting, or tears. The cognitive aspect of catharsis consists of the contents of consciousness during the reexperiencing of an emotional event, whereas its somatic aspect consists of physical sensations and motoric expressions of emotion. The two components usually occur together and are part of a natural sequence of actions—what is meant by "having a feeling."

Sometimes, however, one component can occur without the other. When we cry at the movies, for example, our tears are triggered by cinematic images that stimulate personally meaningful associations —associations that usually remain unconscious. In these instances catharsis is experienced somatically but not cognitively. By contrast, cognitive catharsis often occurs unaccompanied by motoric expression, as when patients remember and describe painful experiences of loss without weeping. Optimum therapeutic benefit takes place when both components are present. Merely talking about an emotionally significant event is not cathartic unless the attendant feelings are expressed in tears, laughter, or angry shouts. And although strong expressions of feeling may ease tension and relax defenses, they do not significantly enhance the work of psychodynamic psychotherapy unless the patient becomes cognizant of their original source.

An even less clear distinction occurs when patients give vigorous expression to emotions triggered by recent events—emotions that were never repressed. The experience of a patient who suffers an acute trauma and then cries about it at the next therapy session would not appear to satisfy our strict definition of catharsis. Yet the strength of emotion expressed in therapy often indicates that some of these feelings were blocked from previous expression by social circumstances, conflict, or chronic emotional restraint. For this reason such an immediate expression of feeling also is likely to be cathartic, and probably includes some breaching of defenses.

Finally, since catharsis encompasses the idea of recollection and expression subsequent to the actual, stimulating event (rather than directly acting on feelings and their impulses), it might be best to limit its definition to expressions not aimed directly at their object. The patient who cries or yells in the presence of a therapist avoids the felt danger of retaliation from the object of those feelings. To express feelings directly toward their object may bring relief, but, unlike catharsis, it is a complete sequence of actions that develops within the context of everyday life. Catharsis, on the other hand, is a kind of substitute expression in a context—therapeutic or artistic—other than the natural one.

Strictly speaking, catharsis is not a therapeutic technique in the way that, say, clarification and interpretation are. It is not something the therapist does, but a process that occurs in the patient. To be precise, the therapist elicits catharsis. However, for purposes of balance within this volume, the phrase "elicitation of catharsis" has been shortened to "catharsis."

Another term often used in conjunction with catharsis is *abreaction*. Some authors employ the terms synonymously; others distinguish between them, treating catharsis as a therapeutic process and abreaction as its result. Although such a distinction could be maintained, the more common usage is to treat the terms synonymously, as is done here.

HISTORY

Catharsis in Drama and Ritual

Long before Breuer and Freud (1895) developed their cathartic technique, catharsis figured in the ancient traditions of drama, ritual, and healing. Used, deliberately or unwittingly, to change behavior, catharsis played a prominent role in Aristotle's concept of the theater (Aristotle, 1951); in ancient religious and magical healing rituals (Malinowski, 1955); in mesmerism and hypnotherapy (Brenman & Gill, 1947); in drug-induced treatment of the traumatic neuroses of war (Watkins, 1949); in religious revivals (McLoughlin, 1959); and in rituals of mourning (Gorer, 1965). The list is too long to elaborate here (c.f. Nichols & Zax, 1977; Scheff,

1979), but some implications from the rich history of cathartic rituals are relevant to the practice of psychodynamic psychotherapy.

Debate over the value of catharsis can be traced at least as far back as ancient Greece. Plato, the ultimate rationalist, condemned theatrical drama for arousing the passions and thereby undermining the state. His pupil Aristotle (1951) responded with praise for the cathartic powers of theater, for its ability to present "incidents arousing pity and fear in such a way as to accomplish a purgation *(Katharsis)* of such emotions." Aristotle believed that emotions are aroused and purged to the degree that the audience identifies with the pain and tribulations of the tragic hero, and he argued for the therapeutic benefits of such an experience.

This ancient dispute illustrates two opposing views of catharsis, which continue until the present day. The question still remains: Is catharsis a way of provoking the passions, or of purging them? The answer, it turns out, is: Neither.

Direct or vicarious participation in activities (classical tragedy or social psychological experiments) that provoke feelings is not catharsis; catharsis involves releasing or uncovering dormant feelings by breaching emotional resistance. Moreover, catharsis cannot purge people of their emotions, because emotions do not have concrete, physical properties, nor are they malevolent. Catharsis is not a puring of feelings; it is an uncovering and expression of them. Yet Aristotle's concept continues to characterize most of the thinking about catharsis as a process of actually expelling bad "objects." The danger of this perspective lies in the invalid notion that feelings can and should be expelled. Many critics (e.g., Binstock, 1973) have pointed out the misguided nature of these purgative metaphors, but have gone on to reject the utility of the cathartic process. As we shall see, however, catharsis has a history of reported success, and even some scientific support (Nichols & Zax, 1977).

Many ancient healing rituals were deliberately cathartic, based upon the Aristotelian belief that catharsis provides a purgation and a rebirth into a purified state. Even when catharsis is an unwitting by-product of occult ceremonies, it still produces a feeling of relief and clarified thinking. Cathartic healing rituals and religious rites are preceded by the expectation that catharsis will occur and begin with various devices to overcome resistance so as to facilitate emotional release. Visitors to Mesmer's "baquet" were prepared for catharsis by the tales told of the procedure and by the elaborate staging of Mesmer's theatrical performances. Shamans and folk healers typically began their healing ceremonies by performing feats of magic to demonstrate their power, to enhance the expectation of success, and to generate an emotionally charged atmosphere. Once primed, emotional arousal was heightened by drum beating, chanting, shrieking, and convulsive dancing. Defenses were further weakened by the use of alcoholic drinks, narcotics, and psychedelic mushrooms.

These ritualized ceremonies enabled participants to shed traditional inhibitions and to depart from social norms of emotional restraint on the grounds that they were not responsible for their behavior. The emotions expressed and the impulses displayed were attributed to demons within, which were believed to be purged in these emotional rites. Although apparently therapeutic (Nichols & Zax, 1977), these cathartic ceremonies did not work by exorcizing demons, either in the form of "evil spirits" or of "repressed affects." Instead they provided a culturally sanctioned outlet for experiencing and expressing significant memories and their attendant emotional responses.

From the perspective of modern psychodynamic psychotherapists interested in lasting personality change, one limitation of these cathartic rites was inherent in their infrequency and ritualized nature. Isolated from everyday experience, catharsis was insulated rather than incorporated into daily living in a way that supported sustained acceptance and expression of feeling as an ongoing feature of a well-integrated life.

Moreover these prescientific, cathartic procedures appealed to occult rationalizations to justify expressions of feeling; and although these justifications may have helped surmount resistance, they cast emotional expression as involuntary and magical, rather than as a natural and healthy reaction. Modern cathartic rituals, such as encounter groups, also fail their participants if emotional expression is limited to isolated contexts rather than promoted on an ongoing basis (Lieberman et al., 1973; Nichols & Zax, 1977). Whenever ritualized performances are believed necessary for the display of strong feeling, the results are probably limited to tension reduction and suggestion. Treating emotions as evil spirits, subject to revelation and ceremonial purgation, is unlikely to alter habits of emotional suppression in everyday life.

The Cathartic Method of Breuer and Freud

The "cathartic technique" developed by Breuer and Freud is the well-known beginning of both psychoanalysis and modern emotive psychotherapy. The cathartic technique was discovered serendipitously by Breuer during his treatment of Anna O. (Breuer & Freud, 1895). In the course of his work with this patient, Breuer discovered that her severe hysterical symptoms were relieved when she reexperienced traumatic events under hypnosis. By encouraging her to associate to the origins of her symptoms, permitting her to describe these events in reverse chronological order, and allowing her to express her accompanying feelings without interruption, Breuer helped Anna O. to resolve the symptoms. This case history illustrates two basic premises of psychodynamic psychotherapy: (1) that neurotic symptoms are at least partly based on buried conflictual feelings, and (2) that these feelings can be recovered. Little was required of the therapist other than not to interfere with the release of pent-up feelings.

It is significant that Breuer hit upon the cathartic method by chance, and that it worked with very little input from him. That catharsis seemed to happen spontaneously, once released and not blocked, suggests that it is a natural and powerful therapeutic mechanism. This contention is further supported by the fact that several other therapists have described their discoveries of cathartic therapy as similar. They were surprised by a patient's sudden and vigorous expression of emotion, and found that if they just let it happen, without interfering, the process of catharsis was profoundly therapeutic. Jackins, who developed reevaluation counseling (1962); Janov, who developed primal therapy (1970); Casriel, who developed new identity therapy (1972); and Moreno, who developed psychodrama (1959), have all described this experience.

After hearing Breuer's account of the treatment of Anna O., Freud began to use the cathartic method himself, and the two men collaborated in writing up their findings. In *Studies on Hysteria* (Breuer & Freud, 1895), they described the details of the cathartic technique and outlined the traumatic theory of neurosis. Treatment of hysterical symptoms required that patients be hypnotized and then urged to recall the events associated with the onset of symptoms. Breuer and Freud wrote:

> We found, at first to our greatest surprise, that the individual hysterical symptoms immediately disappeared without returning if we succeeded in thoroughly awakening the memories of the causal process with its accompanying affect, and if the patient circumstantially discussed the process in the most detailed manner and gave verbal expression to the affect.

Because Breuer and Freud stressed that affect was associated with the resurrection of traumatic memories, it is commonly thought that theirs was an intensely feeling-oriented treatment. This, however, apparently was not the case. A careful reading of *Studies on Hysteria*, as well as subsequent papers by Freud, suggests that he was always more concerned with uncovering memories than with promoting affective expression. In Chapter I of *Studies*, Breuer and Freud reported that both repressed ideas and "strangulated affect" are responsible for causing hysterical symptoms, but that treatment succeeds because, by recovering the repressed memories and describing them, the affect is drained off through memory and speech. Thus memory and speech are the key therapeutic mechanisms; affect is important merely because it signals the presence of vivid memories. Therapeutic reminiscences are usually accompanied by some feeling, but intense emotional expression is never really essential to the treatment. In Chapter IV, on the psychotherapy of hysteria, Freud made clear that the undoing of repression was his primary aim, and affect only a by-product of removing resistances. Freud emphasized, "Finding the pathogenic reminiscences . . . Which required overcoming psychic forces in the patient which opposed the pathogenic idea becoming conscious (remembered)."

Catharsis in the Evolution of Psychoanalysis

The fact that Freud abandoned "the cathartic method" has been taken as evidence that he made a major transition from an emotional to a cognitive form of treatment. As we have seen, however, he was never really an emotivist, but a seeker after memories, who saw in affect a signal that critical rememberances were being uncovered. In fact he may have been uncomfortable in the face of intense emotional display (Jones, 1953).

For Freud, then, the cathartic method was primarily a tool for overcoming repression and was used only until he found a more reliable tool to serve this purpose. During his cathartic treatment of Elisabeth von R., she reproached Freud for so frequently interrupting the flow of her thoughts with his questions (Breuer & Freud, 1895). Fortunately, he listened to her complaint, and thus began the technique of free association, which proved a more reliable and more thorough way of uncovering early memories.

Developments in technique and theory progress in a circular pattern. When Freud saw that remembering traumatic childhood events did not produce lasting behavioral change, he rejected the traumatic theory of neurosis and the hydraulic model of emotions upon which it was based. Feelings, he concluded, are not concrete entities that can be stored up and then drained off, but dispositions of action, to be recognized and given appropriate expression. These insights were aided by Freud's discovery of free association, which led him to locate "complexes," or conflicts, at the root of neurotic problems. With theory (traumatic) issuing from technique (cathartic), and new technique (free association) disconfirming the old theory, so, in circular fashion, emerged Freud's conflict theory. It stated that it is not specific early experiences that must be uncovered and verbalized, but disowned feelings and impulses that must be recognized and integrated into the personality. This change in focus led to further deemphasis of the role of catharsis. No longer was catharsis thought to be a fundamental element in psychoanalysis, although it has always been acknowledged to play a subsidiary role.

Freud's goal, in topographic terms, was to widen the sphere of consciousness (Freud, 1904), using interpretation to overcome resistances. This, he believed, must be done at a pace slow enough to permit the ego to assimilate the unconscious material that is uncovered. This approach differed significantly from the cathartic method—which, through the use of hypnosis, forced the patient to give up repressions suddenly and so precluded a thorough exploration of intrapsychic dynamics. In "The Dynamics of the Transference" (1912), Freud pointed out that the patient seeks merely to discharge emotions without understanding them, but psychoanalysis requires that emotions be made conscious and then analyzed. Feelings not only must be expressed, but understood; catharsis is not enough. Freud's statement (1912) that buried feelings must be made actual and manifest so that they can be dealt with directly, however, suggests that catharsis may be a useful part of the process. Ferenczi (1930), Rank (1945), and Reik (1948) all believed catharsis to be essential to successful psychoanalytic treatment.

Like Freud, Strachey (1934) thought that repressed feelings and impulses must emerge in small quantities if they are to be understood. The problem with massive cathartic discharge, according to Strachey, is that it may overwhelm the patient and tend to confirm the danger of uncovering feelings, leading to a redoubling of defenses. Catharsis, as he saw it, covers two processes. As a discharge of affect, it is a useful adjunct to analysis, perhaps even an inevitable accompaniment to "mutative interpretations." Catharsis following an interpretation is a sign that the interpretation has struck home. But, Strachey warned, catharsis alternately may imply libidinal gratification, which can impede analysis, especially if its true nature goes unrecognized. That is, a patient may consider the analyst's acceptance of the patient's feelings as encouragement to act on the impulses behind them. This is a misuse of the term catharsis. Perhaps because of this mistaken view, Strachey believed that the effects of catharsis are lasting only in cases where the predominant etiology is a traumatic event, as in the neuroses of war.

Bibring (1954) expressed views similar to Strachey's, stating that catharisis was only part of Freud's treatment and never a "one-act" therapy. When hypnosis was replaced by free association, catharsis (or emotional reliving) was considered less a directly curative agent than a means of convincing patients of the reality of their repressed impulses. What was at first thought of as the principal therapeutic tool came to be accepted only as an adjunct to the process of acquiring insight through interpretation.

In evaluating Strachey's and Bibring's criticisms of catharsis, it is important to bear two points in mind. First, the catharsis being referred to means talking about significant events with feeling, and not the intense expression of feeling through sobbing and yelling recommended by modern emotivists. "Verbalizing repressed affect" may have a quite different therapeutic potential than intense and sustained somatic-emotional discharge (Nichols & Zax, 1977). Second, treating catharsis as an adjunct to interpretation may exaggerate the role of interpretation. The cliché that psychoanalytic therapy works by achieving insight through interpretation may be misleading. Interpretation and insight may succeed by removing

defenses so that patients can experience the archaic parts of their personalities. (A similar view is suggested by Kohut, 1977.) In this case interpretation might be a vehicle for achieving catharsis.

Fenichel (1945) expressed what is still the mainstream opinion of catharsis when he said that it demonstrates to the patient "the existence and
intensity of his emotions." Another way of stating this is to say that
catharsis provides the patient with a "sense of conviction about the reality
of his unconscious processes" (Greenson, 1967). When cognitive awareness is coupled with intense feeling, patients are more likely to accept the
significance of their insights.

Modern analysts also believe that catharsis is a useful way to resolve
symptoms that derive from acutely traumatic incidents. Greenson recommends that patients be encouraged to express as much feeling as possible because of the relief it provides, thus enabling them to continue the
hard work of analysis. This form of catharsis not only furnishes relief,
but also prevents present traumas from becoming pathogenic.

Catharsis plays a more prominent role in short-term, dynamic psychotherapy (e.g., Davanloo, 1980; Mann, 1973; Sifneos, 1979), where
analytic technique has been modified to make it more active and cathartic.
These practitioners believe that, by becoming increasingly passive, psychoanalytic psychotherapists have needlessly lengthened the duration of
treatment. Short-term, dynamic psychotherapy is more anxiety provoking
(e.g., Sifneos, 1979) and carthartic (e.g., Davanloo, 1980) than long-term
psychoanalytic psychotherapy (e.g., Langs, 1973). Short-term dynamic
therapists are in the mainstream of psychoanalytic treatment, but are more
active in "releasing hidden feelings by actively working on and interpreting
resistance or defenses; paying strict attention to the transference relationships; and actively making links between the transference and significant
people in the patient's current life and past" (Davanloo, 1980, p. 45).

Modern Cathartic Therapies

As we have seen, Freud abandoned catharsis and the traumatic theory
in favor of free association and the conflict theory of neurosis. Ironically,
however, most of the emotive therapies that were developed in reaction
against psychoanalysis rest on Freud's early idea that neurosis results from
repressed traumatic events and can be cured by remembering and expressing the association affect (e.g., Janov, 1970).

The pioneer, and intellectual leader, of modern cathartic therapy was
Wilhelm Reich (1949, 1960), who was the first to emphasize sustained
catharsis over a prolonged course of psychotherapy rather than singular,
dramatic abreactions. Recent cathartic therapists have followed Reich's
emphasis on intense catharsis and have borrowed some of his techniques

for achieving it. Many, however, have overlooked his understanding of the complexity and tenacity of psychological defenses. The key to liberating feelings, as Reich understood it, is not to sneak past or bludgeon defenses, but to wage a prolonged siege, gradually wearing them down, so that they will not be quickly resurrected following carthartic release.

Although he made it central, Reich never treated emotion as the only valid expression of one's humanness, and his therapy emphasized understanding as well as catharsis. People not only feel, but also think and act; no therapy can succeed without addressing all three aspects of the human personality. It is unfortunate that Reich's influence led to a reactive shift away from rationality. The humanistic myth that surrender to feelings and passive acceptance of impulses lead to fulfillment spawned therapies devoted to purging, not liberating, emotions. Therapists that limit their focus to only one of these dimensions come into and out of vogue. The 1960s saw the popularization of several cathartic therapies, including psychodrama (Moreno, 1958), encounter groups (Goldberg, 1970), re-grief therapy (Volkan, 1972), primal therapy (Janov, 1970), bioenergetics (Lowen, 1967), Gestalt therapy (Perls, 1969), reevaluation counseling (Jackins, 1965), feeling therapy (Hart et al., 1975), and new identity therapy (Casriel, 1972). Subsequently some of these approaches (e.g., feeling therapy) as well as some of their offshoots, (such as feeling-expressive therapy (Pierce, et al., 1981), have incorporated cognitive and behavioral strategies in addition to catharsis. But the spotlight of attention shifted away from cathartic approaches, first to behavioral therapies and then to cognitive ones. Therapies that aim only at catharsis were very successful at developing powerful techniques for eliciting feelings. Unfortunately an exclusive focus on emotion, as if there were no place for reasons and no need for action, is more likly to help patients put up with their problems than to achieve the understanding necessary to master them.

Psychodynamic psychotherapy, unlike these other approaches, has always aimed at treating the whole person and achieving major personality reconstruction. The idea that such therapy focuses on understanding to the exclusion of feelings and behavior is a popular misconception that, unfortunately, is not limited to the public. It also pervades the thinking of those in the psychodynamic tradition who neglect the role of emotions and catharsis in treatment, who do not understand that, instead of substituting reason for feeling and action, psychoanalytic therapy should combine them.

THEORETICAL ANALYSIS

Catharsis and the Nature of Emotions

Most discussions of catharsis are muddled by unclear thinking about the nature of emotions. Emotions, being abstract and complex, are difficult to describe, and hence most people resort to metaphor and analogy in doing so. Typically the language of emotion is the language of water. Sadness, "wells up," anger "boils," happiness "bubbles over," and grief "comes in waves." These watery substances all flow toward a dam, conscious expression, which may be lowered or raised. Although evocative, such descriptions tend to concretize and reify emotions.

Psychoanalysis perpetuated the ordinary language habit of personifying emotions, cloaking the confusion with a veneer of scientific respectability. The idea that repressed affects "build up inside" and need to be "discharged" implies that unexpressed feelings are accumulated and must be drained or harm will result. The underlying premise is that emotions are concrete entities that are capable of being stored and requiring a container (Ayer, 1946; Ryle, 1959; Schafer, 1976). By saying that anger is "kept inside," "let out," or "ventilated," we legitimize Freudian metaphors of inner and outer space (Rabkin, 1970) and, in the process, portray people as passive recipients of their feelings. When people are said to "struggle with their feelings," it seems that the feelings are somehow outside them—or inside them—but not of them. This is contrary to a basic goal of psychodynamic psychotherapy—to help people realize how much they actively (consciously or unconsciously) create their own lives, even if they fail to recognize it.

The following clinical vignette illustrates how clinicians commonly treat emotions as objects.

> Three years after they married, Mrs. X's husband was killed in an automobile accident. Her grief was so immense that she could hardly bear it. To cope with her loss, she repressed her grief and anger, burying these feelings deep inside. For the following two years, she was able to function, but she was lonely, frightened, and anxious. Eventually she became so unhappy that she sought psychotherapy. In therapy her grief, which had been kept inside for so long, welled up to the surface, until at last she was able to discharge it. As her repression lifted, she was able to ventilate her grief and anger, crying and sobbing, until finally she cried herself out.

In this description grief is said to have been repressed, stored, and finally discharged. But where was it stored? Where did it go when it was discharged? And what was left in its place? If these questions seem absurd, it is because they reveal the fallacious implications of our careless metaphors for emotions. Feelings cannot be stored or discharged, because they are not physical objects.

Experience can be divided into a number of logical components, including actions, thoughts, and feelings. But the mere possibility of subdividing the phenomenology of experience into different components does not mean that each of these components actually functions independently of the others.

The fact that we call something a feeling makes it seem to be a thing.

To feel is to do something, not to have something. "Feelings" are not separate from actions; they are both facets of a single process. Any experience entails many complex processes. "Feelings" are what is meant by certain qualities involved in experiencing, including bodily sensations, thoughts, and even actions. The feeling of anger is not a thing that exists separately from and causes hitting or shouting. It does not reside in a place, inside or outside, nor can one be filled with it. Anger is not an entity; its referents are physiological arousal, thinking of hitting someone, clenching one's teeth, yelling, and so on.

Catharsis as the Completion of an Interrupted Emotional Action

If feelings are not concrete and cannot be stored or discharged, what is catharsis and how might it be therapeutic? Catharsis is not a discharge of quantities of psychic energy. It is remembering something with feeling and carrying out the expressive actions that are part of what is meant by "having feelings." That this invariably also involves breaching defenses against expressing feelings is important to remember when considering the nature of catharsis. The idea of catharsis requires the experience of overcoming restraint. Unless the impulse to express feelings were thwarted, we would not sepak of catharsis. If Mr. Potts spanks Tommy and Tommy cries, that is not catharsis. Only if Tommy does not cry when spanked does the possibility of catharsis at a later time arise. Thus catharsis is a label for completing (some or all of) a previously restrained or interrupted sequence of emotional expression. The emotional expression is that which would have occurred as a natural reaction to some experience, had that expression not been thwarted.

Let us see how the catharsis of Mrs. X's grief can be described as the completion of a previously blocked sequence of predictable actions. When her husband died, she was so shocked and hurt that she avoided thinking about it. During that terrible time, she tried anything she could to avoid facing the full significance of her loss. She strained to hold back her tears and sought desperately to think of other things. Unfortunately, by continuing to avoid thinking about what happened and actively struggling to resist her impulse to grieve, she was in fact prolonging her preoccupation with her lost husband. Afraid to face the painful memory of his death, but unable to forget it, she forestalled the natural process of grieving. Unable to let go of the past, or to take hold of life in the present, she was miserable.

Finally, she decided to do something, and so began psychotherapy. There she realized that her prolonged resistance was more harmful than the experience of facing the memory she resisted. With the therapist's help, she determined to face the reality of her loss, concluding that it would be preferable to remember and feel the pain than to stay as she was. Now, instead of avoiding memories of her husband and his death, she recalled them vividly. She remembered the horrible details of the accident, and how much she loved her husband. Naturally her thoughts were attended by strong feelings. She shuddered and wept until she was convulsed with sobs.

Mrs. X's remembering and crying could be described as "discharging affect," "releasing old feelings," "ventilation," or "uncovering her grief." All of these locutions imply that some emotional entity was inside of her, unchanged, like a restless spirit striving to get out. But, since emotions are not substances and cannot be stored, there are no "old feelings." Her emotional reaction (crying about her husband) did not exist inside her. It existed only in the conditional mode; it is what she *would have* done *if* she had thought about her husband. Freud, (1915) expressed a similar opinion in his paper "The Unconscious" (p. 111). There he argued that latent memories do exist in the unconscious, but that:

> A comparison of the unconscious affect with the unconscious idea reveals the significant difference that the unconscious idea continues, after repression, as an actual formation in the unconscious, whilst to the unconscious affect there corresponds in the same system only a potential disposition. . . . "

Describing catharsis as the completion of an emotional action sequence has practical consequences that bear on psychodynamic technique. To say that feelings are actions rather than things avoids divorcing patients from their emotions, and stops them from disclaiming their emotional actions (Schafer, 1976). Mrs. X's therapist was able to help her experience catharsis by interpreting the activity behind her apparent passivity. "Not feeling" is simply a different kind of experiencing (resistant, effortful, distracted) than "feeling" (accepting, completing, expressive). Her grief was not locked inside of her, nor was she "doing nothing" about it. Instead she was fixedly and insistently holding back: avoiding crying, trying not to think of her husband, busily preoccupying herself with other things.

The therapist helped her overcome her resistance by pointing to what she was doing—holding back—and not to "the grief." He drew her attention to her activity and the motives for it. When her husband died, it had seemed inadvisable to her to think about it; she sought to spare herself the pain. Later, after she recognized that she was actively avoiding crying, she redefined the significance of refraining from grieving. She now saw that instead of protecting herself, she was prolonging her suffering. This led to a cognitive transformation that brought about further emotional change.

THERAPEUTIC EFFECTS OF CATHARSIS

Psychodynamic psychotherapy is a process of discovery during which resistances are overcome so as to enable patients to claim responsibility for their actions and experience archaic parts of their personalities. Once they become aware of previously avoided or denied aspects of the self, patients are better able to integrate basic impulses into their lives, gratifying some and finding substitute outlets for others.

Catharsis enhances this discovery. When resistances are sufficiently relaxed (by confrontation and interpretation) to permit catharsis, patients learn that it is safe to feel previously warded-off emotions. As anxiety-producing emotions are enacted, patients are exposed to the dangers they had previously avoided. As more and more feelings are expressed, patients progressively learn to tolerate them. The result is a desensitization of latent feelings and unconscious longings.

The following are the specific mechanisms whereby catharsis is therapeutic: reducing chronic emotional suppression, which includes temporary regression, relaxation of defenses, and reduction of rigid overcontrol; learning to accept the self through the empathic response of the therapist; confession; overcoming preoccupation with past events and correcting misleading cognitive constructions; and becoming more feelingful.

Reducing Emotional Suppression

Emotional suppression is ubiquitous, with both healthy and unhealthy consequences. Defending against the threat of punishment for expressing feelings is the beginning of psychological defenses, which blunt the full range of emotional experiencing and expression, impoverishing the personality. Defensive reaction to feelings has adaptive as well as maladaptive implications. Control and delay may enable feelings to be channeled into appropriate outlets, thus permitting wishes to be gratified more effectively. Although some taming of impulses and restraint on emotions are necessary if people are to live together in harmony, "surplus repression" (Marcuse, 1955), which diminishes the quality of life, is all too common in industrial societies. One way in which children learn to avoid feeling painful emotions is to feel less of anything. Eventually most become so accustomed to restraining their emotions that they cease to be aware of it. Parents unwittingly confuse the expressive and instrumental functions of emotions, and punish their children for crying not only when they are demanding or complaining, but also when they are hurt or frightened. Consequently children learn to suppress their feelings and deny their needs. As they grow older, they mask their feelings even further, in order to manage the impressions they create on others (Goffman, 1959). Bowing to cultural stereotypes, boys are especially prone to hide their sadness, and girls their anger.

Of the many experts who agree that emotional suppression is widespread and maladaptive, few accept catharsis as an antidote. Nevertheless people continue to seek out cathartic experiences. Horror films and "tear jerkers," roller coasters, sporting events, and circus clowns all owe much of their appeal to the fact that they stimulate our emotions and furnish a ritual outlet for their expression. Although we may not be consciously aware of the sources of our distress, these experiences provide relief through somatic-emotional catharsis. We may not know why we are crying or laughing, but we do know that it feels good to be expressive for a change. The pleasure that follows emotional expression may also account for the popularity of encounter groups, est training, and many forms of emotive psychotherapy.

In psychodynamic psychotherapy regression facilitates exploration of the unconscious by reopening intrapsychic conflicts and fostering transference. Catharsis potentiates regression because when patients cry, they are behaving as they did when they were children—they are openly vulnerable. Crying, laughing, and yelling are preverbal forms of expression, and they powerfully evoke childhood associations.

Catharsis and regression are also important elements in the creation of transference and countertransference. By crying a patient says, "When I hurt, I feel sad and unprotected. And when I cry, I remember and expose the hurt, just as when I was a child." The act of crying leaves the patient unguarded; as long as the patient is crying, he or she has dropped the pseudoadult pretense of not needing anything from anybody. This is consistent with Winnicott's (1958) concept of giving up the "false self system" and Guntrip's (1969) notion that to become fully adult, one must let go of the "pseudoadult self." These and other writers recognized that most of us expend much of our energies denying and suppressing basic needs and feelings. Some patients begin to express these needs and feelings directly; others sense but reject them, acting almost belligerently contrary to how they feel. With the first group, therapists can begin by helping them to acknowledge their longings and express them energetically. The second group requires considerable analysis of defenses before they can permit themselves to regress.

Catharsis and regression in the patient also make very specific demands on the therapist. Psychotherapy is a shared experience, unconscious as well as conscious, for both therapist and patient. As the patient experiences more intense and more primitive feelings, so does the therapist. The baby's cry signals the parents to help in some way, but it also distresses them. Parents begin to react punitively when the baby's emotional expression evokes their own unpleasant affect. Subsequently the expression of

dysphoric affect is not only unpleasant, but dangerous; it leads to punishment. Unless comfortable with a wide range of emotions, the therapist
is likely to inhibit the patient's exploration of self. An overly rigid therapist
tends to hinder the patient's "regression in the service of the ego" (Kris,
1952) by conveying discomfort with raw feelings and primitive experience.

Critics (e.g., Lowy, 1970) say that catharsis means losing control,
implying that control is mature and healthy—not something one should
lose. There are two flaws in this argument. First, control is neither categorically good nor categorically bad. Second, catharsis entails giving up
control temporarily and purposefully, not losing it. There are times when
most people need to exercise greater control. Many of us, for example,
would profit from eating less and exercising more. On the other hand,
most people need less, not more, control over the expression of their
feelings. The average person's emotional life is like a pool in a public park:
The contours are nicely ordered, but the water inside is captive and
lifeless. Learning to "lose control" enables the water to run freely, making
the person more alive—better able to be playful, to get angry, or to laugh
at a joke.

The fear of losing control is based on a sense that the self is not solid,
competent, or stable. If it were, would one worry so much about letting
go? The more pronounced the self-doubt, the more rigid is the control.

Like any powerful mechanism of change, catharic uncovering has the
potential for harming, as well as for helping. The exposure and expression
of guarded feelings must be gradual enough for the patient to experience
and understand them without being overwhelmed by anxiety. This requires that defenses be reduced gradually, not prematurely blasted away
by relentless confrontations or emotional gimmickry (as sometimes occurs
in encounter groups and cathartic therapies). In addition patients must
be quite clear about the difference between accepting feelings and acting
upon them uncritically. The therapist should encourage catharsis at a
gradual pace, and then help the patient to understand the implications of
his or her feelings before beginning to test their expression outside the
safety of the treatment room.

Mr. Y sought therapy for help in overcoming a chronic sense of fatigue and
malaise. Despite his excellent physical health and outwardly successful life,
the patient was always tired and vaguely discontented. It soon became
apparent to the therapist that Mr. Y was unconsciously furious at his wife
for her clinging dependency, which he allowed to control him and narrowly
circumscribe his leisure time. In response to her nagging and apparent
helplessness, Mr. Y had abandoned many friends and several hobbies in
order to stay home with his wife. Although he blamed her for his decision
to accede to her demands—real and projected, he did not express anger,
or even resentment, for fear that if he did so, she might reject him, or that
the anger might get out of control and destroy her.
    At this juncture an inexperienced therapist might be tempted to confront

Mr. Y with his anger and insist that he express it to his wife. Fortunately, Mr. Y's therapist realized that precipitate expression of his anger would expose Mr. Y to guilt and anxiety as well as possible retaliation from his wife. Proceeding cautiously, the therapist began to analyze Mr. Y's defenses against anger. Once he understood that he was holding back, and some of the reasons for doing so, Mr. Y was finally able to experience and express angry feelings in therapy sessions. Doing so provided him with a great sense of relief and further understanding about his relationship with his wife.

He now was eager to confront his wife with his newly discovered outrage. Again, however, the therapist urged caution. Together they considered how his wife might react to Mr. Y's expressions of anger and assertiveness. This helped Mr. Y consider how he would feel about and respond to his wife's reactions. Eventually he was able to assert himself to his wife, without exploding with fury that he now understood was directed partly at his mother for her control and partly at himself for putting up with it.

Learning to Accept the Self Through the Emphatic Response of the Therapist

Neither the expression of feeling nor its suppression can be understood outside of the social context. One of the major consequences of emotional expression is to evoke affect in others. The patient's cathartic expression also stimulates an emotional response in the therapist. The therapist's reaction will be an admixture of immediate affective sharing of the patient's feeling state and a restimulation of incompletely resolved emotional reactions in the therapist's own life. Even though part of the therapist's emotional reaction may be to personal experience, the empathic response helps the therapist to feel with, and so better understand, the patient. The therapist's conscious or unconscious identification with the patient's experience ("I know that hurts, I've been there myself") intensifies understanding and acceptance. This deeply felt, empathic response stimulates unconscious mirroring of the patient's nuclear self (Kohut, 1977). Furthermore, the therapist's acceptance of the patient's private feelings is a powerful confirmation of the patient's worth, self, and identity. The therapist who concentrates on feeling what the patient feels will manifest empathy spontaneously, which is far better than an aloof therapist who verbalizes an understanding of feelings not really shared.

Confession

Confession is another therapeutic mechanism potentiated by catharsis. Although sometimes dismissed as prescientific or nonspecific, confession has always played an important role in helping (Frank, 1961) and is a major ingredient of most forms of psychotherapy.

At one time or another, most people violate their own deeply ingrained, personal standards. These transgressions generate guilt and shame, leading to diminished feelings of self-worth. Because shame is painful, these guilty secrets are prototypic of the kind of memories and feelings that are re-pressed. As long as they remain unconscious, even trivial offenses of childhood can needlessly perpetuate self-recrimination and reproach.

Cathartic confession of embarrassing deeds and conflictual feelings helps patients reveal parts of the self that they had not dared to admit, even to themselves. These revelations, in turn, permit patients to reclaim disowned aspects of the self, while enabling their therapists to support and confirm them as basically worthwhile. Because their emotional re-actions are conflicted, patients expect their therapists to condemn or oth-erwise treat them harshly, as significant early figures once did. This expectation leads patients to keep their feelings concealed, believing them to be part of the self that is unacceptable. If they can be encouraged to express these private feelings, however, and if the feelings expressed meet with acceptance, then transference-inspired expectations are discon-firmed.

Although therapists should accept their patients' feelings, they should avoid giving parental reassurance, and must distinguish between feelings and attributions of blame or guilt. By avoiding judgments, favorable or unfavorable, the therapist leaves the patient in a better position to accept his or her own experience and self. Acceptance, not judgment, allows the patient to conclude: "If the therapist can accept my feelings and past deeds, I must not be such a terrible person after all."

Overcoming Preoccupation with the Past

Freud believed that behavior is shaped by early life experiences, many of which have been forgotten. Too often we react to current situations not on their own merits, but as shadowy reproductions of the past. To make matters worse, most people struggle to resist the influence of the past by trying to forget it. Unfortunately, as Santayana observed, those who remain ignorant of the past are condemned to repeat it.

Psychodynamic psychotherapy helps liberate people from the domin-ion of the past by rediscovering it, cognitively and emotionally, and then subjecting its influence to rational evaluation. In the absence of feelings and catharsis, however, this rediscovery tends to be an arid, intellectual process, devoid of real conviction. Remembering and discussing the past expands our understanding of its influence, but remembering without feeling tends to emphasize conscious and cognitive material, and yields more summary description (usually distorted by attributions adopted from other people) than experiential exploration of visceral attitudes and feelings. Catharsis potentiates a vivid and penetrating exploration, leading to a more profound self-discovery.

Psychodynamic psychotherapy is an uncovering process, aimed at expanding awareness of feelings and impulses. As early as 1894, Freud, in "The Neuro-Psychoses of Defense," recognized that in any repression it is the affect more than the idea that is repressed. Therefore, when defenses are reduced enough to unearth the libido from its hiding place, strong feeling is likely to emerge. If it is simply talked about, rather than felt, real awareness will not take place. But when strong emotional catharsis attends the discovery of unconscious wishes, patients tend to be convinced of their reality.

Not only does catharsis demonstrate the intensity of wishes and feelings, it also helps to complete the expression of blocked feelings. This further lessens the preoccupation with the past and fosters clearer and more rational awareness. Catharsis is helpful in extinguishing conditioned emotional reactions and enabling enhanced stimulus differentiation. Since traumatic experiences are painful and lead to avoidance, similar experiences in the future recapitulate these reactions. If the pain was extreme, these reactions may generalize to new situations that only faintly resemble the original. Through catharsis the experiences can be remembered vividly, with full emotional expression. Because this occurs in the context of therapy, no painful consequences are likely to ensue. With no punishment forthcoming, emotional upset, as well as withdrawal and avoidance, begins to abate. With repetition the conditioned emotional reaction is extinguished and the patient enjoys an enhanced ability to differentiate present from past reality.

Lessening the grip of the past is, of course, only part of the process of taking hold of life in the present. Here too catharsis has a useful role to play. Although it is more than a vehicle for lessening tension, it certainly does accomplish that. Crying, laughing, and angry shouting are tension reducers. Opinions to the contrary confuse these forms of somatic-emotional expression with feelings that are aroused but expressed only partially, or not at all. Far from being trivial, tension reduction in the context of psychotherapy helps to countercondition anxiety, leaving patients in a better position to turn their attention to the present with renewed awareness and clarity. The period immediately after cathartic release is a ripe time for analysis and change of maladaptive patterns of behavior.

Becoming More Feelingful

Finally, carthartic expression is a powerful vehicle for helping patients become more feelingful. Often overlooked by those who see catharsis as an expulsive discharge, increased expressivity nevertheless may be the most important consequence of therapeutic catharsis. Catharsis does not expel ancient affects, and thus the form or process of emotional expression may be of even greater value than its content. Catharsis does not get rid of feelings, but it does help patients free themselves of chronic habits of emotional suppression and restraint.

The fact that the long-range effect of becoming more feelingful is more therapeutic than the short-range effect of any particular cathartic expression helps to explain why it is more important to reduce defenses than to breach them temporarily.

Catharsis in therapy helps people to express their feelings fully, and feeling fully is part of being fully alive. But patients must also learn how to express emotions appropriately and effectively. As therapy begins, patients' feelings may be vague and undifferentiated. They may describe themselves as "upset," "confused," or "anxious." Following cathartic expression, feelings are increasingly flexible and differentiated. Then they can be more directly expressed to others. as well as able to serve as signals and incentives for effective action.

SUMMARY AND CONCLUSIONS

Two periods of keen interest in cathartic treatment followed Breuer's and Freud's cathartic method and the proliferation of emotive therapies in the 1960s. These approaches were based on the traumatic theory of neurosis and they treated emotions as foreign bodies that must be purged to achieve psychological well-being. More psychodynamic writers view the former as merely a footnote to the evolution of psychoanalysis, and the latter as part of a misguided shift from rationalism to emotionalism in psychotherapy. These critics now accord catharsis only a palliative function in reducing traumatic tension and an adjunct role in facilitating free association and uncovering unconscious material.

Proponents of catharsis, on the other hand, tend to exaggerate its therapeutic potential and to see it as a panacea applicable to all psychological problems. Underlying this position is the Rousseauian view that people are naturally healthy and that only socially enforced emotional suppression stands in the way of personal happiness and fulfillment. From this perspective catharsis is seen as sufficient to liberate people from their repressions and automatically to free them to become self-actualizing.

Both critics and proponents identify catharsis with exorcism, albeit dressed up in technical language. The notion that catharsis consists of cleansing people of accumulated feelings rests on an appealing but incorrect assumption about the nature of emotions. Although emotions *do* seem to build up inside us if we do not express them, they really do not. Feelings appear to be stored because emotional reactions to old experiences are often as fresh and as vivid as if they were occurring at the time.

Catharsis is not like opening a door to let something out—something existing inside, unchanged. Emotions are not concrete entities capable of being stored and discharged. Although we can separate feelings from other aspects of experience for convenience, they do not have a separate existence. "Not feeling" is an active process of avoiding. Catharsis is the completion of a previously interrupted or blocked emotional expression.

Because feeling is a central aspect of human experience, psychotherapy must deal with feelings. People think feel, and act, and if psychodynamic therapy is to treat the whole person, it must consider all three aspects of human experiencing. Catharsis plays an important role in psychodynamic psychotherapy, where it helps patients confront and learn to tolerate previously warded-off emotional aspects of experience. Understanding catharsis as the completion of previously blocked emotional actions has important implications for practice that will be explored in the following chapter.

REFERENCES

Aristotle, *The art of poetry*. New York: Odyssey Press, 1951.

Ayer, A.J. *Language, truth and logic*. New York: Dover Publications, 1946.

Berkowitz, L. *Aggression: A social psychological analysis*. New York: McGraw-Hill, 1962.

Bibring, E. Psychoanalysis and the dynamic psychotherapist. *Journal of the American Psychoanalytic Association*, 1954, *2*, 745–770.

Binstock, W.A. Purgation through pity and terror. *International Journal of PsychoAnalysis*, 1973, *54*, 499–504.

Brenman, M., and Gill, M.M. *Hypnotherapy*. New York: International Universities Press, 1947.

Breuer, J., and Freud, S. (1895) *Studies on hysteria. Standard edition*, vol. 2. London: Hogarth Press, 1955, pp. 1–310.

Casriel, D. *A scream away from happiness*. New York: Grosset & Dunlop, 1972.

Davanloo, H. A method of short-term dynamic psychotherapy. In H. Davanloo (Ed.), *Short-term dynamic psychotherapy*. New York: Jason Aronson, 1980.

Fenichel, O. *The psychoanalytic theory of neurosis*. New York: Norton, 1945.

Ferenczi, S. (1930) The principles of relaxation and neocatharsis. *Final contributions to the problems and methods of psycho-analysis*. New York: Basic Books, 1955.

Frank, J.D. *Persuasion and healing*. Baltimore: Johns Hopkins Press, 1961.

Freud, S. (1894) The neuro-psychoses of defense. *Standard edition*, vol. 3. London: Hogarth Press, 1953, pp. 41–62.

Freud, S. (1912) The dynamics of the transference. In: *Collected papers, Volume II*. New York: Basic Books, 1959.

Freud, S. (1904) Freud's psychoanalytic method. In: *Therapy and Technique*. New York: Collier Books, 1963.

Goffman, E. *Presentation of self in everyday life*. Garden City, N.Y.: Anchor, 1959.

Goldberg, C. *Encounter: Group sensitivity training experience*. New York: Science House 1970.

Gorer, G. *Death, grief and mourning in contemporary Britain*. London: Cresset Press, 1965.

Greenson, R.R. *The technique and practice of psychoanalysis, Vol. I*. New York: International Universities Press, 1967.

Guntrip, H. *Schizoid phenomena, object relations and the self*. New York: International Universities Press, 1969.

Hart, J., Corriere, R., and Binder, J. *Going sane*. New York: Jason Aronson, 1975.

Jackins, H. *Elementary counselor's manual*. Seattle: Rational Island Publishers, 1962.

Jackins, H. *The human side of human beings*. Seattle: Rational Island Publishers, 1965.

Janet, P. *Psychological healing: A historical and clinical study*, Vols. I and II. New York: Macmillan, 1925.

Janov, A. *The primal scream*. New York: Dell, 1970.

Jones, E. *The life and work of Sigmund Freud, Vol. I*. New York: Basic Books, 1953.

Kohut, H. *The restoration of the self*. New York: International Universities Press, 1977.

Kris, E. *Psychoanalytic explorations in art*. New York: International Universities Press, 1952.

Langs, R. *The technique of psychoanalytic psychotherapy, Vol. I*. New York: Jason Aronson, 1973.

Lieberman, M.A., Yalom, I.D., and Miles, M.B. *Encounter groups: First fads*. New York: Basic Books, 1973.

Lowen, A. *The betrayal of the body*. New York: Macmillan, 1967.

Lowy, F.H. The abuse of abreaction: An unhappy legacy of Freud's cathartic method. *Canadian Psychiatric Journal*, 1970, *15*, 557–565.

McLoughlin, W.G., Jr. *Modern revivalism*. New York: Ronald Press, 1959.

Malinowski, B. Magic, science and religion. In: J. Needham (Ed.), *Science, religion and reality*. New York: George Braziller, 1955.

Mann, J. *Time-limited psychotherapy*. Cambridge, Mass.: Harvard University Press, 1973.

Marcuse, H. *Eros and civilization*. Boston: Beacon Press, 1955.

Moreno, J.L. *Psychodrama, Vol. II*. New York: Beacon House, 1958.

Moreno, J.L. Psychodrama, In: S. Arieti (Ed.), *American handbook of psychiatry*, Vol. II. New York: Basic Books, 1959.

Nichols, M.P. and Zax, M. *Catharsis in psychotherapy*. New York: Gardner Press, 1977.

Patterson, C.H. *Theories of counseling and psychotherapy*. New York: Harper & Row, 1966.

Perls, F.S. *Gestalt therapy verbatim*. Lafayette, Calif.: Real People Press, 1969.

Pierce, R., Nichols, M.P. and Dubrin, J. *Feeling-expressive psychotherapy*. New York: Gardner Press, 1981, in press.

Rabkin, R. *Inner and outer space.* New York: Norton, 1970.

Rank, O. *Will therapy and truth and reality.* New York: Knopf, 1945.

Reich, W. *Character-analysis.* New York: Noonday Press, 1949.

Reich, W. *Selected writings.* New York: Noonday Press, 1960.

Reik, T. *Listening with the third ear.* New York: Farrar, Straus, 1948.

Ryle, G. Feelings, In W. Elton (Ed.), *Aesthetics and language.* Oxford: Basil Blackwell, 1959.

Schafer, R. Requirements for a critique of the theory of catharsis. *Journal of Consulting and Clinical Psychology,* 1970, *35,* 13–17.

Schafer, R. *A new language for psychoanalysis.* New Haven, Conn. Yale University Press, 1976.

Scheff, T.J. *Catharsis in healing, ritual and drama.* Berkeley, Calif.: University of California Press, 1979.

Sifneos, P.E. *Short-term dynamic psychotherapy.* New York: Plenum, 1979.

Strachey, J. The nature of the therapeutic action of psychoanalysis. *International Journal of Psychoanalysis,* 1934, *15,* 117–126.

Volkan, V.D. The linking objects of pathological mourners. *Archives of General Psychiatry,* 1972, *27,* 215–221.

Watkins, J.G. *Hypnotherapy of war neuroses.* New York: Ronald Press, 1949.

Winnicott, D.W. Metapsychological and clinical aspects of regression within the psychoanalytical set-up. In: *Collected papers.* New York: Basic Books, 1958.

Wolberg, L.B. *The technique of psychotherapy.* New York: Grune & Stratton, 1977.

5
Catharsis: Clinical Application

MICHAEL P. NICHOLS, Ph.D.
AND LAWRENCE C. KOLB, M.D.

Unmentioned but hardly unnoticed among the accoutrements of modern psychodynamic therapists are the paper tissues used to stem the flow of tears frequently produced by patients during their treatment. Unfortunately too many therapists automatically respond to tears by stemming them.

Some catharsis takes place during psychodynamic psychotherapy, whether or not the therapist purposefully intends to stimulate it. Most experienced practitioners believe that abreaction in the course of free association is a significant marker of therapeutic movement, as well as an event that produces a sense of personal relief and increased awareness of self. But many are unsure of the relative value of catharsis, and even more are unsure how to promote and encourage cathartic expression.

Catharsis did not cease, nor was it banished, when Freud turned from hypnotic uncovering to free association. Its role changed; the focus and conviction of the therapist were modified. He or she no longer attempted to force an abreactive response associated with the uncovering of a repressed memory in the immediate expectation of a cure. The limits of that technique in bringing permanent resolution to neurosis had been established. Psychoanalysis through free association superseded the abreactive effort. In the intervening years cathartic techniques were seldom discussed among most psychoanalysts—but this was not true of all. Ferenczi (1955) reported on his clinical experiences with neocatharsis—the recurrence of intense hysterical physical symptoms as the analytic process approached an ending. He noted such carthartic abreactions especially as he modified his therapeutic stance from one of strict adherence to the "principle of frustration" to one that included his "principle of indulgence." Neocatharsis involved sudden spasms and paresthesias, violent emotional movements, vertigo, and altered states of consciousness, followed by amnesia for what had taken place. To Ferenczi these late cathartic presentations differed from the "paleocatharsis" that occurred during the early phase of the therapeutic process. In later reenactments the patient reported a sense of actuality, a concreteness of actual recollection of an early traumatic event. The experience seemed to add significance to the recollection of the original traumatic event.

Bibring (1954) defined catharsis as one of the major principles and procedures applicable to all psychotherapeutic methodologies independent of their theoretical bases. Bibring summarized the use of catharsis in earlier psychotherapeutic efforts as follows: Single therapeutic abreaction was indicated only for those with the simplest of three forms of hysteria defined by Freud; that is, retention hysteria where only damming of affect is conceived as etiologic (Breuer & Freud, 1895). For the treatment of those other forms (hypnoid and defense hysteria) where splitting was thought to occur, cathartic therapy required a discharge of affect through verbalization in association with detailed reminiscence of the traumatic event. Therapists thought that for these more complex hysterical constellations, the totality of emotional tension first needed to be discharged to avoid remnants that might be left dissociated and so form the force for continued symptom formation. Then the idea associated with the trauma had to be conducted into consciousness to bring about an associative resolution.

Beyond these steps an adaptation of the decatheted idea needed to take place by working with the fully conscious personality. With the introduction of free association, catharsis, no longer considered curative, was envisaged as a technique of assistance in acquisition of insight following interpretation. This latter conception of abreactive reactions did not demand maximum intensity of affective discharge, but rather allowed maximum play of ego-adaptive function to bring the revealed unconscious into association with the totality of the personality. To Bibring the curative value of emotional expression is unrelated to abreaction per se, but occurs when other therapeutic principles (such as clarification and interpretation) are applied during later treatment sessions as the newly revealed material is "worked through."

Loewald (1955) carried forward the discussion of catharsis. To him catharsis goes beyond the undoing of regression; it moves unconscious neuronal traces onto a higher level of integration. He believed that what is effectively abreacted comes from predominanatly somatic memory traces laid down in the yet-undeveloped or immature state of the psychological apparatus. The abreactive reaction of recollection, affective discharge, and verbalization allows transformation of primary into secondary process activity as material recollected is now absorbed into a complex of associated memories and related to other experiences. This to him constituted the process of working through—each recollection is modified to become a newer and more mature version of the original partial reminiscence.

Each of the earlier commentators on catharsis recognized the tension-relieving aspects of catharsis, as well as the influence of the therapist's presence upon the patient. Yet the transactional connotations of the patient–therapist relationship were not explicitly described. Ferenczi (1955) related the neocathartic outbursts to his more accepting, less distant and depriving therapeutic posture. Bibring mentioned as a consequence of catharsis both existence within of a clearer, more objective perspective on experience and the gratification of being "accepted" and being "understood" through acceptance by the therapist, which also gives ego gratification for various narcissistic needs. In the therapeutic setting, emotional eruption or induced catharsis takes place with the patient acting as a conscious observer of his or her self reaction in company with the therapist. Thus he or she becomes aware of hidden affective and emotional forces within his or her self and perceives in addition the therapist's accepting attitude to his or her emotionality, no matter its intensity or incongruity. In many instances the latter perception provides immediate relief from hidden expectations of shame or guilt engendered by others at the earlier moment of the traumatic incident or fantasized thereafter through punitive superego representations.

Aside from the permissive, nonjudgmental, and understanding posture of the therapist, which encourages any and all expressions of feeling in the patient, little if any information exists with regard to the active interventions employed to produce or respond to intense catharsis. Catharsis in psychodynamic psychotherapy takes place both spontaneously and as a consequence of clarifications or interpretations. In this respect the stimulating effect of the therapist's interventions is not unlike that of the hypnotic therapist who attempts recovery of a repressed event and abreaction of the associated affect. There exists covertly in the transactional relationship between therapist and patient both an expectant and an accepting set toward revelation and affective expression. Such is inherent in their shared expectant hope of relief of suffering with recovery and working through of repressed memories.

CONDITIONS THAT PRODUCE CATHARSIS

Catharsis, particularly when it is intense, is such a dramatic event that its occurrence seems extraordinary. Sessions in which patients remember

vividly and express feelings vigorously about old experiences are powerfully emotional. As therapists we remember these sessions as special
events. Since intense catharsis is unique and dramatic, we tend to assume
that special conditions are required to produce it. In fact there are a variety
of special procedures designed to produce catharsis, including hypnotism,
sodium pentathol, and role playing. These special techniques seem particularly necessary if one views catharsis as purging feelings that are locked
inside the patient. However, once catharsis is understood to be the expression, not the expulsion, of feeling, it can be seen as a quite natural means
of experiencing.

Experiencing and expressing feelings is a natural part of ongoing experience. Before they are socialized, children cry when they are sad, laugh
when they are happy, and scream when they are angry. Why then is
catharsis in psychotherapy so infrequent? *The answer lies not in the
nature of emotions, but in specific actions of the patient, techniques of
the therapist, and the nature of the therapeutic alliance.*

By the time they reach psychotherapy, most patients have learned
well to avoid expressing their feelings. They do this because of chronic
defenses against experiencing and expressing feelings, and because they
expect other "more important things" to happen in psychotherapy.

Therapists tend to expect and elicit material from their patients that
fits their theories of therapy. Behavioral therapists elicit descriptions of
behavior and its consequences; psychodynamic therapists elicit ideas more
than they do feelings. When a psychodynamic therapist approaches a
patient, his or her agenda is to gather information about the patient's
problems, current living, and early experience. The therapist does this
by asking questions and listening. Not only do many psychodynamic
therapists avoid explicitly pressing for feeling expression, but their own
discomfort with strong affect may cause them to discourage such displays.

Catharsis occurs spontaneously as a function of the intensity with
which patients focus on their experience and the degree to which their
defenses are relaxed. Relatively well-defended patients (obsessional personalities) are only likely to experience catharsis when they are focusing
on very dramatic and intense experiences, such as a death or other significant loss. Less well-defended patients (hysterical personalities) experience and express feelings much more readily.

Patients will experience catharsis if (1) they focus intensely on their
experience, (2) their defenses are relaxed, and (3) they are aware of the
empathic and accepting receptivity of the therapist. Therapists have little
to do with the first of these conditions other than to be aware of it. In
fact most people have a sufficient number of experiences about which
they have unexpressed feelings that this does not really distinguish patients
who seek psychotherapy.

The therapist's job then is to do two things—listen in such a way as to communicate interest and acceptance of feelings, and counter defenses against emotional expression when they seem to be present.

The style of listening that promotes catharsis is focused and intense, but also completely accepting. The therapist indicates active involvement by sitting close, looking at the patient, and making comments to indicate that he or she is following what the patient is feeling. This style of listening is more intimate and affectively charged than is sitting back, glancing around, or taking notes.

In addition to focusing intently on what the patient is saying and feeling, the therapist must avoid probing for nonaffective material. Questions designed to obtain information or produce insight may interfere with eliciting feelings, as the following clinical example illustrates.

> Mrs. K. came to psychotherapy upset over an impending separation from her husband. Early in the first session, she began to weep slightly as she described how much she loved him and how afraid she was of his leaving her. At this point the therapist intervened to ask what made her sure he was going to leave. Mrs. K. blew her nose, wiped her eyes, and began to explain why she thought her husband was going to leave.

What might have been cathartic relief for Mrs. K. was aborted by the therapist's intrusive questioning. The therapist received some information (which could have been obtained later), but Mrs. K. left the office as upset and confused as when she arrived. Feelings aroused, but incompletely expressed, are as tension making as complete feeling expression is tension reducing.

Sometimes, however, the patient interrupts or blocks his or her own potential cathartic response. Here the patient's defenses, instead of the therapist's questions, interfere.

> Mr. B., who sought help with his social life, was a man who covered his insecurity with smug bravado. In an early session, he was describing an upcoming social engagement. Thinking this an excellent opportunity to explore Mr. B.'s anxiety and low self-esteem, the therapist asked him to express his feelings about the impending event. Mr. B. proceeded to criticize the people he was going to be with and to downgrade the occasion. Rather than acknowledge, or even experience, his own sense of inadequacy, the patient had learned to attack and criticize. His "You can't fire me, I quit!" attitude, which left him lonely and friendless, prevented him from getting in touch with his feelings during psychotherapy.

When patients' defenses block their own expression of feelings, the therapist must deviate from the stance of listening and accepting. In short the therapist's task—paradoxically—is to not interfere and then interfere. The trick is to be sufficiently sensitive and attuned to the patient to listen openly to whatever the patient says, and to be alert to defenses that come into play when affective material is approached. Among the common signals that anxiety associated with feelings is being defended against are smiling, nervous laughing, changing the subject, looking away, or lighting a cigarette.

As any student knows, whenever resistances crop up, the psychodynamic therapist analyzes them. Yes—and no. Eventually resistances must be analyzed to achieve the lasting reduction of defenses necessary to integrate disowned feelings and impulses. However, at a moment of potential feeling expression, analyzing resistances may lead more to cognitive exploration than to catharsis. If feelings are sufficiently close to the surface, the therapist is often well-advised simply to block or circumvent resistance, postponing the analysis until later.

> Mr. B. continued to belittle the people he was expecting to be with. His apparent boredom, rigid posture, and flat, affectless tone of voice helped tip off the therapist that he was defending against feelings of fear and insecurity. Instead of pointing this out, the therapist simply said, "Tell me how scared you are." At this Mr. B. slumped in his chair and began to cry. "Yes, I'm scared, goddam it."

This intervention was successful because the therapist accurately recognized that Mr. B.'s fear was close to the surface. Were he more defended, this maneuver would have been counterproductive, serving only to increase the resistance. In cases where the patient's resistance is stronger and the feelings less accessible, it is sometimes productive to reflect and exaggerate the resistance. This outflanks the patient and helps make the resistance ego alien.

> In a later hour, Mr. B. was describing his relationship with his father. Again he was covering his own feelings of insecurity by attacking and criticizing his father. Now, however, the therapist judged Mr. B.'s fear to be too well hidden simply to be pointed to. Instead the therapist accepted and magnified Mr. B.'s condemnation of his father.
> *Therapist:* He sounds like a real bastard.
> *Patient:* Well, not exactly a bastard.
> *Therapist:* You didn't give a damn what he thought, did you?
> At this Mr. B. recognized his own avoidance and began to drop it as he went on to describe how he feared his father, and felt he could never measure up to his father's high standards.

Beyond these general considerations of the conditions that produce catharsis we must consider the question of cathartic techniques in more detail. There are those who believe that the techniques of psychotherapy can be neither taught nor described, that therapy is an art not a science. We believe that this half-truth is limiting when it comes to assisting patients to face sincerely their affective expressions. Here, unfortunately, many therapist's natural tendencies lead them to collude with patients' resistance to avoid and suppress intense feeling expression. Cathartic techniques *can be* described and *should be* taught, not to be used indiscriminately or by rote, but to be incorporated into a carefully thought-out strategy of treatment (see Introduction) and to be submerged within the therapist's own personality and style. Having a variety of techniques available—and sufficient theory to place them into proper context—expands the therapist's repertoire and enables the therapist to be more flexible and effective.

TECHNIQUES FOR ELICITING CATHARSIS

Techniques for eliciting catharsis include (1) emotional focusing, (2) supporting spontaneous emotional expression, (3) countering defenses, (4) facilitating the expression of unconscious thoughts and feelings, and (5) emotional working through.

The first two categories (focusing and supporting spontaneous expression) are all that take place in superficial forms of psychotherapy and are often thought to be all that is involved in catharsis. This is true only when catharsis is defined as speaking freely and with some feeling. However, as discussed in the previous chapter, catharsis also involves breaching defenses and uncovering unconscious material as well as emotional working through. In fact therapy that is limited to manifest content and readily available affect does *not* produce unconscious material and, therefore, should not be considered psychodynamic therapy (Langs, 1978). Saying so should not, however, be taken as minimizing the importance of the first two categories, both for reducing tension and for potentiating subsequent exploration of the unconscious.

Emotional Focusing

Productive psychotherapy takes place in a concentrated and focused atmosphere. Although not as single-mindedly focused on affect as are many emotive approaches (e.g., Janov, 1970), psychodynamic therapy cannot be the cool, dispassionate, and intellectual enterprise often portrayed by its detractors. Patients must experience their feelings before the feelings can be analyzed (Greenson, 1967); otherwise patients will deny, isolate, and intellectualize them.

A common error is to interpret transference reactions when they are first voiced and before the affect behind them has been experienced or expressed.

In her fourth hour of treatment with a psychiatric resident, Mrs. L. men-

tioned that she had been annoyed last week when the therapist was late.
"Yes!" he said, "You were angry at me for letting you down, just as you
had been angry with your father for never paying attention to you." Mrs.
L. acknowledged that this was probably true, but with little conviction.
Because she had yet to feel anything like the full force of her rage at being
disappointed by the therapist, the idea that such feelings stemmed from
childhood reactions to her father remained an interesting possibility to her,
but not an emotionally felt conviction. Prematurely interrupted, her transference reaction never yielded access to her unconscious.

Psychodynamic therapy is both experiential and analytic. Thomas
Scheff used the metaphor of distance to describe how therapists modulate
the amount and intensity of their patients' emotional arousal. Not enough
distance is overwhelming; too much distance is passionless. Optimal or
"aesthetic distance" (Scheff, 1979) is a balance. Scheff believes that, when
optimally distanced from their emotions, people simultaneously can be
participants in and observers of their experience. Greenson (1967) speaks
of an "experiencing ego" and an "observing ego," and states that the
successful patient is one who can move back and forth between these two
types of experiencing. When the patient is carried away by painful feelings
and memories, the experiencing ego is in the foreground. Little understanding of the meaning of the emotions and memories occurs at that
moment. Later, when the affect has been thoroughly expressed, the patient
is amenable to rational analysis of the experience.

Many of the routine practices of psychotherapists are designed to
produce an atmosphere of focused intensity. The quiet and privacy of the
consulting room create a therapeutic milieu that is set off and distinct
from everyday reality. Moreover, the therapist's nonjudgmental acceptance, empathic concern, neutrality, and absolute confidentiality all generate trust and a sense of safety. These standard conditions provide enough
ego support to relax resistances and enhance regression.

In addition to these usual procedures, there are a variety of techniques
that therapists can use to increase further the emotional intensity of a
session. Choosing them depends upon the therapist's comfort level and
purpose at the moment. Sitting closer to the patient increases the intimacy
of the therapeutic relationship, raises the patient's anxiety, and brings the
patient's emotions closer to expression. Discouraging various tension-relieving rituals such as smoking or fidgeting also raises the affective intensity. Eye contact and tracking and reflecting the patient's feelings intensify
the affective tone. The following example illustrates how a therapist can
enhance emotional focusing in the psychotherapeutic atmosphere.

Dr. D. received a referral, described as a man undergoing a delayed grief
reaction for his wife. Although the man's wife had been dead for nearly a
year, he remained depressed and apathetic, apparently because he had not
yet actively mourned her loss. Armed with this information, Dr. D. resolved
to concentrate on focusing the patient's feelings in the first session.

When the patient, Mr. F., arrived for the first visit, Dr. D. sat quite close to him, engaged him in steady eye contact, and confined his interventions to supportive comments and reflections of feeling. Dr. D. postponed many of the usual informational interrogatories and concentrated instead on helping the patient experience his feelings.

Although Dr. D. was hoping to get to his patient's grief, his primary agenda was to focus feelings, and he was careful to accept whatever feelings spontaneously emerged rather than introduce his own influence on the material that unfolded. Therefore, when Mr. F. spoke of being confused and uncertain about seeking therapy, the therapist accepted these feelings and made reflecting and supportive statements about the confusion. The fact that Dr. D. did not push him to speak about his wife came as a great surprise and relief to Mr. F. Halfway through the session he began to cry, saying, "It is such a relief to have someone understand how I feel. Everyone keeps pestering me about my wife. My friends tell me to forget about her, and my minister tells me that I should remember her and cry about it. I've been so confused that I can't figure out how I feel."

Once these feelings had been expressed and worked through, Mr. F. was able to turn his attention to his loss. Again the therapist was careful to accept the patient's feelings as they unfolded, always avoiding probing for the "important" feelings.

If the therapist had pushed for the so-called "important" feelings, the patient may have responded with a half-hearted compliance to produce associations that blocked genuine cathartic expression.

Supporting Spontaneous Emotional Expression

Patients will express their feelings spontaneously whenever the press of environmental experience is affectively intense, their own defenses are relaxed (or weakened), and the therapeutic milieu is appropriately safe. Although few therapists deliberately attempt to suppress feeling expression, many do so inadvertently by being insufficiently aware of the need to support such expression. Two categories of therapist responses are required to support and encourage spontaneous expression of feelings. The first is characterological and dispositional. The therapist must be comfortable in the face of emotional display and have the capacity to tolerate a wide range of material. Furthermore, the therapist must consciously and unconsciously accept the notion that affective expression is important and should usually be encouraged. This inherent tolerance for and interest in emotional experience will be felt by patients and will enhance their level of experiencing, even without any deliberate use of technique.

Several years ago a young resident conducted an analytically oriented group therapy session with a group of inpatients. At one point one of the group members, Mr. R., began to hallucinate the image of his long-deceased brother. "It's John, it's my brother, John! I can see him calling out to me. He's begging me to help him."

At this poit many clinicians would become extremely uncomfortable and probably attempt to "calm the patient down." Fortunately the resident was composed enough that he did not need to do so. For about ten minutes, the patient imagined his brother, spoke to him, and then cried profusely for his loss. When he finished crying, he was noticeably relieved and able to participate in a very significant and rational discussion of the meaning of his lost relationship with his brother.

Secondly, there are specific techniques that can be used to support and encourage spontaneous expression of feelings. The first and most obvious of these is reflecting feelings. This requires an empathic understanding of what the patient is feeling and the ability to comment upon it in a way that helps the patient explore more intense feelings. Because people are usually defensive about whatever they are feeling, most reflections should be slightly more intense than the feeling stated by the patient. Thus if a patient says, "I'm unhappy today," the therapist might respond with, "You're feeling pretty miserable, aren't you?"—deepening the feeling and encouraging further expression. The patient's agreement ("Yes, I do feel miserable") is not as valid a confirmation of the intervention as is the subsequent revelation of previously blocked material. Reflection, like other interventions, is aimed at uncovering more material, not at gaining verbal assent.

Since many people are uncomfortable in the presence of affective expression, they usually respond to others by telling them—in a variety of "nice" ways—not to feel that way. "There, there, honey. Don't cry, I'll buy you another one." "Stop crying, it doesn't really hurt, does it?" Even when people thank us for something, we say, "Oh, don't mention it," or "It's nothing. Don't make a big deal of it."

So regularly do these well-intentioned efforts to suppress emotional expression of feelings take place that most people learn to shut down their own feelings. When patients cry a little or become angry, they often stop themselves and express embarrassment. "Oh, this is silly," or "Well, I'd better forget about that." When this occurs, simple statements of encouragement from the therapist will help prolong the expression. "No, stay with it." "That's good, let it all out." As long as such comments continue to produce catharsis, they are all that is needed. When the defenses are stronger and the feelings more blocked, the therapist must work to counter the defenses.

Countering Defenses

Ultimately defenses must be analyzed for fundamental personality change to occur. Therapists, however, need not always confront or interpret defenses before stimulating catharsis. Sometimes simply countering defenses unblocks catharsis. At other times more concentrated analysis of defenses must take place before catharsis is possible.

If simple encouragement of feeling expression is insufficient to overcome resistance, encouraging *affective* expression of the resistance may.

> Mr. A., an aggressively masculine man and successful lawyer, sought therapy shortly after his wife announced her intention to leave him. Although her leaving was a profound narcissistic blow, he did not permit himself to experience his feelings of hurt and rejection for fear of appearing weak and vulnerable. Instead he took up the first few treatment sessions ruminating about "What's best for the children" and "I'd like to explore my various options." In fact Mr. A. did have several realistic problems to solve and plans to make, but the defensive energy he was expending in order to suppress his grief left him with few resources for rational analysis and planning. The therapist, therfore, resolved to help Mr. A. experience the hurt he was avoiding and express his sadness.
>
> Unfortunately Mr. A's defenses were too firmly entrenched to permit spontaneous expression of his genuine emotional reaction to his wife's leaving. When the therapist asked how he felt, Mr. A. responded by saying, "What's done is done. The question now is where do I go from here?" Even more explicit probing was ineffective. When the therapist suggested that Mr. A. must feel hurt, the patient consistently denied it, saying such things as: "It takes more than a little bad news to get me down," and "I can manage very nicely on my own, thank you."
>
> Realizing that further attempts to elicit sadness directly would only serve to intensify the resistance, the therapist switched tactics and began to reflect the resistance. By commenting in a slightly exaggerated way on the resistance, he hoped to make Mr. A feel his own particular way of defending himself and to begin to experience the defense as ago alien.
>
> The following interchange occurred in the next session. Mr. A. began by reporting, "Well I guess it's definite; my wife's moving out next week."
> *Therapist:* That must hurt.
> *Patient:* No use crying over spilt milk.
> *Therapist:* You're right. What's done is done.
> *Patient:* Exactly. I don't give a damn what she does.
> *Therapist:* You don't really need her, do you?
> *Patient:* Well. . . (His facial expression clouds over.)
> *Therapist:* In fact, you don't need anyone.
> At this point this patient began to weep softly.
> *Patient:* Yes I do. "I really love her!"
> At which he burst into sobs.

This interchange, in which the therapist simply mirrored the patient's defenses, enabled the patient to give up his denial. Once there was no longer a need to combat the suggestion that he might be prone to "weak" feelings, a sudden switch occurred. As soon as he began to experience the defensiveness of his position, he was able to drop it. This was sufficient for him to begin to experience some of his previously warded-off grief. Although this countering of defenses did not resolve them, it did demonstrate them graphically, and enable them to be breached sufficiently to permit a carthartic response.

Breaching defenses in no way gainsays the need to analyze, at a later time, the resistances that are the manifestation of defensive mechanisms. In nonanalytic forms of psychotherapy, breaching defenses may be all that occurs. However, in psychodynamic psychotherapy, while we may occasionally use techniques to breach defenses, we do so because the timing is such that emotional expression may be close to the surface. Furthermore, the aim is not simply to achieve catharsis for its own sake. Instead the catharsis achieved when the defense is blocked seems to demonstrate the defensive function of the resistance, as well as to manifest the affect and the impulse behind it, greatly enhancing the ability to analyze the resistance.

Another way to deal with resistance to emotional expression is simply to confront it, pointing to its existence in such a way as to suggest that it should be dropped. Freud's "pressure technique" (Breuer & Freud, 1895), insisting that patients overcome their resistance, is not without its uses. An effective method is to point out the activity (avoiding feelings) that lies behind the patient's apparent passivity (not feeling). This draws the patient's attention to his or her own activity, and enables the patient to switch from avoidance to expression of feelings. After catharsis an optimum time exists to clarify the nature of the patient's defenses and the motives for their operation, as shown in this example.

> Mrs. C. called an hour before her scheduled appointment to report that she would be unable to attend because her car had broken down. The therapist accepted her explanation and thanked her for calling, but reiterated that he charged for missed appointments. In the next session, Mrs. C. denied that she had any feelings about last week's phone call, although the therapist assumed that she might be feeling a great deal. Having developed a careful and thorough formulation of Mrs. C's dynamics, he was aware of her use of denial and displacement to defend against feelings of hurt and anger and so he was alert to subtle evidence of her resistance in the session.
>
> She then related a series of incidents that had occurred during the week in which several people had been inconsiderate and unhelpful to her. Her exaggerated response to several trivial slights was a transparent displacement of her reaction to the therapist. Because he judged her emotional response to him to be close to the surface, he probed it directly, rather than discuss her resistance.
>
> *Therapist:* Yes, and who else are you angry at?
> *Patient:* You mean, you? [Here she paused for a few moments and then began to cry.] Yes, I did feel let down. Why couldn't you have been nicer, more understanding? [Now she cried freely.] My parents were never there when I needed them . . . and now you. Nobody really cares about me. Saying this she became blocked and was silent.
>
> Although she had acknowledged her hurt and disappointment, she still showed signs of being emotionally constricted. Instead of accepting her feelings, she was now resisting them. What had changed?
>
> Frequently feeling expression becomes blocked at a point of transition from one feeling to another. Anger frequently flows into sadness, and

sadness sometimes becomes anger. Many people, however, can express one but not the other of these feelings. Mrs. C. was able to acknowledge her sadness, but not her anger. When she was a child and mistreated by her parents, she learned to mask her fury, because she was punished severely for any expression of anger. She did, however, get some sympathy when she transformed the anger into a kind of helpless sadness. A sad little girl is much easier for parents to accept than an angry one. As she grew older, she continued to suppress angry reactions, while occasionally acting sad and disappointed. Although she avoided the danger of direct confrontation by so doing, she became a dependent person and often felt powerless and hopeless. Aware that if she could express her anger at him she would not need to feel so dependent and helpless, the therapist acted to push past her resistance.

Therapist: Tell me how angry you were that I charged you last week.
Patient: I wasn't angry. Goddamnit, I already told you!
Therapist: You sound angry.
Patient: Well you're always pushing me.
Therapist: Tell me about that.

Mrs. C. went on to describe how angry she got when the therapist pushed her to open up and confront her feelings. And "Yes," she said, "I was good and pissed off that you charged me for last week." In fact once she began to express her anger, she continued for several minutes, giving full vent to feelings of resentment toward the therapist, toward her husband, and toward her parents.

After this cathartic release, Mrs. C. appeared much calmer and more relaxed. Now the therapist interpreted her resistance and the motive behind it, explaining that by acting hurt instead of angry she hoped to make people feel guilty. Thus her defensive transformation of anger into sadness was a means of retaliating without taking the risk of open, angry confrontation.

Understanding that resistance is an active process, "doing something" as opposed to "not doing something," suggests that is can often be circumvented by observing how the patient is resisting and then simply asking him/her to stop acting resistantly. This technique is particularly appropriate for characterological defenses, manifest as body armor (Reich, 1949), which do not readily yield to interpretation. Asking patients to alter rigid posture, facial expression, tone of voice, or pacing of speech will often unblock feelings. "Sit up straight and tell me that." "Don't smile." "Look at me." "Say it louder." "Slow down, say that again." These are interventions of this kind.

Words, the very medium of psychodynamic psychotherapy, are often used to avoid feelings. This is most obvious in the excessive verbiage of the intellectualizing patient. In fact most people present their stories in well-practiced language, sure to minimize the expression of affect. Visual imagery is a useful technique to block the defensive use of language.

Mrs. O., a mildly depressed hysteric, began each session with a breathless account of her husband's latest slights. For the first few minutes, she would deliver a rapid fire account of all the things he did to hurt her and then ask

the therapist, "What should I do?" At first he simply listened to these
weekly diatribes, hoping that they might be cathartic. However, after consulting with his supervisor, he realized that although she had strong feelings
about her husband, her verbal haranguing was blocking open expression
of those feelings.

Mrs. O. began the next session with her usual rapid-fire narrative of
abuse. But this time the therapist interrupted.

Therapist: Stop talking for a minute and close your eyes.

Patient: What do you mean?

*Therapist:*Just try it. Stop talking and close your eyes.

Patient: Okay.

Therapist: Now keep your eyes closed, and just look at your husband. Take
a good look, keep looking at him and think about how he treats you.

Mrs. O. was silent for a few minutes. Slowly her breathing became more
rapid, and her lower lip started trembling. She burst into loud sobs, calling
her husband by name: "Bob, Bob! Why don't you love me?"

The therapist's use of visual imagery to block this patient's defensive
use of words did not resolve the defense, but it did interrupt it long
enough to achieve meaningful expression of the hurt she was so accustomed to masking.

It is important that therapists do not attempt to demand feelings.
Demanding feelings is intrusive and ineffective. Instead the therapist helps
make room for feelings by clearing away resistances. Resistances fractionate, constrict, and filter the affect out of experiencing. While blocking
resistances the therapist must not push the patient to experience anything
in particular. Instead his or her implicit message is, "Stop your usual
resistant presentation, then turn your attention to the memories and experiences that emerge. Don't look for any particular feelings, simply take
what comes."

Breaching resistances may be sufficient to permit cathartic expression
of feelings previously warded off, but such expression is usually brief,
automatically cut short before full, intense somatic-emotional catharsis is
achieved. Full feeling expression is trained out of us. As soon as catharsis
is begun, it is aborted. To prevent this and promote intense catharsis, the
therapist must intervene to help intensify and prolong cathartic expression.

When cathartic expression begins, nothing need be done as long as it
continues. But as soon as it is cut short, the therapist should direct the
patient to stop resisting and express more feeling.

Mrs. O. cried briefly after calling out to her husband, but became embar-
rassed, and asked for a tissue. Instead of complying, the therapist asked
her to keep her eyes closed and keep calling to her husband. As she did so,
her crying intensified, until she was wracked with grief. When this crying
subsided, the therapist, recognizing that she still had more crying to do,
told her to keep thinking about her husband. Now, as she silently visualized
her husband, the therapist spoke as her alter ego: "You do everything you

can for him and still he doesn't love you. And it hurts you so bad you can't stand it. . . ." Each time the patient attempted to dry her eyes the therapist kept her with her feelings. After several minutes, when no more tears were forthcoming, he asked, "And who else used to treat you this way?"

Many therapists are sufficiently unused to, and uncomfortable with, strong expression of feeling that they settle for partial catharsis when more could easily be achieved. Many dynamically oriented therapists are prone to commence interpretation immediately after the briefest outpouring of emotion. The foregoing example demonstrates a useful sequence to follow: seek full expression of the immediate emotional conflict; trace this sequence to its historical precipitants; and only then initiate interpretation. Fenichel (1935) wisely pointed out that emotionality can interfere with insight. His proposed solution, "taking distance from the affect," is less effective, however. The best way to reduce emotionality is not to avoid or suppress it, but to release it, by promoting full feeling expression. Following this a clarifying shift occurs and patients, now less preoccupied with avoiding feeling, are able to see things more clearly. In short, while catharsis without analysis is incomplete, analysis without catharsis is ineffective.

Among the most powerful means of circumventing defenses and achieving catharsis are drugs and hypnosis. Although these approaches reached their zenith in treating traumatic neuroses during the world wars, they are still practiced and continue to prove useful with traumatic stress reactions.

Drug and Hypnotically Induced Cathartic Therapy

Abreaction brought about through the hypnotic technique or through altering the state of consciousness by administration of drugs retains its usefulness in the treatment of the acute posttraumatic stress disorders. Emotional expression allows the patient to accept his/her affect as other than dangerous. Furthermore, with the diminution in anxiety associated with the emotionally charged recollection, the event is retained in consciousness and dissociation is less likely.

It appears that drug-released abreactions may be obtained from a much wider range of the population than abreactions brought about by hypnosis. Certainly the majority of physician psychotherapists find this technique more congenial in application in spite of the greater risk to the patient. Assuredly a variety of levels of altered states of consciousness (including complete lack of arousability and anesthesia) may be induced in all with widely used anesthetics. Yet the numbers of individuals in whom one may attain, through drug induction, a state of light narcosis in which the individual remains arousable and articulate is unknown. In a recent comparative study (conducted by Dr. Kolb) of young Viet Nam combat veterans suffering chronic or delayed posttraumatic stress disorders and having histories of repetitive dissociative episodes of violent acting out as panic attacks, it was found that during narcosynthesis, 13 of 18 immediately responded to the stimulus of meaningful auditory stimulus (a 30-second display of combat sounds) with age regression to the traumatic experience (temporal and spatial disorientation) and abreaction through affective verbal and motor activity in reenacting that scene. Of those who had been tested for hypnotic suggestability beforehand, only three of 18 were found to be highly hypnotizable (scoring 5 on the Stanford Clinical Hypnotic Scale), a percentage similar to that found by Hilgard (1965) in the general population.

That hypnotic and narcosynthetic techniques achieve differing levels of consciousness seemed demonstrated in one highly hypnotizable man who was successively exposed to the combat sound stimuli in a hypnotic trance and later under light drug-induced narcosis. While he was hypnotized, the sounds induced only tearing, but the emotional abreaction that all the other men achieved with drug-induced narcosis did not take place.

Grinker and Spiegel (1945) categorically state that pentothal narcosis is more frequently successful than hypnosis in eliciting abreaction and removing amnesias. They reject the criticism put forward by Hadfield that pentothal narcosis is a crude, though sometimes necessary, assault on so sensitive an organ as the mind. Furthermore they find no difference between "assault" by hypnosis and "assault" by narcosynthesis. To them use of either technique through suggestion alone to reduce symptoms is unlikely to produce lasting effects. They conceive of abrection under a drug as narcosynthetic in that the ego, devoid of the stress of anxiety while sedated, synthesizes the isolated and pathogenically repressed material. And to them the patient's ego, supported by the transference to the therapist, synthesizes the original ego-alien abreacted emotional experiences as well as related feelings separated by dissociation. Thus hostility and fear are recombined as derivatives of the same stress; the patient perceives his or her anger as consequent to his or her isolation in the traumatic incident.

Of the clinical data cited earlier, we agree with Grinker and Spiegel (1945) that abreaction under drug narcosis exposes levels of repression that are unlikely to be achieved through the hypnotic technique. Psychodynamically it is suggested that the drug-induced state acutely impairs those areas of cerebral activity related to superego functioning to a greater degree in a large number of persons than does hypnosis. The suppressive and repressive defensive structures are thus inhibited to a greater extent.

To obviate the essential weakness of drug-induced abreaction, that is, the failure of recall of material on awakening, one of the authors (Dr. Kolb) now routinely has such abreactive states recorded by audiovisual techniques, which are later reviewed with the patient and with others if he or she requests.

The argument presented by some that the use of cathartic techniques (whether hypnosis or drug-induced abreaction) represents an assault upon the psyche seems specious. Just as the lancing of an abcess allows a patient to obtain immediate relief from pain and protection from spread of infection, so does catharsis offer immediate relief and potential benefit to those whose psychological processes have been severely constrained by a major traumatic incident. Overwhelming of the psychological processes by reexposure either through the emotional recall during abreaction or by verbal or audiovisual review later on has not led to greater personality disorder—and quite the opposite for the vast majority of patients so treated.

Facilitating the Expression of Unconscious Thoughts and Feelings

Interpretation has been called the decisive technique of psychodynamic psychotherapy (Greenson, 1967). To the degree to which psychodynamic therapy is a cognitive treatment, this is probably true. But psychodynamic psychotherapy is also an intense means of discovering the self—not just learning about the self, but experiencing it. Sometimes progress results from insight, but frequently personal advancement is simply a process of transformation: a sudden shift occurs, and the person is changed. Often this is a highly emotional process, like a tightness coming unstuck, and catharsis signals that release. Understanding may facilitate this process, either by preparing the way for or following the experiential shift, but the shift is often an intensely cathartic experience, much more affective than cognitive.

Just as preparation is necessary for mutative interpretations, much work needs to be done before intense catharsis of unconscious material is possible. And just as profound insights into the unconscious rarely occur spontaneously, profoundly cathartic experiences rarely occur spontaneously in psychotherapy. Both kinds of breakthoughs require careful preparation and specific techniques from the therapist.

Therapists who limit themselves to manifest content are not dealing with the unconscious and are not functioning as psychodynamically oriented therapists. Similarly, therapists who limit their attention to emotions that are spontaneously expressed or readily uncovered are severely limiting the potential inroad into the unconscious that intense catharsis makes possible. This deep and intense work involves more than a momentary affective eruption, briefly expressed and leisurely analyzed.

Much of the preparation for intense cathartic uncovering involves facilitating spontaneous cathartic expression and countering defenses (as described). Once this work is done, more intense feeling-oriented expression becomes possible. Intense cathartic probing of the unconscious requires opening avoided areas of content, vigorously opposing resistance, and intensifying and prolonging subsequent affective expression.

In general, moving toward the past and toward fantasy leads closer to the unconscious. Affects aroused by current reality, especially when they seem exaggerated, can be used as a bridge to the past and to fantasy. After acknowledging and reflecting feelings associated with a current incident, the therapist can help intensify the experience and expression of feelings in the present context. Asking the patient to repeat those phrases that have the potential for eliciting more affect may be useful.

> Miss R., a 14-year-old girl depressed following her parents' divorce, was describing the recent death of her puppy, Timmy. Although she obviously had a strong attachment to the dog, she masked her feelings with a rapid-fire delivery.
> *Patient:* Oh, I loved him, but he was only a dog, and Mommy says I can get a new one, and besides. . .
> *Therapist:* Hold It. [Pause] Tell me again that you loved him.
> *Patient:* Yes, I loved him, but. . .
> *Therapist:* No, stop. [Pause] Just tell me you loved him.
> *Patient:* I loved him. I loved him. Timmy!
> Now having stopped long enough to experience her feelings, the patient achieved a strong cathartic response.

Once feelings have been expressed about a current incident—but only after as complete expression as possible has been achieved—the therapist may probe for similar experiences in the past.

> *Therapist:* You really did love, Timmy, and it sure hurt when he died. When have you ever felt that way before?
> *Patient:* Do you mean when somebody died?
> *Therapist:* No, not necessarily. Just when have you felt anything similar in the past?

Using the affect rather than the content as a bridge to the past is useful in circumventing the defenses that are encoded verbally.

When affectively charged incidents are recalled, but minimal feeling is actually expressed, a useful technique is to inquire as to "what might have been." Feelings may be more associated with what the patient wanted or hoped for than with what actually transpired. The phrase, "What did you need (want) to say or do?," may uncover impulses that were suppressed or repressed. Alternatively, asking "What would you have liked for him to say or do?" can bring out submerged wishes for nurturance or acceptance. What these techniques have in common is that they are used to explore affect that often goes unnoticed when the anamnesis is limited to events that actually took place.

When unconscious thoughts and feelings are uncovered, therapists should push for cathartic expression, rather than simply touch on the material and then analyze it. Analysis of material that is only partially manifested and incompletely experienced as real—in the treatment—makes for a sterile analysis.

Once unconscious material is "real-ized," patients may be brought to concentrate on their feelings. Asking questions such as "What's the worst of it?" or "Where does it hurt the most?" intensifies the emotional reexperiencing and helps to pinpoint critical aspects of the material. Affect, or lack of it, betrays the importance of the material (A. Freud, 1936).

Part of feeling better after catharsis is not that feelings have been ventilated or gotten rid of, but that unhappy feelings have been differentiated and focused. Experience is no longer colored gray, with vague uneasiness or dissatisfaction. Instead something very specific has been experienced as painful. The relief inherent in really knowing that "here it hurts" is that knowing carries the implication that only that hurts, not everything. Furthermore pinpointing a problem makes it easier to solve. It may be felt as a painful and difficult problem, but at least it is clear what the problem is.

Emotional Working Through

If catharsis were a process of expelling pathogenic affect, it would not need to be repeated more than once. It is not. Since catharsis is not an expulsive, but an expressive, means of helping patients overcome resistances to becoming more feelingful, it is not the one-shot process originally described by Freud (Breuer & Freud, 1895). In fact cathartic working through is similar to interpretative working through (Greenson, 1967). Resistances are stubborn and crop up repeatedly like summer crabgrass. Emotional working through combines repeated confrontation of resistance, in its many guises, with repeated encouragement of cathartic expression.

In working through the choice of techniques will depend in part upon whether the focus of treatment is on the core personality conflict or on derivative psychic functions. The depth and extent of emotional probing vary quantitatively, but the choice of techniques is qualitative and discrete. The more the change sought is a definitive personality change, the more the working through needs to include a regressive, emotional rediscovery of infantile and early childhood emotional reactions. The broader the goals of treatment, the broader—and earlier—the patient's reexperience of feelings and impulses must be.

Mr. N. originally sought treatment to overcome anxiety that was interfering with professional productivity. During two years of weekly treatment, he achieved a dramatic reduction in anxiety, was able to work with great energy, and enjoyed considerable professional advancement. Everything was going well, and Mr. N. felt he had overcome all of his problems. And yet he was not happy.

At this point patient and therapist agreed to meet twice weekly and to shift the focus of treatment from current professional adaptation to an analytic exploration of Mr. N.'s obsessional personality and social isolation. A few weeks later, a dramatic and highly cathartic session took place. In the middle of an otherwise remarkable session, Mr. N. suddenly recalled a dream that had previously been repressed. In the dream the patient was walking down a dark city street in a rough neighborhood. He remembered being frightened, anticipating the possibility that someone might attack him. He turned into an alley, and began to hear footsteps. Terrified, he ran as fast as he could. Still the footsteps kept coming. He turned a corner, and was confronted with a dead end. Trapped, he turned around to face his attackers. Out of the darkness, his pursuers emerged. Instead of robbers, they were his wife and children, reaching out to him, asking him to let them love him and be close to him.

At this point in his narration, the patient was overwhelmed by the emotional recognition of how afraid he was to let people be close to him. He collapsed into a paroxysm of deep, aching crying and sobbing. "All they want is my love, and I'm so afraid!! I've been running away from people all my life . . . I'm so alone!" The realization of what his isolation cost him struck the patient like a hot iron and he continued crying, painfully, heart-wrenchingly crying, for several minutes.

This dramatic and cathartic session was a turning point in Mr. N's treatment. With the therapist's help, he realized that his obsessive preoccupation with various things and activities served to defend him against the anxiety of being close to people. This understanding in turn inspired him actively to pursue more closeness in a variety of relationships.

Mr. N's subsequent progress was steady, but not constant. His obsessional mechanisms of defense were not easily overcome. So long had they safeguarded him against the fear of being with people that he continued to experience a periodic recrudescence of his defenses, and his fears. The emotional working through included a variety of cathartic recollections of early experiences of being close to people and feeling insecure, rejected or trapped. Often these memories were accompanied by such a strong experience of painful emotions that both patient and therapist were tempted to fool themselves that no further such cathartic uncovering was necessary. Happily, though, they persevered, continuing to probe for repressed memories and warded-off affect until finally Mr. N's treatment was satisfactorily completed.

Emotional working through, following a major cathartic breakthrough, involves periodic analysis of resistance, which is the manifestation of major defensive mechanisms. The resistance and underlying defenses do not so much change or multiply as they reappear in a variety of new contexts. Working through includes continued cathartic uncovering and encouragement of behavior change as well as analysis and reduction of resistance. The behavior change, which goes on largely outside the treatment room, continues to produce new material for subsequent work.

A Cautionary Note

The usual hazards of discussing techniques *in vitro* are even greater with catharsis. Skillfully conducting psychotherapy requires attention to the patient, technique, and therapeutic relationship. Considerations of technique must not be allowed to interfere with comprehensive assessment of the patient or awareness of the therapeutic relationship. For example, while asking Mrs. O. to close her eyes and notice what feelings emerged was an effective technique, it would be extremely inappropriate with a paranoid patient.

Since transference is essential to psychodynamic psychotherapy, it is important to consider catharsis in relation to transference and the transference neurosis. Both are similar in that they are based on the resurrection of past experiences. However, the use of active techniques such as role playing to promote catharsis must not interfere with or subvert the development of transference. Too much activity or self-disclosure on the part of the therapist fills in too many of the blank spaces that should be left as a screen onto which the patient projects his or her expectations and fantasies. Furthermore, therapists must not be overzealous in promoting catharsis as to direct the content of the patient's productions. A woman suffering from a pathological grief reaction probably will need to recall and express feelings about her lost loved one. But she must get to this when she is ready; the therapist clears the way, but does not direct the route. The material of every session should come from the patient and not be influenced by inappropriate intrusions from the therapist.

SUMMARY AND CONCLUSIONS

Those who would fractionate experience think of behavior as the province of behavior therapists and feeling as the domain of experiential therapists, leaving only the intellect to analytic therapists. Thus psychodynamic treatment has been wrongly stereotyped as purely cerebral. While we may separate acting, feeling, and thinking for convenience, in reality they do not exist separately. Any therapy that aims to treat the whole person must deal with all three aspects of experiencing.

Unfortunately many therapists, as well as patients who gravitate toward psychodynamic treatment, do so because they are comfortable with thinking and not with feeling. Thus the stereotype tends to become a self-fulfilling prophecy. In the previous chapter, a strong case is made for the value of catharsis in psychodynamic therapy; here techniques for eliciting catharsis are described.

Part of the "technique" of eliciting catharsis is not so much a particular intervention as an acceptance of the value of affective expression, and an acknowledgement that intense focus on experience and relaxation of defenses are the preconditions for cathartic exploration.

Without interest and support, conveyed by words and gestures, patients' fears and uncertainties make them hesitate to explore and express feelings. Life has taught them to expect to be judged or ignored when they risk sharing feelings, and they transfer this expectation onto their therapists. The therapist who would change this pattern of emotional suppression cannot, therefore, simply remain neutral and abstinent; he or she must take pains to listen with interest and demonstrate acceptance of feelings by making empathic comments.

Eliciting catharsis requires alternating between two stances, accepting and supporting patients when they express feelings spontaneously, and actively confronting them when resistances block feelings. The standard practice of analyzing resistances as they emerge sometimes can be postponed until after catharsis is stimulated. Simply breaching defenses when feelings are close to the surface permits a cathartic release that reduces anxiety and graphically demonstrates the impulse behind the defense.

Resistance is an active process—something the patient does, not something he or she has. It can be blocked by observing what the patient is doing and then interrupting it or giving the patient something else to do. Asking the patient to speak louder or to stop smoking are examples of interrupting defensive behavior. Using visual imagery in place of a verbal monologue illustrates giving the patient something else to do.

The hydraulic model of emotions suggests that once defenses that dam up affect are lowered, the feelings bottled up inside will come bubbling out. In fact some emotional expression may begin almost spontaneously as soon as defenses are breached. This expression tends to be brief and superficial, however, because full expression has long been trained out of most people. Emotional expression is not locked up "inside" waiting to get out; it is a habit that must be practiced. Therefore, blocking defenses only prepares the way for deep cathartic expression. It is essential not to abort the cathartic process as soon as it is begun by rushing in to throw a cold interpretation over the emotional fire. Instead therapists should simply accept and encourage feeling expression as long as it occurs.

Even without interference from a therapist, patients will usually stop their own emotional expression soon after it begins. To prevent this interruption, and to intensify and prolong emotional expression, the therapist must intervene by blocking defenses and opening avoided content areas. Exploration of the past and of fantasy are especially likely to lead to unconscious emotions. In short, little other than passive acceptance is required to permit some spontaneous cathartic expression, but active work is needed to produce deep cathartic uncovering. Finally, since catharsis is more than expelling ancient affect, it needs to be worked through to wear down defenses against future feeling and experiencing.

Many of the techniques described in this chapter call for a far more active stance than is typical in psychodynamic psychotherapy. This increased activity creates a problem if it becomes so consistent that the patient is allowed to become passive and dependent upon the therapist's initiative. Therefore, such active techniques are advisable only occasionally to produce emotional breakthroughs. An even greater danger than becoming overly active is becoming directive. The therapist who demands a particular feeling ("You *must* be angry at your wife. Let's hear about it") or regularly suggests certain content areas for exploration ("Let's talk about your job today") risks destroying the climate of free association and spontaneity necessary for psychodynamic psychotherapy.

Regardless of the techniques used to circumvent resistance, it is important to bear in mind that the therapist does not demand that feelings be expressed, but simply makes room for them by clearing away defenses. Feeling expression should always be accepted, it can often be encouraged, but it can never be wrung out of patients.

Catharsis can be thought of as both an end in itself and a means to an end. In itself catharsis is desirable as part of complete experiencing and unconstrained feeling expression. Moreover, defenses against affect are defenses against impulses. Liberating feelings only uncovers the impulses. Once that is done, both the impulse and the defense must be subject to rational scrutiny. Although we have advocated occasional efforts simply to block defenses in order to release feelings, we do not lose sight of the fact that the ultimate aim is to analyze the defense, the feeling, and the impulse behind them.

REFERENCES

Bibring, E. Psychoanalysis and the dynamic psychotherapies. *Journal of the American Psychoanalytic Association*, 1954, *2*, 745–770.

Breuer, J., and Freud, S. (1895) *Studies on hysteria. Standard edition*, vol. 2. London: Hogarth Press, 1955, pp. 1–310.

Fenichel, O. (1935) Concerning the theory of psychoanalytic technique. *Collected papers*. New York: Norton, 1953.

Ferenczi, S. The principles of relaxation of neocatharsis. *Final contributions to the problems and methods of psycho-analysis*. New York: Basic Books, 1955.

Freud, A. *The ego and mechanisms of defense*. London: Hogarth Press, 1936.

Greenson, R.R. *The technique and practice of psychoanalysis, Vol. I*. New York: International Universities Press, 1967.

Grinker, R.R., and Spiegel, J.P. *Men under stress*. Philadelphia: Blakeston, 1945.

Hilgard, E.R. *Hypnotic susceptibility*. New York: Harcourt, Brace & World, 1965.

Janov, A. *The primal scream*. New York: Dell, 1970.

Langs, R. Validation and the framework of the therapeutic situation: Thoughts prompted by Hans H. Strupp's "Suffering and psychotherapy." *Contemporary Psychoanalysis*, 1978, *14*, 98–114.

Loewald, H.W. Hypnoid state, repression, abreaction and recollection. *Journal of the American Psychoanalytic Association*, 1955, *3*, 201–210.

Reich, W. *Character-analysis*. New York: Noonday Press, 1949.

Scheff, T.J. *Catharsis in healing, ritual and drama*. Berkeley, Calif.: University of California Press, 1979.

6
Manipulation: History and Theory

GEORGE AINSLIE, M.D.

Manipulation is the direct creation or inhibition of patients' motives. Its therapeutic purpose is either to induce motives that are beneficial in their own right, or to recreate motivational patterns as laboratory examples that demonstrate something to the patient. In the former context, Bibring (1954) mentioned ways of motivating the patient for the therapeutic process; in the latter, ways to foster what could be called corrective emotional experiences.

The other maneuvers described in this book are forms of discussing the patient's beliefs about his/her motives. Manipulation directly calls upon these motives in one way or another; it becomes a substantive part of the patient's world. For this reason manipulation as a therapeutic technique cannot be well separated from many other transactions in which people try to influence one another. Manipulation, or, in a less one-sided sense, bargaining, has always been the basic interpersonal transaction, and manipulative techniques are often applicable both within and outside of therapy. For instance, the calculated introduction of medals for conduct in Queen Victoria's army (Farwell, 1972) seems identical to the modern manipulation of patients' conduct in a token economy. Some extremely coercive manipulations have been masked as therapies. The electrical aversion "therapy" used in Germany and Austria to treat combat neuroses in World War I, for example, was not really different from the pikes with which sergeants of old drove their men into battle (Freud, 1920b, p. 211). Such abuses make us suspicious of manipulations as therapy. However, even the most nondirective therapists manipulate their patients, as we shall see.

This chapter discusses manipulation as it is applied to psychotherapy. The term *psychotherapy* best includes all learning-based treatments that deal with a patient's ambivalence. It thus excludes somatic and environmental therapies, therapies to which the patient has no significant resistance (simple education, for instance, or biofeedback), and therapies with which the patient has little motive to cooperate (e.g., a token economy that subsidizes socially desirable behaviors by regressed or retarded patients).

Ambivalent patients are those whose symptoms are motivated but who perceive them as undesirable. Patients' participation in their symptoms is a great mystery. Why do phobic and obsessional patients give such importance to objects they know to be trivial? Why do sex offenders and substance abusers indulge in behaviors they know they will regret? Such paradoxes defeat common sense, thus giving rise to psychotherapy as a profession. The brand of psychotherapy one practices, and the use one has for manipulation within that therapy, has a lot to do with one's theory of why ambivalence develops. When we have discussed this relationship, it will be possible to define places for manipulation within insight-oriented therapy and as a supplement to it. First, however, it is important to review the history of manipulation within psychotherapy.

HISTORY

For many years after Freud's acceptance by the psychiatric community, psychotherapy meant his specific technique for helping patients develop insight into the roots of their ambivalence. Since this technique was a radical departure from the highly manipulative and suggestive methods with which he began, it was natural for him and his followers to emphasize the inappropriateness of these methods in the new therapy. Experience soon showed that the temptation to prescribe beliefs and behaviors for the patient could be overwhelming. Thus analytically oriented therapists have stayed on guard against it, and have been understandably uncomfortable with the variety of manipulative techniques that began to be introduced—or reintroduced—by behaviorists in the 1950s.

The fact remains, however, that dynamic psychotherapy was never entirely free of manipulative tactics. Although it is remarkably hard to find written discussions of manipulation within this therapy, certain tactics have been advocated ever since Freud's classical writings on technique, and no one now advocates an attempt at complete therapist neutrality

(Thompson, 1950, p. 107). Some analytically oriented writers have even reported positive results from the inclusion of frankly behavioral maneuvers in their therapies.

Covert Manipulation

To create conditions favorable to analysis, Freud sometimes set up motivational contingencies indistinguishable from those of the modern behavior therapist. He motivated patients both directly, through his fee-setting practices and control over termination, and indirectly, by proposing rules for self-control that patients had to enforce on themselves.

Freud (1913, p. 127) was succinct about his reason for "leasing" a daily time slot to his patients rather than billing by the visit: "Under a less stringent regime the 'occasional' non-attendances increase so greatly that the doctor finds his material existence threatened"; and not only that, but this happens "just when the work promises to be especially important and rich in content." To correct this situation, he set up a contract whereby the patient did not save money by giving in to the frequent temptation to miss a session, but rather lost money.

Likewise, Freud advised against free treatment even when the analyst could afford to give it, because he found it created counterproductive motives in his patients; to offer sexual favors, for example, or to "oppose an obligation to feel grateful." "The absence of the regulating effect offered by the payment of a fee to the doctor makes itself very painfully felt; the whole relationship is removed from the real world, and the patient is deprived of a strong motive for endeavoring to bring the treatment to an end" (Freud, 1913, p. 123). Conversely, if a patient's resistence became unmovable, Freud (1918) might threaten to terminate the therapy to get the patient moving.

Freud (1913, pp. 134–137) also demanded that his patients adopt certain rules of conduct. In fact the "fundamental rule" was not a simple rule of thumb but a principle of self-control; patients violated it "in every analysis" not because it was difficult to understand, but because they could not tolerate the affect that resulted from obeying it. Freud (1914a, p. 153) also dealt with each patient's frequent urges to act out repressed material in therapy "by making him promise not to take any important decisions affecting his life during the time of his treatment."

Even Freud's (1919) suggestion that therapists portray themselves as emotionally neutral served a manipulative end. The purpose was not just to maintain the therapist's objectivity, but also to create a specific motivational state in the patient: "As far as his relations with the physician are concerned, the patient must have unfulfilled wishes in abundance. It is expedient to deny him precisely those satisfactions which he desires most intensely and expresses most importunately."

Thus Freud's break with manipulative technique, although real and dramatic, was only relative.

In the past 30 years, there have been many proposals about therapist activity. The least aggressive are the kind made by Langs (1974, vol. 2, p. 294), who merely says that a therapist should be responsive but limit any responses to those that are "nondeviant, realistic, appropriate, centered on the needs of the patient, and largely conscious." Stevenson (1959) suggested "indirect techniques to stimulate new behavior," but the ways he recommended were those of most "direct" or "brief" therapists who have published subsequently—accelerated interpretations to hasten insight, rather than the manipulation of patients' motives. At the other end of the spectrum, some authors have suggested that the therapist should regulate the patient's motivational disposition from moment to moment. As interpreted by Havens (1976, pp. 13–14), for instance, Harry Stack Sullivan recommended reconstituting the patients' perception of the interview situation by a number of "tools" that included "timing, the expression of non-verbal attitudes (tone, affect, specific vocabulary, etc.) and the creation of a dialectic between the patient's supposed reality and the more factual reality (through transitional statements and those particularly transitional statements I call counterprojective remarks)." The goal is to reduce the patient's motive to fight the therapy. For instance, the last-named remarks include "role-playing plus a great deal else that is best called counterroleplaying. By distinguishing the therapist sharply from what the patient perceives him to be, these statements lessen the anxiety resulting from the projection, paving the way for the continuing establishment of fact" (Havens, 1974, p. 26). Jay Haley (1963, pp. 41–85) has described a number of ways in which orthodox therapists could be interpreted to be controlling the patient, but advocates the still more manipulative methods used by Milton Erickson: The therapist should estimate the patient's most likely reaction to the therapist's behavior and then behave in such a way that it drives the patient in the desired direction—support the inhibited patient's inhibitions to make him or her feel confined by them, give the rebellious patient conspicuously nondemanding tasks to undermine the urge to rebel, and so forth. A similar technique has been described under the name of paradoxical intention (Frankl, 1960). Many other highly controlling activities have been proposed, but will not be described.

Short of such thorough controlling of the patients' motives, a number of more modest suggestions have been made that are consistent with a nondirective stance. Freud's suggestions about concrete details such as seating, lighting, and rules for payment have been enlarged upon. For instance, Langs (1974, vol. I, pp. 45–46) said that a desk in the office provided structure but might suggest a barrier between therapist and patient; on the other hand, a small table might suggest a "boundary" without becoming a "barrier." (See also Haveliwala et al., 1979, pp. 18–31.) More important is the therapist's use of physical or vocal mannerisms to influence the patient's affect: "A positive transference state is induced as rapidly as possible by means of imitating the patient as well as using his own words" (Murphy, 1965, p. 10). Therapists may also use such tactics to draw patients' attention to a conflictual area. They may be deliberately short to make the patient aware of his or her avoidance of anger, or may use an expression favored by a patient's family member, or be significantly silent so that a patient may notice his or her transference feelings (e.g., Brockbank, 1970). Aull and Strean (1967) described therapist silence as an intervention that should be used judiciously; for instance to relieve a patient of a need to perform or to undermine a patient's oral dependency. Then there is Sullivan's (1954, pp. 47–48) "accentuated transition" in an interview: "I usually begin to growl, rather like a ball bearing with some sand in it, just to indicate that something is about to happen. I want to drop what is going on, emphatically; not in such a way that it is forgotten forever, but with such emphasis as to disturb the set, as the old experimental psychologists might call it." In these examples the therapist is not presenting ideas to the patient, but methodically taking on appearances with an eye to how they will move the patient.

Several authors have recently acknowledged, with approval, that insight-oriented therapists' actions and verbal inflections extensively influence their patients' response to therapy (Marmor, 1966; Wachtel, 1977, pp. 251–265; Wolberg, 1977, pp. 47–49; see also beginnings of systematic study by Kelly, 1972). Whether the therapist conceives this part of his or her role in the terms of operant reinforcement theory is probably a matter of taste:

> A medical student once asked the analyst Charles Pinderhughes if a timid young man should not be treated with behavior therapy, to which Pinderhughes replied that he had been doing just that throughout the diagnostic interview: "Didn't you notice that when the boy went on about his nagging doubts and fears, I turned my eyes away and acted bored, while when he began to say something risky I sat forward in my chair and paid the closest attention?"

The "um-hm" of the analyst can shape a patient's behavior with precision. This effect has been described even in Carl Rogers' most nondirective of therapies (Murray, 1956; Truax, 1966).

Overt Manipulation

Most of the manipulations just discussed could be called covert, in that the therapist does not announce them to the patient. Overt manip-

ulations involve bringing motivational pressure to bear on the patient in
ways of which the patient is conscious, or even teaching the patient ways
to rearrange his or her own motives. These have been proposed within
both dynamic and behavioral rubrics, although in the former case they
have usually marked their proponents' departure from therapeutic orthodoxy.

Wilhelm Stekel's (1923, pp. 408–409) practice of "setting tasks" for his
patients, e.g., to free their associations by reciting their life histories with
"epic breadth," did not lead to professional exile, and has been since
advocated from time to time (e.g., Herzberg, 1947). But Ferenczi (1920)
went beyond the pale (Glover, 1955) by carrying this strategy further,
often frankly forbidding one of a patient's habitual activities so as to make
him or her more conscious of the urge to perform it. Wilhelm Reich's
physical demonstrations to patients of their "character armor" led to a
parochial school of therapy, bioenergetics (Reich, 1972; Lowen, 1975).
Similarly, the therapist's restaging of evocative life events to increase
patients' attention to important emotions has been segregated in quasi-
dynamic schools such as psychodrama (Greenberg, 1974) and gestalt therapy (Applebaum, 1976). It is not possible to trace here all the splinter
methods of manipulation that have been proposed (Corsini, 1973, 1981;
Herink, 1980). Many of them no longer aim to help patients gain eventual
dynamic insight.

The other great source of overt manipulative techniques has been
experimental psychology. J. B. Watson and Mary Cover Jones found early
that experimentally induced phobias could be removed by gradual reintroduction of the phobic object (Jones, 1924). Behavioral treatment methods did not become widespread, however, until Wolpe (1958) introduced
therapy by reciprocal inhibition. Since then a very large number of ways
directly to change patients' motivational dispositions have been described
(Kazdin, 1978, pp. 160–232).

Beyond contracting with the patient about a few basic rules, the use
of overt manipulation in dynamic psychotherapy has been controversial.
Proponents have suggested that it cuts the Gordian knot of the genetic
approach to therapy (e.g., Wachtel, 1977); opponents have pointed out
that it may undermine the perceived neutrality of the therapist, or may
offer a treacherous shortcut to the beginning therapist (e.g., Greenson,
1967). Probably, too, many analysts have been repelled by the hostility
with which some behavior therapists have criticized analytic methods
(e.g., Eysenck, 1965). The most extreme advocates of both schools have
made the two therapies seem like opposites that must be pursued, one or
the other, in pure form. However, there have now been a moderate
number of reports of successful combinations of analytic and behavioral
approaches—that is, of alternate use and nonuse of overt
manipulation—within the same therapy.

In some cases behavioral manipulations have provided the self-observations needed for dynamic insight. For example, a 20-year-old man was prescribed a bed-wetting alarm for persistent enuresis, but as the treatment began to be effective, he seemed to be colluding with his mother to disconnect the alarm and thus prolong his dependency on her (Birk, 1970). Once the therapist had confronted the patient with this concrete example of resistance, they could learn about it in psychodynamic therapy.

An even more striking example of a manipulative technique that uncovered motivational conflict is reported by Adler and Morrissey-Adler (1979).

> A hysterically blind young woman, who was incidentally being treated for tension headaches with EMG biofeedback from her frontalis muscle, could not vary her muscle tension level until her fifth session, when the readings suddenly dropped to low levels, rose, and abruptly dropped back down again. At this point, the patient laughed and stated, "I know what's causing my headaches now, doctor, and I don't think I need the biofeedback anymore." When asked what she meant, she replied that she had been struggling to push out of her mind a wish to have an affair because it was a "sinful thought for a God-fearing person." While experimenting with trial and error on the feedback, she allowed herself to picture a detailed image of such an affair, and an immediate decrescendo of the feedback greeted this image. To confirm her impressions, she again put the image out of her mind, again let it in. Her impression was confirmed. The headaches were gone from that point on, as was the blindness.

In the converse approach, psychodynamic interviewing techniques uncover a basic conflict, which is then modified by directed rehearsal in place of the orthodox method of working it through. In one method patients have then been taught systematic muscle relaxation and instructed to spin fantasies of indulging the impulsive side of this conflict, an anxiety-provoking procedure that leads to symptomatic relief and a variable degree of insight (Feather & Rhoads, 1972; Rhoads & Feather, 1974). In another, called implosive therapy, the therapist "presents" the conflictual situation to the patient in such a way that it maximizes the patient's anxiety, and repeats it until the anxiety attenuates through a supposed extinction process (Stampfl & Levis, 1967). Wachtel (1982) reports that dynamic formulation of patients' conflicts is sometimes necessary to avoid misplacement of behavioral interventions. He points out that a patient is often unable to report the crucial motive—for example, fear of success or forbidden anger—and that in such a case, a straightforward behaviorial technique aimed at the patient's manifest complaint will fail.

Recently Olds (1982) has pointed out that overt manipulations can either increase dynamic insight or give the patient practice with new behaviors. Their "cohesive active technique" begins with analytically oriented therapy, but if it "begins to stagnate or become repetitive," the therapist gives the patient direct instruction in behavioral exercises, in-

cluding guided "fantasy rehearsal," self-monitoring, contracts, and paradoxical intention. These exercises should enlarge the patient's repertoire
or else confront the patient with his or her resistance, either of which is
useful. The therapist may then return to an orthodox insight-oriented
technique. This strategy is indeed more cohesive than the manipulative
and uncovering techniques that have simply been intermixed or alternated
on a trial-and-error basis in previous reports (Brady, 1968; Hersen, 1970;
Leventhal, 1968; Segraves & Smith, 1976; Woody, 1968); but the relationship of the two approaches is still uncertain, and Olds worries that
they sometimes may be incompatible.

The history of manipulation within insight-oriented therapy ends here.
It ends on a promising note, for several new combinations of overt manipulation and insight-oriented therapy have been reported. However, it
is far from satisfactory, since it leaves unanswered many questions about
how such combinations can be created on a regular basis and when they
are desirable.

Theoretical Analysis

At least some mixtures of psychodynamic and overt manipulative
techniques apparently are successful. Nevertheless, those writers who
have accepted both analytic and behavioral approaches have tended to
blur the very real differences in their assumptions about the healing process, and, in turn, about the pathogenesis of ambivalence. Some suggest,
for instance, that their differences are largely a matter of therapist temperament—the analyst might tend to be patient, tolerant of ambiguity
and delay, apt to perceive any acting as "acting out," perhaps "tragic" in
his or her world view; the behaviorist may be highly active, suspicious
of phenomena that are hard to observe, demanding tangible results, perhaps viewing the world "comically" in that he or she looks for technical
solutions (Messer & Winokur, 1980). But this is to ignore the therapies
themselves.

Other writers suggest that psychodynamic and behavior therapies are
basically the same (Garfield, 1982; Sloane, 1969; Strupp, 1973). It is true
that these therapies share more than has usually been acknowledged. With
or without overt manipulation, psychotherapists must form a therapeutic
alliance of such a kind that they are not seen as pursuing their own interests
as opposed to those of the patient; they must achieve an emotional engagement with the patient; they try whenever possible to recreate an
important example of the target problem during the therapy session, so
that they and the patient can observe it together [e.g., Freud's description
of the analysis of the transference (1925, pp. 42–43)]; and in some way
they must bring out the motives that are crucial to the patient's symptoms

and permit the patient to weigh them against each other, so that he or she can arrive at a simple stable preference instead of pathological ambivalence [again, see Freud's (1919) insistence that the patient must confront his or her real-life conflictual situation]. However, to make these similarities the means of reconciling manipulative and nonmanipulative approaches is to imply that the specific procedures of each approach are unimportant to the outcome. These comparisons do not resolve the many theoretical differences among the procedures, for instance that insight-oriented technique aims at eliminating defensive processes, whereas overt manipulations seem to strengthen them. More immediately, they do not suggest why a patient or therapist might choose one approach or the other, or how one might combine elements from each. Blanket identification of the two approaches provides no basis for further technical development.

It may be that many of the overt manipulative techniques being developed by behavior therapists can be combined under some or all circumstances with analytic psychotherapy; but most of the work of testing possible combinations remains to be done. Unfortunately there has been no adequate conceptual framework that suggests mechanisms for or relationships among these various techniques. Testing so far has been a matter of trial and error. Yet at some level these techniques must be comparable, since they represent alternative hypotheses about how to relieve the same pathological condition: ambivalence that fails to resolve.

It would be worthwile to find a common denominator that could relate these various techniques to one another and to their common goal. The next part of this chapter reviews the assumptions that have led to the major existing therapies for ambivalence. My argument is that none has the power to prevail over the others, but that all show a simple feature that will permit the beginnings of a taxonomy of therapies. Foreseeable problems in combining nondirective therapy with specific overt therapies are described in this framework.

A BASIS FOR COMPARING DIVERSE TECHNIQUES

When people differ at length about how to do a job, it makes sense to ask whether they are thinking about the same job. Certainly differences of opinion about the nature of therapy may lead to different attitudes toward manipulation. For instance, in discussing how much therapist activity was acceptable, Glover (1955, p. 244) assumed that the object was insight: "So long as the technique is directed at uncovering and interpreting pathogenic material, (it) should be regarded as a variety of psychoanalysis." However, many dynamic therapists since Alexander have aimed not only at interpretation, but at teaching a skill by practice: The job of the therapist may be to modulate his or her attitudes and behaviors in such a way that the patient's "ego is repeatedly exposed to its crucial emotional conflicts, reduced in intensity . . ." (Alexander, 1948, p. 286; see also Rioch, 1943, p. 151). Within such a "corrective emotional experience," a patient learns ego functions as he or she might learn to ride a bicycle, without necessarily being conscious of the process. This view of therapy permits a greater place for overt manipulation, as in the Olds approach just described. Furthermore, those therapists who approve of manipulation make different assumptions about how long it will be needed. Most dynamic and some behavioral therapists regard manipulation as a temporary adjunct to therapy, to be removed like a worker's scaffold when the patient is no longer ambivalent; but many behavioral writers recognize cases where the patient's ambivalence persists, and where the patient must be taught to use "self-management techniques" indefinitely (e.g., Chaney et al., 1978; Meichenbaum, 1977).

Differences in therapists' assumptions run deeper, however. At the bottom of their beliefs about therapy, there can usually be discerned different beliefs about the pathogenic process itself.

The most elementary explanation of ambivalence is that there might be more than one autonomous center of motivation within a single person. The biblical belief that a normally rational person might be possessed by a demon still appears in Western culture, though no longer in the forefront of thought. Even Freud (1920a) once speculated that the id and the ego might be separately motivated, so that the id could experience pleasure while the ego experienced unpleasure. Modern evidence for distinct motivational centers in the brain (Olds & Fobes, 1981) or separate "personalities" in right and left hemispheres (Scola, 1984) might seem to revive this possibility. However, we can be confident in discarding any theory that relies on multiple centers of motivation, according to a simple argument: Most of a person's behaviors are replaceable by most other behaviors, so that there must be one ultimate mechanism that chooses among them. This is not to argue against the possibility of different motives or even anatomically different motivational centers in the brain; only that such motives or centers must complete and be chosen on the basis of some common dimension. There must be, in effect, a final marketplace where the person's preference is decided. It is the occasional failure of this marketplace to produce a stable decision that we describe as ambivalence. How is it that the person's favor is not always auctioned off, as it were, to the highest bidder?

Theories that assume a single marketplace generally invoke a pathological learning or remembering process that lacks "normal," goal-directed controls. Analytically oriented therapists have seen repression as the key to ambivalence, while therapists inspired by the findings of experimental psychology have postulated classical conditioning or superstitious operant learning as the key. Each theory now has a long and respectable history. However, continuing examination of these mechanisms has raised doubts about each as a universal paradigm:

Repression of Motives

Psychoanalytic theory has retained the hypothesis that Freud originally described in his "Project for a Scientific Psychology" (1894/1956, pp. 8–13): that ego-dystonic motives are preserved because the patient represses or distorts some of the available information about them, thus keeping them from coming into equilibrium with other motives. Repression was the prototype of the defense mechanisms, and was said to occur because the person found some perceptions intolerable and shut them out of awareness, unknowingly producing autonomous, unextinguishable motives as a by-product. This hypothesis has remained a cornerstone of insight-oriented therapy; the purpose of this therapy is to let the patient stop repressing the relevant material, so that he or she can see goals in their true proportions: "During treatment unconscious (repressed) material becomes conscious. This increases the action radius of the conscious ego: The ego becomes cognizant of unconscious impulses and thus is able to coordinate (integrate) the latter with the rest of conscious content" (Alexander, 1963).

Just because repression and pathological ambivalence are commonly found together and abate together with therapy, it is not possible to conclude that the process of repression is what keeps one motive from being directly weighted against its competitors. The theory that repression causes ambivalence, rather than responding to it, is not contrary to the known facts in most cases, but it is not a necessary conclusion either. The repression theory is also difficult to integrate with the theories of the other behavioral sciences. Nothing in basic research suggests how a motive can be removed from competition with other motives by a perceptual process. Furthermore, there are clinical examples to which repression seems to contribute nothing.

The most concrete example of clinical ambivalence is furnished by the addictions. An addicted person who wants to break a dependency on a substance also wants not to, and clear expressions of these conflicting wishes are readily observable. In this example the role of consciousness in creating or curing the ambivalence is hard to discern. People who eventually will be addicted to a substance do not seem to use repression or other defense mechanisms in any unusual way. Examination of psychological functioning in young adulthood cannot predict, for instance, who will become alcoholic (Kammeier et al., 1973; Vaillant, 1980), and the notoriously widespread difficulty of giving up a cigarette habit even when the person is strongly motivated to do so does not seem to be related to psychopathology. It is illuminating that Freud found his self-analysis useless against his own habit of smoking cigars, despite the fact that he was concerned about the effect of cigars on his health and finally died of mouth cancer (Schur, 1972). There seem to be some examples, at least, where ambivalence does not depend on repression.

Conditioning

Classical conditioning became a popular theory of pathogenesis shortly after its first clear description by Pavlov. J. B. Watson showed that a child's fear could be transferred to an arbitrarily chosen stimulus by pairing this stimulus with a loud noise, and that a fear thus implanted was hard to extinguish (Cohen, 1979, pp. 142–144). Some early writers in the behavorist school described maladaptive behavior itself as being conditioned, so that there might be, for example, conditioned alcohol-drinking responses or conditioned phobic avoidances. Interestingly, this awkward theory was similar to an early psychoanalytic theory: some stereotyped behaviors represent an exact replay of behaviors that had happened to occur during special "hypnoid" states of consciousness (Breuer & Freud, 1895). Neither theory lasted very long in its original form, although references to "conditioned" motor behaviors are still occasionally encountered (e.g., Smith, 1982). However, after goal-directed ("operant") learning was clearly differentiated from classical conditioning in the 1930s, O. H. Mowrer (1947) proposed the conditioning theory of pathogenesis in its modern form. According to this "two-factor" theory, visceral states, particularly emotions, become maladaptively conditioned by chance pairings with environmental stimuli, and the patient then performs ordinary goal-directed behavior to seek or avoid the stimuli. This theory was applied to psychopathology in Dollard and Miller's influential book, *Personality and Psychotherapy* (1950), which provided an intuitively satisfying explanation of how the defensive processes described by psychoanalysis might be providing relief from conditioned emotions.

The first therapy inspired by behavioral experiment was the extinction of deliberately induced conditioned fears in children (Jones, 1924). Countless later therapists have discerned Watson's laboratory paradigm underneath their patients' behaviors, which seem to be "controlled by a stimulus" (Kanfer, 1975). They have undertaken to undo the supposed incidents of classical conditioning that made their patients phobic, say, or gave them perverse sexual appetites, by means of direct manipulations (Eysenck & Rachman, 1965, pp. 4–7; Rachman, 1968; Wolpe, 1969, pp. 4–12).

Experiments over the past 15 years, however, have shown that classically conditionable behaviors can also be controlled by operant reinforcements. These findings have called into question the existence of classical conditioning as a separate principle of reinforcement (Hearst, 1975). Once a response can be governed by either of two reinforcing principles, the same argument applied as to two reward centers: There must be a final common mechanism that determines how much force each principle will have. In fact several aspects of the conditioning process suggest that it is not a separate reinforcing principle at all, but just one route by which operant reinforcement can come to control behavior. The reinforcers in classical conditioning, unconditioned stimuli, can all serve as operant reinforcements or punishments as well; classically conditioned responses can be eliminated, or even reversed, by differential operant reinforcements; and when conditioned responses are examined in detail, they are found not to be identical copies of the unconditioned response that have been transferred whole to a new stimulus, but new responses differing in many particulars from the unconditioned response (Ainslie & Engel, 1974; Atnip, 1977; Siegel, 1983).

Likewise, in our clinical example of substance abuse, operant reinforcement seems to underlie supposedly conditioned appetites. Substance abusers are often said to have developed conditioned emotional responses to the trappings of ingesting their substance—bars and shot glasses, or needle parks and "works," for instance—in such a way that the sight of these stimuli will overwhelm all other motives and cause a loss of control even after years of abstinence. But drug and alcohol abusers on experimental wards develop craving if, and only if, the substance is scheduled to be available on that particular day, with the environmental stimuli held constant (Meyer, 1981). Similarly, smokers who never smoke at certain times do not develop craving at those times. It has even been reported that withdrawing narcotic addicts stop developing physiological symptoms of need for narcotics when these are punished by shock (Wolpe et al., 1980). The appetite for these substances is probably best understood not as blind association, but as a goal-directed preparatory response that has been rewarded in the presence of certain cues by consumption of the substances.

Superstition or Other Misguided Operant Learning

An experimental model of goal-directed learning was described by Thorndike (1905) at the turn of the century. It was not until the 1940s that investigators described systematic errors that could develop in this kind of learning, errors that were not necessarily corrected by greater practice. Animals' tendencies to develop seemingly random bits of behavior and keep them even after they become otherwise efficient at getting the reward have been likened to human superstitions, and, by extension, to clinically maladaptive behaviors (e.g., Gambrill, 1977, p. 34; Skinner, 1948). If there is some fundamental tendency for goal-directed behavior to move off course and stay off course, the argument runs, then such a process could be an important pathogen.

A closer examination of the laboratory "superstition" that seems to run counter to reward, however, has shown that it is not caused by random pairings of behavior and reward, but by a species specific preparedness to respond to particular features of the test situation (Staddon & Simmelhag, 1971). In effect there have simply been additional, intrinsic rewards that earlier experimenters did not recognize.

Meanwhile many behavior therapists have assumed by analogy to the older model that some kind of overly narrow, albeit goal-directed, learning has led to maladaptive "habits" in their patients (e.g., Eysenck, 1960). The reason for the pathological narrowing is usually not developed. Likewise cognitive therapists take negative cognitions about the self to be the pathogenic agents of their patients' ego-dystonic behavior, but do not explain why their patients should have selectively formed such cognitions (Ellis, 1977; Shaw & Beck, 1977).

Some interpersonal therapists have proposed to free therapeutic strategy from the implications of the repression hypothesis by recognizing cases where symptoms are learned and maintained by a deceptive learning situation. For instance, a patient who believes that he or she has dangerous dependency needs becomes extremely independent, thus making those dependency needs even more importunate, and so on. In such situations the patient seems innocently to misinterpret his or her failures to mean that he or she is not performing enough of what is in fact the failure-producing behavior, and so tries even harder at the wrong thing (Wachtel, 1977, pp. 41–75). Again it is not clear why the patient should be so deceived, or why he or she should defend this deception against the therapist's attempts to point out the error. Simple misinformation is not ambivalence, and should respond to straightforward teaching.

Such a response rarely happens with psychiatric patients, least of all in our basic example, substance abuse. Substance abusers have many superstitions (e.g., Ikard et al., 1969), and often get into vicious circles of tension and chemical relief, but education is notoriously ineffective in treating them. After thousands of encounters with their substance, they continue to oppose their own better judgment by ingesting it. Even prolonged experience with substance-free living is not adequate to prevent a continuing tendency to lapse into addiction.

Reliance on any specific theory of motivational conflict is probably premature, if for no other reason than that all have persisted after years of vigorous competition with each other. Repression, classical conditioning, and inefficient learning are widely observed phenomena, but their role in generating motives for ego-alien behavior remains speculative (Ainslie, 1984). In the present review, we should not assume that any known pathological learning process is responsible for ego-alien behavior. Nevertheless we can still use a comparative approach if we return to the most elementary fact about ego-alien behavior and follow its implications.

The motives for ego-alien behavior must have the potential to be dominant some of the time. Ego-alien motives would not be a threat unless at some times they could control the person's decision-making process long enough to undermine the ego's projects. Even such intrapsychic processes as phobic anxiety and obsessional doubt must be preferred to their alternatives long enough to admit them to consciousness, if we accept both behavioral and analytic evidence that paying attention is a motivated process (Ainslie, in press; Erdelyi, 1974). That is, if the expected value, or reinforcing effect, of the incentives for an ego-syntonic behavior and an ego-alien alternative are graphed as a function of time, the line for the alien incentive must spike above the line for its syntonic alternative at some times; otherwise it would not pose a problem.

Such temporary preferences for generally unpreferred alternatives might occur because of surges in unconscious motivation, or happenstances of conditioned stimuli, or errors in judgment caused by faulty learning, as the hypotheses just reviewed have held. They could conceivably occur because of random oscillation in the evaluation process (Hull, 1943, pp. 304–321). The author has proposed still another theory based on the function by which human and animal subjects discount delayed goals: A hyperbolic curve of declining reward effectiveness as a function of delay, which has been described for both animal and human subjects (deVilliers & Herrnstein, 1976; Baum, 1975), predicts a temporary change of preference from a larger, later reward to a smaller, earlier alternative during the time the latter is imminently available, and this change has now been observed directly (Solnick et al., 1980; Ainslie & Herrnstein, 1981; Ainslie & Haendel, 1983). This, too, would create ambivalence that fails to resolve, because competing rewards are dominant at different times.

Whatever its cause, the alternation of incompatible preferences is apt to be the greatest planning problem any person faces. In effect it creates two conflicting kinds of interests within the person: long-term interests based on the all-over preponderance of the rewards in a particular kind of situation, and short-term interests based on temporary preferences for generally unpreferred alternatives. As Freud (1911) and therapists from many other schools have pointed out, the short-term interests tend to predominate only when the rewards on which they are based are imminent. Interests are motivational states, not separate organs or homunculi;

but during the times they are dominant, they have all the person's knowledge and skills at their disposal. The many theories that have likened ambivalence to a struggle among separate people have not been entirely wrong.

In the conflict between short- and long-term interests, each side can be expected to learn the tactics made available by the conditions that created them. The long-term interest is somewhat in the position of Ulysses when he had to sail past the Sirens; it has the advantage of foresight and can adopt tactics to forestall the foreseeable change of preference. The short-term interest has the advantage of taking its turn last, and will prevail whenever it has not been forestalled in advance. The conflict of these interests over time is sufficient to explain most familiar patterns of clinical impulsiveness and defenses against them.

CLASSIFICATION OF SYMPTOMS BY THE DURATION OF TEMPORARY PREFERENCES FOR THEM

Temporary preferences may be arranged according to their durations, which affect the way they are experienced both quantitatively and qualitatively. Cycles of original preference, reversal, and return to the original preference fall roughly into four orders of length, which can be defined by the way the two parts of the ambivalence are experienced (Table 1).

Sellouts

The most ego-syntonic zone contains activities that are clearly pleasurable but for which some people develop an aversion after a period of years. These people report that the pleasure of such activities is of an inferior quality or even treacherous, leading to a dysphoric sense of dis-

Table 1
Zones of Temporary Preference

Exemplar	Distinguishing Feature	Duration of Cycle
Sellouts	Ambiguous aversive phase	Months to years
Addictions	Clear periods of pleasure and aversion	Hours to days
Itches	Ambiguous pleasurable phase, but patient is conscious of participating	Seconds
Pains	Never pleasurable, no participation	Fractions of second

sipation after years of indulgence. As a psychiatric problem, the complaints based on this kind of conflict are the hardest to understand because they arise in an apparently healthy life-style: the person is successful at a job but undergoes a mid-life crisis because he or she is not getting the expected satisfaction; the person is successful in romance but begins to lose interest, and so on. Often these conflicts are seen in philosophical or religious rather than clinical terms. For instance, the seven deadly sins perceived in medieval times (lust, wroth, avarice, pride, envy, sloth, and gluttony) are activities that can be highly stable and may never be renounced or even questioned, but which tend to prove unsatisfactory in the long run. There is no accepted generic term for these slowly changing preferences with a clear-cut attractive phase and an ambiguous or variably experienced aversive phase, but sometimes they have been called "sellouts" and that term is used here.

Addictions

Where temporary preferences are briefer, the change of preference is marked and unambiguous. These activities are identified as addictions. Here an influence of proximity on the temporary preferences is especially evident. An alcoholic plans not to drink, manages not to drink if sufficiently distant from the opportunities, becomes overwhelmingly tempted when faced with an imminent chance to drink, but later wholeheartedly regrets this lapse. These activities include not only substance abuse but many thrill-seeking behaviors, such as gambling compulsively, courting fights, and running risks with the law, as well as more briefly preferred activities such as the ritualized sexual offenses (e.g., exhibitionism, voyeurism), and kleptomania.

Itches

If the temporary preference for an activity is briefer still, the person's perception of this preference will be marginal. It is apt to be experienced as an unaccountable urge that is not called pleasurable. The prototype of such activities is an itch, which the person wants to be rid of and which will abate if ignored, but which the person usually maintains because of brief preferences for the sensation of scratching. Other activities in this range are unwanted personal habits such as nail biting, bruxism, psychogenic coughing, mannerisms of gesture and speech, rage in people who suffer from tantrums, and many dysphoric thought patterns that feel to the person as though he or she is participating in or "going along with" them: obsessions, pathological doubts, hypochondriacal worries, and the like. Perhaps the self-induction of seizures in epileptics who have this ability should also be placed here.

Pains

Activities with the briefest attractive phase are not experienced as pleasurable at all, and people do not report that they participate in them. It feels as though they "happen to" the person, and their attraction can only be inferred from the fact that they can compete for attention with incentives that are clearly rewarding (Ainslie, in press). The prototype is physical pain, which is unambivalently avoided, but which nevertheless usually competes successfully for the person's awareness. However, highly involving activities such as combat or competitive sports can often keep pain out of awareness (Beecher, 1959, pp. 157–190), as can the structuring of attention used to promote anesthesia in dentistry and obstetrics (Melzack et al., 1963; Licklider, 1961); conversely pains are notoriously worse in the quiet time that precedes sleep. Pains clearly trade in the same market as rewards, and thus must use the same currency; but the fact that they reinforce only attention, not motor behavior, implies that their period of dominance must be shorter than the latency of motor responses, and thus that pains belong at the short end of the continuum of temporary preference durations. Their seemingly continuous unrewarding-but-hard-to-ignore quality is well accounted for as the perceptual summation of repeated very brief reinforcements followed by relatively longer periods of disruption of other sources of reinforcement (Ainslie, 1975, and in press).

Phobias follow a similar pattern. They are experienced as unwelcome, yet they are in equilibrium with other motivated processes and must repeatedly be admitted to consciousness, just as an urge to look down from a dizzy height or to notice the precariousness of highway driving may becken to one but cannot arbitrarily preempt one's attention.

This hierarchy of four neat time zones should not be taken too literally; it is presented only to suggest a relationship among seemingly disparate symptoms. Cycle durations of preference–change undoubtedly form a continuum, and there is no reason to suppose that these conceptual zones correspond to real clusters along this continuum. Classifying particular dystonic mental processes as itches or pains, by determining whether the person notices a participatory component, is especially difficult in practice. Nevertheless these rough categories will simplify the discussion of therapeutic strategies against temporary preferences.

CLASSIFICATION OF TACTICS AGAINST TEMPORARY PREFERENCES

Threatened with the occurrence of such temporary preferences, people use a variety of tactics to precommit their future choices (Ainslie, 1982).

Many of these tactics are familiar to analytically oriented therapists as defense mechanisms, but since this term is also used to describe the avoidance of painful affect, it is apt to be ambiguous. One might "defend" oneself against an intolerable affect, then have to "defend" oneself again against the behavioral tendency engendered by this distortion of perception. Whether or not they are thus causally related, these two kinds of defense are distinct processes. For instance, a person might identify with Christ in order to deny an intolerable feeling of helplessness, or to control an impulse to get into fights, and in either case it would be called a defense mechanism (A. Freud, 1966). All schools regard defense mechanisms in the former sense as harmful. Defense mechanisms in the latter sense are controversial. They can be overused, they have side effects, and if one regards the problem of temporary preference itself as curable, they may be unnecessary. Nevertheless it is just these mechanisms that overt manipulations seek to strengthen and improve. Four basic kinds are discernible in the literature of both analysis and behavior therapy; they are reviewed at length in Ainslie (1982) and only summarized here.

Extrapsychic Mechanisms

Devices of the extrapsychic kind involve arranging for either physical or social action upon the person's future self. Behavior therapists have described many ways in which a person can set up outside forces that will influence the person later. Psychodynamic writers have described how someone may act up to attract the attention of a person in authority, who will then serve as a guard and prevent the occurrence of more serious impulsive behavior. This maneuver has been called asking for controls.

The potential committing power of these devices is obviously variable, and their usefulness also depends on whether the environment makes them available. Devices that enlist other people's influence, probably the most practical of the extrapsychic devices, also depend on one's social style—whether one leaves oneself vulnerable to the opinions of other people.

Control of Attention

Repression, which Freud (1914b, p. 16) at one time held to be the cornerstone of all defensive processes, controls behavior by keeping attention away from information about the availability or proximity of the poorer alternative. A similar process has been described by some behavior therapists, but as a useful recommendation for avoiding impulses called "stimulus control" (Kanfer, 1975, pp. 309–355; Goldiamond, 1965).

The disadvantage of attention control as a defense against impulses is that it may hinder the gathering of useful information, possibly leading to serious gaps in the person's orientation to reality.

Preparation of Affect

Freud (1894, p. 58) initially included in his concept of repression the disconnection of thoughts from feelings, a distinct process he later named isolation of affect: A person pays attention to experiences that would be expected to cause emotionality, but reports feeling no emotion (Freud, 1926, pp. 120–122, 163–164). This may be understood as an example of precommitment if we notice the effect that an emotion has on subsequent motivation. It is commonly recognized that basic emotions such as anger, sexual arousal, and fear are, up to a point, vicious circles. After the emotion has been aroused, there is a lower threshold for further emotional activity of the same kind, until some satiation point has been reached (Skinner, 1953, pp. 235–236, 239–240). If a person expects an emotion to make an otherwise unpreferred reward temporarily dominant, he or she may commit him or herself to forgo the reward through early inhibition of that emotion.

Early inhibition of affects is probably a powerful means of precommitment, although this device costs whatever reward is dependent on that affect for its consumption. For instance, the person who controls sexual temptations by the early avoidance of sexual affects runs the risk of losing the capacity for sexual enjoyment.

A person can also decrease the attractiveness of a particular activity by cultivating a contradictory affect. For instance, when entering a situation he or she expects to provoke unwanted tender feelings, the person might forestall these feelings by summoning up rage at the earliest opportunity. Conversely, a person who is worried about rage might cultivate tender feelings. Examples of this device have been discussed under the name "reversal of affect" (A. Freud, 1966, pp. 20–40; Freud, 1915, pp. 126–127). This device has also been proposed by behavior therapists (who call it "covert sensitization") as a means of spoiling a person's appetite for addicting substances (Cautela, 1967). It seems to represent a special case of general strategy: finding activities that reduce one's appetite for, or increase one's appetite for the alternative to, a particular reward. This general strategy has been called reaction formation (A. Freud, 1966, pp. 37–38; Freud, 1926, pp. 157–158).

The disadvantage of this strategy is that the activities that counteract a particular temptation may not happen to be otherwise productive. The need to maintain a close balance of emotions might greatly reduce the person's reward-getting efficiency.

Private Rules

The three kinds of precommitment already mentioned do not seem to account for the kind of impulse control we call will power, which allows a person to resist impulses while being both attracted by them and able to pursue them. To do this people seem to make private rules that group their temptations into sets, so that each choice involving a temptation becomes a precedent predicting all future choices within the set. By this perceptual change, we are able to stake our expectation of reaching some major goal against each small step in the wrong direction. An overeater, for instance, may adopt a diet that each act of eating must either violate or not violate; thereafter any act of overeating would lead not only to a small gain in weight but to a major fall in the person's expectation of sticking to the diet in the future. This tactic of staking the credibility of a long-term goal on each choice that threatens it has been described as will power, acting on principle, making promises to the self, and beta control (Kanfer & Karoly, 1972). It does not correspond to any single psychodynamic defense mechanism, but seems to be at the heart of what are called "compulsive controls."

Private rules can be distinguished from ordinary rules of thumb by the asymmetrical motivational pressure they focus on each relevant choice. A person has no great tendency to break a rule of thumb, for instance, not to order yellow vegetables in restaurants because they are usually bland. If the person decides to order them, he or she risks nothing but current enjoyment, which will govern his or her keeping or changing the rule. If the person, however, feels an urge to order dessert despite a private rule not to eat rich food, and gives in to the urge even once, the precedent will damage his or her subsequent ability to follow the rule. "Every gain on the wrong side undoes the effect of many conquests on the right" (Bain, 1886, p. 440).

Private rules depend a great deal on the particular arrangement of those facts outside of the person's control that are potential truce lines between long- and short-term interests. This is so because even a powerful long-term interest, which the person would never choose to abandon all at once, can be defeated by the gradual growth of exceptions. In any given choice governed by a rule, the person's long-term interest is to say, "It's a matter of principle," whereas the short-term interest proposes, "Just this once." If the proposed exception produces a greater expectation of imminent reward than an expectation of fall in aggregate, discounted future reward, it will succeed, and in all probability be institutionalized as a loophole: "I always get drunk on New Year's Eve." "We mustn't stint expenses on Johnny's birthday." "It's all right to vent aggression against blacks (whites, orientals, etc.)—they don't count."

This fourth strategy, making private rules, seems to be the most effective means of precommitment. Unfortunately it is also subject to the most complex and far-reaching side effects.

Overuse of private rules can be expected to produce compulsive symptoms. The interdependency of the relevant choices transforms a diffuse array of decisions into a single, highly charged dichotomy, which results in more consistent behavior toward temptation. People with little skill at formulating rules or who believe themselves to face unusually strong impulses might compensate for these problems by increasing the scope of their private rules. Increasing the tendency to classify their behaviors as legitimate or not would give their experience a dry, rational, lawyerly quality, since they would choose their actions less and less for their intrinsic value, and more according to whether they met the terms of a rule. Increasing the interdependency of their rules would give every choice a cataclysmic, life-or-death quality, since the expectation of being able to resist a wide realm of impulses would be riding on it. They would be likely to make a diehard stand on a small matter of principle, even if the case at hand exemplified the principle only by the most far-fetched flight of symbolism, since they would incur an enormous fall in expectations if they perceived themselves to have violated any component rule. They would come to feel that they acted at great peril, and begin to examine each choice with such care as to render themselves utterly indecisive.

Even a moderate user of private rules will realistically fear that he or she has reduced the ability to control impulses after a lapse. A frequent response will be to evade the information that so alters the person's expectations: (1) He or she may fail to notice the information (i.e., repress it) or fail to relate it to the rest of his or her knowledge (i.e., deny it). This activity could seriously undermine the ability to control himself or herself with rules. (2) The person may stop trying to follow the rule in its original form, but "regress" to a less difficult rule, thereby abandoning an area of functioning to the sway of a short-term interest. For example, a person who normally resists thoughts of danger while driving, or self-conscious feelings while talking in public, or the urge for a cigarette under social pressure, may have his or her will "broken" by a conspicuous failure in one of these endeavors. If the person preserves related rules by abandoning the one in question, he or she is apt to experience a loss of control of these urges when driving, or talking in public, or facing smoking peers. They will form large, stable loopholes. If such loopholes do not go on to destroy the entire rule, they may form circumscribed lacunae in the person's impulse controls, which may even be experienced as an automatism or irresistible urge. The person "automatically" will panic in traffic, freeze while speaking, or reach for a cigarette. In such a lacuna, it will be very hard for a long-term interest to retrieve enough credibility to bet against subsequent urges. An encapsulated symptom will persist.

Any of these four precommitting tactics—outside controls, diversion of attention, preparation of emotion, and private rules—may also become maladaptive if the person misidentifies too many motives as being counter to long-run interests. If a person feels endangered by any temptation to get angry, for instance, or by normal hunger or sexual desire or spontaneous emotion, then attempts at self-control will bring less satisfaction rather than more, and a therapist who tries to strengthen those controls will find the patient strangely unmotivated to cooperate. Furthermore, the person who rules out all anger may find that this rule is sometimes overwhelmed when he or she drinks, leading the person to distinguish periods of drinking from the rest of experience as a permanent loophole where the rule against anger is ineffective. If he or she then seeks help to control the drinking, even measures taken well in advance of the opportunity to drink may not be adequately motivated, since their effect is to shore up the original, over-inclusive rule against anger. The therapist needs to be alert for precommitting devices that cost more than they are worth.

A CRITICAL TAXONOMY OF OVERT MANIPULATIVE TECHNIQUES

The groundwork has now been laid to organize manipulative techniques in terms of how they help the patient forestall temporary preferences.

Analytically oriented therapy seems to follow two strategies in a variable proportion: (1) to reduce the patient's defensiveness against the objective perception of reality, defensiveness that particularly distorts those aspects that engender guilt; and (2) to arrange reexposure to situations that bring ego-dystonic motivational pressure to bear, so as to improve the patient's skill at defense in the other sense of the word—against impulses. Overt manipulation can have a role in both strategies.

In the first strategy, the use of behavioral exercises to spotlight resistance has already been described. Structured teaching about the patient's guilt and maladaptive reaction to it will be described under "cognitive therapy." The latter therapy, however, seems to offer not a supplement to the insight-fostering techniques described elsewhere in this book, but rather an ostensibly more rapid alternative. Regarding the second strategy, exercises to guide corrective emotional experience have also been mentioned. These are now discussed in more detail, according to the apparent site of action of the impulse-controlling skills they develop. They seem to be compatible with insight-oriented techniques.

There has not been enough study of overt manipulation within insight-oriented therapy to permit an account of which combinations work, on whom, and when. There are now reports, however, of numerous manipulations undertaken by themselves as definitive therapies. Many of these reports are quantitative, and some even controlled, with long-term follow-up. Since this literature by no means shows that "all have won and all must have prizes," it is worth reviewing before one combines any given manipulation with nondirective technique.

Extrapsychic Tactics

Since Ulysses had himself tied to the mast to sail past the Sirens, a large number of extrapsychic precommitting tactics have been described. Their active principle is either physical or social.

Physical measures have been directed mainly at the addictions. Where they have been evaluated as sole therapies, their success has been limited. Disulfiram cannot usually sustain sobriety over periods of months (Fuller & Roth, 1979), appetite suppressants are ineffective (Munro, 1979), and methadone, although able to maintain large numbers of addicts heroin-free (Bale et al., 1980), itself induces an ego-dystonic state. However, combination with a broad behavior therapy program aimed at social behaviors has been reported to raise the six-month sobriety rate for disulfiram dramatically, to nearly 100 percent (Azrin et al., 1982).

Inducing illness to spoil the appetite for a substance (oversmoking, alcohol + emetine) has sometimes been reported to be successful, but only as part of a larger program of therapy (Bernstein & Glasgow, 1979; Nathan & Goldman, 1979). As has been noted, a simple resort to classical conditioning as an explanation is probably inadequate. An empirical answer is lacking. The noxious experience may give patients a vivid, unpleasant memory they can rehearse when faced with temptation, but only if they are motivated to do so. Such a memory would resemble the "coverants" that will be described later. In a similar way, some homosexuals have been reported to change their sexual preferences after shock paired with homosexual stimuli, but only if their homosexuality was dystonic for them to begin with (Birk, 1971).

Such gadgets as refrigerator locks and timed cigarette cases, are usually proposed as part of a multiple-treatment approach and have not been evaluated separately. Drugs to control pain and fear should be mentioned here; these sometimes are beneficial but often are insufficient in themselves to eliminate "pain behavior" (Fordyce & Steger, 1979) and phobic avoidance (Marks, 1976).

Social contingencies are also directed mainly at addictions, but sometimes at sellouts. Side betting—that is, contracting with a therapist, family member, or other monitor to forfeit something of value if the person indulges in the bad habit—has been said in case reports to work, but neither controlled studies nor large numbers of cases have been available. An exception is Paxton (1981), who found that contracts not to smoke were effective while in force, as long as the side bet was large enough. Adherence to a course of therapy itself has been increased by making it necessary for the refund of a deposit (St. Lawrence, 1981). In contrast to therapist contracts, self-help groups that bring social influence to bear on the behavior have been remarkably successful for alcoholism (Alford, 1980) and seem to be effective in opiate abuse (Nurco & Makofsky, 1981), overeating (Anonymous, 1981), gambling (Scodel, 1964), and social regression in mental patients (Low, 1976). They also have time-tested applications in the forms of monastic and other religious groups for people concerned with character traits such as pride and selfishness, and the armed forces for those concerned with timidity.

Social contingencies are not much used to control very brief preferences. Perhaps itches and pains are too immediately available to their sufferers and/or too concealable for social influence to be an effective countermeasure.

The virtue of extrapsychic therapies is that they are direct and can often be controlled or verified by the therapist or third parties. However, they are also potentially the most destructive of a therapeutic alliance. The creation of external forces that interfere with temporary preferences may tempt the patient to drop internal efforts at self-control. Thus the therapist may find he or she is speaking for the patient's long-term interest in opposition to the patient, who comfortably speaks for the short-term interest. This seeming advocacy by the therapist of one side of the patient's ambivalence may be avoided by serving only as a source of information to the patient, and letting the patient do any actual contracting with others. If the therapist thus retains a nonvoting status in the patient's life, there is no reason he or she cannot conduct an analytically oriented therapy at the same time. The therapist could, for instance, explore the role of a patient's smoking in rebelling from authority while at the same time administering an oversmoking program, so long as the patient's genuine control of the options is clarified where needed.

These extrapsychic procedures tend not to internalize and usually have to be continued indefinitely if they are to be effective (Ayllon & Azrin, 1968; Paxton, 1981).

Attention Control

The tactic of attention control involves keeping oneself from noticing information that an unwanted but seductive reward is available. It is effective mainly against painlike activities. Good hypnotic subjects are capable of gating out even intense pain (Hilgard & Hilgard, 1975); since a hypnotist is not always needed to guide the hypnotic process after the patient has learned self-hypnosis, this is classified as an intrapsychic process. Many patients obtain relief from dental and obstetrical pains with attention-patterning exercises (Howitt & Stricker, 1966; Melzack et al., 1963). A common-sense way of dealing with phobias is to direct attention away from where the phobic object might be (e.g., "Don't look down"), but this is obviously a stopgap tactic, and results with direct hypnotic suggestion for phobias have been disappointing (Schneck, 1954; Wolberg, 1948).

Attention control is intuitively appealing to many people as a way of controlling temporary preferences with longer dominant periods as well. Cautionary phrases such as "Speak of the devil and he'll appear" advise people to "forget about" temptations or keep their minds occupied, and there are religions that teach that to sin in fantasy is tantamount to sinning in deed. This approach, however, is of dubious value for temporary preferences with longer dominant periods than pains have, and there seems to be little clinicians can add to patients' intuitive knowledge. The behavior therapy technique called "stimulus control" might seem to use this approach, but actually does not. Patients with addictive disorders are advised to avoid reminders of the availability of the target activity: not to subscribe to betting sheets, not to window shop in stores that sell fattening foods, not to watch people drinking alcohol, and so forth (Goldiamond, 1965; Kanfer, 1975). But these usually involve changing the actual environment rather than simply directing attention and are thus properly members of the extrapsychic category. They are almost always recommended as part of a larger program of precommitting tactics and have not been evaluated singly.

Rather than finding more ways a patient could use attention control, therapists are more often faced with a patient's overuse of this approach, leading to serious gaps in his or her self-knowledge.

Preparation of Affect

This tactic involves early inhibition of emotions that would foster temporary preferences if allowed to gain momentum, or the cultivation of emotions that are apt to have the contrary effect. There has been little written about reducing the appetite for maladaptive activities by nipping it in the bud. Wolpe's (1969) thought-stopping technique might sometimes serve this purpose against activities in the itch range. The obsessional patient is told to be alert to the beginnings of any characteristic obsessions and to say "stop," aloud or silently upon detecting one. The activity being avoided, however, is usually the problem behavior itself, not the beginning of a larger temptation to come, and Wolpe's therapy just teaches the patient to make a private rule against symptomatic thinking in much the same way as if it were an overt behavior. With regard to affects that are in danger of growing, it is probably hard for a therapist to augment a patient's own intuitive sense that one should not try to cultivate them. Indeed patients are apt to carry this spontaneous stratagem too far, producing isolation of affect.

On the other hand, many strategies have been described to undermine unwanted appetites by cultivating a contradictory process. Classical conditioning originally seemed an ideal method of doing this, perhaps even going so far as to extinguish the appetites themselves. Just as basic research was questioning the existence of conditioning as a principle of choice, however, clinical trials were showing that conditioning techniques cannot change appetites, even though they are said to be moderately successful in helping patients change their behavior. Gradual reexposure to a phobic stimulus while the patient relaxes has been a successful treatment for phobias, supposedly through the extinction of a conditioned fear (Rachman, 1968) or conditioning of a response (relaxation) incompatible with fear (Wolpe, 1969); but the relaxation itself has not proved to be a necessary element of the therapy, which requires only regular practice in approaching the phobic object (Marks, 1978). Likewise, conditioning techniques have been unable to create enough aversion to drinking, smoking, or homosexuality to make them effective as the sole therapy for these behaviors; conditioned responses themselves are rarely documented in reports of these trials (Wilson, 1978; Hunt & Matarazzo, 1973; Lichtenstein & Danaher, 1976; Clairborn et al., 1972). Where this therapy works, it seems to do so despite the failure of the supposedly conditioned pathological appetite to extinguish. The fact that placing the punishment *before* the response seems to work as well as after argues against the occurrence of true conditioning (McConaghy & Barr, 1973).

Although the pairing of the target activity with aversive experiences has not proved sufficient to erase appetites, some success has been reported with giving patients a behavior to counteract the appetite each time it is in danger of occurring. This is the point of "habit reversal," a technique aimed at itchlike activities. The bruxist is taught to react to the urge to grind his or her teeth, for instance, when it first appears, or even when circumstances make it likely to appear, by engaging in a contradictory activity such as tightening the masseter muscle (Rosenbaum & Ayllon, 1981; Azrin & Nunn, 1973). Similar tactics have been found to work in controlled studies of mouth biting, lip sucking, and similar habits (Azrin et al., 1982) and in compulsive hair pulling (Rosenbaum, 1981).

Temptations with longer dominant periods are undermined in fantasy by the covert operant or "coverant," an emotionally evocative image a patient is advised to entertain when it is needed to interfere with a target appetite (Homme, 1965; Cautela & Bennett, 1981). A patient trying to give up smoking, for instance, would be advised to imagine that the cigarette smoke was automobile exhaust or some other disgusting substance. The target behaviors are mostly addictions; in fact, Cautela has said that he deliberately conceived the therapy to deal with the addictions (Cautela & Bennett, 1981). It seems to act by custom-designing an array of disgusting or deflating images like those that obsessional patients spontaneously think of when faced with sexual or other temptations. These images, which temporarily compel attention because of their vividness, represent a sort of iatrogenic itch, which might also be the mechanism of the ostensible conditioning therapies; when imagined and actual punishments for unwanted homosexual urges were compared recently, they were equally effective (McConaghy et al., 1981). Obsessional persistence of these images could conceivably be a side effect of covert sensitization as a therapy, but examples of this problem have not been reported. However, because of the emotional charge of these images, the therapist who wants also to do nondirective work with the patient should probably be careful that the patient supply them himself or herself rather than take examples from the therapist. Furthermore, the evidence thus far is that coverant techniques do not do as well as techniques requiring actual practice, and should not be substituted for them when actual practice is possible (Kazdin, 1977).

The converse of covert sensitization is covert reinforcement, the cultivation of activities that are desirable in their own right (Cautela & Bennett, 1981). Positive affects that have habitually lost out to unwanted ones have been reported to regain the advantage if rehearsed systematically. For instance, a patient who has completed assertiveness training may find that the assertiveness itself inhibits anxious or depressive modes of thought (Galassi et al., 1975; Liberman et al., 1976). Wolpe's (1969) belief that systematic relaxation inhibited the onset of phobic anxiety through "reciprocal inhibition" has already been discussed. Assignment of specific exercises to strengthen key behaviors does not interfere with insight-oriented therapy, and was in fact developed within the latter school before it was proposed by behavior therapists (Herzberg, 1947). Insofar as the patient has previously been afraid of these behaviors, a regular regimen of practice also represents systematic exposure, a rule-rebuilding technique to be described presently.

Private Rules

This tactic involves the classification of single choices as precedents for larger categories of choice, so that each single decision affects the person's expectancy of a long-range, cumulative outcome. Private rules are less tangible than the other tactics against temporary preferences, and for that reason authors who deal with impulse control tend to neglect them or to describe them in terms of concrete operations. Nevertheless they are probably the most effective and flexible form of self-control. They have been used against temporary preferences of all durations. They seem to be the only practical approach, aside from some social precommitments described earlier, to controlling sellouts.

Therapy to improve the operation of private rules is directed at either of two problems: (1) The patient has broken a rule repeatedly, leading to formation of an encapsulated area where his or her will seems to have no power; or (2) the patient's rules have been formed badly, so that they forbid rewards under too few or too many circumstances, or in the wrong circumstances.

1. The process of restoring a rule after it has lost its credibility requires the patient (a) to have a series of experiences in which the patient observes himself or herself, following the rule, and/or (b) to change in some conspicuous way so that the patient's past behavior does not seem to predict future behavior.

2. Giving the patient successes generally means restricting the degree of challenge to the rule by limiting its scope. Alcoholics Anonymous recommends limiting resolutions of sobriety to one day at a time. Therapists dealing with phobias reintroduce the phobic object gradually in such a way that the patient does not run away from it—a class of treatment called systematic exposure or desensitization. The first desensitizations of phobias tried to build up private rules against the fear response itself, calling for relaxation in the face of exposure to increasingly evocative phobic objects; but dealing with the emotional response has not been found to be as effective as dealing with the retreat from the feared object (Marks, 1978). As with covert imagery, the vicarious treatment is less effective than the treatment involving actual practice. The latter approach does not try to overcome the fear response itself, but systematic prevention of avoidance behavior seems to achieve that result. In a similar way, chronic pain has been treated effectively by eliminating the patient's pain-associated behaviors (Fordyce & Steger, 1979).

Reducing the tendency to panic by using medication during reintroduction of the phobic object has been found not to impede the progress of this approach (Hafner & Marks, 1976). The technique of flooding, or implosion, reduces the urge to panic by giving such prolonged exposure to the phobic object that the urge habituates, permitting the patient to see himself or herself facing the object calmly. Flooding has been found to be sometimes as effective as gradual reintroduction but no more so, only in some patients, and only as long as the patient does not withdraw before the fear has attenuated (Gelder, 1975; Marks et al., 1971).

With symptoms in the itch area, the tactic of strengthening self-control by giving the patient experience with a habituated temptation is called paradoxical intention. The patient with a compulsive ritual is advised to overpractice it, or the patient with an obsessional worry about fainting is told to try to faint (Frankl, 1960). As has been noted, overpractice has been used with addictions, too, but only when it can induce actual aversion; the strategy of giving the will practice with a fatigued opponent is probably not practical at that end of the continuum.

In doing systematic exposure, some therapists train not only relaxation but active mental exploration of the anxiety-provoking situation and of the responses open to the patient, thus supposedly "inoculating" the patient with stress (Meichenbaum, 1976) so that varied encounters with stimuli for fear (Goldfried, 1971; Suinn & Richardson, 1971), pain (Levandusky & Pankratz, 1975), anger (Novaco, 1976), or addiction (Chaney et al., 1978) no longer will lead to sudden losses of control. This activity may result in actual restructuring of the person's private rules, which is discussed in the next section.

b. Conspicuous change, a credible new deal for the patient's will, is hard for a therapist to arrange or even suggest, although Alcoholics Anonymous calls for an abrupt change of "persons, places, and things." Perhaps the repetitive rediscoveries of self-help techniques, with new rationales and new terminologies, that fill the therapeutic literature (Corsini, 1981) and nonfiction shelves may also serve this purpose. By the time a patient seeks help, however, he or she has usually exploited the "New Year's resolution" principle to death, a problem that has been dealt with extensively by theology but not by psychotherapeutic writers.

2. During the past decade, techniques of examining and suggesting changes in patients' private rules have developed rapidly. To bring will power to bear on a class of behaviors, it is necessary only for the patient to define the class, that is, to begin to perceive these behaviors as precedents predicting his or her behaviors under the other circumstances within the class. To allow a patient to abandon a rule that costs more than it is worth, it is necessary for that patient to distinguish between that rule and others that should not be abandoned.

The prototype of the newly made rule is the diet, which divides the relevant behaviors into observances and lapses. The mere act of counting the occurrences of an unwanted behavior may create pressure to abandon it by making each occurrence affect an allover count. This effect has been exploited as "self-monitoring," (Broden et al., 1971; Fremouw & Brown, 1980), and has been reported to gain potency if the patient establishes concrete rewards or punishments to be consumed or not, depending on his or her behavior (Mahoney, 1972). The procedure is then called "self-reward" or "self-punishment," but the term is misleading: The patient obviously cannot coin sources of reward that have been otherwise outside of his or her grasp; rather the patient changes a simple rule never to do

X so that it reads, "Never do X without accepting punishment Y." This change might be useful in buffering the rule from being actually broken if the patient is occasionally overwhelmed by temptation (Ainslie, 1975), but otherwise seems to add nothing. The "self-talk" recommended for some immature patients may also work by strengthening personal rules, since it makes categories for self-monitoring inescapably clear (Meichenbaum, 1977). Some therapists have described extensive programs for developing patients' rules under such names as will training, reality therapy, and direct action therapy (Glasser, 1965; Greenwald, 1973). The risk of being too aggressive in this regard is that patients will see the rules as the therapist's demands rather than as proposals to restrain motives they themselves do not want to become dominant. Proponents of these rule-building programs so far have not evaluated this risk.

Because people hesitate to abandon rules for fear that they will see themselves as having broken them, there is a tendency for private rules to become ever more inclusive. Thus a major need for therapy is to free the patient from rules that renounce too much reward. This is the emphasis of the cognitive therapies, which prescribe conscious, logical analyses of the patient's ways of solving problems, and, particularly, of arriving at judgments about oneself (Beck, 1976; Ellis, 1977). Sometimes these seem to be purely didactic, or conflict-free, as when a therapist gives a schizophrenic patient specific information about what which communications sound bizarre to the listener (Meichenbaum, 1977). However, cognitive therapy often seems to impart information, that one would expect to be already in the patient's grasp. Examples of college teachers who commit "logical errors" of overinclusiveness, substituting a part for the whole, and so on, with regard to their self-judgments while otherwise retaining razor-sharp critical faculties cannot represent cases of simple ignorance or naiveté. Rather these patients seem intimidated by the risk of appearing indulgent toward their impulses, and, therefore, to classify most examples of enjoyment as dangerous precedents just to be on the safe side. Their therapy involves discrediting the most inhibiting rules according to announced principles, so that these patients will not fear that their rules will completely unravel.

In examining the most fundamental private rules, such as those restricting fantasy and other autistic activities ("reality testing") and those that establish the conditions for self-esteem, cognitive techniques begin to resemble clarification and interpretation. They represent an attempt to bypass the long, Socratic ripening process required for interpretation, by finding distortions that can be demonstrated to patients from their spontaneous speech. It is not clear to what extent the benefits of persuasiveness and speed are offset by a tendency for patients to form dictionary insights.

Existing manuals of cognitive therapy take little notice of motivation, and thus of motivational conflict. They present no hypotheses about how maladaptive cognitions form, other than simple error; they do not describe resistances to changing these cognitions or guidelines for selecting which cognitions are more apt to be of clinical importance. At the moment cognitive therapy constitutes little more than permission for behaviorally oriented therapists to experiment with insight-oriented techniques. Because of the similarity of its operations to clarification and interpretation, it probably should not be combined with traditional psychodynamic procedures, lest the patient became confused about just how much initiative he or she is supposed to take. As experience clarifies the motivational "economics" of cognition, however, cognitive therapy may develop concepts and procedures that can be incorporated effectively into short-term dynamic therapies.

SUMMARY

Psychotherapy is the psychological treatment of ambivalence. Diverse therapeutic strategies have arisen from different theories about why people sometimes remain ambivalent despite adequate familiarity with the available choices. Most of these theories fit into one of three categories: (1) repression, (2) classical conditioning, or (3) superstitious or otherwise misguided operant learning. This chapter has not tried to resolve the differences in these theories; rather, manipulative techniques have been discussed in terms of how they deal with the most disruptive aspect of ambivalence—temporary preference for alternatives that are generally unpreferred. Four ranges of duration of temporary preference are distinguished: sellouts (slowest), addictions, itches, and pains (fastest).

Many *covert* manipulations are used in the insight-oriented psychotherapies, that is, those therapies that try to correct distortions of motivation caused by the operation of the defense mechanisms. These distortions may be a basic cause of ambivalence, as Freud held; alternatively, they may be side effects of a frequent tactic to counteract ambivalence, the making of private rules. In any case, insight-oriented therapists have used varying amounts of covert manipulation to improve their patients' motivation for treatment or to elicit demonstrable examples of the patients' motivational conflicts.

Overt manipulations—that is, those that are discussed with the patient—either give the patient some means of precommitting his or her choices in advance to forestall these temporary preferences, or, more naturally, teach the patient how to improve spontaneous precommitting tactics. Four kinds of tactics are discussed: extrapsychic tactics, control of attention, preparation of emotion, and private rules. Some should be more compatible with insight-oriented therapy than others, but the actual trial of such therapeutic combinations has just begun. The careful avoidance of coercion, in fact and in appearance, may permit both the use of insight-producing techniques and the direct teaching of impulse-forestalling skills within the same therapy.

REFERENCES

Adler, C., and Morrissey-Adler, S. Strategies in general psychiatry. In: J.J. Basmajian (Ed.), *Biofeedback: Principles and practice for clinicians*. Baltimore, Md.: Williams & Wilkins, 1979.

Ainslie, G. Specious reward: A behavioral theory of impulsiveness and impulse control. *Psychological Bulletin*, 1975, *82*, 463–496.

Ainslie, G. A behavioral economic approach to the defense mechanisms: Freud's energy theory revisited. *Social Science Information*, 1982, *21*, 735–779.

Ainslie, G. Behavioral economics II: Motivated, involuntary behavior. *Social Science Information*, 1984, *23*, 247–274.

Ainslie, G. Aversion with only one factor, In: M. Commons, J.A. Nevin, and H. Rachlin (Eds.), *The effects of delay and of intervening events on reinforcement value*. Cambridge, Mass.: Ballinger (in press).

Ainslie, G., and Engel, B. Alteration of classically conditioned heart rate by operant reinforcement in monkeys. *Journal of Comparative and Physiological Psychology*, 1974, *87*, 373–382.

Ainslie, G., and Haendel, V. The motives of the will. In: E. Gottheil, T. Skoloda, H. Waxman, and K. Druley (Eds.), *Etiologic aspects of alcohol and drug abuse*. Springfield, Ill.: Charles C. Thomas, 1983.

Ainslie, G., and Herrnstein, R. Preference reversal and delayed reinforcement. *Animal Learning and Behavior*, 1981, *9*, 476–482.

Alexander, F. *Fundamentals of psychoanalysis*. New York: W.W. Norton, 1948.

Alexander, F. The dynamics of psychotherapy in the light of learning theory. *American Journal of Psychiatry*, 1963, *120*, 440–448.

Alford, G.S. Alcoholics Anonymous: An empirical outcome study. *Addictive Behaviors*, 1980, *5*, 359–370.

Anonymous. Overeaters Anonymous: A self-help group. *American Journal of Nursing*, March 1981.

Applebaum, S.A. A psychoanalyst looks at gestalt therapy. In C. Hatcher and P. Himmelstein (Eds.), *The handbook of gestalt therapy*. New York: Jason Aronson, 1976.

Atnip, G. Stimulus and response-reinforcer contingincies in autoshaping, operant, classical, and omission training procedures in rats. *Journal of the Experimental Analysis of Behavior*, 1977, *28*, 59–69.

Aull, G. and Strean, H. The analyst's silence. In J. Lindon (Ed.), *The psychiatric forum*, vol. 2. New York: International Universities Press, 1967, pp. 81–87.

Ayllon, T. and Azrin, N. *The Token economy: A motivational system for therapy and rehabilitation*. New York: Appleton Century Crofts, 1968.

Azrin, N., and Nunn R. Habit reversal: A method of eliminating nervous habits. *Behavior Research and Therapy*, 1973, *11*, 619–628.

Azrin, N., Nunn R., and Frantz-Renshaw, S. Habit reversal vs. negative practice treatment of self-destructive oral habits (biting, chewing, or licking of the lips, cheeks, tongue, or palate). *Journal of Behavior Therapy and Experimental Psychiatry*, 1982, *13*, 49–54.

Azrin, N., Sisson, R. Meyers, R., and Godley, M. Alcoholism treatment by disulfiram and community reinforcement therapy. *Journal of Behavior Therapy and Experimental Psychiatry*, 1982, *13*, 105–112.

Bain, A. *The emotions and the will.* New York: Appleton, 1886.

Bale, K., Van Stone, W., Ruldan, J., Engeling, T., Elashoff, R., and Zarcone, V. Therapeutic communities vs. methadone maintenance: A prospective controlled study of narcotic addiction treatment design with a 1 year follow-up. *Archives of General Psychistry*, 1980, *37*, 179–193.

Baum, W. Time allocation in human vigilance. *Journal of the Experimental Analysis of behavior*, 1975, *23*, 45–53.

Beck, A. *Cognitive therapy and the emotional disorders.* New York: International Universities Press, 1976.

Beecher, H. *Measurement of subjective responses.* New York: Oxford, 1959.

Bernstein, D.A., and Glasgow, R.E. Smoking. In: O.F. Pomerleau and J.P. Brady (Eds.), *Behavioral medicine: Theory and practice.* Baltimore, Md.: Williams & Wilkins, 1979, pp. 233–254.

Bibring, E., Psychoanalysis and the dynamic psychotherapies. *Journal of the American Psychoanalytic Association*, 1954, *2*, 745–770.

Birk, L Behavior therapy: Integration with dynamic psychiatry. *Behavior Therapy*, 1970, *1*, 522–526.

Birk, L., Huddleston, W., Miller, E., and Cohler, B. Avoidance conditioning for homosexuality. *Archives of General Psychiatry*, 1971, *25*, 314–323.

Brady, J.P. Psychotherapy by a combined behavioral and dynamic approach. *Comprehensive Psychiatry*, 1968, *9*, 536–543.

Breuer, J., and Freud, S. (1895) *Studies on Hysteria.* In: J. Strachey and A. Freud (Eds.), The *standard edition of the complete psychological works of Sigmund Freud*, Vol 2. London: Hogarth Press, 1956.

Brockbank, R. On the analyst's silence in psychoanalysis: A synthesis of intrapsychic content and interpersonal manifestations. *International Journal of Psychoanalysis*, 1970, *51*, 457–464.

Broden, M., Hall, V., and Mitts, B. The effect of self-recording on the classroom behavior of two eighth grade students. *Journal of Applied Behavior Analysis*, 1971, *4*, 191.

Cautela, J. Covert sensitization. *Psychological Reports*, 1967, *20*, 459–468.

Cautela, J., and Bennett, A. Covert conditioning. In: R.J. Corsini (Ed.), *Handbook of innovative psychotherapies.* New York: Wiley, 1981, pp. 189–204.

Chaney, E., O'Leary, M., and Marlatt, G.A. Skill training with alcoholics. *Journal of Consulting and Clinical Psychology*, 1978, *46*, 1092–1104.

Clairborn, W., Lewis, P., and Humble, S. Stimulus satiation and smoking: A revisit. *Journal of Clinical Psychology*, 1972, *28*, 416–419.

Cohen, D. *J.B. Watson: The founder of behaviorism* London: Routledge & Kegan Paul, 1979.

Coleman, S., and Gormezano, K. Classical conditioning and the law of effect: History and empirical assessment. *Behaviorism*, 1979, *7*, 1–33.

Conn, J.H. The myth of coercion through hypnosis. *International Journal of Clinical and Experimental Hypnosis*, 1981, *29*, 95–100.

Corsini, R.J. (Ed.) *Current psychotherapies.* Itasca, Ill: Peacodk, 1973.

Corsini, R.J. (Ed.) *Handbook of innovative psychotherapies.* New York: Wiley, 1981.

deVilliers, P., and Herrnstein, R. Toward a law of response strength. *Psychological Bulletin*, 1976, *83*, 1131–1158.

Dollard, J., and Miller, N. *Personality and psychotherapy*. New York: McGraw-Hill, 1950.

Ellis, A. The basic clinical theory of rational-emotive therapy. In: A. Ellis and R. Grieger (Eds.), *Handbook of rational emotive therapy*. New York: Springer, 1977, pp. 3–34.

Erdelyi, M.H. A new look at the new look: Perceptual defense and vigilence. *Psychological Review*, 1974, *81*, 1–25.

Eysenck, H.J. *Fact and fiction in psychology*. Harmondsworth, England: Penguin, 1965.

Eysenck, H.J. Learning theory and behavior therapy. *Journal of Mental Science*, 1979, *105*, 61–75.

Eysenck, H.J. (Ed.) *Behavior therapy and the neuroses*. New York: Pergamon, 1960.

Eysenck, H.J., and Rachman, S. *The causes and cures of neurosis*. San Diego, Calif.: Knapp, 1965.

Farwell, B. *Queen Victoria's little wars*. New York: Harper, 1972.

Feather, B., and Rhoads, J. Psychodynamic behavior therapy: Clinical aspects. *Archives of General Psychiatry*, 1972, *26*, 503–311.

Ferenczi, S. (1920) The further development of an active therapy in psychoanalysis. In *Further contributions to the theory and technique of psychoanalysis*, London: Hogarth, 1950.

Fordyce, W.E., and Steger, J.C. Chronic pain. In: O.F. Pomerleau and J.P. Brady (Eds.), *Behavioral medicine: Theory and practice*. Baltimore, Md.: Williams & Wilkins, 1979, pp. 125–154.

Frankl, V. Paradoxical intention: A logotherapeutic technique. *American Journal of Psychotherapy*, 1960, *14*, 520–535.

Fremouw, W.J., and Brown, J.P. The reactivity of addictive behaviors to self-monitoring: A functional analysis. *Addictive Behaviors*, 1980, *5*, 209–217.

Freud, A. *The ego and the mechanisms of defense*. New York: International Universities Press, 1966.

Freud, S. (1894) Project for scientific psychology. In: J. Strachey and A. Freud (Eds.), *The standard edition of the complete psychological works of Sigmund Freud*, Vol.1. London: Hogarth Press, 1956.

Freud S. (1911) Formulations on the two principles of mental functioning. *Standard* edition, Vol. 12. London: Hogarth Press, 1956.

Freud, S. (1913) On beginning the treatment. *Standard edition*, Vol. 12. London: Hogarth Press, 1956.

Freud, S. (1914a) Remembering, repeating, and working through. *Standard edition*, Vol. 12. London: Hogarth Press, 1956.

Freud, S. (1914b) On the history of the psycho-analytic movement. *Standard edition*, Vol. 14. London: Hogarth Press, 1956.

Freud, S. (1915) Instincts and their vicissitudes. *Standard edition*, Vol. 14. London: Hogarth Press, 1956.

Freud, S. (1918) From the history of an infantile neurosis. *Standard edition*, Vol. 17. London: Hogarth Press, 1956.

Freud, S. (1919) Lines of advance in psycho-analytical therapy. *Standard edition*, Vol. 17, London: Hogarth Press, 1956.

Freud, S. (1920a) Beyond the pleasure principle. *Standard edition*, Vol. 18. London: Hogarth Press, 1956.

Freud, S. (1920b) Memorandum on the electrical treatment of war neurotics. *Standard edition*, Vol. 17. London: Hogarth Press, 1956.

Freud, S. (1925) An autobiographical study. *Standard edition*, Vol. 20. London: Hogarth Press, 1956.

Freud, S. (1926) Inhibitions, symptoms and anxiety. *Standard edition*, Vol. 20. London: Hogarth Press, 1956.

Fuller, R.K., and Roth, H.P. Disulfiram for the treatment of alcoholism. *Annals of Internal Medicine*, 1979, *90*, 901–904.

Galassi, J.P., Kostka, M.D., and Galassi, M.D. Assertive training: A one year follow-up. *Journal of Counseling Psychology*, 1975, 451–452.

Gambrill, E., Behavior modification. In: *Handbook of assessment, intervention and evaluation*. San Francisco: Jossey-Bass, 1977.

Garfield, S. Eclecticism and integration in psychotherapy. *Behavior Therapy*, 1982, *13*, 610–623.

Gelder, M. Flooding: Results and problems from a new treatment for anxiety. In: T. Thompson and W.S. Dockens (Eds.), *Applications of behavior modification*. New York: Academic, 1975.

Glasser, W. *Reality therapy*. New York: Harper & Row, 1965.

Glover, E. *The technique of psychoanalysis*. New York: International Universities Press, 1955.

Goldfried, M. Systematic desensitization as training in self-control. *Journal of Consulting and Clinical Psychology*, 1971, *37*, 228–234.

Goldiamond, I. Self-control procedures in personal behavior problems. *Psychological Reports*, 1965, *17*, 851–868.

Greenberg, I. *Psychodrama: Theory and therapy*. New York: Behavioral Publications, 1974.

Greenson, R. *The technique and practice of psychoanalysis*. New York: International Universities Press, 1967.

Greenwald, H. *Direct decision therapy*. San Diego, Calif.: Edits, 1973.

Hafner, J., and Marks, I. Exposure in vivo of agoraphobics: The contributions of diazepam, group exposure and anxiety evocation. *Psychological Medicine*, 1976, *6*, 71–88.

Haley, J. *Strategies of psychotherapy*. New York: Grune & Stratton, 1963.

Haveliwala, Y., Scheflen, A., and Ashcraft, R. *Common sense in therapy: A handbook for the mental health worker*. New York: Brunner-Mazel, 1979.

Havens, L. *Participant observation*. New York: Aronson, 1976.

Hearst, E. The classical-instrumental distinction: Reflexes, voluntary behavior and categories of associative learning. In: W. Estes (Ed.), *Handbook of learning and cognitive processes*. Hillsdale, N.J.: Erlbaum, 1975.

Herink, R. (Ed.) *The psychotherapy handbook*. New York: Meridian, 1980.

Herson, M. The use of behavior modification techniques within a traditional psychotherapeutic context. *American Journal of Psychotherapy*, 1970, *24*, 308–313.

Herzberg, A. *Active psychotherapy*. New York: Grune & Stratton, 1947.

Hilgard, E. *Divided consciousness: Multiple controls in human thought and action*. New York: John Wiley & Sons, 1977.

Hilgard, E., and Hilgard, J. *Hypnosis in the relief of pain*. Los Altos, Calif.: Kaufmann, 1975.

Homme, L.E. Perspectives in psychology: XXVI. Control of coverants, the operants of the mind. *Psychological Record*, 1965, *15*, 501–511.

Howitt, J.W., and Stricker, G. Objective evaluation of audio analgesia effects. *Journal of the American Dental Association*, 1966, *73*, 874–877.

Hull, C. *Principles of behavior*. New York: Appleton-Century-Crofts, 1943.

Hunt, W., and Matarazzo, J. Three years later: Recent developments in the experimental modification of smoking behavior. *Journal of Abnormal Psychology*, 1973, *81*, 107–114.

Ikard, F., Green, D., and Horn, D. A scale to differentiate between type of smoking as related to the management of affect. *International Journal of the Addictions*, 1969, *4*, 649–659.

Jones, M.C. The elimination of children's fears. *Journal of Experimental Psychology*, 1924, *7*, 382–390.

Kammeier, M., Hoffman, H., and Toper, R. Personality characteristics of alcoholics as college freshmen and at time of treatment. *Quarterly Journal of Studies on Alcohol*, 1973, *34*, 390–399.

Kanfer, F. Self-management methods. In: F. Kanfer and A. Goldstein (Eds.), *Helping people change*. Elmsford, N.Y.: Pergamon, 1975.

Kanfer, R., and Karoly, P. Self control: A behavioristic excursion into the lion's den. *Behavior Therapy*, 1972, *3*, 398–416.

Kazdin, A.E. Research issues in covert conditioning. *Cognitive Therapy and Research*, 1977, *1*, 45–58.

Kazdin, A.E. *History of behavior modification*. Baltimore: University Park, 1978.

Kelly, F.D. Communicational significance of therapist proxemic cues. *Journal of Consulting and Clinical Psychology*, 1972, *39*, 345.

Langs, R.J. *The technique of psychoanalytic psychotherapy*, New York: Aronson, 1974.

Levandusky, P., and Pankratz, L. Self-control techniques as an alternative to pain medication. *Journal of Abnormal Psychology*, 1975, *84*, 165–169.

Leventhal, A.M. Case report: Use of a behavioral approach within a traditional psychotherapeutic context. *Journal of Abnormal Psychology*, 1968, *73*, 178–182.

Liberman, R.P., King, L.W., DeRisi, W.J., and McCann, M. *Personal effectiveness: Guiding people to assert themselves and improve their social skills*. Champaign, Ill.: Research Press, 1976.

Lichtenstein, E., and Danaher, B.G. Modification of smoking behavior: A critical analysis of theory, research and practice. In: M. Hersen, R.M. Eisler, and P.M. Miller (Eds.), *Progress in behavior modification*, Vol. 3. New York: Academic Press, 1976, pp. 70–132.

Licklider, J.C.R. On psychophysiological models. In: W.A. Rosenblith (Ed.), *Sensory communication*. Cambridge, Mass.: M.I.T. Press; New York: Wiley, 1961.

Low, A. *Mental health through will training*. West Hanover, Mass.: Christopher, 1976.

Lowen, A. *Bioenergetics*. New York: Coward, McCann, & Geoghegan, 1975.

Mahoney, M.J. Research issues in self-management. *Behavior Therapy*, 1972, *3*: 45–63.

Marks, I. Psychopharmacology: The use of drugs combined with psychological treatment. In: R. Spitzer and D. Klein (Eds.), *Evaluation of psychological therapies: Behavior therapies, drug therapies and their interactions*. Baltimore: Hopkins, 1976.

Marks, I. Exposure treatments: Clinical applications. In: W.S. Agras (Ed.), *Behavior modification: Principles and clinical applications*. Boston: Little, Brown, 1978, pp. 204–242.

Marks, I., Boulougouris, J., and Marset, P. Flooding in desensitization in phobic disorders. *British Journal of Psychiatry*, 1971, *119*, 353–375.

Marmor, J. Theories of learning and the psychotherapeutic process. *British Journal of Psychiatry*, 1966, *112*, 363–366.

McConoghy, N., Armstrong, M., and Blasczyski, A. Controlled comparison of aversive therapy and covert sensitization in compulsive homosexuality. *Behavior Research and Therapy*, 1981, *19*, 425–434.

McConaghy, and Barr, R. Classical avoidance and backward conditioning therapy of homosexuality. *British Journal of Psychiatry*, 1973, *122*, 151–162.

Meichenbaum, D. A self instructional approach to stress management: A proposal for stress inoculation training. In: C. Spielberger and I. Sarason (Eds.), *Stress and anxiety in modern life.* New York: Winston, 1976.

Meichenbaum, D. *Cognitive behavior modification: An integrative approach.* New York: Plenum, 1977.

Melzack, R., Weisz, A.Z., and Sprague, L.T. Strategems for controlling pain: Contributions of auditory stimulation and suggestion. *Experimental Neurology*, 1963, *8*, 239–247.

Messer, S., and Winokur, M. Some limits to the integration of psychoanalytic and behavior therapy. *American Psychologist*, 1980, *25*, 818–827.

Meyer, R. Conditioning factors in alcoholism. Paper presented at American Psychiatric Association, May 1981.

Mowrer, O.H. On the dual nature of learning—A reinterpretation of "conditioning" and "problem-solving." *Harvard Educational Review*, 1947, *17*, 102–148.

Munro, J. Clinical aspects of the treatment of obesity of drugs: A review. *International Journal of Obesity*, 1979, *3*, 171–180.

Murphy, W. *The tactics of psychotherapy: The application of psychoanalytic theory to psychotherapy.* New York: International Universities Press, 1965.

Murray, E.J. A contact analysis method for studying psychotherapy. *Psychological Monographs*, 1956, *70*, 1–32.

Nathan, P.E., and Goldman, M.S. Problem drinking and alcoholism. In: O.F. Pomerleau and J.P. Brady (Eds.), *Behavioral medicine: Theory and practice.* Baltimore: Williams & Wilkins, 1979.

Novaco, R. The treatment of chronic anger through cognitive and relaxation controls. *Journal of Consulting and Clinical Psychology*, 1976, *44*, 681.

Nurco, D.N., and Makofsky, A. The self-help movement and narcotic addicts. *American Journal of Drug and Alcohol Abuse*, 1981, *8*, 139–151.

Olds, D.D. Stagnation in psychotherapy and the development of active technique, *Psychiatry*, 1981, *44*, 133–140.

Olds, M., and Fobes, J. The central basis of motivation: Intracranial self-stimulation studies. *Annual Review of Psychology*, 1981, *32*, 523–574.

Paxton, R. Deposit contracts with smokers: Varying frequency and amount of repayments. *Behavior Research and Therapy*, 1981, *19*, 117–123.

Rachman, S. *Phobias: Their nature and control.* Springfield, Ill.: Charles C. Thomas, 1968.

Reich, W. (1933) *Character analysis*, 3rd ed., New York: Farrar, Straus, & Giroux, 1972.

Rhoads, J.M., and Feather, B.W. The application of psychodynamics to behavior therapy. *American Journal of Psychiatry*, 1974, *131*, 17–20.

Rioch, J. The transference phenomenon in psychoanalytic therapy. *Psychiatry*, 1943, *6*, 147–156.

Rosenbaum, M. The habit reversal technique in treating trichotillomania. *Behavior Therapy*, 1981, *12*, 473–481.

Rosenbaum, M., and Ayllon, T. Treating bruxism the habit reversal technique. *Behavior Research and Therapy*, 1981, *19*, 87–96.

St. Lawrence, J. Efficacy of a money deposit contingency on clinical outpatients' attendance and participation in assertiveness training. *Journal of Behavior Therapy and Experimental Psychiatry*, 1981, *12*, 237–240.

Schneck, J. The hypnoanalysis of phobic reactions. In: L. Lelson (Ed.), *Experimental hypnosis*. New York: Macmillan, 1954, pp. 465–476.

Schur, M. *Freud: Living and dying*. New York: International Universities Press, 1972.

Scodel, A. Inspirational group therapy: A study of Gamblers Anonymous. *American Journal of Psychotherapy*, 1964, *18*, 111–125.

Scola, D. The hemispheric specialization of the human brain and its applications to psychoanalytic principles. *Jefferson Journal of Psychiatry*, 1984, *2*, 2–11.

Segraves, R.T., and Smith, R.C. Concurrent psychotherapy and behavior therapy. *Archives of General Psychiatry*, 1976, *33*, 756–763.

Shaw, D., and Beck, A. The treatment of depression with cognitive therapy. In: A. Ellis and R. Griegs (Eds.), *Handbook of rational emotive therapy*. New York: Springer, 1977, pp. 309–326.

Siegal, S. Classical conditioning, drug tolerance, and drug dependence. In: R. Smart, F. Glasser, Y. Israel, H. Kalant, R. Popham, and W. Schmidt (Eds.), *Research advances in alcohol and drug problems*, Vol. 7. New York: Plenum, 1983, pp. 207–241.

Skinner, B.F. "Superstition" in the pigeon. *Journal of Experimental Psychology*, 1948, *38*, 168–172.

Skinner, B.F. *Science and human behavior*. New York: Macmillan, 1953.

Sloane, R.B. The converging paths of behavior therapy and psychotherapy. *American Journal of Psychiatry*, 1969, *125*, 877–885.

Smith, J.W. Aversion conditioning hospitals. In: E. Kaufman. and E. Pattison (Eds.), *The American encyclopedic handbook of alcoholism*. New York: Gardner, 1982.

Solnick, J.V., Kannenberg, C.H., Eckerman, D.A., and Waller, M.B. An experimental analysis of impulsivity and impulse control in humans. *Learning and Motivation*, 1980, *11*, 61–77.

Staddon, J.E.R., and Simmelhag, V.L. 'The superstition experiment': A reexamination of its implications for the principles of adaptive behavior. *Psychological Review*, 1971, *78*, 3–43.

Stampfl, T., and Levis, D. Essentials of implosive therapy, a learning theory-based psychodynamic behavioral therapy. *Journal of Abnormal Psychology*, 1967, *72*, 496–503.

Stekel, W. *Conditions of nervous anxiety and their treatment*. London: Kegan, Paul, 1923.

Strupp, H.H. On the basic ingredients of psychotherapy. *Journal of Consulting and Clinical Psychology*, 1973, *41*, 1–8.

Stevenson, I. Direct instigation of behavioral changes in psychotherapy. *Archives of General Psychiatry*, 1959, *1*, 115–122.

Suinn, R., and Richardson, F. Anxiety management training: A nonspecific behavior therapy program for anxiety control. *Behavior Therapy*, 1971, *2*, 498–510.

Sullivan, H.S. *The psychiatric interview*. New York: Norton, 1954.

Thompson, C. *Psychoanalysis: Evolution and development*. New York: Nelson, 1950.

Thorndike, E.J. *The elements of psychology*. New York: Seiler, 1905.

Truax, C.B. Reinforcement and nonreinforcement in Rogerian psychotherapy. *Journal of Abnormal Psychology*, 1966, *71*, 1–9.

Vaillant, G. Natural history of male psychological health, VIII: Antecedents of alcoholism and morality. *American Journal of Psychiatry*, 1980, *137*, 181–186.

Wachtel, P. *Psychoanalysis and behavior therapy: Toward an integration.* New York: Basic Books, 1977.

Wachtel, P. What can dynamic therapies contribute to behavior therapy? *Behavior Therapy*, 1982, *13*, 594–609.

Wilson, T.G. Alcoholism and aversion therapy: Issues, ethics and evidence. In: G.A. Marlatt and P.E. Nathan (Eds.), *Behavioral approaches to alcoholism.* New Brunswick, N.J.: Publications Division, Rutgers Center on Alcohol Studies, 1978.

Wolberg, L. *Medical hypnosis.* New York: Grune & Stratton, 1948.

Wolberg, L.R. *The technique of psychotherapy.* New York: Grune & Stratton, 1977.

Wolpe, J. *Psychotherapy by reciprocal inhibition,* Stanford, Calif.: Stanford University Press, 1958.

Wolpe, J. *The practice of behavior therapy.* New York: Pergamon, 1969.

Wolpe, J., Groves, G., and Fisher, S. Treatment of narcotic addiction by inhibition of craving: Contending with a cherished habit. *Comprehensive Psychiatry*, 1980, *21*, 308–316.

Woody, R. Integrating behavior therapy and psychotherapy. *British Journal of Medical Psychology*, 1968, *41*, 261–266.

7
Manipulation: Clinical Application

REUBEN J. SILVER, Ph.D.

Psychoanalytically oriented therapists recoil from the idea of manipulation in psychotherapy. For one thing, the concept is associated with a type of control that is foreign to the very essence of dynamic psychotherapy—helping patients resolve unconscious conflicts through understanding. Understanding is primary; change is secondary.

In dynamic therapy modification of behavior and of attitudes is valued, but as a by-product of interpretation and insight. Psychodynamic therapists want their patients to achieve insight to empower them to solve their own current and future problems. Understanding leads to growth and the possibility of becoming a mature and independent being, a state of autonomy that is considered incompatible with techniques of control.

Another source of distrust of manipulation is the belief that it rests on trickery and deceit. Those who advocate openness, honesty, and genuineness oppose any form of manipulation. However, even Freud (1937), who opposed the idea of manipulation, used it. His treatment of Bruno Walter (Sterba, 1951) serves as a good example. The famous musical conductor consulted Freud because of severe pains in his right hand that prevented him from conducting. Freud responded by telling Walter to take a three-week holiday in Sicily. On his return he was still unable to use his right hand. Freud then advised him to resume conducting. When Bruno Walter protested that he could not take the responsibility for upsetting a performance, Freud replied, "I'll take the responsibility." Walter began conducting and eventually lost his symptom.

One could argue that Freud abandoned analytic principles in his treatment of Bruno Walter. As the reader will discover, however, analytic clinicians use many manipulative techniques—wittingly and unwittingly. Manipulation should be used cautiously; when we use it, we should not do so blindly. The question is not: Should manipulation be used in psychotherapy? The question is: How, when, and under what conditions are such techniques helpful?

Before proceeding to discuss these points, we need to define the term.

DEFINITION

Bibring (1934), in his classic paper, defines manipulation as "employment of various emotional systems, existing in the patient, for the purpose of achieving therapeutic change." The implication is that the therapist's activity triggers psychological mechanisms within the patient. Maneuvering the forces within the patient helps achieve the analytic goal of understanding. Bibring's definition does not address the issue of informing the patient of the purpose of the manipulation.

In contrast to Bibring, Greenson (1967) has a more restrictive view of the technique. For him manipulation involves "an evocative activity undertaken without the knowledge of the patient." The narrowness of Greenson's definition may stem from his strict adherence to the classical psychoanalytic model. His illustrations, for example, are geared exclusively to the development of insight. However, other uses of manipulation are consistent with the analytic model. The agoraphobic patient serves as a good illustration. Telling such a patient to spend 15 minutes each day in longer and longer walks away from the safety of the home is manipulative, but not devious.

Bibring excluded advice and guidance from his definition of manipulation. He believed that these activities were not curative. Advice and guidance, however, are not inconsistent with analytic principles, provided that they are based on an understanding of the patient's motivations and conflicts.

Manipulation that is devious and does not produce increased understanding in the patient is inconsistent with analytic principles. On the other hand, manipulation that changes behavior in a way that ultimately leads to more insight is an appropriate technique for analytic clinicians. Such therapists use manipulation, not to take control, but to give their patients eventually more control over their own lives.

In dynamic psychotherapy manipulation is a supportive expediency. It is an activity initiated by a therapist who has a clear goal in mind. The decision to communicate the goal to the patient will depend on the purpose of the manipulation and the patient's psychological status, that is, the dynamics. In using manipulation, dynamic therapists will consider the patient's defenses, needs, and conflicts. For example, therapists might explain their reasons, to agoraphobic patients, for the directive to expose themselves to the feared object. Yet for an acutely status-conscious, paranoid patient, changes in the seating arrangements would not be discussed.

Techniques are manipulative to the degree that they induce direct changes in a patient's perceptions, attributions, and behavior. The maneuvers are specific, planned, and goal directed.

Therapists may alter the patient's perception of a situation or event. The change may involve having the patient attribute different motives to other people, viewing the self differently, or perceiving the external environment from another perspective. Manipulation may, of course, involve direct attempts to modify either the internal or external environment of the patient. Encouraging the patient to leave the parental home is an example of a direct environmental manipulation. Prescribing an antidepressant medication alters the patient's internal environment. Prescribing a task for a patient is designed to alter the external environment.

Analytically oriented therapists consider manipulation a "parameter of a technique." Eissler (1953) defines a parameter as a deviation from the basic technique of interpretation. He lists the criteria for the use of any parameter:

1. It is used when interpretation does not suffice.
2. The parameter must be kept to a minimum.
3. When no longer needed, the parameter must be replaced by interpretation.
4. The effect of the parameter on the transference will be dissolved by interpretation.

Eissler correctly indicates that manipulation is used as a temporary measure that later must be scrutinized in the therapeutic situation. The meaning that the specific intervention had for the patient must be explored and the reasons for its choice must be understood by the patient.

SUGGESTION AND MANIPULATION

Manipulation is similar to suggestion. Both are direct actions by a therapist designed to change the patient. Both are supportive measures. Both have one of two goals: symptom relief, or a technical goal of en-

hancing the therapeutic process. The main distinction rests in the degree
to which each makes use of positive transference. Suggestion relies heavily
on the prestige and authority of the therapist. The indirect methods of
suggestion, however, as exemplified in the work of Erickson (Rossi et al.,
1983), are indistinguishable from manipulative techniques. Moreover,
manipulation probably will not be effective unless there has developed a
degree of positive transference.

Freud's treatment of Bruno Walter illustrates the difference between
suggestion and manipulation. Freud's statement, "I'll take the responsibility," presupposed a basic positive transference and, therefore, represented suggestion. The technique worked because the composer believed
in Freud's healing powers. On the other hand, sending Bruno Walter to
Sicily to enjoy the countryside was an uncomplicated manipulation in
which environmental stress was decreased.

DANGERS

Manipulation may be useful; it may also be destructive. As Langs
(1973) correctly indicates, the dangers of manipulation are many. He
believes that "direct advice and manipulation are generally to be avoided
in insight therapy" (p. 550). He would, of course, use such techniques
in an emergency situation, especially if the life of the patient were in
danger. Even then, however, Langs would resort to manipulation only
if interpretation did not diffuse the risk.

Patients may view manipulation as an assault or as an unwanted intrusion. They may respond by leaving therapy, becoming more resistant
to the therapist's interventions, or by a feeling of rage toward the therapist.
Some patients feel so helpless in the face of manipulation that they are
unable to convey the extent of their anxiety in the treatment sessions.
Those who are unable to voice disagreement with an authority figure may
pretend to accept the manipulation. In reality, they may become more
distrustful of their therapist. The result is increased passive resistance and
a censoring of the material presented in the session. Accordingly the threat
to the therapeutic alliance is real, especially if the assigned tasks are selected on the basis of inadequate information and understanding. Since
premature interventions are always dangerous, therapists should avoid
reaching decisions until they have evaluated their patients thoroughly.

For a variety of reasons, patients may not complete their assignments.
The task may be too difficult; the patient may need to rebel against
authority; the basic dynamics may have been misunderstood; the strength
of the resistance was underestimated; or the nature of the positive trans-

ference was misjudged. Under these conditions a struggle between patient and therapist may ensue. The resulting conflict works against the therapist's stance of neutrality. The "real relationship" takes on added importance and contaminates the interchanges. Intrapsychic exploration gives way to a feud.

Perhaps the greatest danger in the use of manipulation involves countertransference. Sometimes therapists offer advice, guidance, and assignments that are based upon their own needs rather than those of the patient. Manipulation may be based on the need to control the patient. At other times the technique permits acting out against the patients. Manipulation should not be based on the therapist's anger, seductiveness, impatience, or need to infantilize the patient. Consequently analytic workers should guard against the possibility that their manipulative maneuvers are based on their own psychopathology. One way to defend against the intrusion of countertransference is to be certain that the manipulation is aimed at enhancing the therapeutic process or facilitating the development of insight. In general it is best to act as if the maneuver will need to be analyzed.

The danger of countertransference is illustrated in the following vignette.

> In the course of her treatment, an attractive 32-year-old woman complained of the behavior of her husband. She described his various irresponsible acts, including persistent illicit sexual encounters. Believing that the patient was in a self-destructive relationship, the young male therapist instructed her to seek a temporary separation. At the next session, she appeared near panic. She had been unable to comply with the directive. Her panic, it was learned later, was based upon her belief that the therapist was motivated by his wish to use her sexually. Actually the therapist's advice was based upon his values about the rights of women. Nevertheless his intervention reflected his needs, rather than his patient's needs.

TECHNICAL MANIPULATION

Manipulation that is designed to enhance the process of therapy is referred to as technical manipulation (Bibring, 1954). In general there are two types of such maneuvers; positive manipulation, which aims to produce favorable attitudes in the patient; and negative manipulation, which attempts to remove obstacles that the patient has toward treatment. The following example illustrates the use of a negative technique.

> A father was concerned about his 26-year-old son, who had grown increasingly withdrawn and isolated, though he continued to function independently as a graduate student. Despite his father's suggestions, the son had

not consulted a therapist. Finally the father, taking matters in his own
hands, made an appointment for the son, which the young man accepted
without protest. However, upon arriving at the therapist's office, he expressed his fury at his father's action. He complained that he had been
treated in an infantile manner. He was also angry with the therapist, who,
he believed, had colluded with his father. Yet the patient considered himself
to be trapped because he did not wish to offend his father. The therapist
responded by emphasizing that he would see the patient only if he himself
wanted to be seen, thereby reestablishing that the patient was a responsible
adult capable of making his own decisions.

The intervention was manipulative because it used the patient's need to
please an authority figure to redefine the conditions of treatment.

A more common occasion for the use of manipulation to decrease
initial resistance to treatment is exemplified by deliberate use of tentative
interpretation.

A patient who has developed a reaction formation to his passivity responds
to any sign of domination with anxiety and rejection. A therapist will use
this knowledge, in a manipulative manner, to decrease the patient's negative
attitude toward therapy. In offering interpretations to such patients, one
might say, "I don't know if this applies but . . . ," or, "Could you perhaps
be saying . . . ?" Another possibility would be, "This may be way out, but
see what you think."

Analytic therapists employ many manipulative techniques in an attempt to engender positive feelings toward therapy. Let us consider six
manipulations that foster the therapeutic alliance.

Creating a Therapeutic Atmosphere

Despite insightful conceptualization, some therapists have difficulty
in keeping patients in treatment. The fault may lie in their failure to foster
a therapeutic alliance, without which patients may not persevere in the
painful task of treatment. One important ingredient in developing the
alliance is the creation of a therapeutic atmosphere (Dewald, 1972).

The proper climate in treatment may be achieved by the manner in
which therapists listen and by the way in which they respond to patients.
Accurate and appropriate empathic communication plays a key role in
maintaining the therapeutic alliance. Failure to convey accurate empathy
may drive the patient from treatment. The following case history is instructive.

The patient, a 24-year-old woman being seen by a male student intent on
adhering to the analytic model, began insisting that he ask her questions
and lead her. She was interpreting his silence as a sign of his lack of concern.

Rather than responding to her discomfort, he continued his silence or repeated the basic rule of free association. After two such sessions, the patient left a message that she was withdrawing from treatment. Fortunately, she agreed to appear for the next session to discuss her discontent. In that hour the student, realizing that she needed to feel that her discomfort was appreciated, responded with empathic statements that focused on her discontent. The change in attitude toward him was remarkable. In this example the therapist was using manipulation since he was attempting to change the patient's perceptions and attributions of the therapy situation

Sometimes excessive empathy is detrimental to the therapeutic process. The patient may perceive such responses as false reassurance and as a sign that exploration is unacceptable to the therapist. Empathic comments may assume an unduly intrusive characteristic and, paradoxically, may be seen as judgmental. Thus, reflection of feelings then becomes a sign that the therapist agrees with the self-derogatory attitudes or thinks of the patient as a weak creature who needs to be coddled. The danger of misperceptions is increased when therapists rely on voice quality (Truax & Carkhuff, 1967) to convey empathy rather than saying precisely what they mean.

The dilemma for therapists is how much empathy they should show. In one sense the answer is simple: therapists should display enough empathy to keep the therapeutic atmosphere intact. Eissler's (1953) rule, which says that the parameter should be kept to a minimum, can be a source of guidance.

Tact

Tactfulness strengthens the therapeutic alliance. Painful material should be presented in a way that permits the patient to accept the interpretation and integrate it. The consequence of lack of tact is evident in the following case.

The patient, a 35-year-old married woman, was reporting on her periodic feelings of depression, which she thought occurred about once a year and which lasted for a few days. The psychiatrist, who was seeing her for evaluation, responded that she was incorrectly reporting the situation. He told her that she had mood swings every two to three months that lasted for about one week. He also proclaimed that with her positive family history of depression, he considered her to have a bipolar disorder. The patient was crushed. In retrospect, she thought he might be right. Nonetheless she considered herself to have been betrayed and humiliated. She did not return for treatment.

Encouraging the Patient's Participation

Active listening encourages patients to share their intimate secrets. Therefore, therapists resort to a variety of techniques to communicate their interest in the material that is presented. Not only do they look interested, but their posture conveys that attitude. They avoid the faraway look and the preoccupied expression. If they find themselves bored during a session, they should suspect that countertransference is at work. At the very least, boredom implies a lack of appreciation and understanding of the patient's dynamics.

An appropriate nod of the head, an interjected, "I see," or the non-committal "M-hmm," conveys the therapist's interest. Remembering the details of the patient's narrative conveys an attitude of active listening. On the other hand, when therapists forget things they have heard, they should not pretend that they remember.

Periodically therapists must respond to the material they hear. However, active listening limits the degree to which therapists may indulge in inductive leaps. Patients interpret statements that are too far beyond their awareness as a sign of inattentiveness and lack of understanding. They may also believe that the therapist is a genius and they are stupid. Therapists who make this type of statement should consider whether or not they are motivated to achieve any of these results.

Perhaps the most important aspect in encouraging the patient's participation is the safety of the situation. A calm attitude in the face of the patient's distress adds to the feeling of security. Regardless of the content of the patient's associations, the therapist remains shockproof. This stance signifies that since moral judgments are suspended during the hour, patients need not fear retaliation for their utterances.

An example of tolerant and accepting attitude is given in the following case vignette.

> The patient, a 38-year-old highly anxious and obsessive woman, was reporting on her tendency to overreact to any change in her work routine. Since she was employed in a busy medical practice, she was frequently subjected to many changing circumstances in her daily routine. While she was relating these conditions, we both heard a loud cracking sound, indicating that some glass was shattered in the outer room. We were both startled. The patient asked if I wished to investigate. I replied that there was time at the end of the hour to do that. My response implied that nothing was more important during that hour than her therapy.

Seating Arrangements

The seating arrangement and the office decor are manipulative in nature. Dim lights create an atmosphere of intimacy that encourages patients to disclose details about themselves. Sitting upright implies an equality between two adults. The use of the couch induces relaxation, which diminishes anxiety and promotes regression. Should the couch be too threatening, however, the therapist will move the patient to the upright position. Yet the advantage of the couch is that it permits the expression of feelings that might otherwise produce incapacitating anxiety. The behaviorists (Wolpe, 1973) are correct in postulating that relaxation and anxiety are incompatible. Some people may experience excessive anxiety if they are asked to sit quietly in a chair. If that happens to be the case, the patient should be permitted to walk about the office.

The seating arrangement assumes increased significance with paranoid patients who notice the minutia of their environment and read meanings into neutral situations. Therapists should minimize the possibilities for distortion. With very suspicious patients, for example, therapists generally do not place themselves between the door and the patient. Paranoids might misinterpret such an arrangement as a deliberate attempt to block the exit. Further distortion then becomes possible.

For the status-conscious patient, the relative heights of the chairs may become an issue. To avoid such problems, some therapists insist that all office chairs be identical. For the same reason, it may be unwise to sit behind a desk during the treatment hour. The formality and distance implied in that seating may inhibit the patient from disclosing intimate material. Yet other patients cannot tolerate any hint of closeness. They welcome the barrier of the desk and the aloofness of such an arrangement. An office decor that is too cosy sets a tone of friendship that can be seductive.

Manipulating the seating arrangement is a nonverbal technique aimed at changing the patient's attributions. Such maneuvers will be successful to the degree that they meet the needs and address the conflicts of the patient.

The value of attending to the seating arrangement is illustrated by a case example given by Briggin and Zinberg (1969, p. 201).

> The first time Mr. B. entered the psychiatrist's office, he took the seat farthest from the therapist. The interview was halting and difficult. On reflection, the therapist realized that the patient had taken a soft deep chair, which resulted in his being lower than the therapist. The therapist felt that this was upsetting to Mr. B. because it interfered with his desire to be in control at all times. As a result the interview was unproductive. Before the patient's next appointment, the therapist changed the arrangement of the chairs so that the farthest seat was a firm straightbacked leather one. Mr. B. took the chair and it was clear that he felt more in control and therefore could allow himself greater freedom. The content of the interview material supplied further evidence for this view.

Limitation on Time

The standard 45- or 50-minute session is another example of manipulation. Usually therapists begin and end the session on time and avoid interruption. The manipulation involves keeping the treatment setting constant. Consequently the patient's responses are assumed to be the result of intrapsychic promptings rather than artifacts of the situation.

Understanding that the limitation on time is manipulative may encourage therapists to experiment with the length of the session. At times it may be appropriate to have long sessions as Freud did in his treatment of Gustav Mahler, the composer (Jones, 1957). Mahler had consulted Freud with a problem of sexual impotence, which threatened his marriage. Although the treatment was based on insight, Freud spent four continuous hours with Mahler, part of which involved strolling through the gardens. The reason for such a long session is not specified. Nor is the effect of this procedure on the transference mentioned. It is likely, however, that a great deal of positive transference was generated. Since the treatment was limited to this one session, Freud could not have interpreted the transference.

Forty-five minutes might be excessively long for other patients. Therapists working with frightened, withdrawn, schizoid people may wish to limit the treatment time to 20 or 30 minutes. Under some circumstances, it is appropriate to permit the patient to terminate the contact. Usually, however, the therapist remains in control of the length of each meeting. Regardless of the changes in duration of the session, therapists should have a clear understanding of the reason for any deviation. As with all matters, countertransference may have dictated the maneuver.

No Major Decisions

Dynamic therapists ask patients to refrain from making major changes in their lives without first discussing the matter in treatment. If this is not followed, patients may act out by making major alterations and thereby sabotaging the therapeutic situation. The imposition of restrictions is clearly manipulation. The aim is to control the patient's environment. In that sense the restriction is slightly more subtle than directing the patient to move to another apartment, obtain a job, leave the parental home, enter a hospital, or take medication.

Many patients have a strong reaction to this rule. Some will report temptations to violate it. Others may engage in direct rebellion, a not infrequent occurrence. To each of these responses, the therapist will react by scrutinizing its meaning and implication for the transference.

The prohibition against major life changes without adequate discussion has the advantage of keeping external crises to a minimum. Eruptions in the patient's life usually provoke emergency procedures in which the therapist is apt to lose sight of the nature of the resistance. Equally important, interpretation, the primary tool, is discarded.

The rule of suspending major decisions must be flexible (Weigart, 1954). Too strict adherence to the command may result in premature termination. Some patients perceive the rigidity of the therapist as identical to the attitude of a feared parent. As a result, future plans become taboo topics. Not wishing to offend their therapists or incur their wrath, patients may be unable to discuss any contemplated change.

Not infrequently patients use the rule to rationalize their refusal to consider major changes, preferring the dependency implicit in avoiding personal growth. Therapists must be alert to that possibility.

MANIPULATION IN EMERGENCY SITUATIONS

Even the most conservative analytic therapists agree that manipulation is justified in an emergency. As we have noted, Langs (1973) endorses such maneuvers if the patient's life is in danger. The following case is instructive.

> The patient, a 35-year-old woman with borderline features, threatens to terminate therapy because of her continued feelings of hopelessness and despair. A highly moralistic woman, she is horrified by her growing sexual attraction to a man whom she has known for many years. Although she has not revealed her desires to this man, she fears that she might. Were she to have an affair, she believes her husband would divorce her, and her two small children would never wish to see her. My attempts to have her explore her feelings merely increase her distress and she threatens to leave my office and never return. She expresses regret for having shared her secret fantasy. Although she believes that I have tried to help her with her problems, she is convinced that she is hopeless and that I too have given up on her. As she places her hand on the doorknob, she announces that she intends to kill herself later that day.
>
> The hour is up and I must make a decision. Do I tell the next patient, who is waiting for me, that I must extend the time for this woman? Would that signal her that I have as much despair as she? I respond by saying that I wish her to return home and to call me later that evening when we can decide on the need for an appointment the following day. My message is that she is a responsible adult who is capable of making important decisions.

In life-threatening situations, active intervention may take a variety of forms, including violating the patient's confidence, talking to significant others, or protecting the patient by close monitoring of activity, all of which alter the patient's external environment. Such extreme interventions may hamper the continued use of the analytic model. Emergency procedures violate the basic tenets of the dynamic approach. They encourage therapists to relinquish the goal of insight. Control of behavior temporarily supersedes understanding as the primary objective.

The degree to which these antianalytic techniques were used will determine the feasibility of resuming psychodynamic treatment. If dynamic therapy is reinstituted, the deviation will need to be analyzed. Upon close scrutiny the deviation may turn out to be seen as unnecessary or as a product of the therapist's own anxiety. Such mistakes should be acknowledged. If the damage to the transference cannot be repaired, and if dynamic therapy is desirable, referral to another therapist is appropriate.

THERAPEUTIC MANIPULATION

Some dynamic therapists (Alexander & French, 1946) believe that the basic ingredient of psychotherapy is a corrective emotional experience. Alexander (1956) used this construct to explain the impact of the therapist's personality on the outcome of treatment. He considered it impossible to be completely free from the influence of countertransference—regardless of the therapist's personal adjustment. Therapist attitudes interact with the dynamics of the patient, sometimes in a beneficial way, sometimes in a detrimental manner. An illustration from Alexander (1956, pp. 95–96) may be helpful.

> (The patient, who was described as inhibited, depressed, and withdrawn) was the son of a wealthy merchant who indulged his son financially and emotionally. . . . (The son) detested his father. At the beginning of treatment we agreed on a modest fee. . . . A few weeks (later) the value of the German mark decreased. . . . I neglected to adjust his fee. . . . (The patient then reported a dream suggesting guilt feelings over having his therapy for nothing.) I still deferred changing his fee. In the next interview, he declared he could not continue treatment with me because I reminded him of his father. . . . (The patient was referred to another therapist who charged him ten times Alexander's fee. The patient remained in treatment to a successful conclusion.)

Alexander postulated that the therapist reacted in the same indulgent manner as did the father. The other analyst, however, provided a marked contrast, which permitted the patient to have a new experience with a father figure. As a result, a different method of responding to authority was facilitated.

When the goal of treatment is a corrective emotional experience, manipulation, especially of transference, assumes added significance. If, for example, the father's overindulgent behavior contributed to the problem, the therapist would deliberately adopt a more stringent attitude. When the issue is one of a harsh rejecting parent, the therapist becomes a benevolent, accepting, warm person. Which role to assume will depend on the patient's dynamics. The basic principle is "to re-expose the patient, under favorable circumstances, to emotional situations which he could not handle in the past" (Alexander & French, 1946, p. 66).

The work of Whitaker and Malone (1953) can be viewed as an extreme application of this approach. They advocated provoking anger if that expression constituted a corrective emotional experience. At times they were exceedingly rude to their patients in the hope of eliciting the underlying fury.

Alexander's approach has the merit of bringing life into the treatment room. Unfortunately, it places unrealistic demands on the therapist. It is unlikely that any one person could play the great variety of roles that the method mandates. Strict adherence to the model would require an appropriate match between the needs of the patient and the personality of the therapist. If the assortive mating between patient and therapist were faulty, a referral to an appropriate clinician would be necessary. Unfortunately, adequate data concerning the effect of matching are lacking. Moreover there is no compelling support for the belief that assuming a role is a more powerful tool than interpretation.

Dynamic therapists might reserve this approach for patients who are refractory to interpretation. If the patient is responding with extremely intense transference feelings that threaten the continuation of treatment, the therapist is justified in manipulating the transference. Decreasing the frequency of the sessions may diffuse a potentially explosive situation. A shift from weekly to biweekly sessions might be a sufficient change in the treatment schedule. The decision to manipulate the transference, however, should be made at the initial evaluation interview. At that point the therapist decides on the frequency of sessions and on the use of the face-to-face arrangement.

In addition to altering the frequency of meetings, the therapist may need to change the stance toward the patient. Becoming more empathic and less aloof may be essential if treatment is to continue with a dynamic focus. However, therapists should recognize that they are responding to a crisis situation. Eventually the question must be answered: Can the patient tolerate an approach aimed at understanding unconscious conflicts? Not all patients can and, therefore, not all patients are suitable for insight-oriented treatment. People who live from one crisis to the next are not likely candidates for insight therapy, nor are those with insatiable dependency needs. Those patients who refuse to explore their psyches should not be treated in a dynamic mode. Unmotivated, nonverbal persons with incapacitating symptoms are best treated by other methods.

Therapeutic manipulation is frequently used in brief consultations. In these instances the therapist uses the patient's defensive system to effect a desired outcome. A case in point is given by Briggin and Zinberg (1969, p. 203).

(The patient, a middle-aged man for whom bedrest had been prescribed, refused to comply and threatened to leave the hospital.) The psychiatrist's interview revealed that the patient stressed independence, dominance, and control . . . (which were) a denial of intense passive longings . . . The order (bedrest) aroused fears that he would become totally passive, dependent, and helpless. The manipulation attempted to put him in control of his therapeutic regime. He was allowed to schedule his own medication and dose himself. Any sedation had particularly frightened him because . . . (it) resulted in his thinking processes becoming less acute. (Consequently all procedures were explained thoroughly as a way of having him feel in control of the situation.) He became much more accepting of the medical regime.

If this patient had continued in dynamic therapy, more work would have been necessary. His need for control would have been exposed and the nature of his defenses would have been analyzed. Eventually, the patient would have gained understanding into his problems.

MANIPULATION IN NONANALYTIC THERAPIES

In contrast to dynamic workers, strategic therapists use manipulation as the primary intervention tool. They believe that insight is neither desirable nor necessary. Rather than self-understanding, the goal of treatment "is to influence the client in such a way that his original complaint is resolved to his satisfaction. This can be done by interdicting the problem-maintaining behavior . . . or by altering the client's view of the problem . . ." (Fisch, et al., 1982, p. 127). Strategic therapy, therefore, is primarily a series of techniques aimed at symptom relief. For this reason dynamic therapists who use strategic manipulations must modify these maneuvers so as not to preclude the patient's future development of insight.

Reframing

A clearly manipulative technique, reframing (Watzlawick et al., 1974; Watzlawick, 1978; Fisch et al., 1982) involves a redefinition of the problem behavior and hence a change in the patient's perception of the symptom. The therapist reinterprets the meaning of the behavior and postulates a plausible reason for its existence. The relabeling could be negative, neutral, or positive. The last has been called positive connotation (Selvini Palazzoli et al., 1978).

An example from Fisch et al. (1982, p. 135) illustrates the use of redefining an undesirable behavior in positive terms.

A depressed man describes himself as a workaholic. He admitted that he pushed himself mercilessly, never took more than two or three days vacation, and then only rarely. The therapist was able to reframe his depression as a beneficial force by explaining to the patient that his depression was forcing him to stay away from work and take it easy at home—a luxury, if not a necessity, that he would never purposefully allow himself. The patient found this explanation a profound and useful interpretation.

Another way of using reframing is indicated by Watzlawick's (1978, p. 143) vignette in dealing with a rebellious teenager and his parents.

In the presence of the teenager, the therapist can usually reframe the situation by pompously invoking his "long clinical experience" with cases of this kind and asserting that the youngster is not really insolent, but is reacting to a deep-seated, existential fear of growing up and of losing the comfortable safety of childhood.

To the adolescent this redefinition is unacceptable. Therefore, if he continues to misbehave, he admits to the accuracy of the definition. Rebellion no longer means rebellion; it means fear, an alternative that the adolescent rejects.

Reframing is effective provided that the patient accepts the new definition. The therapeutic task, therefore, requires the clinician to prevent the patient from rejecting the new label. If a therapist has enough charisma, the patient may not be able to negate the changed meaning. Even more powerful would be to have the people in the environment act as if the new definition were correct. Under those conditions the patient is unable to disconfirm the meanings attributed by the clinician.

One of Bergman's (1982, p. 218) cases demonstrates the power of the group in implementing this technique.

(After a long state hospital stay, a patient placed in a community residence, persists in speaking gibberish, pacing for hours, and then whining.) We apologized to Luigi for trying to change him and for not recognizing that he was actually a spy from the state hospital. He was encouraged to speak gibberish, which was (reframed) as a code needed to safeguard his cover as a spy. (The patient's pacing was reinterpreted as a method to receive the signals from the hospital that the transmission had been received.) Although the patient tried to disagree with the relabeling, the staff remained united and insisted that a spy always denies his identity.

Dynamic workers who use such maneuvers would insist that the reframing be an accurate reflection of the patient's problem. In that sense reframing would be equivalent to a direct interpretation, made somewhat prematurely and aimed at a change in the patient's perception of himself or herself. Dynamic workers who redefine problems may utilize the concept of interpretation upward (Langs, 1973) to achieve a change in the

patient's attitude. In contrast to strategic therapists, the analytically oriented clinician utilizes the patient's dynamics in postulating a cause for
the behavior. For example, when the analyst interprets upward a patient's
unconscious wish to suckle at the breast as a need to be loved and cared
for, a new definition is given to a basic problem. The dynamic worker
remains interested in the accuracy of the formulation. For the strategic
therapist, the validity of the rationale is irrelevant. The strategic therapist
requires only that an intervention provoke change. The dynamic therapist
requires something more: that the change be a product of growth through
understanding. Insight provides patients with a method to solve their own
problems—both current and future ones.

Symptom Prescription

Patients who present with disturbing symptoms usually report unsuccessful attempts to rid themselves of the problem. The anxious person
has made many attempts to relax. If that method has worked (and often
it does), the patient is unlikely to come for therapy.

Symptom prescription presents the patient with an unexpected task,
namely, being asked to engage in the behavior that prompted the consultation. Instructions to bring on the symptom, paradoxically, decrease
the problem behavior that may have been maintained by the anxiety
associated with the patient's preoccupation. Behavioral psychologists have
demonstrated that deliberate practice of a bad habit weakens that response.

The treatment of impotence will serve as a useful illustration of the
technique.

> The patient struggled with various procedures to solve his sexual failures.
> The harder he tried when he was with a woman, the less likely he was to
> achieve an erection. A strategic therapist would do the unexpected: instruct
> the patient to plan on being impotent, using a rationale to make the as-
> signment plausible. For example, the patient would be told that he should
> concentrate on the thoughts that he had at the time of the impotence so
> that he could learn the precise triggers for his impotence. Basic to this
> approach is the belief that changes in the context in which the symptom
> occurs diminish the problem behavior.

Another vignette may be useful.

> A young woman, the mother of two preschool children, presented with
> extreme anxiety associated with some recent intrusive thoughts. For about
> the past two weeks, she had had the recurring thought, "What if I took a
> knife and stabbed my two children?" She was acutely distressed by these
> "impulses," which she dated to her husband's recent transfer to another
> military post. She and her children were scheduled to join him within a
> week.

Since time was of the essence, I proceeded as follows: I told her it was necessary for her to learn whether she became anxious and then had the disturbing thought, or whether the thought preceded the anxiety. The discrimination was described as one that required considerable practice to make successfully. Accordingly, her task was to have as many anxiety attacks as she could. When she became disturbed, she was to ask herself, "Was I anxious and then had the thought, or did I have the thought and then become anxious?" She was also instructed to determine what was going on in her mind at the time she experienced the anxiety and/or had the intrusive thought. An additional task of keeping a log of her practice sessions was imposed.

The patient returned a few days later, much calmer, and reported that she was not having the intrusive thoughts. She was rejoining her husband the next day.

In this example, dynamic considerations were not used in formulating the intervention. The patient needed quick relief from her symptoms. At most only a few sessions were available. It should be noted, therefore, that a shift to a more dynamic approach would have been exceedingly difficult.

A more subtle use of the technique is illustrated by the following case.

The patient, a 22-year-old single, male, college senior, sought treatment because of intense anxiety associated with disturbing thoughts related to sexual promptings. He was highly stimulated by images of married women having coitus with strangers. A moralistic young man, he considered sex outside of marriage as wicked and sinful. As he related his concerns, his tension mounted and he pleaded with me for a direct method to stop these intrusive thoughts. To make matters worse, he believed that other people knew of his preoccupation.

Since his anxiety was increasing and his ego seemed fragile, I resorted to symptom prescription. I said, "I wonder about the degree to which you are aware of the nature and degree of the distress that you feel. Perhaps you might wish to set aside some time each day when you could try to bring on the anxiety by thinking about women having sexual relations. Should you so decide, you may want to learn where you feel the anxiety, what specific image brought on the distress, and how the feeling spreads and intensifies."

Psychodynamic clinicians who use symptoms prescription encourage their patients to discuss the thoughts, emotions, wishes, impulses, and fantasies that occur during the assignment. The ultimate goal is insight. Unanalyzed compliance may be based on irrational modes of relating, including masochism, seduction, and childish wishes to please an omnipotent parent.

Restraining

Restraining is a paradoxical technique in which the patient is urged not to change. Although the patient is given a task, he or she is told not to try to solve the problem or make much progress in completing the assignment. As an example, let us consider the patient who has incapacitating anxiety when she drives a car. She is instructed to sit behind the wheel of the car, but refrain from driving. To make the maneuver plausible, the therapist provides a rationale, such as telling the patient she needs to learn to be comfortable merely sitting in the car. Along with this explanation, the therapist plants another suggestion by adding that should the patient have the urge to drive, she will inhibit that impulse. In the step-by-step approach (Fisch et al., 1982), all assignments related to driving are stated as restraints. "I want you to drive no more than around the corner." Since mastery of the task is deemphasized, the therapist does not give approval for progress.

Among the most important restraining techniques are the injunctions "to go slow" and to recognize "the dangers of improvement." With these manipulations no specific task is assigned. The instructions, which are vague, emphasize that the patient should avoid trying to change rapidly. Much of the discussion consists of the therapist developing a rationale for the danger of quick improvement. Fisch et al. (1982) illustrate this approach in the treatment of a depressed man. They tell him that he should go slowly and not attempt to do much during the week. When he returns feeling improved, they reemphasize the need to slow down, and the dangers of rapid progress are again enumerated. Additionally the patient is asked to think about the untoward consequences of any alteration in the symptom picture.

These approaches have been recommended for patients who demand, from the therapist, immediate symptom relief. While the patient insists on a quick cure, the therapist argues for the status quo.

Dynamic workers would employ the technique differently. By interpreting the patient's wish for immediate relief of symptoms, they would convey the message of going slowly. They would also focus on the needs that the symptom satisfies. Therefore, it would not be inconsistent with an analytic model to tell the patient to go slowly. The dynamically oriented clinician who uses restraining techniques bases the intervention on a different understanding of the patient's problems, namely, unconscious conflicts. As a result, the restraining maneuvers are perceived by both the patient and the therapist as being secondary to the primary tool of interpretation.

CONCLUSIONS

Strategic interventions are the state of the art of manipulation. They do deliberately and skillfully what psychodynamic therapists often do unwittingly and haphazardly. But manipulations have limits and dangers even when not based on countertransference. For one thing, their use risks depriving patients of autonomy and growth. Behavior change, which may be based on blind compliance, could replace the analytic goal of insight. Psychodynamic therapists are not content merely with producing behavior change. They want their patients to be competent to solve their own problems.

Analytically oriented clinicians should only employ manipulation in a conscious, deliberate manner to achieve a specific goal. The particular maneuver should be based upon an understanding of the patient's unconscious motivation and his or her personality structure. Psychodynamic therapists resort to manipulation only when necessary and only when interpretation is inadequate or inappropriate. When directives are used, they must remain subservient to the larger goal of understanding. It is through insight that patients grow and become autonomous human beings. Self-understanding permits patients to solve their own problems, now and in the future. With insight, patients have a method of meeting successfully the stresses encountered in living.

These assumptions dictate that manipulative maneuvers should be kept to a minimum and analyzed when they are no longer necessary. Violation of this rule may be destructive to the use of insight-oriented therapy. But if used judiciously, manipulation can add an important dimension to psychodynamic treatment.

REFERENCES

Alexander, F. Psychoanalysis and psychotherapy. *Journal of the American Psychoanalytic Association*, 1954, *2*, 722–733.

Alexander, F. *Psychoanalysis and psychotherapy: Developments in theory*. New York: W.W. Norton, 1956.

Alexander, F., and French, T. *Psychoanalytic therapy: Principles and applications*. New York: Ronald Press, 1946.

Bergman, J. Paradoxical interventions with people who insist on acting crazy. *American Journal of Psychotherapy*, *36*, 1982, 214–222.

Bibring, E. Psychoanalysis and the dynamic psychotherapies. *Journal of the American Psychoanalytic Association*, 1954, *2*, 745–770.

Briggin, C.S., and Zinberg, N.S. Manipulation and its clinical application. *American Journal of Psychotherapy*, 1969, *23*, 198–206.

Dewald, P. *The psychoanalytic process: A case illustration*. New York: Basic Books, 1972.

Eissler, K.R. The effect of the structure of the ego on psychoanalytic technique. *Journal of the American Psychoanalytic Association*, 1953, *1*, 104–143.

Fisch, R., Weakland, J.H., and Segal, L. *The tactics of change: Doing therapy briefly*. San Francisco: Jossey-Bass, 1982.

Freud, S. (1937) Analysis terminable and interminable. *Standard edition*, vol. 23, London: Hogarth Press, 1964, pp. 209–253.

Greenson, R. *The technique and practice of psychoanalysis.* New York: International Universities Press, 1967.

Haley, J. *Strategies of psychotherapy.* New York: Grune & Stratton, 1963.

Haley, J. *Uncommon therapy: The psychiatric techniques of Milton H. Erickson, M.D.* New York: W.W. Norton, 1973.

Jones, E. *The life and work of Sigmund Freud,* Vol. 2. New York: Basic Books, 1957.

Langs, R. *The technique of psychoanalytic psychotherapy,* Vol. 1. New York: Jason Aronson, 1973.

Rossi, E.L., Ryan, M.O., and Sharp, F.A. (Eds.) *Healing in hypnosis: The seminars, workshops, and lectures of Milton H. Erickson,* Vol. 1. New York: Irvington, 1983.

Selvini, Palazzoli, M., Boscolo, L., Cecchin, G., and Prata, G. *Paradox and counterparadox.* New York: Jason Aronson, 1978.

Sterba, R. A case of brief psychotherapy by Sigmund Freud. *Psychoanalytic Review,* 1951, *38*, 75–80.

Truax, C.B., and Carkhuff, R.R. *Toward effective counseling and psychotherapy: Training and practice.* Chicago: Aldine, 1967.

Watzlowick, P. *The language of change.* New York: Basic Books, 1978.

Watzlawick, P., Weakland, J., and Fisch, R. *Change: Principles of problem formation and problem resolution.* New York: W.W. Norton, 1974.

Weigert, E. The importance of flexibility in psychoanalytic technique. *Journal of the American Psychoanalytic Association,* 1954, *2*, 702–710.

Whitaker, C.A., and Malone, T.P. *The roots of psychotherapy.* New York: Blakeston, 1953.

Wolpe, J. *The practice of behavior therapy.* New York: Pergamon Press, 1973.

8
Confrontation:
History and Theory

RONALD J. KARPF, Ph.D

Voltaire once declared that he would not debate any person who had not defined the terms of the discussion. Accepting Voltaire's wisdom, I will begin by defining the technique of confrontation. It does not necessarily mean "to challenge," as the dictionary has it, although the therapist may want to challenge the patient's resistances at the appropriate time. Instead, as Paolino (1981, p. 8) says, "Confrontation is a technique in which the therapist forcefully directs the patient's attention to something of which the patient is unconscious, preconscious, or conscious." To qualify as a basic technique of psychodynamic psychotherapy, confrontation has to be consciously directed with a specific purpose in mind (Paolino, 1980). A confrontation may serve many purposes, depending on the context of the psychotherapeutic situation. It is the conscious intent of the psycho-therapist, however, that differentiates a confrontation from a counter-transference-based response. In fact no matter how accurate an intervention may be, and despite the fact that the therapist has to have ready access to his or her unconscious, if a confrontation is based on preconscious or unconscious responses, it may be said that countertransference had a preemptive role in its delivery (Karpf, 1980a; Spitz, 1956).

Other definitions of confrontation emphasize these same processes. For example: Confrontation is "a technique designed to gain a patient's attention to inner experiences or perceptions of outer reality of which he is conscious or is about to be made conscious" (Buie & Adler, 1973, p. 127). Some descriptions of confrontation are more dynamic: "Confron-

tation designates interventions which connect something kept from consciousness by reality-distorting defenses (denial, projection, introjection)"
(Binstock, 1981, p. 5). Thus a confrontation may be aimed at intrapsychic
events such as defenses or resistance, or at external events in the patient's
life.

An integral part of every confrontation is the forceful insistence of the
message and the preparation for interpretations and insight (Paolino,
1981). The adaptive context of the therapy situation (Langs, 1976) is
important to a confrontation. The adaptive context is the real relationship
between patient and therapist. A confrontation brings this real relationship
into focus so that the pathological and intrapsychic conflicts can then be
analyzed. The message does not have to be a declarative statement. The
use of humor, surprise, or an unusual phrase or tone of voice may all be
quite forceful. Unlike clarification or interpretation, confrontation is not
intended to produce insight and working through (Bibring, 1954). It is
intended as a preparatory intervention, setting the tone for an interpretive
remark (Compton, 1975), or it may be an end in itself, directly challenging
the reality-distorting defenses and improving judgment. As part of the
interpretive process, a confrontation is crucial to the effectiveness of a
forthcoming clarification or interpretation (Greenson, 1967). As an end
in itself, it communicates displeasure with a certain behavior or aspect of
psychic function and implies that the patient should examine it.

In a classical analysis, the confrontation and the patient's reaction to
it must be analyzed so that they do not become a technical parameter
(Eissler, 1953). This need not be the case in face-to-face psychodynamic
psychotherapy. Psychotherapy permits a wider range of appropriate interventions than does a psychoanalysis, although the differences between
the two are not always sharply demarcated (Langs, 1973; Stewart, 1975).
The terms "therapy" and "therapist" are used in this chapter rather than
"analysis" and "analyst" because they are more encompassing. Nevertheless, the variables of intensity, duration, and frequency will always differentiate a therapy from an analysis.

HISTORY

Before 1910 catharsis, confrontation, and reconstruction were the principal techniques in Freud's repertoire. In this year, however, the founder
of psychoanalysis changed his viewpoint toward what today is modern
psychoanalysis or ego psychology. He emphasized that "finding out and
overcoming the 'resistances' " was the major work of the psychotherapist
(Freud, 1910). Freud emphasized that the ego must be prepared for the

analysis of resistance (Karpf, 1977, 1981). Earlier Freud was not so circumspect in his treatment. A reading of his cases suggests that he often used confrontation as a technique to force the unconscious into consciousness, rather than to interpret resistance (Freud, 1905, 1909a, 1909b). As the goal of treatment became the study of the repressing forces, confrontation moved into the background, subordinate to interpretation.

Classical psychoanalysis took root as Freud's focus on technique increased (Freud, 1911, 1912, 1913). Anna Freud's (1936) study of the defense mechanisms clarified the analysis of repressing forces. Nevertheless the approaches to defining interventions were nebulous (Glover, 1937; Lorand, 1946). Therapists seemed to feel that only experience and intuition were necessary on their part to make the patient's unconscious conscious. In those times it did not matter so much what the therapist did as long as it led to symptom resolution. Freud had never defined the therapist's interventions. He used a variety of terms—such as interpretation, explanation, instruction, construction, and reconstruction—almost interchangeably.

A major advance in the history of technical interventions came in 1954 when Bibring published his classic paper on technique (Bibring, 1954). Here he elaborated five techniques that have both technical and curative applications: suggestion, abreaction, manipulation, clarification, and interpretation. These techniques can be utilized in varying degrees, but they form a hierarchical structure: Insight through interpretation is the principal agent and the other four are subordinate to it. Confrontation as a technical and curative intervention was not mentioned. Bibring's descriptions of manipulation and clarification, when combined, constitute much of the contemporary definition of confrontation. Manipulation's purpose was to mobilize the existing forces in the patient that would further the goals of treatment. Clarification's goal was to make the preconscious conscious. Confrontation, as defined in the present discussion, does just these things. The forced insistence by the therapist to get across a message mobilizes the patient's fear of rejection by the therapist and his or her reliance on an external authority. In addition, by directly challenging the avoidance defenses, attention is drawn to the preconscious, making it conscious. For example, confronting the patient about driving recklessly on the expressway challenges his or her avoidance of the danger involved. Later this may be interpreted as an inappropriate expression of aggression.

Not everyone accepted Bibring's announcement of principles. Eissler (1953) introduced the term "parameters," meaning deviations. According to this most of Bibring's principles are nonanalytic. Eissler felt that only the question and the interpretation were necessary in an analysis. All other interventions were nonanalytic and were to be used only in unusual situations. These extra-analytic interventions eventually must be analyzed for the therapy to be deep and successful.

Devereux (1951), who was one of the first to use the term "confrontation," defined confrontation differently than we do today. In fact it sounded much like Bibring's use of the term "clarification." Devereaux said that confrontation was a rewording of the patient's own statements, with nothing added or subtracted. Its intent was to force the patient to pay attention to something he or she had just said, to interrupt the flow of associations when they were veering away from the main issue at hand. Devereux's article had little impact on the field.

The classic textbook (in addition to Nunberg, 1932) used in many training institutes was Glover's *The Techniques of Psychoanalysis* (1955), first published in 1928. Although he never used the term "confrontation" specifically, Glover spoke of modifications in basic psychoanalytic procedures. They were to be used as injunctions to patients who defensively gratify their libidinal impulses in a manner that stalemates their therapy. Glover spoke of the indications for suggestions and forceful directives, reminding the therapist that they may be countertransference-evoked responses. His descriptions of the active techniques contain many of the factors present in the contemporary definition of a confrontation.

Greenson's *The Technique and Practice of Psychoanalysis* (1967) superseded Glover's text. Greenson explictly used the word "confrontation," saying that a confrontation was the first step toward analyzing the patient's material. First the confrontation makes evident to the conscious ego what has been avoided during the analytic hour. Then a clarification focuses the psychic phenomenon. Finally, an interpretation makes the unconscious phenomenon conscious. Working through allows the psychic material, now conscious, to become fully integrated into the character structure, making for structural change in personality.

A few years later, an entire book was devoted to confrontation as a curative technique in psychotherapy (Garner, 1970). Here confrontation was presented as the delivery of a forceful statement and a follow-up question. It was to be used for an emotional problem that was central but only vaguely recognized, and stated succinctly in a positive, almost authoritarian tone: "Stop believing that you are the world's meanest person. What do you think or feel about what I told you?" The first part of the statement, it was believed, helped relieve guilt and anxiety. Moreover it strengthened transference phenomena by its authoritarian nature. The second part of the confrontation, however, permitted the patient to work out a satisfactory solution to his or her conflicts by encouraging independent thought and reality testing. Although Garner's approach, when used in a framework of psychoanalytic therapy, may have merit under certain circumstances, it is not applicable to a wide range of patients and does not entirely fit the definition of confrontation used in the present discussion. It does not seem applicable as a preparatory intervention leading to an interpretation and insight (Greenson, 1967; Compton, 1975). Its application with impulse-ridden characters to block acting out tendencies could be explored by clinical investigation.

The late 1960s and early 1970s were times of social upheaval. Confrontation meant violent clashes between the counterculture and the establishment. Perhaps in response to these sociocultural events, more and more work on the technique of confrontation was published. At the same time, the exploration of the widening scope of indications for psychodynamic therapy (A. Freud, 1954a; Jacobson, 1954; Stone, 1954) prompted psychodynamic therapists to deal more explicitly with essentially nonneurotic transference constellations, such as those seen in borderline personalities, psychotics, and patients with characterological disturbances. Although Eissler (1953) recommended against modifications in classical technique, some therapists began to use confrontation as a salient vehicle in therapy (Adler & Buie, 1972; Buie & Adler, 1973; Kernberg, 1975, 1980). The new discoveries concerning the narcissistic personality (Kohut, 1971, 1977) have also given credence to the use of confrontation as a mode of intervention to be added to Bibring's (1954) other five. Today confrontation is accepted as a valid technique to be used with patients suffering from a diversity of psychopathology.

PRINCIPLES OF TECHNIQUE

For us to understand how best to use confrontations, some salient questions need to be explored. How is a confrontation formed? When should the therapist intervene with a confrontation? How should the therapist evaluate the effect of a confrontation? If a particular confrontation is effective, what accounts for its effectiveness? Without considering the response of the patient, one cannot get far. Does confrontation ever lead to insight? If it does not, how can we distinguish insight from the responses that a confrontation evokes? Finally, what is the proper role of confrontation in the whole therapeutic process?

Freud defined the purpose of psychoanalysis in his famous phrase, "Where id is, there shall ego be." By the very nature of the force that confrontation implies, it exposes something as conflictual where no conflict had previously been apparent. It is a type of intervention that creates conditions without which the analytic procedure would be impossible. Confrontation makes possible the desired dynamic effect of an interpretation; it may thus be regarded as a preparation for an interpretation.

On the other hand, a confrontation may be judged successful in its own right, without leading to an interpretation. It may break through resistance that is hindering the flow of associations. Franz Alexander

(1950) used a confrontation under just these circumstances. He was il-
lustrating his concept of the corrective emotional experience, but his clinical work may be appreciated even by those who do not agree with this
theory.

Alexander's patient was a young, overindulged man who was experiencing difficulty in interpersonal relationships. This patient whined a
great deal, complained, and was extremely demanding. He critized Alexander whenever a clarification or interpretation was made. His appearance
was unappealing; he was frequently dirty and disheveled. Finally, after
the patient protested that Alexander was no different from any of the
other people in the patient's life, Alexander confronted the young man
with the statement that it was no wonder no one liked him if he behaved
in such an unpleasant manner, especially when someone was trying to
help. This confrontation had a striking effect on the patient. Whereas
formerly a therapeutic alliance had been precluded, now the therapist and
patient could collaborate in the analytic work. Alexander's approach illustrates how a confrontation can be effective at an impasse in the therapy,
and particularly how it may strengthen the therapeutic alliance. Although
a confrontation penetrates the reality-distorting defenses in a forceful
manner, the therapy can be enhanced if this intervention is delivered
empathically. How is a confrontation formed and why does the therapist
intervene when he or she does?

Arlow (1980) wrote a comprehensive discussion of the inner workings
of the therapist in the genesis of an interpretation from which we may
learn about the genesis of a confrontation. Freud focused on the therapist's
inner experience as a guidepost to the proper understanding of the patient's
mental life. According to later writers (Reich, 1966), if the therapist has
been properly analyzed, the correct intervention appears automatically in
the therapist's mind in the form of free association.

What is involved in understanding confrontation is the constructive
use and understanding of countertransference. This issue is a continuing
controversy in the literature, and it may be said that the Kleinian school
of psychoanalysis can be distinguished from the classical school by its
treatment of countertransference in the genesis of interventions. The followers of Melanie Klein (e.g., Racker, 1968), by emphasizing the process
of projective identification, believe that the patient induces the therapist
to reflect directly what the patient is unconsciously wishing by projecting
his or her inner life onto the therapist. Thus if the therapist is feeling
angry, then this is an accurate reflection of a projected introject from the
patient's past. An analysis of the therapist's feelings becomes identical
with an analysis of the patient's transference. This Kleinian approach is
particularly harmful when one considers confrontations. To use a confrontation, the therapist must be aware of the potentially traumatic effect
that his or her anger, frustration, or other dysphoric affect will have upon

the patient. The Kleinian approach seeks to validate these emotions in the patient whereas the classical approach seeks to control them. Only the classical approach avoids the harmful consequences of countertransference and its use in confrontations.

Classical therapists such as Spitz (1956) and Arlow (1980) believe that countertransference is but one part of the therapist's relationship to the patient. Having been analyzed and, therefore, knowing his or her own personal equation, the therapist recognizes that he or she may be angry because that is what the patient is saying. After a while this passive–receptive role is abandoned in favor of a more active stance. Through the process of introspection, the therapist becomes aware of personal associations to the patient's material. The range of associations to what the patient is saying are almost infinite. Finally a connection is made between what the patient is reporting and what the therapist is thinking. The repetition of certain themes, material appearing in related sequences, and the convergence of data in a similar context all gell into a hypothesis about the patient's mental functioning (Arlow, 1980).

At this point the therapist's inner experience is transformed into an intervention, usually an interpretation. Often, however, the therapist's intuition seems to call for a preparatory confrontation or clarification. "A confrontation can be made in the form of a question or even an inarticulate gesture or sound that turns the patient's attention towards something just said or done, or interrupts the patient's associations when they are taking the patient away from some issue that the therapist thinks should hold the patient's attention" (Paolino, 1981, p. 8). The ego must be prepared for insight. Sometimes the intervention fails, although the context of therapy seemed to indicate that the ego was ready for an interpretation. The patient may reject it, ignore it, show no insight, or blindly acquiesce. At this point resistance is rearing its head. The patient may continue to regress or to become more uncooperative.

Now the therapist begins to feel frustrated, piqued, or downright angry. Controlling countertransference becomes a salient issue because the therapist will feel a desire to overpower the patient's defenses and resistance. Rationalizations for sadistic intent or for the need to control the patient become primary issues. The feeling of being in a struggle with the patient is unavoidable. At this time the transitory identification made with the patient in the initial passive–receptive role becomes significant in intuiting how forceful to be. Will negative transference manifestations be engendered or will the therapeutic alliance be rent? Will the patient be hurt or traumatized by the intervention? Will the person be made more amenable to insight, the *raison d'être* for uncovering psychotherapy? The nonverbal communications, timber of voice, facial expression, body posture, and gestures (Karpf, 1980a) all give clues to the timing and dosage of the confrontation. The nature of both the therapist's and the patient's characterological defenses and communicative styles also influences the process.

The ingredients of force and urgency are communicated to the patient in a confrontation. The patient's response to an effective confrontation is readiness to examine some behavior that had previously been taken for granted. No insight is imparted, for that is not the goal of this intervention. A confrontation that is not delivered with the proper tact, or is offered in a hostile manner, can be quite disastrous and traumatizing.

An illustration of an effective confrontation that resulted in immediate behavioral change—but no insight—was in the treatment of a young man with a schizotypal personality.

The patient was having difficulties in interpersonal relationships at his job and frequent squabbles with his new wife. His reality testing was mildly distorted, as was his judgment, to conform to his strong need states. He was most likely to misinterpret reality in charged emotional situations; he could not anticipate the consequences of his behavior, and his judgment was habitually so defective as to interfere with his occupation and his marriage. Unable to regulate and control his drives, affects, and impulses, he usually acted on his strong urges, and had poor frustration tolerance. This man's object relationships were characterized by a schizoid detachment rather than a total withdrawal. He was interested in people, but he rarely understood other people's feelings and motives.

I was the third therapist he had seen in a matter of months. The patient always complained that the other therapists did not understand him. It was difficult to form a working alliance with this young man because he related on such an egocentric basis. Always implied was the threat that if his transference needs were not immediately gratified, he would "punish" me by terminating his treatment and consult yet another therapist. Soon the patient began coming late to his sessions with a myriad of excuses ranging from traffic congestion to babysitting problems. At first I let the sessions run late, gratifying his transference wishes for an all-giving mother. Gradually the sessions were ended on time, regardless of when the patient arrived. In Bibring's (1954) terminology, this was exercising a manipulation in order to mobilize the patient's psychic functioning in the service of treatment. The patient was not yet ready for an interpretation. He induced feelings of frustration, helplessness, and anger. The manipulation of the session did not seem to have any effect on his lateness. At last the patient was confronted with his resistance. I asserted that his excuses for lateness did not always appear honest and that honesty was essential if we were to have any sort of therapeutic relationship. I also said that if he did not begin to arrive on time for his appointments, I would transfer him to another therapist. Perhaps, I said, I was not the right person for him to work with.

The young man responded with shock and surprise, typical reactions of a patient to a confrontation. His attention was forcefully thrust toward an issue that threatened his treatment. The intervention was quite effective, because after that the patient was punctual, and when he was late, he was now willing to explore the reasons. In fact after the confrontation the therapeutic alliance solidified.

This is an example of an intervention in the initial stages of treatment before an interpretation is appropriate. It was preparatory in the sense that it set the stage for later insight. There were many times in the psychotherapy of this very disturbed young man when my interpretations were ignored. I remember one session in particular when his reactions to me were taking on a bizarre coloration. He was in the throes of primitive rage, with no obvious reality precipitant. At first I tried connecting his reaction to his mother. When this did not lead to insight, I decided to combine my interpretation with a confrontation. Just when he was making a demand on me that was characteristic of his infantile conflicts with a maternal object, I said to him in a forceful, declarative way, "I am not your mother!" The effect, once again, was to startle him and neutralize his rage. He began to discuss his mother instead of focusing all his attention on me.

As this example illustrates, confrontation can be combined with another intervention. There are often no sharply demarcated classifications concerning when a confrontation ends and a clarification or interpretation begins. Interventions are more often blends then they are pure examples of a specific technique.

Before leaving the principles of technique for a confrontation, I would like to clarify a technical error based on a negative countertransference. The therapist's personal analysis and character structure will influence the way he or she resolves problems about forcing, being forced, hurting, and being hurt. Maintaining self-awareness will avoid bias and negative countertransference.

Once I had the experience of treating a histrionic young women who was seductive and at the same time phobic about being raped. She was quite an attractive patient and my initial countertransference problems were of a positive nature. The patient had entered therapy when an automobile accident left her with a fear of driving. Displacements of oedipal longings for her father seemed to occur with all males regardless of their characteristics. The neighborhood she had to travel was a dangerous one, so her reality testing was good. What she did not understand was her seductive behavior with males and her oscillating wishes for intimacy and distance. This young woman often responded to my interpretations in a compliant but unfeeling manner, with no real indication that she understood what I was saying. One day, in a mood of pique, and not having my wits about me, I confronted the patient with her seductive behavior toward men by simply saying that much of her fear of rape would be diminished if she stopped acting in such a seductive manner. The effect of a successful confrontation is to lead the way toward insight. What aspect of her behavior or inner workings of her psychic functioning could she have become aware of without analyzing it? This is, of course, a rhetorical question, asked so that the purpose of a confrontation may always be kept in mind—to prepare for an interpretation or to effect some immediate change without insight when an interpretation failed.

In any case the patient was predictably shocked, the usual reaction to a confrontation. On the other hand, no insight was engendered. In fact she came to her next session with a dream that a close friend had betrayed her trust and made a sexual overture toward her, representing the traumatic effect the confrontation had had. The patient felt violated and unconsciously

angry. My countertransference-based intervention had no effect other than
to create further resistance and to hinder our therapeutic alliance.

Timing, dosage, tact, style, and self-awareness are as important for
the effective delivery of a confrontation as they are for an interpretation.

CONFRONTATION IN THE TRANSFERENCE

The phenomenon of transference is central to understanding psychodynamic psychotherapy. It may be defined as the present experience of
past relationships, usually pathogenic (Meissner & Nicholi, 1978). During
uncovering therapy the patient transfers feelings and behavior originating
with parental figures onto the therapist, forming a transference constellation, either neurotic, borderline, or psychotic, depending on the nature
of the psychotherapy (Karpf, 1980b).

The therapeutic alliance counterbalances the inappropriate repetitions
of the past manifested in the transference. The term "therapeutic alliance"
was introduced by Zetzel (1956), and refers to the working relationship
between the healthy part of the patient's ego and the therapist's analyzing
ego. It is essential for an analysis of the transference. In her seminal
article, Zetzel contrasts the classical viewpoint with the Kleinian one in
regard to the "split" in the patient's ego that allows the alliance to take
place. The Kleinians view the entire relationship between therapist and
patient as transference, and understand this relationship in terms of the
early mother–infant relationship. The technique of confrontation may
best be understood from the classical position, which emphasizes the
necessity for a sound therapeutic alliance in performing psychotherapy.
As I will make clear, a confrontation often has the effect of securing the
foundations of a shaky alliance.

Allied to the concept of transference is the acknowledgment that the
therapist may interfere with the unfolding of the transference manifestations of the patient by countertransference. Essentially, countertransference is transference emanating from the therapist. It must be kept out
of treatment. The more that external reality—aside from the therapeutic
alliance—is kept away from the treatment, the more the group of genetically founded intrapsychic fantasies known as transference may unfold.
The real relationship between patient and therapist, with the therapeutic
alliance as one sector, is often contrasted with the distortions of transference (Menaker, 1942). The idea that the transference can be "contaminated" (Greenacre, 1956) or "safeguarded" (Greenson, 1967) is a logical
consequence of the classical psychoanalytic position.

By remaining anonymous and fulfilling the mirroring function, and adhering to the rule of abstinence, the therapist safeguards the transference from inappropriate contamination. The transference is analyzed when it becomes a resistance, and also when it has reached the highest possible level of intensity, making it amenable to insight for the patient. Greenson (1967) described the facets of a series of technical steps in analyzing the transference, with confrontation beginning the process.

The task of confrontation in analyzing resistance is to get the patient to understand that he or she is resisting, to be followed later by clarifications and interpretations that help the patient understand *why* he or she is resisting, *what* he or she is resisting, and *how* he or she is resisting. Sometimes a confrontation is unnecessary in demonstrating resistance if the resistance is obvious to the patient. Usually, however, reality-distorting defenses conceal the obvious from the patient. Then a confrontation is essential. The vividness of the resistance and the extent of the psychopathology as manifested by the patient's reasonableness will be the factors influencing when and if to confront. In the clinical vignette offered earlier concerning the schizotypal young man who continued to come late to the sessions, it was necessary to wait for a considerable period of time, until the intensity of resistance had reached its maximum, for a confrontation to be made.

Greenson (1967) offered an illustration of confrontation that complements the author's vignettes. Premature attempts at confrontation to demonstrate resistance are a waste of time, and actually may create new resistances that will be difficult to analyze at a later time. In Greenson's example his patient was coming a few minutes late to each session. To have pointed this out to her on the spot would have been a technical error. It would have distracted the patient. Instead Greenson waited for other instances of resistance in the sessions until the patient no longer could deny that she was avoiding something. The effect of the confrontation was to bring the patient's preconscious motivation into awareness, making it amenable to interpretation and insight. For the confrontation to be maximally effective, the therapist must let the resistance develop. Then the forcefulness and accuracy of its effect on the patient eventually will lead to curative insight.

One other instance when a confrontation is appropriate occurs when the interpretive process has gone awry. At times misunderstanding of the patient may invoke an incorrect interpretation. At other times the therapist's countertransference will intrude on the process and an interpretation may not only be inaccurate, but also mildly traumatizing. At still other times a negative therapeutic reaction (Freud, 1923) may occur to a valid interpretation, leading to a worsening of symptomatology. A negative therapeutic reaction is an increase of pathology attributable to intrapsychic aspects of the patient and not to the therapist's errors in technique (Sandler et al., 1970). The special roles of negativism (Olinick, 1964) and masochism (Asch, 1976) have been identified as prime contributing factors.

The validating process within the therapist will alert him or her to the fact that the interpretive process has failed and to the reasons for its failure. If misunderstanding or countertransference has contributed to an invalid intervention, it must be corrected. On the other hand, if a negative therapeutic reaction has occurred, appropriate action must be taken. An incorrect intervention would lead to a redoing of the whole interpretive process, starting with demonstration of the resistance by a confrontation. Negative therapeutic reactions, however, often lead to self-destructive acting out. In these instances a confrontation is the intervention of choice.

In acting out, denial and other reality-distorting defenses may lead to life-threatening behavior. A shock to the patient's psychic equilibrium is needed to block this behavior and make him or her amenable to insight. Often the best shock is a confrontation. This is especially true with narcissistic and borderline persons. Neurotic acting out occurs because it unconsciously relieves inner tension and provides parital discharge of warded-off impulses (Fenichel, 1945). The essential process is a displacement from repressed memories to present derivatives. On the other hand, borderline, narcissistic, and other nonneurotic forms of acting out take place because repression and other processes of internalization have failed. In these conditions acting out may take the form of suicidal gestures. On other occasions the patient's employment or marriage may be threatened. The forceful intrusion of a confrontation upon the defenses of splitting or other forms of projection will have a salutary effect upon the ego function of judgment. Since acting out is essentially a process of reenactment—reliving, or living out, rather then remembering—it is most frequent in patients with impulse-control problems. These patients have difficulties anticipating the consequences of their actions. Forcing them to come to grips with these consequences and to take responsibility for their behavior ultimately will lead to internalization of their conflicts, making the patients amenable to insight.

PARAMETERS OF TECHNIQUE

Any discussion of the technique of confrontation would not be complete without considering its relationship with the so-called "parameters" or deviations in technique as set forth by Eissler (1953). Is a confrontation a parameter of technique? It was Freud, of course, in his papers on technique (e.g., Freud, 1913), who set the ground rules and boundaries of the therapeutic relationship. He advocated that the therapist be like a surgeon who puts aside his or her personality when operating. The therapist should be like a mirror, showing the patient no more and no less than he or she projects onto the therapist. The therapist must also remain neutral and strictly adhere to the rule of abstinence for analysis to occur. The therapist should set aside an hour for the patient and lease it for a set fee, to be paid on a monthly basis. Freud also described the use of a sofa and the therapist's position out of sight behind the patient, although face-to-face encounter is more generally practiced in psychoanalytic psychotherapy. In any case Freud let the area of technical precepts concerning the ground rules of treatment lay fallow. Ferenczi (1921) advocated educative and active measures under certain conditions. Before Freud died he offered an analysis of his treatment of the Wolf Man (Freud, 1937). Freud asserted that setting a time limit could be a very effective technique in treatment, although it would not guarantee success. He felt that such steps were necessary with patients who suffered alterations of their ego. This is also the viewpoint of Eissler (1953).

Eissler defined parameters of technique as quantitive and qualitative deviations from the basic model that requires interpretation as the exclusive therapeutic tool. With unmodifiable ego dysfunctions, parameters may be introduced, but never beyond the unavoidable minimum, and they should be used only when they subsequently can be analyzed. Parameters are those deviations in technique to be used with patients suffering developmental ego arrests. All other alterations in standard technique and in the basic framework have been called "deviations" and "modifications" (Langs, 1976). At times these may compromise the therapeutic outcome. Recent work with borderline personalities (Kernberg, 1975) speaks specifically of the confrontation being a necessary modification in technique, although it is not felt that the therapeutic outcome is compromised. In fact, with these severely disturbed patients, confrontational style actually enhances the therapy.

Is a confrontation a parameter or deviation of technique? If it is, then many of the other interventions described in this book would be also. Perhaps this question is best answered by reiterating the purposes of a confrontation. Any intervention that has as its purpose the replacement of interpretation and eventual insight is a deviation that may threaten the therapeutic outcome. All interventions subserve the final goal of insight and should be judged on that basis. Thus, if a confrontation is offered to stabilize a weak therapeutic alliance, it is not a modification in technique, because the whole purpose of the therapeutic alliance is to create the conditions necessary for analysis of the transference to occur. If a confrontation is offered as a preparatory introduction in the interpretive process, then, once again, it is quite appropriate because it leads to insight. If a confrontation is delivered because the therapist is frustrated or angry, then, although not a deviation, it is an inappropriate countertransference-based response. Rarely is a confrontation a deviation that would threaten the therapeutic outcome. More commonly it is countertransference. A confrontation is not difficult to analyze because it evokes so many unconscious fantasies and transference manifestations. If it is a parameter at all, it should be termed a "minor" parameter rather than a "major" parameter. It is unlike the writing of a prescription for medication, which is a major parameter and an often unanalyzable modification in technique.

Perhaps one should remember Anna Freud's (1954) injunction for flexibility in the ground rules and Stone's (1961) call for the human qualities of the therapist to be part of the framework. Stone discussed the need for all interventions to be neutral maneuvers. He viewed the whole therapeutic situation as taking place along an axis between the poles of gratification and frustration. The therapeutic situation is stringent enough, he asserted, to allow some minor, social gratifications. Stone discussed the ground rule of anonymity and questioned whether it was appropriate for the therapist indiscriminately to withhold information about himself or herself. He considered that it is less detrimental to the therapy for the patient to discover that the therapist is human than for the therapist to use stiff, unreal attitudes and practices. Although not specifically mentioned by Stone, a confrontation reveals the human side of the therapist more often than many other interventions. A confrontation, by intruding on denial, projection, or avoidance, separates what a person is from what he or she would like to be (Weisman, 1973). It is a demythologizer.

CONFRONTATION IN THE THERAPEUTIC ALLIANCE

In addition to Freud, Sterba (1934) and Bibring (1937) made explicit the cooperative factors in the therapeutic relationship. The mature and rational capacities of the patient to work toward the goals of therapy were emphasized by Zetzel (1956) in her concept of the "therapeutic alliance" and Greenson (1965) in his idea of the "working alliance." Moreover, recent writers stress the differences between the classical analytic stance toward the patient and that in other therapeutic persuasions, by emphasizing the concept of the therapeutic or working alliance (Curtis, 1980).

On the other hand, purists (Brenner, 1980; Langs, 1976) see no need for the concept and feel that the human qualities of the therapist are best exemplified by quiet understanding and empathic interpretations. As so often happens, these radical purists run the risk of allying themselves unintentionally with the Kleinians, who accentuate the total relationship as transference and call for immediate and deep interpretation of primitive anxieties. What the classical analysts are realistically concerned about is that the working alliance may be a rationalization for deviations in technique, and unnecessary deviations at that. The real purpose of the therapeutic alliance is to further the goals of psychodynamic therapy, not to subvert it—a caveat that those who work with borderline and other non-neurotic syndromes often forget. A confrontation that stabilizes the therapeutic alliance does not lead to insight, but is not a deviation in technique because it furthers the analytic goals of treatment. A confrontation is not a deviation in technique if it is not a technical error based on faulty knowledge, lack of empathy, or countertransference. Confronting the patient with an unpaid bill, for example, helps reestablish the working alliance, the ground rules, and the boundaries of the therapeutic relationship. Without such noninterpretive confrontations, the work cannot proceed.

Viewing the therapeutic alliance as mild positive transference resolves the difficulties. There are always analyzable transference components of the alliance, just as there are precipitates of reality in every transference manifestation. Nevertheless recent clinical research (Karpf, 1980a) points to the inevitable reality factors that must be recognized in any therapeutic relationship. Ignoring the nonverbal components—the kinesic and proxemic aspects—of therapy hinders the working alliance and creates bastions of preformed transference reactions that may be difficult to analyze later in the treatment. Confronting the patient with attitudes toward decorations in the office, clothing styles, and even such touchy issues as ethnic and generational differences, will help to create a viable working atmosphere and the eventual constellations of the infantile neurosis toward the therapist. As clinicians we often treat patients who have political and cultural attitudes that we find morally repugnant. When this happens the most effective strategy is to maintain a neutral and mirroring function, while confronting those conflicts that hindered effective collaboration against the patient's misery. Often attitudes are preconscious and must be made conscious by a forceful confrontation. Not only statements, but sometimes such nonverbal pronouncements as grunts of approval or disapproval, may make an attitude amenable to eventual interpretation and insight.

Warnings, prohibitions, threats, or verbal punishments are occasionally appropriate in emergency situations. These types of confrontations have been termed "heroic" interventions, to distinguish them from "routine" confrontations in the interpretive process (Corwin, 1973). They arouse abandonment anxiety and the need to please the therapist. They also call for immediate behavioral change. These dramatic confrontations should only be used in the face of destructive acting out or when the treatment is threatened. They are analyzable parameters of technique. The therapist eventually must analyze the primitive anxiety and terror aroused by this type of confrontation. The patient may be traumatized, but is likely to realize at some level that the caring and humaness of the therapist prompted the intervention.

SUMMARY

Confrontation only recently has been recognized as an appropriate intervention in psychoanalytic psychotherapy. Freud and his students used it, and contemporary therapists use it still. At times the confrontation is the initial step in the interpretive process. At other times it is a viable intervention in its own right. It aids in the analysis of transference and it structures the therapeutic alliance. It is occasionally a parameter of technique, but more often it is not. It may be a countertransference-based response, but usually is an appropriate intervention to id derivatives. All in all it is a fitting stone in the edifice of psychodynamic psychotherapy.

REFERENCES

Adler, C., and Buie, D. The misuses of confrontation with borderline patients. *International Journal of Psychoanalytic Psychotherapy*, 1971, *1*, 109–120.
Alexander, F. (1950) Analysis of the therapeutic factors in psychoanalytic treatment. In: F. Alexander (Ed.), *The scope of psychoanalysis.* New York: Basic Books, 1961.
Arlow, J. The genesis of interpretation. In: H. Blum (Ed.), *Psychoanalytic explorations of technique.* New York: International Universities Press, 1980.
Asch, S. Varieties of negative therapeutic reaction and problems of technique. *Journal of the American Psychoanalytic Association*, 1976, *24*, 383–408.
Bibring, E. Therapeutic results of psychoanalysis. *International Journal of Psychoanalysis*, 1937, *18*, 170–189.
Bibring, E. Psychoanalysis and the dynamic psychotherapies. *Journal of the American Psychoanalytic Association*, 1954, *2*, 745–770.
Binstock, W. *Clarification.* Unpublished manuscript, 1981.
Blum, H. (Ed.) *Psychoanalytic explorations of technique.* New York: International Universities Press, 1980.
Buie, D., and Adler, G. The uses of confrontation in the psychotherapy of borderline cases. In: G. Adler and P. Myerson (Eds.), *Confrontation in psychotherapy.* New York: Science House, 1973.
Compton, A. Aspects of psychoanalytic intervention. In: B. Fine and H. Waldhorn (Eds.), *Kris study group monograph VI.* New York: International Universities Press, 1975.
Corwin, H. Therapeutic confrontation from routine to heroic. In: G. Adler and

P. Myerson (Eds.), *Confrontation in psychotherapy*. New York: Science House, 1973.

Curtis, H. The concept of therapeutic alliance: Implications for the "widening scope." In: H. Blum (Ed.), *Psychoanalytic explorations of technique*. New York: International Universities Press, 1980.

Devereux, G. Some criteria for the timing of confrontations and interpretations. *International Journal of Psychoanalysis*, 1951, *32*, 19–24.

Eissler, K. The effect of the structure of the ego on psychoanalytic technique. *Journal of the American Psychoanalytic Association*, 1953, *1*, 104–143.

Fenichel, O. Neurotic acting out. *Psychoanalytic Review*, 1945, *32*, 197–206.

Ferenczi, S. (1921) The further development of an active therapy in psychoanalysis. In: S. Ferenczi, *Contributions to the theory and technique of psychoanalysis*. New York: Basic Books, 1955.

Freud, A. (1936) *The ego and the mechanisms of defense*. New York: International Universities Press, 1966.

Freud, A. Discussion. The widening scope of indications for psychoanalysis. *Journal of the American Psychoanalytic Association*, 1954a, *2*, 607–620.

Freud, A. Problems of technique in adult analysis. *Bulletin of the Philadelphia Association for Psychoanalysis*, 1954b, *4*, 44–70.

Freud, S. (1905) Fragment of an analysis of a case of hysteria, *Standard edition*, vol. 7, London: Hogarth Press, 1953, pp. 3–124.

Freud, S. (1909) Analysis of a phobia in a five-year old boy. *Standard edition*, vol. 10, London: Hogarth Press, 1955, pp. 3–149.

Freud, S. (1909) Notes upon a case of obsessional neurosis. *Standard edition*, vol. 10, London: Hogarth Press, 1955, pp. 153–318.

Freud, S. (1910) The future prospects of psychoanalytic therapy, *Standard edition*, vol. 11, London: Hogarth Press, 1957, pp. 89–96.

Freud, S. (1911) The handling of dream interpretation in psychoanalysis. *Standard edition*, vol. 12, London: Hogarth Press, 1958, pp. 89–96.

Freud, S. (1912) The dynamics of transference. *Standard edition*, vol. 12, London: Hogarth Press, 1958, pp. 89–96.

Freud, S. (1913) On beginning the treatment. *Standard edition*, vol. 12. London: Hogarth Press, 1958, pp. 12–144.

Freud, S. (1923) The ego and the id. *Standard edition*, vol. 19. London: Hogarth Press, 1961, pp. 3–66.

Freud, S. (1937) Analysis terminable and interminable. *Standard edition*, vol. 23. London: Hogarth Press, 1964, pp. 209–253.

Garner, H. *Psychotherapy: Confrontation problem-solving technique*. St. Louis: Warren H. Green, 1970.

Glover, E. The theory of the therapeutic results of psychoanalysis. *International Journal of Psychoanalysis*. 1937, *18*, 125–132.

Greenacre, P. Re-evaluation of the process of working through. *International Journal of Psychoanalysis*, 1956, 37, 439–445.

Greenson, R. (1965). The working alliance and the transference neurosis. In: R. Greenson, *Explorations in psychoanalysis*. New York: International Universities Press, 1967.

Greenson, R. *The technique and practice of psychoanalysis*. New York: International Universities Press, 1967.

Jacobson, E. Transference problems in the psychoanalytic treatment of severely depressive patients. *Journal of the American Psychoanalytic Association*. 1954, *2*, 595–606.

Karpf, R. Psychotherapy of depression. *Psychotherapy: Theory, research, and practice*, 1977, *14*, 349–353.

Karpf, R. Nonverbal components of the interpretive process in psychoanalytic psychotherapy. *American Journal of Psychotherapy*, 1980a, *34*, 477–486.

Karpf, R. Modalities of psychotherapy with the elderly. *Journal of the American Geriatrics Society*, 1980b, *28*, 367–371.

Karpf, R. Individual psychotherapy with the elderly. In: A. Horton (Ed.), *Mental health interventions with the aging*. New York: Praeger, 1982.

Kernberg, O. *Borderline conditions and pathological narcissism*. New York: Jason Aronson, 1975.

Kernberg, O. Some implications of object relations theory for psychoanalytic technique. In: Blum (Ed.), *Psychoanalytic explorations of technique: Discourse on the theory of therapy*. New York: International Universities Press, 1980.

Kohut, H. *The analysis of the self*. New York: International Universities Press, 1971.

Kohut, H. *The restoration of the self*. New York: International Universities Press, 1977.

Kris, E. *Explorations in art*. New York: International Universities Press, 1952.

Langs, R. *The technique of psychoanalytic psychotherapy, volume one*. New York: Jason Aronson, 1973.

Langs, R. *The therapeutic interaction, Volume II: A critical overview and synthesis*. New York: Jason Aronson, 1976.

Lorand, S. *Technique of psychoanalytic treatment*. New York: International Universities Press, 1946.

Meissner, W., and Nicholi, A. The psychotherapies: Individual, family and group. In: A. Nicholi (Ed.). *The Harvard guide to modern psychiatry*. Cambridge, Mass.: Harvard University Press, 1978.

Menaker, E. The masochistic factor in the psychoanalytic situation. *Psychoanalytic Quarterly*, 1942, *9*, 171–186.

Nunberg, H. (1932) *Principles of psychoanalysis*. New York: International Universities Press, 1955.

Olinick, S. The negative therapeutic reaction. *International Journal of Psychoanalysis*, 1964, *45*, 540–548.

Paolino, T. *Confrontation: A historical perspective*. Unpublished manuscript, 1980.

Paolino, T. *Twenty minute lecture on technique*. Unpublished manuscript, 1981.

Racker, H. *Transference and countertransference*. London: Hogarth Press, 1968.

Reich, A. (1966) Empathy and countertransference. In: A. Reich (Ed.), *Psychoanalytic contributions*. New York: International Universities Press, 1973.

Sandler, J., Holder, A., and Dare, C. Basic psychoanalytic concepts: VII. The negative therapeutic reaction. *British Journal of Psychiatry*, 1970, *117*, 431–435.

Spitz, R. Countertransference: Comments on its varying role in the analytic situation. *Journal of the American Psychoanalytic Association*, 1956, *4*, 256–265.

Sterba, R. The fate of the ego in analytic therapy. *International Journal of Psychoanalysis*, 1934, *15*, 117–125.

Stewart, R. Psychoanalysis and psychoanalytic psychotherapy. In: A. Freedman, H. Kaplan, and B. Sadock (Eds.), *Comprehensive textbook of psychiatry*. Baltimore: Wailliams & Wilkins, 1975.

Stone, L. The widening scope of indications for psychoanalysis. *Journal of the American Psychoanalytic Association*, 1954, *2*, 567–594.

Stone, L. *The psychoanalytic situation.* New York: International Universities Press, 1961.

Weisman, A. Confrontation, countertransference, and context. In: G. Adler, and P. Myerson (Eds.), *Confrontation in psychotherapy.* New York: Science House, 1973.

Zetzel, E. Symposium: Current concepts of transference. *International Journal of Psychoanalysis,* 1956, *37,* 368–376.

9
Confrontation: Clinical Application

ZVI LOTHANE, M.D.

Dr. Nichols appeared apologetic when he invited me to write a chapter on confrontation. He expressed regret that the more prestigious topic of interpretation had already gone to someone else, leaving me with a much more modest assignment. He was surprised when I accepted with alacrity. For I profess a healthy respect for confrontation. It has been dawning on me for sometime now that, contrary to the official story, the leverage of psychotherapy derives not from interpretation, but from confrontation. It is confrontation that is a source of learning for the sufferer, often much more so than interpretation. Furthermore, one may not be able to draw clear boundaries between the traditionally established estates of clarification, confrontation, and interpretation. It may be impossible to tell where confrontation ends and interpretation begins.

To understand the concept of confrontation, we need a preparatory discussion to orient us about the field in which confrontation plays a role, so that we can understand the role it does play. According to the official story, the so-called patient is suffering from anything ranging from problems in living to maladjustment to so-called mental illness, to which a professional applies a treatment called psychotherapy, analysis, or simply therapy. It is also often stated that the primary tool of such therapy is interpretation; that interpretation offers insights to the patient; and that insights make the patient change. It is implied that interpretation is the summit of all other therapeutic measures, which are seen as preparatory or adjunctive. This conception of psychotherapy as a craft is tacitly based on an analogy with medicine and surgery. Just as in somatic therapy, the expert, the physician or surgeon, diagnoses ulcers in the intestines and prescribes the right kind of pharmacological or surgical treatment, so in psychological therapies the expert, the psychotherapist, diagnoses the patient's psychological ills and applies the right interpretation, which creates change and cures the patient. However, a disturbing fact has been causing sleepless nights to both the recipients and the providers of psychotherapy; namely, all too often the right interpretations are given and insights are acknowledged, but the patient refuses to change.

The professional and popular literature both are full of statements praising or condemning psychotherapy, touting its various methods and modalities, polarizing people into those who "believe" in it and those who do not. People debate whether psychodynamic therapy is superior, inferior, or worthless as compared with behavior modification, or drugs. A striking difference leaps to mind, however, between the realms of somatic and psychological therapies. Whereas in both realms, reference is made to the theoretical and empirical dimensions of the discipline, the distinction between the theoretical and empirical is clear in the realm of the somatic, and most confused in the realm of the psychological. Thus, for example, two surgeons who advocate different surgical techniques for ulcerative colitis will not, by virtue of this fact, see themselves as belonging to opposing and hostile schools of surgery. Neither will the surgeons fight each other because they have differing views on the theory, say, of transfer of substances across cell membranes. The picture is very different in the psychological realm. Psychodynamic and behavioral clinicians are very often at each other's throats because of the difference in the theories about the species to which they subscribe. In this sense we are not very far from the theological wars of the Middle Ages. Do we believe in the unconscious, the Oedipus complex, penis envy, the self, or deconditioning and reinforcement? What cures the patient—the right theory and the right technique or the right quality of relationship between the participants? Are interpretations a specific mode of treatment or are they effective because of a placebo effect, that is, are based on nothing more than mere suggestion?

I hope the foregoing discussion highlights a confusion between what is fact and what is inference in the psychological realm. To further our discussion of the concept of confrontation, I would like to generate some agreement about how to view the field and how to act in it. I propose that the psychological model differs essentially from the medical model. In the psychological realm, we are dealing with human character as it reveals itself in love and in action, in conflicts of conscience and choices made about such conflicts. Psychotherapy continues the tradition of the moralist, the dramatist, the novelist, and the educator. It is not a cure of conditions, but more in the nature of child rearing and education. Just as in these processes, learning and change are a result of an interaction between two persons, so in psychotherapy the teacher can only have an effect if the student wants to learn. Just as there is no learning by the student without homework, there is no analysis without self-analysis. Interpretations do not create insights and change; they can only be the occasions for setting in motion processes of self-scrutiny and, possibly, an impetus to change. What changes are we talking about? They are changes in the habits that make up a person's character, habits of dealing with moral conflicts and actions according to recurrent stereotypes of character. Since change means changing habits, there is no contradiction but only complementarity between psychotherapy and behavior modification.

An early teacher of mine, Dr. Angelo Madonia, used to say that he was forever baffled by the question of whether psychotherapy works. Of course it works, was his answer, because life works. Psychotherapy works or fails to the extent that life's enterprises end in success or in defeat. My own conviction is that psychotherapy works because love works (Lothane, 1982b; 1985). Toward the end of his career, Sigmund Freud, who contributed more than anyone else to the enterprise of psychotherapy, spoke of analysis as an after-education (Lothane, 1984b). In the course of my most recent study on transference (Lothane, 1984d), I discovered that another abiding paradigm in Freud is the *love model*. Freud's whole life was a struggle with the demons of love. He encountered it in Breuer's (his mentor) and his own dealings with hysterics toward the end of the 19th century, and rediscovered it full force in the 20th century, toward the end of his life, when he unabashedly spoke of love in "The Question of Lay Analysis" (Freud, 1926). I view the psychotherapeutic relationship as a love relationship ruled by ethics and by its own moral code. It is a love relationship, whose purpose is to teach and learn about love.

To continue with the topic of confrontation, we may begin by considering the everyday uses of the concept and then examine what is added to them in their technical applications. The relationship between ordinary words and technical terms in psychotherapy is not the same as the relationship between ordinary usages and scientific usages.

The referents of scientific technical terms, as in physics or chemistry, are narrowly and precisely defined, based on empirical or experimental criteria. The same cannot be said of the technical terms of psychodynamics and psychotherapy. The boundary between the ordinary and the technical usages is often blurred and imprecise. This stems from two facts: (1) the therapeutic situation itself is not that far removed from ordinary life experiences, and (2) the technical terms of psychodynamics often are not determined scientifically but ideologically, or even politically at times, to satisfy the political and polemical needs of an ideological cult (Lothane, 1983b).

Confronting has these meanings according to standard dictionaries: (1) coming together to face one another, (2) comparing, (3) challenging. It is a concept that qualifies human relations and interactions. Confronting in human relations, once invoked, immediately, momentously, and radically implies the qualities of love, power, and justice in these relations. The concept of confrontation also implies the notion of purpose and choice in human action. Thus to say that a person confronts another immediately presupposes that he or she confronts the other with a purpose deriving from love, power, or justice. Confronting, therefore, is an action whose ethical dimension needs to be spelled out. Confronting can be right or wrong depending on the quality of the purpose that informs it.

It also flows from the foregoing that the difference between confronting in ordinary life circumstances and confronting in the context of the psychotherapeutic situation has similarities and differences. As posited earlier, the psychotherapeutic relationship is a special instance of a love relationship ruled by the ethics of the situation. Whenever we consider confronting, we should be asking ourselves these questions: For the sake of whom? In the name of what? To what end? In love or in hatred? Truthfully or deceitfully? Selfishly or altruistically? To gratify or to frustrate? To reveal or to conceal? To enlighten or to confuse? To heal or to harm? To serve or to use? Then, too, is the confronting for the benefit of the patient or for the benefit of the therapist? Is it done out of concern for the other's welfare, as in true friendship, or to aggrandize oneself, to triumph, to be right?

People confront each other as who they are, what they do to each other, and what they have. What people are in terms of their appearance, the words they utter, the acts they perform, and the attitudes they choose to display—all these are in the realm of the overt and the observable. They are on the surface, and can be witnessed and recorded. Compared with these, motives of actions are covert, secret, hidden in the depths. They either can be *confessed* by the actor or inferred by an observer. It was the followers of Franz Anton Mesmer (such as Count de Puységur), the forerunners of Sigmund Freud, who as practitioners of psychotherapy (without calling it by that name) stumbled on the submerged continent of the inner depths of the mind—the hidden motives of human action. Novelists and dramatists, of course, knew all that before, as did ordinary men and women. Freud used the catchword "the unconscious" to refer to the complexities of conflict and motivation lying in the hidden depths.

It is usually said that confrontations deal with and are aimed at the surface, whereas interpretations are aimed at the depths. If this is given, then it follows that as confrontations are concerned with overt conduct, they aim at words, deeds, and gestures that are witnessable and thus ascertainable. Confrontations deal with facts. By contrast interpretations are concerned with inferences about facts. Interpretations are constructions, conjectures, and, perhaps, merely guesses put on facts. Interpretations are assumed, derived, construed, fabricated meanings and intentions applied to what people say and do (Lothane, 1984a).

Freud delineated interpretation, first in the epoch-making *The Interpretation of Dreams* (Freud, 1900), and some 35 years later in the *New Introductory Lectures* (Freud, 1933) and other works. In *The Interpretation of Dreams*, the definition of the concept of interpretation and the delineation of the definitive psychodynamic method of treatment and research (the method of free association) went hand in hand. In that work Freud clearly juxtaposed the interpretations of dreams according to the methods of divination, as in the "Egyptian Dream Book," (i.e., according to a fixed symbol key) versus the new method of decoding dreams on the basis of the dreamer's own associations to the dream as a whole or to its various elements. It is of interest to note that the pseudoscientific method of divination and the scientific method of physical diagnosis share a common methodological denominator—a fixed cause-and-effect correlation between the cause hidden in the depth and the effect seen on the surface—and that this can be discovered by an expert in interpretation. By contrast the personal key to the unlocking of the dream's deeper mysteries, determined by individual and not generic causes, was in the possession of the dreamer, not of an external diviner or interpreter. In short, analyzability was the analyzee's responsibility. Toward the end of his career, in the *New Introductory Lectures*, Freud noted the limits of interpretation: that one should always be aware of the difference between interpreting from a text and interpreting into it. At any given time, and with any sequence of the material, the question is whether the interpreter is reading the sender's meanings or putting his or her own meanings into the received message. Furthermore, it should be appreciated that these limits are invoked from the vantage point of *semiology*, the discipline that deals with the correspondence and reference between the signifier and the signified. However, as I have shown elsewhere (Lothane, 1983a), semiology and the pursuit of meaning address the content of the sender's messages, but not their intent. The other vantage point is that of *axiology*, the discipline that deals with values. The meaning of meaning is twofold: *perceptual* identity and correspondence on the one hand, and *personal* intention and moral values on the other. Meanings are read; intentions are read, confronted, and acted upon. Specifically the question can always be asked whether the observed speeches and acts are confrontations of friendly or hostile, loving or hating, intentions. Whereas perceptual identity can be ascertained immediately and unmistakably (we see a cow and we know it is a cow instantly), the identity of intentions may or may not be self-evident. Time is the test for the truthfulness of intentions.

From the time Freud was struck with the discovery of meaning, to his last work dealing with it (Freud, 1937), he remained most vocal about the meaning of ideational content and considerably less so about intent, although he was not silent concerning the latter. His 1912–1915 papers on technique addressed the issues of honesty, candor, and responsibility quite clearly. Most therapists today have followed in Freud's footsteps in considering content over intent. Szasz (1965) is a notable exception. You will not find the concept of confrontation in the index to the *Standard Edition* of Freud's works, and the existing literature on confrontation also is rather limited.

Devereux (1951, pp. 19–20) has given the following definition of confrontation.

> Confrontation, which differs appreciably from interpretation, consists essentially in a rewording of the patient's own statements, especially in the form of "calling a spade a spade." Nothing is added to the patient's statements, nor is anything subtracted therefrom, with the exception of the actual wording, which is viewed as an attempt to gloss over the obvious. In simplest terms, confrontation is a device whereby the patient's attention is directed to the bare factual content of his actions or statements to a coincidence which he has perceived, but has not, or confesses not to have, registered.
>
> . . . [in confrontation] the analyst utilizes primarily his secondary thought processes. Consequently confrontation is an *analytic* device only in so far as it leads to the production, or to the mulling over, of some new material, *which is eventually interpreted* in terms of the logic of the unconscious.
>
> . . . in contrast to genuine interpretations, which demand an unusual appropriateness in timing, confrontations may, in most cases, be made whenever the analyst notices something which the patient does not profess to know or is not aware of knowing

Devereux (1951, p. 20) goes on to stress the following as the hallmark of an interpretation.

> A genuine interpretation is an act whereby the *quality of intelligibility* is added to the patient's own statements and acts. Substandard additions are not interpretations but an attack upon the patient's autonomy as a person . . . An interpretation must add "nothing" to that which is being interpreted, and must be intelligible to the listener—i.e., there must be a psychic readiness for it and a possibility of utilizing the interpretation. (Emphasis in the original.)

He then reaches the following conclusion.

> If we read only thus far, we may gain the impression that there is no real difference between an interpretation and a confrontation. Actually, the two differ as much as an interpretation differs from a mere rewording, or from drawing someone's attention to something which the latter perceives but fails to register. The crucial difference between the two is the overwhelmingly greater significance of psychic readiness for the effectiveness of interpretations.

In the foregoing analysis, Devereux makes a number of distinctions. There is a difference between psychotherapy defined as a *science* and "craft lore" and *service*. Since the readiness of the patient is a crucial consideration, it follows that the service aspect is much more important than the science aspect. Incidentally Devereux's chosen criterion of scientific validity derives from gestalt psychology, a matter of no immediate concern to us here. His other invoked scientific concern, the logic of the unconscious, is not operationalized in his paper at all, other than being linked to irrationality. Another distinction concerns the difference between surface manifestations and depth meanings. Without so naming it, Devereux here is on rather familiar grounds; that is, those generally subsumed under the rubric of resistances. Thus the difference between confrontations and interpretations is not maintained at the level of extrinsic, or formal, criteria (i.e., from the vantage point of the observer), but at the level of the intrinsic, personal criteria of the recipient of these ministrations. In this Devereux falls in with the well-known classical therapeutic prescription to approach the patient's productions from the surface, from what is known and what the patient is ready for, with the idea of turning the patient's attention to his or her own productions, of increasing the degree of awareness of self and thus providing a stimulus toward further self-inquiry, and, it is hoped, a desire to change. It is difficult to see how these recommendations essentially augment the everyday implications of the word "confront," in the sense of facing, comparing, or challenging.

Greenson (1967), a later exponent of the classical psychodynamic technique, did not add anything new to the state of the art as reflected in Devereux's paper. He maintained that to analyze means to engage in any one of the activities of confrontation, clarification, interpretation, and working through; but the only marked difference between him and his predecessor is the focusing on the patient's feelings and analyzing of resistances. Greenson spoke of confrontation as a demonstration to the patient's "reasonable ego," its modes of not knowing, not paying attention, resisting. He followed the classical prescription of analyzing "resistances before content." His notion of a working alliance carries the implication of absence of resistance. But such lack of resistance implies a consensus between the patient and the therapist about their mutual vested interests, goals, and pursuits, presumably on behalf of the patient. Such a consensus is either self-evident, or is itself a result of the specific work of analysis and persuasion (working through) on the part of the therapist that is, for some reason, accepted by the patient. The implication is that since such matters of consensus are self-evident to the clinician, they should also be self-evident to the client, or else he or she is resisting. But who has the right to resist whom? Why should the patient agree with the therapist's judgment of what is right unless he or she chooses to? We return to these issues in the section on confronting as challenging.

As for feelings, a similar index of doubt applies as in the case of the interpretation of ideas and their referents. The therapist presents the patient with an *inference*: You seem to be angry. But this might be a reading into rather than from the patient's conduct. The patient may seem to be angry but actually may be contemptuous or envious or disgusted. Again, who is the legitimate judge of one's feelings? As I have argued elsewhere (Lothane, 1984d), the ultimate boundary between "neutral" interpretation and "biased" persuasion may be an illusion. The bottom line of all psychotherapy is the therapist, like a teacher or parent, doing the utmost to persuade the patient, (student or child) to follow a certain course of action or code of ethics, of which the therapist presumes to be the better judge, for the good of the patient's (or student's) soul.

A similar course was pursued by Robert Langs a decade ago (Langs, 1973, 1974). Langs does not hold to a sharp distinction between confrontations or interpretations (Langs, 1973, p. 85). He speaks of confronting the patient "with his unrealistic wishes" (p. 82). He considers confrontations to be directed at the manifest material and deems them to be "critical in assisting the patient to modify and correct ego dysfunctions" (p. 418). He also feels that confrontations are used to advantage to overcome situations of stalemate, manipulation, or attack upon the therapist, but also to confront "misperceptions, defenses, and resistances" (p. 432). In another context he speaks (Langs, 1974, pp. 268, 273) of the therapist who "confronts without condemning" the patient's "inappropriate" productions. He also refers to underuse and overuse of confrontations, calling the overusers "confrontationists."

A decade later, Langs (1982) has moved perilously close to confrontationism. In what he claims to be his new and original method, he has given a new twist to "the logic of the unconscious." In a curious way his method incarnates Lacan's dictum that the unconscious is the discourse of the other. Langs scans the patient's stream of verbalizations for allusions and references to stimuli arising from the therapist primarily, and for utterances about the patient's own life and concerns secondarily (Lothane, 1984c). Thus, claims Langs, even though the patient is talking about his or her own life and loves manifestly, ie consciously, the truth is that latently, or unconsciously, he or she is *really* talking about his or her real though unconscious perceptions of the conduct of the therapist. Whereas Langs earlier spoke of this possibility predominantly in terms of it being a silent hypothesis (Lothane, 1980a), he has since converted such conjectures to convictions. However, at least since Descartes' *Cogito ergo sum*, one is much safer expressing convictions about what one thinks or feels oneself, and less so about what others think or feel. The person's intentions are his or her own and the person may speak the truth or lie about them, as he or she chooses. Although Langs had gone to considerable pains to define his criteria for intervening, based on the *therapist's* reading of the patient's derivative communications, all he has established are probabilities, not certainties. Also, feelings as such are not recognized in his system as it is limited to dealing with ideas, either manifest or unconscious, as inferred by the expert.

One consideration is conspicuously missing from Langs' as well as most other published discussions: It is not stated whether the therapist should wait for the patient's invitation to offer an interpretation. The implicit assumption is that the therapist is the expert on the unconscious and so knows best. Everything is spelled out except what motives guide the therapist, in a given situation, to engage in a certain action toward the patient. An uninvited intervention is called an intrusion. An interpretation, since it is in the realm of inference, can easily be a delusion, under the sway of the zeal to heal, or any other self-serving motive. We are now ready to discuss the three aspects of confrontation.

ASPECTS OF CONFRONTATION

Confronting as Coming Together

To confront is to come together, face to face, with another person, as embodied in the root meaning of the word "confront," from the Latin word *frons*, meaning forehead or face. People confront each other as friends or foes, as collaborators or competitors, pursuing congruent or conflicting purposes. They may come together to help or to hinder, to heal or to hurt. Two people confronting each other for the first time need to settle at once whether they agree or are in conflict. People confront each other as who they are, what they do, and what they have.

In the context of the contract known as psychotherapy, there is a person (a patient) confronted by and confronting another person (a counselor or psychotherapist). Each pursues his or her own interests, purposes and goals. The objective of the initial encounter is to determine whether the two people confronting each other are at cross-purposes or share a common goal. The seekers of psychotherapy are people unhappy in love. They are usually in conflict with their character, conscience, and conduct, and with their customary ways, or habits, of coping with their character, conscience, or conduct. What do they seek? Comfort, always; counsel, sometimes; change, rarely and reluctantly. The seller of psychotherapy first must understand the central purpose of the buyer, and what he or she is willing to counter with in this encounter.

The provider or vendor of the services of psychotherapy, whether in an institutional or entrepreneurial setting, is offering a service and plying a craft. Ideally it should be a craft exercised to meet the interests of the client. In reality, a different picture prevails.

Institutions, while paying lip service to the idea of serving the best interests of their clients, primarily live for themselves. In any institution the needs of the rank and file come before the needs of the clients. For example, mental hospitals or psychiatric wards in general hospitals are forever worried about budgets and rates of occupancy. On medical wards of general hospitals, patients with so-called psychosomatic illnesses rarely seek psychiatric consultations on their own initiative. This is not to deny that they very often have emotional conflicts. The fact remains, however, that it is the nurses, social workers, and doctors—those who have the power to frustrate or gratify the needs of the patient—who call in the psychiatrist to calm a patient raging or complaining against them. In institutes teaching the craft of psychoanalysis, students commonly "convert" a "psychotherapy case" into an "analytic case." They act to satisfy the requirements of a curriculum committee, or a supervisor pursuing pet theories, and not primarily in the interests of their client.

Institutes of psychotherapy offer ample syllabuses devoted to psychodynamic or psychotherapeutic techniques. Technique comes from the Greek word *techne*, which originally meant art and craft. Technology, derived from the same root, has come to mean the manipulation of machines or being manipulated by machines. In the context of psychotherapy, technique seems to imply a kind of technology, presumably derived from some scientific principles. In the context of psychotherapy, however, we are not dealing with the sciences in terms of their subject matter (inanimate matter), but with science in the sense of rigor of thinking and of examining evidence in support of any claim made in the name of that science. The answer to the question of whether psychotherapy is a branch of science or of the humanities is that it is neither, although it partakes of some of the characteristics of each.

It is a matter of scientific technology to treat syphilis with penicillin but it is a matter of humanistic personology (love and ethics) to treat compulsions with conversation. Personology here implies that psychotherapy is a personal relation based on the capacity of persons to establish emotional contact, communion, and communication, and so create a climate conducive to learning, and possibly change. Such a climate, of an emotional kind, is based on the quality we call liking. Liking is beyond semantics, semiology, biology, cosmology, and technology. It is an instinctive, immediate reaction to people who can feel together. Such feeling together is conveyed by the old Greek word *sympatheia*, which means what it says: *sym*, together, and *pathos*, feeling. This is exactly rendered by the word compassion: *com*, together, and *passion*, feeling. Compassion is the quality of being a fellow sufferer, of having been there and thus able to understand another person. The Germans have two words to convey these ideas: *mitfuhlen*, the capacity to understand somebody else's feelings, to feel with them; and *Mitleid*, or the capacity to feel somebody else's suffering, compassion. The old and important word "sympathy" has now been preempted by the nouveau-riche word "empathy," a neo-Greek translation of the German work *einfuhlen*, which means to feel oneself into (a word on which Heinz Kohut has made his fortunes). Sympathy has, in modern English, been degraded to condolences, as charity has been reduced to alms giving. In their original meanings, charity stood for selfless love, and sympathy for liking (Lothane, 1985).

The essential confrontation between two people in an encounter has to do with basic questions: Do we like each other? Are we in some ways like each other? Are there bonds of sympathy between us? Are we *sympathique, sympatisch, simpático* to each other? Do we share something in common? Will the shared feelings stand us in good stead when the going gets rough? Will the mutual liking make for enough patience to be able to stay the course? Or is there dislike, antipathy, the reverse of sympathy? If so, maybe we should part company instead of vainly trying to play it for keeps.

My advice to beginners and veteran psychotherapists alike is to heed such signals about themselves and their patients, for the good of all concerned. It will save much unnecessary suffering, and will make for better results. The bottom line of psychotherapy is to be able to influence the other to change his or her habits of character and conduct. Such changes are achieved at the cost of overcoming tremendous inner resistances. What is required is weaning through love tempered by discipline and responsibility.

Confronting as Comparing

When an atmosphere of reciprocity, mutuality, dedication, and care prevails between the two persons, that is, if there is an emotional communion between them, there also will be communication. The love model and the communication model go hand in hand. Having dealt at some length with the aspect of communion, let us now consider the concept of interpretation in relation to confrontation.

I propose to show here that what is traditionally referred to as "making interpretations" and "giving insights" amounts to two people confronting—that is, comparing their opinions, views, and perspectives. Insights given are not insights taken, even though we can speak of them in metaphors borrowed from taking in and assimilating drugs and foods. We are talking here of ideas expressed by one person, of thoughts put into words by a speaker that are then rethought by the listener, used to set in motion his or her own thinking in order to compare his or her thoughts with those of the interlocutor and then decide whether to agree or disagree with the ideas offered.

There is also the evocative power of feeling. The academicians may treat of cognition and emotion, but in the human encounter, there are no ideas without feelings and no feelings without ideas.

Even though we are told that the truth shall set us free, truths about ourselves are only accepted from those whom we like and respect. Freud referred to this as positive transference, and Greenson renamed it "the working alliance." The name does not matter as long as we understand that it is the readiness to be influenced, to be inspired by mutual love and respect, which is the requirement for success in parenting, education, and psychotherapy.

When a mood of compatability, mutality, and collaboration prevails between the two participants in the psychotherapeutic dialog, then a setting is created for psychotherapeutic work. Our present focus is on mutually evocative processes of thinking and feeling between the two participants. It is an activity of communication and contemplation. The emphasis here is on what is presented to the mind's eye. It is a matter of comparing each person's inner vision of the other, of using the power of imagination to visualize a narrative told in evocative words (Lothane, 1981b, 1984b). The mutual function in question is the listener's ability to visualize what words describe, ie the ability to recreate in one's own thinking and in mental images, that is in pictorial thought, the scenes, events, feelings, visceral sensations, and moods depicted by the speaker. To communicate through words is to be able to put something across to a listener such that the listener is able to say in return, "I get the picture in my mind that your words stand for and I understand what you are saying to me. Let me acknowledge your vision and tell you what I have visualized in turn."

This function of *imaginative visualization* operates in every human communication through words, and the situation is only one of the many in which its operation is manifest. If it were not for this ability, we could never understand what people say to us, or read a book and "see" what it describes. I have discussed this function (Lothane, 1977) and connected it with the work of my teacher, Otto Isakower, on the analyzing instrument (Lothane, 1981b, 1984b).

The analyzing instrument was Isakower's metaphor, following Freud, to refer to processes of communication that prevail in the near-dream atmosphere of the therapeutic situation, when the participants give themselves over to free association and free communication. In Isakower's conception, the patient and the therapist "share a worktable in the mental laboratory." When they abandon goal-directed selection and self-conscious criticism and allow their thoughts to emerge freely and effortlessly, these thoughts lead them to important discoveries. The two participants stimulate each other to an ever-widening mobilization of thoughts. It is seen here that free association and imaginative visualization combine to create conditions conducive to illuminating meanings, to forming mental sights and insights (Balter et al., 1980; Lothane, 1981).

It can be seen from the foregoing that the spontaneous emergence of mental images is akin to the spontaneous emergence of daydreams and dreams. Like dreams, such images emerge in consciousness, the outcroppings of preceding preconscious mental processes. Again, such processes occur in every waking state. But they occur more readily in sleep and in the near-sleep atmosphere of the therapeutic encounter, which is deliberately once-removed from ongoing waking concerns because the purpose is to foster a focus on inwardness—on the activities of remembering and dreaming. Remembering and dreaming are activities that are characterized by the presence of mental images: the images of memory and the images of the dream, of all grades of vividness, ranging from those that are faint to those that emerge with hallucinatory ultraclarity.

When the two participants in the imaginative communication speak their images, they engage in one variety of confrontation. They confront each other with their visions for the sake of comparing them. There is no question here of judgment, no imposition of values. One image commands no special authority over the other. The images as seen and verbalized are offered for mutual contemplation. The participants converse, compare, and contemplate. The stage on which dreams and images are seen and shown is a dream stage and a theater stage. Similarly, in the therapeutic setting, no real action takes place, only action as remembered, as dreamed of, as enacted (or, as Freud put it, dramatized) for contemplation and catharsis. It is not the scene of real, waking, goal-directed, goal-pursuing action. This is precisely what Freud (1900) meant when he differentiated *material* reality from *psychic* reality. As I have argued elsewhere (Lothane, 1983a), major confusion can ensue when it is not stated at what level human dialog takes place— the level of material or waking reality or the level of psychic or dream reality. Even though dream psychology was Freud's concern throughout his life, the dream was discovered, forgotten, and rediscovered under many different guises during the generations that followed. Its rediscovery is at times as elusive as the dream itself, but none the less real. I have argued that both Lacan and Langs were restatements of Freud's dream psychology (Lothane, 1983b, 1984c).

It is a fundamental fact that Freud's psychoanalytic *method* (free association) is also derived from dream psychology. So is his conception of the so-called mental symptom: the symptom and the dream are similarly conceived and similarly expressed (Lothane, 1983a). The three realms that followed dream psychology in Freud's writings were his *drive psychology* (theories of sexuality), his *sociobiological anthropology* (the theory of the Oedipus complex, of phallocentrically defined female sexuality), and *transference.* His formulations about these three domains led to a very different concept of interpretation from that embodied in his dream psychology. Let us give it a closer look.

What is in question are two different models of explanation, and thus two different models of interpretation, and, as a result, two different models of relating between the patient and the therapist. These divergent models are discernible in Freud himself, and they are also issues with which every therapist has to come to terms in the course of his or her career.

The two models are the historic and the natural–scientific paradigms of causality. They operate according to two different principles of explanation. The historic approach deals with the individual, and the scientific with the generic. In the historic model, the individual is the cause of his or her actions. In the generic model, the person is the effect of impersonal, natural causes. In the historic model, the governing principle is *actualization,* which means that the individual actualizes personal potentialities, propensities, or dispositions in acts of free choice and free will. Even if subject to causes beyond his or her control, the individual is still capable of the unexpected, of the surprising, of free choice that defies all predictions. The generic model obeys the principle of *subsumption,* or *instantiation.* Here the individual event is merely an instance of, is subsumed under, a general law, an occurrence determined by a statistical average, an effect of a universal cause.

The purpose of interpretation has always been to make the unconscious conscious, where the "unconscious" stands for the forgotten and the encoded. Briefly, according to the trauma model of symptom formation, the unraveling of the conscious reminiscence or the conscious screen memory, formed by dynamic forgetting or repression, led to the hidden or unconscious original memory and the recall led to the dissolution of the symptom. In the dream model, the manifest dream content, shaped by the encoding and transforming activity of the dream work, led (through free association) to the hidden latent content and thus resulted in the solution of the dream. Both the memory and the dream were the individual creations of a person with a history. The historic–biographical search was aimed at understanding this particular memory, this particular dream, this particular symptomatic action (Lothane, 1983a, 1984a). Therefore, at the beginning, it was essential to enlist the collaboration of the recaller and the dreamer, to get his or her associations and memories, to dissolve the memory or to solve the dream. Consequently, the first model of therapeutic collaboration was democratic.

When Freud moved from the memory and dream models, (dream psychology) to drive psychology and sociobiology, and thus to a scientific model of explanation, the individual became an instance of the law. Thus in the Dora case (Freud, 1905), Dora was seen as an effect of inhibited sexuality and oedipal fixations, rather than as an author of her actions and decisions in a particular historic context, as acting upon and being acted upon by different characters in her environment. The shift from historic causality to sexological and sociobiological causality was also accompanied by a shift in the personal stance: the earlier democratic attitude now changed into a new autocratic attitude. It is not surprising that Dora became enraged at Freud, felt betrayed by him, and left treatment (Lothane, 1984d). From this point on in Freud's thinking, the generic point of view and a concern with it led to his famous wars of orthodoxy with his disciples—Jung, Adler, and Rank. The libido theory and the Oedipus complex became the shibboleths that separated the believers from the nonbelievers. Clearly orthodoxy went hand in hand with despotism. Doctrinal orthodoxy was paralleled by therapeutic orthodoxy: there were also acrimonious debates and disagreements about how to treat patients, as revealed in the feud between Freud and Ferenczi (Lothane, 1983a).

There is a difference between interpreting according to the dream method and interpreting according to the generic method. The dream method requires both people to participate in field work; they have to produce a piece of original research and it requires some doing. Interpreting according to the generic method supplies the interpreter with a facile formula, a convenient cliché, an easy equation, into which he or she can key in the individual situation and come up with a stereotyped answer, invoking trends and patterns as dictated by the theory. This kind of generic interpreting is more like medical diagnosis than psychotherapeutic work. The intricacies of an individual case can be neatly reduced to a ready-made formula, such as the Oedipus complex, penis envy, castration anxiety, and, lately, developmental arrests, pathology of the self, and identity. I would argue that such interpretations are not genuine interpretations in the spirit of Freud's own method, but are manipulative confrontations of an insensitive kind. The gist of such interpreting is throwing the book at the patient. This is not confronting in the sense of comparing, but confronting in the sense of aggressive challenging.

Before examining the concept of confronting as challenging, something needs to be said about the third main Freudian treatment strategy, which was a departure from dream psychology: interpreting the transference.

Transference has come to mean different things to different people in different situations. The most common meaning is, of course, repeating past experiences with a person in the present; that is, reacting to the person in the present not as that person, here and now, but *as if* a person from there and then. One could also say that it is an automatic, mindless, unreflected enactment of old habits, except that Freud rarely used the concept habit. As I have argued elsewhere (Lothane, 1983a, 1984d), transference as repetition of the past is but an extension of the memory model and dream model. However, there is one more important implication of transference in Freud: since the present behavior is totally unprovoked by the therapist, who merely acts as a reflecting mirror, transference also implies the irrationality of the patient's behavior vis-à-vis the given rationality of the therapist. Another implied meaning of transference is that the patient's behavior is put on or faked, that it is not genuine or sincere. The most noxious implication of transference is (in Freud, and, regrettably, in the hands of many therapists), a way of labeling the patient's behavior as pathological. As John Dewey once put it, give a dog a bad name and hang him. Granted, in all these situations we are dealing with behavior and evaluation of behavior—but who is the final judge? If transference is like a dream, which I think it is, then, as with the dream and memory, the patient and therapist are judges in equal measure, and both can be right or can err in the evaluation of a piece of behavior as transference or as reality, as good or bad. However, as with generic interpretations, a habit has died hard among psychodynamic clinicians who regard themselves as the sole experts on transference, as they thought they were the sole experts on the unconscious. Furthermore, by extending the right to be sole judges, therapists are in danger of remaining blind to their own behavior, of believing they are above all suspicion, and thus viewing their behavior merely as grist for the mill. Again, it is clearly an authoritarian stance, and it leaves the therapist free to put all the patient's complaints, the unjustified as well as the justified, into one basket called transference.

Confronting as Challenging

If to confront means to come together face to face, then every encounter in life is a challenge—in both a good sense and a bad sense. There is opportunity as well as danger in meeting a new face. It is both exhilarating and annihilating to meet a new person. Because we look different, speak differently, think differently, dress differently, and believe differently, we are a treat and a threat to other human beings. In the negative sense, confront is close to affront—shame and humilate.

Confronting, then, can be acting upon the other for the sake of commending or criticizing, enhancing or exploiting, enfranchising or entrapping, playing fair or playing foul, selfishly or selflessly. Whatever the merits of interpretation as being aimed at the depths, confrontation is aimed at the overt surface of human action as witnessable by the participants in the interaction. As soon as we reach the level of action, however, we must note that there is no way to discuss human action without invoking the ethics of this action. Just as behaviorism in the past was described as a psychology without consciousness, so psychoanalysis was at first built up as a psychology without ethics, that is, as though it dealt with biological facts. Freud was of two minds about this, but it is Freud the moralist of the mind, and not Freud the biologist of the mind, who is crucial to the practice of psychotherapy.

Since we are weaving our argument here as a counterpoint of the historic perspective as it illuminates a search for a pragmatic method, we shall note again that in his development as a psychotherapist, Freud first delineated the lawfulness of the process of psychotherapy and only later attended to its ethics. Thus at the end of the 19th century, he defined the process in the *Studies on Hysteria* and in the *Interpretation of Dreams*, and in the early 20th century defined the ethics in the papers on technique in which he addressed the rules of the game. As he laid down the foundations of the ethics of psychotherapy, he also grappled with the intricate problems of transference. In addition to the foregoing functions of transference, the concept had one more important role assignment: to bring law and order into the unruly reality of the love relationship. In this sense transference complemented the procedural function of the analytic couch. To recapitulate: The analytic situation was a place of remembering and dreaming, of a contemplative reexamination of the past, of emotion recollected with a view to obtaining tranquility, a stage on which dreams were enacted but not acted upon. The idea of transference was meant to complement this. The patient's love for the therapist was real as an experienced emotion but the situation was artificial. Thus it required a joint decision by both participants in the venture *not* to treat their love emotions as real but as mere enactments, that is, as transference. In real life an encounter could lead to a real friendship or a real marriage with all their real consequences. In the therapeutic situation, no real consequences to any suit for love were anticipated or encouraged. It often happens that after a successful treatment, the former patient and therapist become lifelong friends. But for the personal relationship to take place, the professional one, based on the principle of service for a fee, must be dissolved first. This is the dividing line between dream reality and waking reality, between transference love and real love: in real love the exchange is based on a barter system, whatever the bartering chips may be, whereas in the clinical situation, the particular love and devotion by professional to client is love for a fee. It is one of the paradoxes of life that filthy lucre is the best safeguard of a clean love.

There is one more aspect to consider in tracing Freud's departure from the ideals and practice of dream psychology, that is, his handling of transference as a resistance. Even as he started with the definition of transference as a manifestation of remembering and enacting past character traits, attitudes, relationships, and the like, it was resistance analysis that became the new cutting edge of his therapy. What was fought on the battlegrounds of transference were wars of resistance. In the hands of many psychodynamic clinicians today, resistance analysis is a method of aggressively confronting the patient in the spirit of a perception that has died hard with the lay public: the therapist is a person who attacks and demolishes resistances and defenses. It is a departure from confronting as comparing and from the conception of the psychotherapeutic encounter as a communication, as a dialog, as remembering and dreaming along with the patient. Confronting as comparing is here replaced by confronting as challenging in an aggressive manner.

Traditionalists are wont to say that they focus on the intrapsychic whereas the revisionists deal with the interpersonal. They elevate the idea of the intrapsychic to the same mystical heights as the idea of "the unconscious." In Freud, however, the ideas of defense and resistance as intrapsychic are derived from the social and interpersonal referents of these words. The concept of repression as inner defense was explicated (Freud, 1910) as an inner replication of political, or outer, repression. The idea of defense (as in the defense neuropsychoses) was an inner method of coping with disappointments caused by a denying hostile environment. Neurotic conflicts meant for Freud that in real-life confrontations the neurotic was unable to meet an opponent as an equal in power but as a helpless child, burdened anachronistically by an attachment to memories and dreams of figures from the past. From the very beginning, the cure of the neurotic meant a liberation from the shackles of the past and an ability to handle oppressors better in the present—the nature of the contract between the two persons involved and how the principles of power, justice, and love are handled by each.

As I have shown elsewhere (Lothane, 1984d), the idea of resistance as a negative phenomenon in human relations was not discovered by Freud at a point when he turned toward resistance analysis and away from dream analysis. He knew of resistance as an opposite of compliance back in his days as a practitioner of hypnotic suggestion. Nor was the phenomenon of resistance unknown to the predecessors of hypnotic suggestion, the magnetists, offspring of the mesmerists in the early 19th century. Resistance is primarily an attitude of disbelief in, distrust of, and disobedience toward an authority. Freud's addressing of resistance, for the first time clearly in the Dora case, was an expression of his vested interest in having the patient do his bidding. Dora's vested interests were sacrificed to those of the adults in Dora's environment, with whom Freud sided against his patient. For example, there is a nebulous allusion to money, presumably not a negligible factor in Freud's collusion with the father, who was paying for the treatment.

Resistance analysis may be nothing but brow-beating of the patient in the service of the therapist's selfish interests. The patient does not owe a therapist trust, belief, or obedience, but only to adhere to an agreed-upon therapeutic contract. There can be no understanding of resistance as an inner self-awareness of the patient, no way to understand inner conflicts, unless there is a voluntary and mutually accepted contract that both parties choose to consider as free from conflicts of interest and as morally binding. It is the therapist's role to propose a contract, and the patient's right to dispose of it. The nonacceptance of the contract is not resistance, but the exercise of the patient's right to agree or not agree to a proposed contract. The only rights the therapist has are to be his or her own person with his or her own domain, method and beliefs, and to hold the patient to the agreement as long as it is in force.

Therapists have often been enjoined to be moral rather than moralizing. Not to moralize means to confront, to face patients with their moral codes—to which they are entitled. If patients do not accept a particular moral code of the therapist, no contract results. Patients may be challenged by the simple fact that a therapist has a moral code, but again they have a right to reject the contract for this reason at the very beginning. Therapists may be moved by similar consideration: they may not like the idea of treating an ex-Nazi, a neo-Nazi, or a crook. This can happen only when the therapy situation is viewed as democratic, not as autocratic. These considerations, of course, pertain to voluntary patients. Psychotherapy is by definition a free enterprise, not a legal psychiatric commitment. This attitude is in the medical tradition itself. Medical patients may refuse treatment or sign out of a hospital against medical advice. The staff might try to persuade patients to stay, but if they are adamant in their refusal, out they go. Nobody stops them at the door to analyze their resistances. The same rights belong to persons in psychotherapy. The only model that applies here is communication, by definition a voluntary enterprise. Sufferers have a right to refuse to play the game of communication, and practitioners have a right to refuse to play if their methods, their privacy, or any of their other rights are not respected by clients. Neither need be labeled as being in resistance. Any contractual agreement implies certain freedoms and certain constraints. The therapeutic contract also carries freedoms and constraints, and both need to be accepted by the parties concerned. The provider has a right to charge and the buyer an obligation to pay. Having defined the situation as professional in this sense, the buyer then has a right to say, not do, to the therapist whatever he or she wants in whatever way he or she wants in whichever language and manner. The buyer pays to speak in the manner he or she pleases. Should the therapist object to that manner of speaking, labeling it as resistance rather than accepting it as a communication, this is counter-resistance, at best, and defrauding the client of the service for which the client is paying, at worst. It is the buyers' right to speak freely, to reflect on what is said, and to draw their own conclusions, as it is their right to dream as they please.

This same focus on the psychotherapeutic agreement and resistance, with the emphasis on its democratic nature, the voluntariness of the contract, and the binding mutual responsibility, has led me to similar realizations about the teaching of psychotherapy. The authoritarian attitudes some therapists have shown toward patients they also invoke toward their students. This stance is reflected in the words "supervision," "supervising," and "supervisee." According to the *Oxford English Dictionary*, a supervisee is a person under police surveillance. The enterprise of psychodynamic teaching has been named supervision, which is a misnomer. Supervision is on-site overseeing of the performance of a junior by a senior, as in the public school system when a supervisor sits in on a teacher's class. It can also be said that a senior surgeon supervises the way in which a junior surgeon performs an appendectomy. But the psychodynamic teacher is not a supervisor, only a listener to a report of a session, in the way a therapist listens to the report of a dream. The supervisor "identifies him or herself—that is, imagines or visualizes him or herself with the student's patient while listening to the student's narrative—and comments on what has happened, what may have happened, and what should have happened.

The exploitative aspect of the "supervision" of psychotherapy resides in the supervisor's advocacy of the patient *against* the student. But in the student–teacher relationship, as in the psychotherapeutic relationship, it is the student who should be the teacher's primary concern, not the student's patient. The patient already has advocates—family, friends, the legal system. Students, on the other hand, need an advocate. They may find such advocacy in their own therapy, should they be so lucky, but they also need it from their therapist-teachers. Students should feel free to speak of their anxieties, problems, and insecurities, without fear of being criticized as being in resistance and defeated, let alone thrown out of the teaching program. The danger here is not so much of the abused patient but of the abused therapist. In my own teaching, I try to strengthen the students, to show them what their rights are, to teach them how to defend these rights against the onslaughts of patients, to help them handle unreasonable guilt, and also to show them their mistakes while respecting their personhood.

Every establishment has its problems with power politics, ideological control, and issues of hurt pride, which result in rage and revenge. The same is true of the therapeutic establishment. Politicians on a campaign trail notoriously use the failures, weaknesses, and character problems of their opponents to discredit them in the eyes of the public. Lawyers for both the prosecution and defense similarly seek to influence a jury. Supervisors of psychotherapy—people with power over others—have played similar games. The therapeutic mode of character tampering, as in the case of politicians, often stoops to the level of character assassination. This tradition goes back to Freud himself, and it has been amply illustrated by the recent rise and fall of Jeffrey Moussaieff Masson, as deliciously documented in the subversive writings of Janet Malcolm (1983) and the chorus of critics who jumped on the bandwagon. Of course, the essential difference between the medical establishment and the therapeutic establishment lies in the following. Medicine teaches an established and agreed-upon body of knowledge, and subjects its students to examinations based upon rigorously defined and standardized criteria, whereas the therapeutic establishment teaches a body of knowledge that cannot even put into a standard textbook, let alone the outpourings of the many schools of therapy, each proclaiming that its own theory is the tried and true path to salvation. With rigorous criteria lacking from the analytic syllabus, the advancement of the student has been ruled to a large measure by the personal tastes or distastes, likes or dislikes, of the supervisors. Although character does play a role in the medical establishment, the therapeutic establishment has nothing *but* character to deal with. Students of therapy have been much more a captive and legally defenseless population than their medical counterparts.

It is against a background such as this that one should evaluate the vogue enjoyed by certain ideological cults in the therapeutic profession. The ideology of Kohut appeals to many students as well as veteran clinicans who have experienced the ravages of lovelessness created by the orthodox analytic establishment. The austere, spartan atmosphere inspired by Heinz Hartmann created a backlash by Heinz Kohut: the cult of self psychology (Lothane, 1983b). Kohut's ideology, a sermon of love masquerading as science and in reality a pseudoscience, is aimed at the love-starved student. The jargon of self psychology contains words such as self-object, the self, and empathy, pale synonyms for sympathy, friendship, love, and devotion toward the patient or the student. By contrast, the ideology of Langs seems to satisfy the needs of guilt-ridden insecure students, who seek absolution for their mistakes in submitting to the blandishments of a hypercritical task master with a promise of a mistake-free technique. Later, students forget their guilt and start complaining (Lothane, 1984c).

The above digression is only an illustration of the principle of confronting as criticizing and challenging in the negative, or violent, way, devoid of charity and compassion for the other sufferer. I will not deny that love is the most complex human tie and emotion, most liable to misunderstanding and abuse. Freud was cynical about love, but Fromm did not rescue it either (Lothane, 1985). Nevertheless a proper use of love is indispensable to properly conducted psychotherapy and teaching.

In what follows I attempt to define some preliminary guidelines, dividing my remarks into two parts: confrontations in the first hour, in the precontract phase, and confrontations within an established contract.

GUIDELINES FOR CONFRONTATION

The First Hour

The purpose of the first hour, or the initial contact (or during whatever time it may take to establish a committed contract), is to establish whether the two potential contractants have a basic sympathy or affinity, and whether they have a commonality of needs and interests. A teacher in my residency once said that there is no issue here of whether the two people like each other; they have come to do a job. I do not know what he meant by liking each other, but I believe that liking, or a basic bond of sympathy, is a precondition for successful work. Two people may confront each other with the attitude of liking each other or they may have an instant dislike and aversion to each other that will remain unshakable.

It is a fact of life that not all people are meant for each other. Nobody—except maybe a saint—can like all people all the time. Saints among psychotherapists, like mathematical geniuses, are probably distributed along a bell-shaped curve. But even saints are not going to be liked by everybody. By "like" I mean a deep and profound resonance, on a conscious level and subliminal level, which takes in qualities of relating, speaking, thinking, expressing oneself, temperament, and many other ineffable characteristics that make for a fit between some people and not between others—the chemistry is or is not right. What is meant here is not instances of overtly expressed dislike, or even hostility, which can be managed if the basic fit is there. I am speaking of a fundamental aversion or distaste for a person by the prospective client, which needs to be acknowledged right there and then.

Since most first encounters are blind dates, I do not recommend charging fees for the first session. It can either be optional, at the client's judgment, or charged after he or she decides to come for a second session, but the first hour should be left as a shopper's privilege. It should leave the parties free to decide whether they are fit for each other. The patient should not pay for having had the misfortune to stumble into a character he or she does not really like. The therapist also has the freedom to say no without offending the person and without making him or her pay for it.

A person's unwillingness to proceed on the basis of dislike should never be questioned but always taken at face value. The client may be abrupt in judgment, acting on impulse, displaying a psychological allergy because the therapist happens to resemble somebody from the past; the client may be missing out on a lifetime chance to have a good therapist—none of this is relevant. The decision to enter a relationship with a person is a fateful one and the decision should be left to the patient's own instincts. Nobody can claim ultimate wisdom in such matters.

The next confrontation is about the business at hand. Does the prospective patient want and need the same things as the therapist is willing to offer? What are the vested interests and needs of both? What are their mutual expectations?

According to an aphorism from the Talmud, the cow wants to give a suck more than the calf is willing to suckle. The mutual interests of both people will be determined by their degree of autonomy, their social and life situations, their belief systems and other characteristics that are expressions of the basic character fit. The patient's autonomy is defined by whether he or she is a child or an adult, self-supporting or supported, self-motivated for treatment or railroaded into it, wants a brief encounter or a long-term haul. The therapist may be a beginner or a veteran, an independent practitioner or beholden to an institutional setting. Thus third parties may be involved in cramping the autonomy and the style of both patient and therapist. The basic character needs to be complemented by a demand and supply fit. This is a continuation of confrontation along the lines of comparison: the two people compare their mutual needs, interests, and expectations, and size each other up in the process. Lawyers talk about the process of discovery in a case. Such a process of mutual discovery begins in the first hour and probably never ends. However, a modicum of agreement has to be reached before the next phase can be undertaken, that is, the phase of commitment.

I have avoided discussing anything related to diagnosis or prognosis, because these represent specialized interests. They are relegated to their respective domains. Without denying the legitimacy of such pursuits, it is clear that these are not of concern to patients. They have not come to fulfill anybody's ambition as a diagnostician, but to determine whether they have an ally and a trustworthy and competent person who can help them with their specific predicament, a person who can give love and teach about love.

Otto Rank is credited with having said that patients will always get out of treatment when they want to. I believe this is sound because it is primarily the patient's, not the therapist's, contract. If the expectations do not fit the therapist's, then it is the therapist's right to decline service and to refer the person elsewhere. The therapist is not entitled to press the other person into the mold of his or her biases, prejudices, expectations, and interests.

The first encounter is no time for confrontations in the sense of challenge or criticism. At this time the therapist has no warrant to challenge anything, only to receive communications and give back communications that should help both people to decide if they are meant for each other. Since there is no contract, nobody owes anything to anybody.

The first move toward the committed contract is strictly up to the seeker of therapy. It is not up to the therapist to solicit the patient. It is my custom not to mention cost in the initial phases of a consultation. If the patient chooses not to bring up the question of money during the first session, the first session is ended without money being mentioned. The decision to talk money is already a step in the direction of possibly buying, but the buyer has to state his or her intentions first.

When a person has decided to move toward a commitment—is able to state his or her purpose and to define what kind of work he or she is willing to do—*then* the therapist is free to define the terms of the working contract and the method. The next step is up to the patient; namely, to accept or decline the proposed work contract. When the two people finally agree on fees, frequency, and formal procedure, then they are ready to go into the next phase, the committed contract.

The Committed Contract

Following the establishment of the committed contract, the proper work of psychotherapy begins, even though it is more accurate to say that this work begins at the moment one person makes the first phone call to the other. In medicine, proper diagnosis leads to proper treatment. Diagnosis means identifying a type or genus of disease according to its indices, as in sleuth work. Here it is the other way around: according to an aphorism attributed to Anna Freud, treatment begins at the word "go," but "diagnosis" never ends—if by diagnosis we mean the continued process of discovery, of revelation, of being taken by surprise, as Theodore Reik put it. Such discovery has already been taking place in the initial precontract phase, as mutually sent-out feelers, to assess the atmosphere and the fit. Now there is agreement to do it all the time.

In the communicational paradigm, confrontation is only one kind of communication, be it as comparison or as challenge. I am for confrontations of the nature of comparisons, of demonstrations, of making implicit things explicit, of making things visible and witnessable. The challenge is to help the other person see something, that is to increase self-awareness and focus attention so that he or she can better see whatever is in the field of vision. Oscar Wilde said that the superficial is the most profound. The Bible is right in insisting that correct perception is one of the hardest tasks to achieve: Eyes they have, but they do not see; ears they have, but they do not hear.

To clarify further an approach to confrontation, I shall invoke the earlier mentioned difference between reality and dream; psychic reality and external reality; the reality of speaking and acting versus that of thinking and feeling; the mode of waking consciousness and that of dream consciousness. There is no denying that like amphibians who live in air and water, we go through our lives living in both worlds simultaneously, living a counterpoint of waking consciousness and dream consciousness. In a given situation, one of the modes may predominate, but the other is never completely extinguished. Thus in sleep we dream, but we also perceive and react to external noises. In the case of sleep walking, we perform a waking function while in a deep hypnotic trance.

In the interhuman realm, speech and gesture are real observable events. Dreams are also real. Words and deeds are also witnessable. The law only recognizes facts that have been witnessed, but it also rules on motives and intentions that are not witnessable.

In the exchanges that occur in psychotherapy, both participants may fluctuate in their perceptions of their words and deeds as waking realities or dream realities. Their exchanges may be viewed as taking place on the plane of overt action, which leads to real-life consequences, or they may be viewed as if they were only happening in the mental theater of dreams, illusions, imaginings. These distinctions are also important to understanding when the words and deeds of the other will be taken as helpful or harmful, as caressing or cruel, as pleasant or painful. It may be fair to generalize that when one addresses the other on the level of the actual and waking reality, while the other is responding at the level of psychic or dream reality, misunderstandings may follow. For these reasons it is of the utmost importance to establish a consensual contractual agreement about what each person is permitted to do to the other within the confines of the contract.

A brief example will illustrate these distinctions. A professional man was committed to ongoing work for a number of years at the time of the following episode. One day, due to a failure of the passenger elevator, he had to reach my office by way of the service entrance and the kitchen. He passed me in the kitchen on the way to my office and I proceeded to join him there immediately. He was convinced that the person he saw while passing through was not me but my twin brother. And, he insisted, it was not me facing him in my office, but my twin. This was proof that I did not really care much about him, that I was treating this work in a totally mercenary fashion, and it proved how little he could trust me. This feeling persisted for many months and years. There was no twin brother, of course, and there was no plot to defraud him. Yet I never challenged this perception, as wild as it was, nor did I interpret anything about it. Call it transference, delusion, illusion, or dream—it comes to the same thing: an image, a fusion of an idea and a feeling (they always go together), was formed by condensing perception, imagination, and memory. He had complained for years of an ineffectual father, while with his older brother, neo-Malinowski style, and mother he had created the triadic constellation. The work of comparison, deduction, analysis, and interpretation was left in this instance to him. Years later, at the time of this writing, I confronted him about the nonreality of this perception, when I requested permission to publish this vignette. He accepted my assertion, while remembering that at the time of the occurrence he was thoroughly convinced of the reality of his perception. He agreed in retrospect that he was at that time working through issues of self-doubt, mistrust, indecision, and dependence in his own life.

At another point in treatment, the patient delared an indefinite suspension of the contract, possibly a termination for good, following a stormy period. He demanded of me time and again to tell him whether to give in to the pressures of his lover to get married. My consistent stance was that it was not my job to recommend personal decisions or choices but only to discuss them. The patient's reaction was to become angry and leave (also leaving a sizable unpaid bill). After sending a number of reminders with no result, I finally had a lawyer send him a letter. The patient not only paid the money owed, but also returned to continue treatment. Contrary to all expectations, my "aggressions" did not destroy anything, but led to a better and healthier contract and continued productive work.

The case illustrates the different paradigms under consideration. It demonstrates that the essence of psychotherapeutic work is to provide a setting in which a person can develop dreams, get hold of emotional experiences, and learn from them, essentially through a feat of self-analysis. It leaves the therapist to function as a benign Socrates; not Socrates the gadfly, but Socrates the midwife to the patient's or student's brain children. It is less a stance of active and meddlesome interpreting than a permissive facilitating atmosphere so that the patient's own ideas and feelings can develop undisturbed to the point of ripeness and self-revelation. An intervention is often an intrusion and interpretation is frequently a delusion, since most of us speak more from self-knowledge than from the certain knowledge of the other. The implication also is that, as noted by Devereux, interpretations and confrontations are not clearly demarcated as they are ideas, feelings, imaginings, and suppositions about what is going on with the other.

Since patients know best where their ideas are coming from, therapists should follow patients where they go, and be aware of the origins of *their own* ideas, attitudes, strivings, needs, and expectations toward their patients. Rather than being experts on the unconscious of their patients, they should be experts on their own. This leaves us free to enunciate the following principle in regard to confrontations. The therapist is entitled to confront the patient whenever the latter attempts to breech or destroy the mutually agreed-upon contract. But even then, the confrontation should take the form of a question, not of criticizing, complaining, or nagging. Rather the therapist should insist on defending professional rights and turf, according to the terms of the contract, and against the onslaught by the patient. Clinicians may defend their rights by silence, by speech, and, if need be, by action. Again, they should be moral but not moralistic, kind but not cruel, firm but not inflexible.

AREAS OF CONFRONTATION

Some areas of confrontation will now be briefly defined. They apply to the committed contract. It means that the two parties have voluntarily agreed to have mutually defined rights and obligations and that each has a right to challenge the other upon default of these obligations. What is challenged are words and deeds, which can be witnessed by both participants.

1. *Persons.* The persons are defined as what goes on between the therapist and the patient and to the exclusion of any third parties, unless agreed upon by the two people.

2. *Place.* The patient is entitled to a private place, free from interruptions and disturbances. The right is to be able to say in that place and during that time whatever he or she wants, not to *do* whatever he or she wants. The place is the therapist's property and as such is inviolable.

3. *Payment.* The therapist is entitled to a fee for time given. The favor of offering free time, no matter how dire the emergency or how trivial the favor, is in the interests of neither. The payment assures professionality and is the best guarantee of the therapist's neutrality. By virtue of paying for service rendered, the patient need feel no compunction about criticizing and berating the therapist; the therapist need not feel personally slighted or attacked. The principle of service for payment is inviolate.

4. *Procedure.* The procedure is that both participants have the right of speech and silence. The patient has a right to speak freely, but is not under any mandate to speak when or what the therapist wants. Similarly the therapist has a right to speak when clinical judgment tells him or her so, not when the patient tries to coerce him or her to do so. Each shall take the consequences of this rule. According to the principle of communication, therapists work with what they get and are not obligated to work with what they have not received—to guess what patients might be thinking.

5. *Primacy of perception.* The principle here is that just as reality is prior to the dream (Lothane 1983a), the conscious prior to the unconscious, trauma prior to a reaction to trauma, so the first order of business is to confront what is perceived—first the facts, then the inferences.

6. *Probity.* Here the contract is definitely more obligatory toward the therapist than the patient. The therapist is obligated to speak truthfully, to deal honestly, to be prompt; the patient is not. Thus the patient is entitled to a fixed hour, but can be late as much as he or she wants and owes the therapist no apologies for lateness. It is up to the patient then to analyze the motives for lateness. Also the patient may tell the therapist any number of lies. The therapist may choose to believe or disbelieve them, but cannot demand truthfulness the same way he or she can demand payment. It is up to the patient to choose between truth and lies.

7. *Parity.* In one area both persons are absolutely equal: in their power to give love and to take love. This is so because parent and child, student and teacher, are also equals in loving, leaving, and learning. Consciously one may lie to the other about what one has taken or given. The unconscious keeper of records, however, has an exceedingly precise ledger of credits and debits. Everybody will be paid according to what they pay in.

8. *Pause.* I use the word pause to refer to termination. Termination is also a one-sided right. The right to fire belongs to the patient. The therapist has no claims in this regard. Lengthy symposia are devoted to the issue of termination. For me the matter is simple: termination is determination to terminate. Psychotherapy is defined as whatever happens between the two points in time, both chosen by the patient; that is, when to begin treatment and when to stop it. The idea of pause is meant to underscore both the transience of life's relationships and their fatefulness. In one of his last papers, Freud (1937) described the futility of any claim to a definitive psychological treatment. All work is by definition transient, all results temporary, anything can return. Both psychotherapy and life work in mysterious ways.

CONCLUDING REMARKS

The suspicion that no clear boundary can be drawn between confrontation and interpretation is upheld here. Rather than maintain artificial definitions, it is more important to seek understanding and clarity of vision in the two great areas of human life: psychological processes and conscientious conduct. The psychological modes of knowledge are perception and imagination, or waking consciousness and dream consciousness, aimed at waking reality and dream reality. But knowledge does not take place in an emotional and ethical vacuum. Waking awareness and dream awareness are used by people involved in love relationships, and thus in power relations, of the fair or unfair kind. Therefore, both confrontations and interpretations ultimately deal with exchanges of love, power, and justice. These principles are seen as guides for both companions traveling together on their terminable or interminable journey.

REFERENCES

Balter, L., Lothane, Z., and Spencer, J.H., Jr. On the analyzing instrument. *Psychoanalytic Quarterly*, 1980, *49*, 474–504.

Devereux, G. Some criteria for the timing of confrontations and interpretations. *International Journal of Psycho-analysis*, 1951, *32*, 19–24.

Freud, S. (1895) Studies on hysteria. *Standard edition*, vol. 2. London: Hogarth Press.

Freud, S. (1900) The interpretation of dreams. *Standard edition*, vol. 4, 5. London: Hogarth Press.

Freud, S. (1905) Fragment of analysis of a case of hysteria. *Standard edition*, vol. 7. London: Hogarth Press.

Freud, S. (1910) Five lectures on psycho-analysis. *Standard edition*, vol. 11. London: Hogarth Press.

Freud, S. (1926) The question of lay analysis. *Standard edition*, vol. 20. London: Hogarth Press.

Freud, S. (1933) New introductory lectures. *Standard edition*, vol. 22. London: Hogarth Press.

Freud, S. (1937) Analysis terminable and interminable. *Standard edition*, vol. 23. London: Hogarth Press.

Freud, S. (1937) Constructions in analysis. *Standard edition*, vol. 23. London: Hogarth Press.

Greenson, R.R. *The technique and practice of psychoanalysis*. New York: International Universities Press, 1967.

Langs, R.J. *The technique of psychoanalytic psychotherapy*, Vol. 1. New York: Jason Aronson, 1973.

Langs, R.J. *The technique of psychoanalytic psychotherapy*, Vol. 2. New York: Jason Aronson, 1974.

Langs, R.J. *Psychotherapy: A basic text*. New York: Jason Aronson, 1982.

Lothane, Z. The art of listening: a critique of Robert Langs. *Psychoanalytic Review*, 1980a, *67*, 353–364.

Lothane, Z. A perspective on Freud and psychoanalysis. *Psychoanalytic Review*, 1981a, *68*, 348–361.

Lothane, Z. Listening with the third ear as instrument in psychoanalysis. *Psychoanalytic Review*, 1981b, *68*, 487–503.

Lothane, Z. Dialogues are for dyads. *Issues in Ego Psychology*, 1982b, *5* (nos. 1, 2), 19–24.

Lothane, Z. Reality, dream, and trauma. *Contemporary Psychoanalysis*, 1983a, *19*, 423–443.

Lothane, Z. Cultist phenomena in psychoanalysis. In: D.A. Halperin (Ed.), *Psychodynamic perspectives on religion, sect and cult*. Boston: John Wright-PSG, 1983b.

Lothane, Z. A new metapsychology—psychoanalysis as storymaking. *International Forum for Psychoanalysis*, 1984a, *1*, 65–84.

Lothane, Z. Teaching the psychoanalytic method. In: L. Caligor et al. (Eds.), *Clinical perspectives on the supervision of psychoanalysis and psychotherapy.* New York: Plenum Press, 1984b.

Lothane, Z. The communicative approach of Robert Langs. In: J. Reppen (Ed.), *Beyond Freud.* Hillsdale, N.J.: The Analytic Press, 1984c.

Lothane, Z. Transference—the sacred cow of psychoanalysis. In press 1984.

Lothane, Z. The reality of love, the love of reality. Presentation at the Second Renaissance Congress in Tokyo, (1985), in press.

Malcolm, J. Annals of scholarship. *The New Yorker Magazine*, December 5, 12, 1983.

Szasz, T. *The Ethics of psychoanalysis.* New York: Basic Books, 1965.

10
Clarification: History and Theory

HERBERT N. BROWN, M.D.

"It seems very pretty," she said when she had finished it; "but it's *rather* hard to understand!" (You see, she didn't like to confess, even to herself, that she couldn't make it out at all.) "Somehow it seems to fill my head with ideas—only I don't exactly know what they are!"

Lewis Carroll
Through The Looking Glass

The term "clarification" was a latecomer to dynamic psychotherapy. It quickly received a warm welcome though; no one quarrels with the value of clarity. The concept is so commonly used in clinical discussions today that it is hard to believe much of the technical literature was written without it. Freud himself only used the word colloquially, even though he wrote extensively (if not systematically) on psychotherapeutic technique.

Edward Bibring (1954) described the introduction of the term by Carl Rogers in 1942, its relevance to psychoanalytic technique following developments in ego psychology and character assessment, and the pivotal place it had found within the psychodynamic therapies by the 1950s. Since then increasing interest in the therapeutic alliance and object relations, together with the advent of self psychology, have extended the context for understanding this fundamental therapeutic technique.

The purposes of this chapter are (1) to trace the development of the concept of clarification within the increasingly sophisticated theories of psychological functioning, and (2) to explore the important niche into which this basic therapeutic technique has evolved in psychodynamic psychotherapy.

SOURCES OF THE CONCEPT AND TECHNIQUE OF CLARIFICATION

Rogerian Clarification

Carl Rogers first introduced the technical concept of clarification. He wished to shift (what he viewed as) the prevailing emphasis in psychotherapy on analysis and diagnosis toward the dynamic process of change. In the preface to *Counseling and Psychotherapy*, Rogers (1942, p. vii) states: "The balance has definitely shifted from diagnosis to therapy, from understanding the individual to an interest in the processes through which he may find help." A few pages later (p. 18), he puts forth his basic psychotherapeutic hypothesis: "Effective counseling consists of a definitely structured, permissive relationship which allows the client to gain an understanding of himself to a degree which enables him to take positive steps in the light of his new orientation."

Rogers' (1942, p. 41) "new approach" to self-understanding was a process of clarification of possible decisions or courses of action. "The counselor's function here is to help clarify the different choices which might be made, and to recognize the feeling or fear and the lack of courage to go ahead which the individual is experiencing. It is not his function to urge a certain course of action or to give advice."

This original technique of clarification, characteristic of Rogers' non-directive, client-centered approach, relies heavily—if not exclusively—upon the therapist restating or verbalizing "in somewhat clearer form" (Rogers, 1942, p. 38) the patient's thoughts and feelings. Rogerian clarification, therefore, purposefully does not go beyond what the patient says and does; in reflecting the patient's statements and behavior, the therapist limits the focus to phenomenology. Indeed there is no need to go further because the goal is only for clients to improve their already conscious perception of themselves and their reality: "The primary technique is to encourage the expression of attitudes and feelings until insightful understanding appears *spontaneously*. Insight is often delayed, and sometimes made impossible, by efforts of the counselor to create it or to bring it about. It is probably not delayed, and certainly never made impossible, by those interviewing approaches which encourage full expression of attitudes" (Rogers, 1942, p. 195).

As incremental improvements in self-perception (clarifications) occur, it is anticipated that changes in behavior will follow. This expectation is based on the supposition (not unique to Rogers) that individual perception is the crucial element in determining behavior. Interpretation, as opposed to clarification, is seen by Rogers in a more "declarative" (Rogers, 1951, p. 28) and explaining mode, even though he sometimes blurred this distinction: "Under certain conditions, it is possible to interpret to the client some of the material which he has been revealing. When the interpretation is based entirely upon statements which the client has made, and *when the interpretation is merely a clarification* of what the client has already perceived for himself, this kind of approach can be successful" (Rogers, 1942, p. 196). Interpretation is not, for Rogers (1942, p. 419), a highly valued technique since "the client can achieve for himself far truer and more sensitive and accurate insight than can possibly be given to him (by the therapist) . . ." The therapist's job is merely to clarify conscious experience; the client's integrative ego processes are expected to do the rest. Clarification in the Rogerian sense means to see as clearly as possible *with* the patient, not to see *for* the patient—or, worse, to lead or guide the patient from a potentially invalid outside vantage point.

By 1951, in *Client-Centered Therapy* (Rogers, 1951), he preferred the phrase "*reflection* of attitudes" to "clarification of attitudes." This modification underlines his sustained emphasis on nondirective empathy—understanding from client's point of view. With the obvious mirroring connotations of reflection, Rogers makes his own interesting change in the famous Freudian mirror simile. (In his 1912 "Recommendations to Physicians Practicing Psychoanalysis," Freud had advised —strikingly consistent, it seems, with Rogers' emphasis—that a doctor practicing true psychoanalysis should, in the face of temptations to reveal personal information, "be opaque to his patients and, like a mirror, should show them nothing but what is shown to him.") Rogers (1951, pp. 112–113) says that "rather than serving as a mirror, the therapist becomes a companion for the patient as the latter searches through a tangled forest in the dead of night." Being a companion foreshadows the recent emphasis in self-psychology on empathic understanding, the modern existential perspective (Havens, 1973, 1974), and certain aspects of Sullivan's interpersonal approach (Sullivan, 1954, 1962). Rogers transformed the therapist's position from that of detached observer to "being with" the patient—joining with the patient and perhaps helping with reflected illumination.

Ego Psychology and Clarification

Freud first required and provided a concept of ego. In the *Project for a Scientific Psychology* (1895), he described the ego as a structural agency for the discharge of tensions through appropriate actions upon the environment. His subsequent interest in libido theory and psychosexual development delayed further elaboration of ego functions until he gradually developed a more complete exploration of the ego position in psychoanalytic theory, during the period from 1923 and 1938. In his final conception of the ego, Freud recognized some autonomous integrative functions; this involved postulating the ego as an active principle, influenced by but independent of libidinal drive energy, and capable of initiating its own activity. Attention shifted from the mediating and defensive functions of the ego to those functions that are adaptive and relatively autonomous from drives. No longer was the ego conceived as helplessly strapped to the horse of the id. The ego was now seen as itself a powerful structure. Interestingly, with her book in 1936, *The Ego and The Mechanisms of Defense,* Freud's daughter, Anna, was probably the first substantial contributor to this theoretical line of development—building on the work of her father and, to some extent, of Wilhelm Reich in 1933.

As this new emphasis on and conceptualization of the ego was amplified and systematized (particularly by Heinz Hartmann, Ernst Kris, Rudolph Lowenstein, and David Rapaport), it became known as "ego psychology." The ego took shape as a general adaptational agency with a problem-solving, organizational role, not simply as a mediator of conflict, and as responding to conflict within the larger adaptational task of fitting in with an "average expectable environment" (Hartmann, 1958). Subsequently, Erikson led the way in understanding that ego development extends over the entire life cycle.

Developments in ego psychology relate to our understanding of clarification because they lend theoretical context to the therapeutic function of bringing to the patient's attention (that is, reflecting to a patient, observing with the patient, restating, or verbalizing for a patient) connections between his or her behavior and ways of thinking, as well as between his or her perspective and the therapist's. It is now theoretically accurate to say that drawing attention to specific features of an individual's ego functioning is, in itself, important.

Shapiro (1965, p. 15), a student of Rapaport's, states "an indispensable prerequisite to understanding the origins of behavior and psychopathology . . . must include careful observation and analysis of the tendency present in the more or less continuously manifest, perhaps mundane, and ordinarily unremarkable dimensions of experience of activity—the continuous way of living, conscious attitude, and overt behavior . . ." Shapiro further argued that the action and behavior of the neurotic person are "in character" because they reflect attitudes and frames of mind that generally characterize that person's consciousness and guide his or her action. While these characteristic attitudes have developed in a self-protective response to conflict or threat, the result, as Shapiro (1981, p. 25) puts it, is a more or less stable restriction of subjective self-experience:

> An estrangement has developed between how this person thinks he feels, on the one hand, and how he actually feels and behaves, on the other. This is *not* an estrangement between conscious and unconscious feelings. It is a gap—or, perhaps more precisely, an incomplete congruence—between

what he self-consciously recognizes, identifies, or articulates as his feelings and the actual, though unrecognized and unarticulated, nature of his subjective experience—the actual quality of his wishes, the actual direction of his interest and attention, his actual frame of mind, estimate of his prospects, all that actually accounts for his action.

Shapiro offers the case example of a man who thinks of himself as worried about his temper. The man's unwitting smile while he discusses this problem reflects secret pleasure with his "manliness" and his power to intimidate his spouse. This attitude is unrecognized and "conscious only in a limited sense" (Shapiro, 1981, p. 28). The man is indeed conscious of the pleasure, but he does not *notice* it; he would remain *unaware* of experiencing it unless it were drawn to his attention, and, especially, he does not connect and contrast it with his preferred view of himself as guilty. Both the therapist's pointing to the connection and the patient's tendency not to notice it in the first place are important. Drawing someone's attention to something known but unnoticed requires the therapeutic technique of clarification; the patient not noticing reflects the operation of defenses and level of conscious awareness. As Elvin Semrad (1980), an admired teacher in the Boston psychoanalytic community, once said: "A good deal of therapy involves a patient's acknowledging, and then bearing and putting into perspective, things that they already know about themselves."

What is historically and theoretically important here is that greater attention is being paid to the primary importance of self-awareness. Later we must take up the subtle, but significant, matter of the degree to which it is advisable, or even necessary, for the therapist to do more than simply reflect a patient's behavior by extending that reflection to include a dynamic formulation.

We should recognize that prevailing social attitudes about drives and strong emotions have changed significantly since the turn of the century. Freud's emphasis on the instincts, particularly sex, is no longer shocking or revolutionary. Modern patients are much less surprised to discover evidence (sometimes called derivatives) of powerful drives. What has become increasingly relevant and interesting, to patients and therapists alike, are the unique ways in which individuals handle their drives and feelings.

The adjustment in theoretical and clinical emphasis brought about by ego psychology is illustrated in the writing about depression by E. Bibring and about anorexia nervosa by Bruch. Bibring (1951) describes the basic mechanism of depression as the ego's shocked awareness of its helplessness in regard to certain of its narcissistic aspirations. Depression is defined as being "primarily an ego phenomenon," that is, like anxiety, a "basic ego reaction" (p. 34), which is essentially independent of the vicissitudes of aggression as well as of oral drives. "According to this view, depression is not primarily determined by a conflict between the ego on the one hand

and the id, or the superego, or the environment on the other hand, but stems primarily from a tension within the ego itself, from an inner-systemic 'conflict' " (Bibring, 1951, pp. 25–26). Bruch (1973, p. 335) makes a similar shift in emphasis. Eating disorders (obesity and anorexia nervosa), previously conceptualized within the structural model, are now seen from an ego perspective.

> The more the psychological disorder is conceived of as expressions of oral dependency, incorporate cannibalism, rejection of pregnancy, etc., the more likely that therapy will follow the classical psychoanalytic model. The concept that the abnormal eating is a late step in the development of the illness, a frantic effort to camouflage underlying problems, or a defense against complete disintegration has only recently been formulated for anorexia nervosa, and is not widely known. With this new orientation the therapeutic focus is on the failure in self-experience and on the defective tools and concepts for organizing and expressing the patient's own needs, and on his bewilderment in dealing with others. Instead of dealing with intrapsychic conflicts and the disturbed eating function, therapy will attempt to repair the underlying senses of incompetence, conceptual defects and distortions, isolation and dissatisfaction.

Note that Bibring places greater emphasis on intra-ego *conflict* (that is, between narcissistic aspirations and perception of capacities); Bruch emphasizes ego *deficits*, heralding the focus in self psychology that is discussed later.

Ego psychology found its most sturdy and appropriately fashioned therapeutic tool in clarification. And as ego psychology penetrated the thinking and practice of psychodynamically oriented therapists, clarification enjoyed increasing appreciation and application. Yankelovich and Barrett (1970, pp. 119, 130) conclude that Hartmann (and the ego psychologists generally) hoisted psychodynamic theory out of the "terrible dilemma," the "dead end," of conceptualizing the outcome of neurotic struggle as inevitably stacked against the relatively weak ego in its battle with the overpowering forces of the id. The use of clarification reflects faith in an ego powerful enough to establish a beachhead against the forces of psychopathology and, eventually, to strengthen and extend outposts so that an entire territory of psychological function can be brought under conscious control.

CLARIFICATION, INSIGHT, AND LEVELS OF CONSCIOUSNESS

Freud (1940, p. 177) emphasized that the "method by which we strengthen the weakened ego has as a starting point an extending of its self-knowledge." Later, Bibring distinguished two basic ways of extending self-knowledge or insight, which he proposed calling "insight through clarification" and "insight through interpretation." These forms of insight differ along lines determined by the nature of the psychological material with which they deal: clarification for conscious and preconscious material, and interpretation for unconscious material.

Referring to insight through clarification, Bibring (1954, p. 755) describes the level of discourse:

> Many, if not all, patients are often rather vague about certain feelings, attitudes, thoughts, impulses, behavior or reaction patterns, perceptions, etc. They cannot recognize or differentiate adequately what troubles them, they relate matters which are unrelated, or fail to relate what belongs together, or they do not perceive or evaluate reality properly but in a distorted fashion under the influence of their emotions or neurotic patterns. In brief, there is lack of awareness (recognition) where awareness is possible.

He goes on to offer classic examples of insights characteristic of clarification (Bibring, 1953, pp. 775–756):

> We clarify the patient's feelings, e.g., when we show him that what he describes as fatigue or feeling of being tired is actually an expression of depression. It is clarification when we elaborate his patterns of conduct, demonstrating to him that he reacts in typical ways to typical situations; or that certain of his attitudes which appear to him unrelated are in fact related to each other, representing various manifestations of the same attitude or that certain reaction patterns from a characteristic sequence, etc. We clarify when we demonstrate to a patient that her enthusiasm about "analytic" minds which are readily aware of and skillfully elaborate difference of thought, feelings, etc., and her idea of two words which have to be kept apart (the clean and the dirty, the fine one and the low one, school and home, father and mother, etc.) and also her heightened interest in the conception of a class society and class struggle, etc., are various expressions of the same attitude. (Consequently, she was less appreciative of "synthetic" thinkers who were going to discover more readily the common denominator between seemingly disparate things.) We clarify when we point out to a patient that his strong, nearly compulsive need to put books on a shelf side by side when they were "separated" by space; that his somewhat contented compulsive laughing when he witnessed people discussing in a friendly manner divergent conceptions of how to tackle a certain problem, or his passion to be the middleman between disputing parties, or his interest in telling people every friendly remark they made about each other, that all this represented related attitudes . . .
> We clarify a patient's reality situation, for instance, when we separate the objective reality from his subjective distorted conception of it, when we make him understand the actual, perhaps neurotic motivations of his love objects' attitudes toward him, whereas he may have misinterpreted them as a rejection or condemnation or attempts to dominate him, etc.

The levels of awareness in these examples of clarification involve psychological material that is not clearly perceived, verbalized, or connected by the patient. Yet we are not dealing with the unconscious and, therefore, not with insight through interpretation. Rather the material is either conscious, in a form that so far has eluded clear perception, or preconscious.

Here we are working with the topographical model—that early aspect of psychodynamic theory that classifies mental operations and contents according to hypothetical levels of the mind: conscious, preconscious, and unconscious. These levels are neither anatomical nor spatial; depth is only a metaphor for accessibility to consciousness. Strachey (1934, p. 150) helps to demystify what it means to be psychologically "deep": "It describes, no doubt, the interpretation of materials which is either genetically early and historically distant from the patient's actual experience or which is under an especially heavy weight of repression—material, in any case, which is in the normal course of things exceedingly inaccessible to his ego and remote from it."

Although it has been largely replaced by structural theory (the tripartite model of ego, id, and superego), the topographic model remains useful in describing the quality and degree of awareness of mental events. Because unconscious and preconscious material can become conscious (one of the well-known goals of psychodynamic treatment is to make the unconscious conscious), this potential does not distinguish them. Rather the distinction has primarily to do with the nature of the material and the nature of the process by which this material becomes part of conscious self-awareness. Unconscious material includes the mechanisms of defense and instinctual drives. Greater effort is required to transform unconscious to conscious, as compared with making the preconscious conscious. Referring to the former, Freud (1933) stated: "This transformation is difficult and takes place only subject to considerable expenditure of effort or possibly never at all." As Bibring commented, this explains the resistance that is aroused generally with interpretation and not with clarification.

But what are the functional implications of such a theory of levels of awareness? What is the spectrum of clinical interactions between patient and therapist that fall in the range of clarification? Bibring (1954, p. 755), again, gets us off to a good start with his observation that clarification "aims at those vague and obscure factors (frequently below the level of verbalization) which are relevant from the viewpoint of treatment; it refers to those techniques and therapeutic processes which assist the patient to reach a higher degree of self-awareness, clarity and differentiation of self-observation which makes adequate verbalization possible." Clarification in this sense involves the therapist taking the lead in putting forth an observation about the patient's behavior or psychological functioning intended to produce or extend insight. There are three fundamental approaches by which the therapist may employ clarifications to this end. The first is conservative, the second is less so, and the third is most bold.

1. With Rogerian clarification, the therapist concentrates on material that is entirely within the range of the patient's conscious awareness—only restating more precisely (more clearly) thoughts and feelings already expressed (less clearly) by the patient. We are on very firm ground here, and that is why Rogers' respectful conservatism is so appealing. This kind of clarification could simply be called *conscious restatement.* Rogers (1942, p. 189) himself offers a clinical illustration:

> "A year ago you wouldn't have talked with the boy at the meeting [an incident she had described]. You wouldn't have admitted to yourself that you were interested in him or that you were attracted to him. Now you can realize it. Of course, what you will do about it will not be simply to follow your impulses, but to decide how far you want to go in following up that interest." She laughed at this and said that she had hardly dared to admit to herself the extent to which this boy had interested her. "But it is true lately that I feel that I want more masculine friends." The counselor added, "And you will be willing to admit that you have both an intellectual interest in them and also an interest in them as boyfriends."

2. Clinical requirements and appropriate therapeutic ambition sometimes call for broader applications of what may still be called clarification. The therapist can link together previously unconnected psychological phenomena of which the patient is specifically and consciously aware only *separate* from each other. This kind of clarification is exemplified by Shapiro's case of the man who is aware of his avowed distaste for anger and, although not simultaneously, his smile. Both attitudes, the former a self-deception (the disavowal) and the latter an affect (the pleasure), are consciously available. We may, therefore, appreciate why Shapiro specificallly renounces the use of the term "preconscious" when discussing this case, preferring instead to characterize the level of awareness in this patient as a current "estrangement" or "incomplete congruence" of self-perception. We could also call this kind of clarification *conscious–conscious linkage.* In this example from Shapiro, the emphasis has been on the lack of coherence in the two consciously held attitudes or feelings, much as in Kernberg's (1966) discussion of the phenomenon (and perhaps motivation) of splitting. The usual approach is the linking up of psychological phenomena that "go together" in the sense of consistent patterns, such as Bibring so elegantly and astutely describes. Yet the generic process has most fundamentally to do with linkage.

3. The most ambitious form of clarification involves the linking together of a conscious thought or feeling with something preconscious (that is, in range but not currently within the patient's attention and not connected). The preconscious material is brought to consciousness by the linkage and the linkage or pattern is established in a simultaneous, mutually reinforcing process. For example, a patient began a meeting by talking about his difficult and anxious effort to decrease the dose of his

antidepressant medication. He next went on to "another subject" (a familiar and rather reliable indicator for clarification): criticizing his wife for her trouble with ending the frequent breast-feeding of their 18-month-old child. The therapist clarified by connecting the "weaning" associated with the patient's own effort to decrease the intake of medication and his wife's struggle. The patient reacted with surprise, followed closely by great interest and intellectual pleasure at seeing something he had not appreciated previously. The connection allowed him to understand better the intensity of his involvement with his wife's behavior, his anger at himself and her, and their complex interactions around this subject. This kind of clarification is usefully called *conscious–preconscious linkage*. It also strengthened efforts toward interpretations relating to this man's desires to be cared for, coupled with his intense fears that such wishes make him vulnerable to the manipulations of women. For instance, one concern about his child was that the prolonged breast-feeding would make for a too needy child (like him), and his concern in the transference was about his conflictual wish for care through medication from the therapist versus his fear of overdependence.

A therapist may maximize the patient's sense of personal freedom as well as show the patient how the process of linkage in clarification is accomplished by simply placing two issues together that were initially perceived as separate. For example, the therapist could simply observe: "A few moments ago you were discussing 'x,' now you are talking about 'y.' " Instead of suggesting a connection, or even wondering aloud if there is one, a pause allows the patient to consider whether the subjects are linked or not.

As Binstock outlines later in Chapter 11, it is most consistent and useful to think of "preconscious" in the clinical context as referring to material that is usually or normally not conscious. However, because of the principles that persuade clinicians to work close to the surface and at points of urgency for the patient, clarifications take into account the ripeness of specific material for comment and highlighting by the therapist. Conscious–preconscious linkages have an obvious advantage here. It is as though the conscious material functions as a platform to which the preconscious material is first attached and then hoisted up.

With such emphasis on the pursuit of insight and the supreme position it consequently achieves in the value system of much psychodynamic psychotherapy, at least two other points of view deserve brief comment. First, as Alexander and French (1946) have asserted: "Insight is frequently the result of emotional adjustment and not the cause of it" and "the role of insight is overrated." They emphasize experience. Dorothy's heroic companions in the *Wizard of Oz*, after successful mastery of challenges requiring brains, heart, and courage, could see in themselves those attributes they thought were lacking. Those same characters could not, however, have been convinced before their journey that such capacities existed within them. Werner Erhard, founder of est, has said: "Insight is the booby prize!" Moreover every therapist knows the enormous impediment to genuine growth and change presented by intellectualization—a relative, though actually a quite distant one, of clarification.

Second, Vaillant (1983), in commenting on Wallerstein's monumental 30-year empirical prospective study (Wallerstein, 1969), recently took up the fundamental question of whether insight is "a precondition of change, a result of change, or just the ideational representation of change." Vaillant concludes that maturation, not insight, is the goal of psychodynamic therapy. Building on Wallerstein's data, he detects a false dichotomy between so-called insight and so-called supportive therapies. What really matters is the development of a more flexible, mature, and adaptive repertoire of defenses and, for this, support is always essential. While all effective therapies are supportive and strengthening (in the sense of providing a holding environment), the important distinction is whether the therapy is "ego maintaining" or "ego building." Psychodynamic therapy can be supportive either in the sense of reducing conflict by offering an auxillary ego or in the sense of regarding conflict as inevitable and enabling development. In this view insight is merely an "intellectual construct"—wonderfully educational, but not the essence of treatment.

For most patients and therapists, the self-understanding provided by clarification is essential to enduringly helpful therapy. We rightly hold high the freedom and power that insight offers. As proclaimed in the *Sermons* by John Wesley (1780) late in the 18th century, we understand something fundamental: "He that is not free is not an agent, but a patient."

CLARIFICATION IN RELATION TO OTHER TECHNIQUES

The techniques of suggestion, catharsis, manipulation, and confrontation discussed earlier in this book all require a dynamic formulation of the patient's unconscious conflicts, character structure, and personal predicament. However, the application of these techniques does not aim primarily to induce the kind of self-awareness we refer to as insight.

Erikson (1950, p. 422) reminds us of the enormously important shift—a "moral step," as he calls it—that took place historically within the evolution of psychoanalysis:

> Here one remembers with gratitude the *moral step* which Freud took when he repudiated hypnosis and suggestion: a matter much too easily rationalized

on the grounds of therapeutic expediency. When Freud decided that he must make the patient's conscious ego face his anxieties and his resistances, and that the only way to cure anxiety is to invite it to be transferred into the doctor–patient relationship, he demanded both from his patients and from his doctors that they realize a step in the evolution of conscience. True, Freud substituted the psychoanalytic couch for the hypnotic one, thus exposing the patient's inhibited will and unavoidable infantile regression to some sadistic and faddish exploitation. But the moral idea was clearly stated for all to behold: the "classical arrangement" was only a means to an end—namely, a human relationship in which the observer who has learned to observe himself teaches the observed to become self-observant.

This phylogenetic change in strategy relates to our exploration of the basic psychotherapeutic techniques as they are employed in the context of any particular psychotherapy. The emphasis on insight, provided by a trained, teaching observer, separates clarification and interpretation from manipulation, suggestion, catharsis, and even confrontation.

Of course a conceptually rigid or dogmatic division here would be misleading. Ducey, in Chapter 2, reminds us how Freud fostered self-awareness in his patient with a postpartum depression through the forceful use of suggestion. Catharsis can release more than emotion; sometimes important memories, and thereby cognitive connections, are released as well. Briggin and Zinberg (1969) offer an example of how insight may occur with repeated manipulation: "Many of our manipulations represent a form of clarification. To tell a patient that it is all right to suffer or all right to want a particular food, for example, is much the same as telling him that he judges himself too harshly or that he carries around a tyrant in his head."

Clarification has a unique role and character even though all psychotherapeutic techniques exist within a complex, interrelated framework. We can learn more about this by focusing on the relationship between clarification and confrontation, on the one hand, and clarification and interpretation, on the other.

Clarification and Confrontation

Greneson (1967, p. 37) calls our attention to the process of analyzing, a condensed expression for the four distinct technical procedures he believes contribute most directly to patient insight: confrontation, clarification, interpretation, and working through. He has obviously made two additions, working through and confrontation, to Bibring's original group of five basic techniques—both specifically aimed at furthering insight. Working through, the nature and merits of which cannot be taken up here, refers essentially to the repetition and elaboration of interpretations. But what about confrontation, and its distinction, if any, from clarification?

Binstock (Chapter 11) points out the similarity between clarification and what Devereaux (1951) calls confrontation: the focusing of the "attention of the patient on something which he perceived but failed to register—or refuses to acknowledge openly. In other words, confrontation is a rather superficial manipulation of cathexis, i.e., of attention." Shapiro's example cited earlier of the man who is pleased with his temper might seem, therefore, to involve confrontation as much as clarification. Indeed, at first glance, there seems to be little to distinguish the two.

Yet, by dissecting the process of gaining insight, Greenson spells out that the patient must recognize that an issue exists in the first place before moving on to sharpen focus and deepen understanding. Moreover, the connotations associated with the two words speak to differences. We find a clue in Devereaux's use of the word "refuses." In contract, when we review Bibring's description of clarification, we are impressed by the predominance of words such as: "show," "elaborate," "demonstrate,"—at most, "point out." The tone differs. Clarification is cooler, more detached; the patient is already in a position to consider what the therapist is observing. Confrontation is more forceful, more assertive, more confrontive. The patient's attention must be captured. There is a corresponding and generally matching tone to the patient's response. The usual reaction to successful clarification is "surprise and intellectual satisfaction" because strong resistance is not stimulated by attention to "vague, not adequately perceived or differentiated (conscious and/or preconscious) factors on a phenomenological descriptive level" (Bibring, 1954, p. 756). The patient's reaction to confrontation is, generally, less calm—to say the least! Many authors have emphasized that patients often respond to confrontation with anger.

Buie and Adler (1973) suggest that Bibring omitted confrontation from his discussion of technique because his work was predominantly with neurotics. While neurotic patients are relatively unaware of the specific, unconscious nature of their dilemmas, they tend to feel internally unhappy. They locate the source of their troubles within themselves, having often experienced something like Zetzel's (1970, p. 237) "hour of truth." Bibring, therefore, presumably had less need (less provocation!) to consider in depth the technical problems encountered by therapists working with psychotic and borderline patients who frequently use "avoidance devices" actually to "prevent awareness of material that is already available to consciousness" (Buie & Adler, 1973, p. 121). Such patients frequently locate the source of their troubles *outside* themselves. Commonly this externalization takes the form of projection or acting out. Vaillant (1980) has offered the marvelously graphic analogy of two men on an elevator: the neurotic is the one who is apologetic and grateful when it is pointed out that his fly is unzipped ("Why, I'm sorry. Thank you.") and the character disorder is the one who responds to a complaint about the unpleasant odor of his cigar smoke by screaming ("Screw you!") or punching the observer.

Confrontation is especially useful in drawing a patient's attention to his or her externalizing or external behavior, thereby moving the therapy toward an intrapsychic focus. Confrontation often implies direct changes in behavior. The holding environment in the therapy is even more necessary for successful confrontation than for clarification. Put another way, because the internal psychological material may be readily available for conscious consumption but is indigestible due to the predominant use of what Vaillant (1971) calls "immature" defenses, confrontation serves the therapist's requirement to counter the effects of these defenses directly. To the extent that it deals directly with unconscious defense mechanisms, confrontation could even be viewed as a particularly forceful and direct kind of interpretation.

Havens (1973, p. 245) takes up with great sensitivity and persuasiveness several of the isues most central to this kind of discussion of clarification and confrontation:

> I believe, myself, that the long period of psychoanalytic confirmation I referred to earlier, with its necessary emphasis on neutrality and objectivity, is a period we are leaving behind. And only our having stayed so long there and drunk so deep of those waters can explain our ever having needed to question the necessity of confrontation in the first place. Of course, psychotherapy and psychoanalysis require both clarification and confrontation; of course, each is helpless without the other; and, of course, there must be inherent conflict between them—hence, the art and perhaps never the science of psychotherapy.
>
> But how, in fact, are we to move the characterological to the symptomatic without destroying the treatment? Often we wait for life to do it—by forcing insight on the patients, through the pressure of circumstances or the criticisms of a friend. Or we may act as Alexander did, by a flash of anger that overrides the patient's resistances and establishes the characterological trait now as a symptom.
>
> The commonest method is neither of these. It is the method Elvin Semrad (1971) succinctly called "the right hand and the left hand." We give with one hand, or we spend the credit we have in hand, while at the same time something unpleasant is pointed out. At the moment of special closeness we chance the separation of the patient from a bit of his character. The closeness makes seeing it the doctor's way possible, a transient identification; and the greater that closeness, the more likely the insight will be kept long enough to be useful. Then the work of understanding can begin. This is not intimacy for its own sake, but to make possible a confrontation and, in turn, analysis.

He then concludes: "Intimacy makes objectivity usable, while objectivity justifies and spends the gained intimacy." There is much to be said for the contribution that confrontation makes to intensity and intimacy in the therapeutic relationship and that clarification makes to objectivity.

Yet even such a compelling generalization may underestimate the intimacy generated by clear, shared intellectual understanding and the objectivity that is galvanized from real emotional engagement.

Not surprisingly it is also Havens (1973) who offers some of the most radical and thought-provoking reflections on clarifications and confrontations, going so far as to suggest a preference for confronting over clarifying.

> Now it can be argued that word confrontation does not belong here, that I am merely describing "clarification." Certainly it could be cogently argued that to get a bit of reality past many of the resistances we meet a quiet clarification will do better than bombastic insistences; the latter are likely, with many patients, to excite more resistances than they overcome. That is plain enough. And throughout I never mean to equate confrontation with bombast, screaming, or emotional outpourings of any particular sort. Someone said that Lincoln could make a fool stop and think with a joke or a glance. Many of the most effective confrontations are that quiet or that homely. The goal is to get the message across, not to be ourselves defeated by the resistances, whatever the method. We want the patients to confront their inner and outer realities and in the long run it is the therapist alone against the resistances.
>
> Much analytic remembering fails to reconstruct the past; perhaps it is too intellectual or too purely perceptual a recollection, and this failure fully to enter the past opens the way to acting it out. For these reasons, confronting, meeting, encountering, such words as these, seem to me to represent better the work to be done in relationship to the past than such a word as clarification.
>
> Of course, as the transference neurosis develops, we will be blamed for the past. That is precisely what we want to have happen. My point is that transference interpretations cannot be convincing if the interpreter does not really understand, first, what he is being blamed for and, second, whether his neutrality and passivity indeed make him resemble in actuality any unfeeling figures of the past.
>
> . . . I am saying that the medium must carry the message, and if the medium is wrong, or if the medium is missing, there will be no message. The anesthetic is perfect, the diagnosis correct, the nurses skilled, the patient ready, but too often the psychiatric surgeon has no knife.
>
> I think the lesson is clear. We must be careful how we teach objectivity and neutrality, for with many students we will too readily suppress what personalities they have. Of course some need to put away parts of their personalities; but on the whole most psychotherapists are hardly an aggressive lot, not particularly loaded with what the world calls personality; and what capacity they have for confrontation is too readily snuffed out.

For our purposes it is fair to conclude that both techniques have their limits and their values, and that the nature of each is made clearer by standing them side by side.

Clarification, Transference, and Interpretation

Comments by the therapist regarding transference phenomena are conventionally called interpretations. This is hardly surprising in that transference reactions are usually unconscious (although the patient may be either intensely or vaguely aware of reacting inappropriately). Yet we know that transference phenomena run the gamut from assumptions about people in everyday relationships to specific, highly structured, and focused reactions to the therapist. Since the therapist can refer to transferential thoughts and feelings that are relatively conscious, preconscious, or unconscious (depending upon the context and current situation), it is more accurate to speak technically of both transference interpretation and transference clarification.

We must look at psychotherapy longitudinally to avoid the misleading conclusions of a static perspective. It is especially true early in the course of psychotherapy that a patient's recurrent misperceptions and deeply imbedded expectations of a therapist are generally not, as described above, consciously available. At this point in treatment, the therapist often takes the lead in making observations about transference manifestation, either because of the emergence of a negative reaction that blocks the therapeutic process or because the patient appears ready to comprehend and seriously consider it (in topographic terms, transference thoughts and feelings are nearing the psychological surface). Although close to the surface, these thoughts are still unconscious. Consequently, this kind of intervention qualifies as interpretive. It is generally met by the reluctance characteristic of responses to interpretations, both because patients commonly feel that the process of interpretation diminishes the personal nature of their relationship with the therapist, and because they resist the content.

Later in therapy the patient may lead the way in transference explorations. For example, he or she might say: "You know, it dawns on me that through this entire discussion I have again been assuming—subtly, but quite distinctly—that you are a threatening competitor who is ready to put me down." The therapist, in clarifying and extending this realization, might reply: "Exactly. It's the same expectant attitude we have observed before. As another example, you were just talking about similar feelings at work this week." If the patient agrees, and if there is no evidence that the attribution was stimulated by a real experience with the therapist [see Gill's (1979) concept of "possible plausibility" in reviewing cues to transference reactions], then the inappropriate displacement from past important relationships can be confirmed through reconstruction. Thus, in the familiar fashion, repetition in the therapy can be transformed into memory and self-understanding.

Toward the end of most successful psychodynamic psychotherapies, transference phenomena have become considerably more accessible to consciousness and references to them are clearly restatements and reminders for the patient. That is, they are clarifications. Another class of common clarifications (or interpretations) about transference reactions refer to the patient and important people other than the therapist. This is particularly prevalent in dynamically oriented treatment of couples.

A comment here about free association is also germane. In psycho-dynamic psychotherapy (as opposed to psychoanalysis), there is generally less opportunity to associate freely. Along with the more intermittent experience of free associating, the interaction between a patient's free associations and the therapist's free-floating attention is less intense and less regressed. The transference (neurosis) does not usually develop so fully and compellingly. Consequently, the amounts of transference re-action, free associative activity, and interpretation are highly correlated. Likewise, clarification becomes the most frequently used and most fun-damental technique in insight-oriented, psychodynamic psychotherapy.

Clarification and Catharsis: Affect in Meaningful Context

Bibring (1954) concludes that any curative value of emotional expres-sion in psychotherapy is not due directly to catharsis itself; abreaction has become a technical (versus a curative) means of providing evidence and conviction for psychodynamic formulations. The original idea of a purely cathartic cure introduced by Freud and Breuer in 1895 has been put to rest. Yet Binstock (1973, p. 500) provocatively reminds us that "naive re-enactments of the discovery of abreaction spring up about us on every hand. Their names are legion, but they constitute collectively a special American therapeutic passion of the present day. They are described as 'experiential,' 'mind-expanding,' 'potential-enhancing,' 'primal,' 'genuine,' 'existential,' and 'real,' and as an added attraction they 'get the anger out.' " We need not agree entirely but it is easy to respect his cogent observation that the "very essence of catharsis, wherever is is encountered, is the minimization of the ego's active participation."

Although Binstock's (1975, p. 225) heart-felt point is different ("I have by no means condemned the enjoyment of histrionics—only the pretense that they constitute treatment"), his last observation helps us to focus on the relationship, the necessary synergism, between clarification and ca-tharsis. The critical point in recovering affect is not the recovery itself; rather it is the opportunity to reexperience the affect within a new cog-nitive structure. Such a structure, this new self-perspective and under-standing, is built predominately with clarifications.

There is perhaps no more persuasive example of this principle than the patient who makes an impulsive suicide attempt. Like Conrad in *Ordinary People*, who suddenly had the enormous guilt he felt for sur-viving his hated older brother reactivated by hearing of his former co-patient Karen's suicide, these patients are unprepared for the feelings they abruptly experience. Only within the new cognitive structure of self-understanding can these patients reexperience such powerful feelings. It is indeed necessary for them to recover and learn to tolerate and manage such painful feelings (frequently of dependence and rage). But experiencing the feelings, in and of itself, is not sufficient for treatment. Recovering affect alone only increases the likelihood of repeated, impulsive, often self-injurious activity. In other words, catharsis is useful only in the context of insight—which, in turn, requires clarification and interpretation.

THE ROLE OF CLARIFICATION IN THE THERAPEUTIC ALLIANCE

While debate swirls around details of the concept of alliance, there is little question that successful psychotherapy requires a consistently respectful, frequently rational, and relatively trusting relationship between therapist and patient. Whether citing Freud's advice in 1913 "It remains the first aim of the treatment to attach him (the patient) to it (the treatment) and to the person of the doctor" (Freud, 1913, p. 139) and in 1940, the analytic "pact" (Freud, 1940, p. 173), Sterba's (1934) emphasis on identification and the "analyzing ego," Fenichel's (1941) "rational transference", Elizabeth Zetzel's (1958) "therapeutic alliance," or Greenson's (1965) "working alliance," the vast majority of clinicians and theoreticians agree that an alliance is essential for psychotherapy. Brenner (1979) stands as the foremost articulate champion of the pure transference position that distinguishing between transference and alliance is neither correct nor useful. Lawrence Friedman's (1969) paper is probably the most sophisticated and even-handed consideration of the therapeutic alliance.

Our focus centers on the role of clarification in the formation, development, and maintenance of the patient–therapist alliance. In the process we must consider what Fairbairn meant when he said (quoted by Guntrip, 1975): "You can go on analyzing forever and get nowhere. It is the personal relationship that is therapeutic." On the other hand, patient and therapist can continue in a relationship indefinitely, with only insight eventually offering help. It seems likely that there must be a dynamic, never fully resolvable tension between personal relationship and insight. But, like catharsis and clarification, there is clearly synergism too.

Bibring (1954) observed that patients respond to successful clarification with intellectual satisfaction and detachment:

> The insight resulting from it provides—so to speak—a bird's eye view for the patient with regard to his attitudes, feelings and impulses, character traits, and modes of conduct, in relation to himself as well as to the environment, his love objects, etc. By seeing his difficulties more clearly and in a more objective realistic perspective he is no longer overwhelmed or

frightened by them: he is less "identified" with them; no longer takes them for granted, nor does he consider them as constitutional parts of his personality; in brief, he is less involved . . . In general, the neurotic problems are not resolved in the process of clarification but are seen in a different light by a detached ego.

Gutheil and Havens (1979) commented that the therapeutic alliance within dynamic psychotherapy can be characterized as three different therapeutic tools (termed rational, irrational, and narcissistic alliance). These three approaches, and even their two basic components (an object relationship and an ego split), are not, however, independent of each other. In fact it is the interaction of the two components, and the technical place of clarification in this synergistic process, that is so important to appreciate.

Zetzel (1970) proposed a "dual approach" to the therapeutic process that emphasized differentiation between the dyadic and triadic aspects of the transference. First, the therapist "must continue throughout to respond intuitively to affect, indicating the patient's basic need to feel accepted and understood as a real person." This Zelzel (1970, p. 186) sees as the "core" of the therapeutic alliance, defined as a "a real object relationship which fosters autonomous ego attributes in patient." She continues (p. 213):

> At that time, the therapist must objectively recognize and interpret verbalizations and non-verbal behavior which reveal wishes and fantasies derived from the transference neurosis proper. Here the analyst serves primarily as the displaced object of unresolved, unconscious, infantile conflict. Successful analysis thus demands, at all times, recognition of the difference between the transference neurosis which is subject to infinite changeability, and the core of therapeutic alliance which, like other basic ego identifications, retains a continuous stable nucleus.

Zetzel sees the therapeutic alliance, therefore, as having primarily to do with "the healthy part of the patient's ego"—a basic capacity of the patient that has its roots in childhood dyadic object relationships and is influenced by the current patient–therapist relationship. The alliance is both felt and perceived, and these two aspects of the therapeutic relationship work together. For the patient in therapy to feel accepted, he or she must have evidence of being understood; the patient must feel a basic sense of acceptance. Clarification contributes in the arena of understanding. Along with a sense of mutual shared insight comes conviction and growing capacity for new perspective, the detachment Bibring and others have described so well. Ultimately felt acceptance follows.

Greenson (1965) begins by emphasizing the role of understanding.

> The fact that the patient is troubled, unknowing, and being looked after

by someone relatively untroubled and expert stirs up the wish to learn to emulate. Above all, the analyst's constant emphasis on attempting to gain understanding of all that goes on in the patient, the fact that nothing is too small, obscure, ugly, or beautiful to escape the analyst's search for comprehension—all this tends to evoke in the patient the wish to know, to find answers, to find causes. This does not deny that the analyst's probings stir up resistances; it merely asserts that it also stirs up the patient's curiosity and his search for causality.

Further along in the same paper (p. 221), Greenson puts it: "The most important contribution of the psychoanalyst to a good working relationship comes from his daily work with a patient. His consistent and unwavering pursuit of insight in dealing with any and all of the patient's material and behavior is the crucial factor." This is not to say—and no one (except possibly Freud in his case reports) conveys this more eloquently than Greenson—that aloof, antiseptic, or mechanistic commitment to intellectual understanding is the goal.

Sullivan (1954), too, advocated this blend of objective, observing perspective, with a tone that he referred to as serious interest and respect. This is partly why he emphasized the importance of offering a summarizing statement to the patient in the early phase of therapy. Certainly Sullivan wished to unveil interpersonal distortions, but his approach served the alliance as well—two observers, together viewing an external focus. The combination of empathic interest and objectivity create the atmosphere required for successful therapy. Returning to Rogers for a moment, we can see how this interest in clarification, reflection, and finally companionship (not only observing and describing, but entering into the experience of the client) captures important elements of alliance formation.

Clarification, therefore, aids in the development and contributes to the stability of the therapeutic alliance—particularly the rational alliance, as described by Gutheil and Havens (1979). The patient's observing ego is encouraged and reinforced. The patient perceives himself or herself as being understood by the therapist and, consequently, increasingly capable of understanding himself or herself. In closing this section, I stress that *all* effective interventions support and enhance the therapeutic relationship.

CLARIFICATION AND SELF PSYCHOLOGY

With so much emphasis on empathy in self psychology, the apparent intellectual detachment of clarification may seem out of place. Nonetheless, while empathy sounds soft and squishy, the actual state of being empathic (and being perceived as being empathic) has some rather hard-nosed and firm foundations. For example, in discussing the facilitation of empathy, Schafer (1983, p. 37) introduces the concept of a "mental model": "Empathizing requires the analyst to construct a mental model or idea of the analysand to use as a framework for responding empathically . . . one empathizes with one's idea of the analysand." Modell (1981) too observes the constant interaction between the I–thou empathic position and the I–it objective–scientific position. He indicates that these are separate stances, between which the psychotherapeutic practitioner oscillates. While such dissection helps to describe the process and practice, there is an unmistakably integrated, synergistic effect from the two perspectives. The interrelationship between cognitive and emotional states requires techniques that deal with both aspects of the human mind.

Self psychology has stimulated a more sophisticated understanding of narcissistic development and a revised approach to treatment—not only treatment of specific narcissistic disorders, but also an approach to the fundamental narcissistic issues encountered with all patients. Freud believed that the narcissistic disorders (by which he meant the psychoses, especially schizophrenia) were not amenable to psychoanalytic treatment because these patients, unlike hysterical and obsessive–compulsive patients, do not develop an analyzable transference. Recognition by Kohut of the intense self-object, narcissistic transferences makes possible analytic and psychodynamic work with patients heretofore viewed as frustratingly inaccessible. The old formula, according to which no mature object love equals no transference, turned out to be inaccurate.

These discoveries, which complement existing theory, imply an expanded role for clarification. As Goldberg (1978) points out in his introduction to *The Psychology of the Self* (and as Kohut himself frequently stated), the classic form of self psychological therapy continues to emphasize insight:

> In *The Analysis of the Self*, Kohut makes it clear that the essential aspect of the analysis of narcissistic personality disorders lies in the *working through* of the narcissistic transference. This is accompanied by the patient gaining insight and is associated with the expansion of the reality ego. The working-through process consists of the ego's repeated reactions to temporary losses of the narcissistically experienced self-object. It results in the acquisition of new psychic structures and functions through the transformation and reinternalizations of the mobilized structures—what Kohut has called transmuting internalization . . . It must be emphasized that a correct or ideal emotional position on the part of the analyst is insufficient by itself; interpretations must carry the brunt of the analytic process.

Although self psychology shifts the emphasis from the sources and implications of conflict to those of defect, treatment remains fundamentally insight-oriented and not simply experiential. Here we are reminded of Bibring's original notion that the various dynamic therapies could be described in terms of their combinations of the basic therapeutic techniques. It would be possible to emphasize manipulation in approaching narcissistic issues and disorders (versus clarification and interpretation). Experiential work would make use of a dynamic formulation from historical, developmental material and the self-object transference in the therapy itself, but then would emphasize a corrective emotional experience—supplying the patient with the kind of self-object missing in proper dose during earlier development. Psychodynamic therapy emphasizes, as I believe Kohut and Goldberg do, insight about the nature of what Kohut (1968) calls the "intense form of object hunger" observed in these patients:

> The intensity of the search for, and dependency on, these objects is due to the fact that they are striven for as a substitute for missing segments of the psychic structure. These objects are not loved for their attributes, and their actions are only dimly recognized; they are needed in order to replace the functions of a segment of the mental apparatus that had not been established in childhood.

Kohut then goes on to describe a man constantly searching for approval. Much of his life was characterized by a depressive, enraged, and withdrawing response to perceptions of lack of understanding or disapproval. This reaction pattern was traced to conscious memories of his father, but memories that had not previously been respected for their intensity and importance. This again emphasizes the role of clarification within the context of self psychological postulates.

Another emphasis of self psychology relevant to clarification relates to the ubiquitous problem of potential divergence between what the therapist intends and what the patient actually experiences. Self psychology encourages therapists to pay more attention to the patient's experience of an intervention. There has, of course, always been counsel to do this—but more in terms of gauging the state of the transference and managing resistance. The new concern here is more the recognition that, for example, a clarification may be experienced as hurtful and nonempathic even if accurate and even if not defended against for traditionally described drive-related reasons. Clearly, in such instances, the offered insight will go by the boards.

CONCLUSIONS

A dynamic tension in psychotherapy builds up between the patient's difficulty in expressing thoughts or feelings and the therapist's sense of what they are. As with Freud's shift from hypnosis to free association, Carl Rogers recognized that, in closing this gap, the patient must experience himself or herself as the crucial active participant if treatment is to be truly and abidingly useful. The patient must have ample opportunity to make the discoveries, to see and to say something first. Therapeutic results are enhanced by methods that encourage the patient to perceive change as the result of internal rather than external factors.

A related aspect of this dilemma was put interestingly by Havens (1980): "How do we give another person freedom, without imprisoning them in our world view?" How, in bringing a patient's conflicts and character out for examination, do we advance insight and shed light without enslaving them in our idiosyncratic beliefs or perceptions? We must convey, even exemplify, the process of open inquiry. We do not supply solutions; we help patients find them. The self-understanding cannot be given, it can only be fostered.

Clarification flirts with this dilemma, but also contributes much toward resolving it. Especially when helping a patient to make connections between what is already known and that which is at the periphery of current awareness (preconscious), the patient takes in not just the specific content, but also the process of self-understanding as well. With clarification the therapist articulates something more clearly or leads the way in such small increments and in such genuinely nonprovocative fashion that the patient feels a sense of expanding self-mastery. Because it is possible to understand something new about one's inner psychological functioning, and because that awareness is not too anxiety provoking, the patient feels empowered, strengthened, emboldened—increasingly in control of his or her life. Articulating a patient's dimly understood patterns of thought and behavior allows the patient to experience his or her way of being as more comprehensible and, therefore, more of a personal choice.

But this requires two preconditions. First, clarification must occur within an interpersonal context where the patient can really say: "No, that's not right." Here the therapist's attitude is crucial; only submission and distortion or struggle and resistance result if the therapist presses rigid conjectures on the patient. Tentativeness is no answer because it contributes to avoidance. Respectful clarity is needed. Ultimately the patient's own independent insight into internal functioning (his or her thoughts, feelings, motives, assumptions. intuitions, etc.) must also be imbued with this same freedom and responsibility. Second, we must appreciate the patient's perspective—the meaning to the patient of what the therapist views and intends as a clarification. This appreciation extends to the emotional climate of the clinical situation, which is mightily, though not exclusively, influenced by the therapist's attitude. The interpersonal climate must be warm enough, well wishing enough, and encouraging enough to facilitate the patient's acknowledging highly defended painful thoughts and feelings. Such a genuinely caring attitude (which specifically includes the therapist's capacity to accept, bear, and put in perspective projective identifications) is not equivalent to saccharin murmurings, meaningless reassurance, or coddling. Support, in this sense, must be part of even the most analytic treatments. Without it any potential for insight is lost. Without a positive interpersonal climate, clarifications feel like rebuffs or criticisms. Other negative reactions are, at least in their transient forms, understandable, and they are expected within the context of our appreciation of negative transference, resistance, and the vicissitudes of the alliance. Yet self psychology and object relations theory, with their exquisite sensitivity to vulnerable self-esteem and helpless dependency, remind us to temper our clarifications with empathically-attuned compassion.

When therapist and patient join in making insight their priority, a process is born that transcends both behavior change and emotional relief. The patient begins—consciously, although not without periodic anxiety and resistance—to aid in the widening and strengthening of self-understanding. The therapist steadily engages the patient's expanding ego. Patient and therapist become colleagues in the now joint endeavor of further "clarifying" a dynamic, working formulation of psychological functioning that is modified and improved through continuous investigation. This formulation includes characteristic modes of resistance. A wonderful paradox unfolds: the therapist may sometimes know more, but the patient is becoming his or her own teacher.

Psychoanalytic theory emphasizes that consciousness is exceptional, that unconscious processes play the significant role in human experience. Clarification performs three technical functions that take unconscious influence into account. These functions range along a continuum of psychological (and historical) emhpasis; that is, from a focus primarily on conscious and preconscious "surface" material to primary emphasis on the preconscious as a transition to the unconscious. Rogerian clarification aims solely at reflecting, sharpening, and refining conscious attitudes and behavior. For ego psychologists, such as Shapiro, clarification means identifying and connecting conscious and preconscious thoughts, feelings, and behavior. Not only does the ego have its own energy, but it can also contemplate its self. The psychodynamic psychotherapist directs clarification down the path which extends toward a profound awareness of unconscious influences (with their roots in drives, early object relations, and repressed memories). Clarification, in this sense, prepares the patient; it sets the stage for ever deeper self-understanding. Variations in the nature and goals of different clinical situations in psychodynamic psychotherapy introduce the possibility of using clarification for any one, or combinations, of these three general purposes.

Much of what is referred to as "interpretation" in psychotherapy (and even in psychoanalysis) is in fact clarification. Clarification always stands on the side of the psychotherapist's steady efforts to separate thought from action. And clarification can also be seen, along with the overarching influence of the therapeutic alliance with which it is so intimately connected, to function as an important strategic transitional object of psychotherapeutic process. Being understood contributes to a feeling of being held (not directly gratified), which, in turn, fosters ego growth.

Clarifications foster the patient's capacity to characterize his or her own intrapsychic and interpersonal state. This capacity ultimately becomes an internalized, self-directed method for maintaining dynamic psychological equilibrium, which then can be enriched periodically by the much less certain, initially unsteady intuitions of self-interpretation.

All psychodynamic, insight-emphasizing therapies concern themselves with the essence of clarification: bringing to the patient's fuller awareness that which is almost known. In clinical practice the distinction between clarification and interpretation blurs. Yet clarification, more than any other therapeutic technique, provides scaffolding for the therapist and patient. Its great values are those of consolidation, structure, and context. Lacking the boldness and penetration of interpretation and confrontation, it does provide an anchor of understanding. As such, it is by no means the sole equipment needed for the larger psychotherapeutic journey of self-discovery, but who would wish to set forth without it?

REFERENCES

Alexander, F., and French, T. *Psychoanalytic therapy: Principles and applications.* New York: Ronald Press, 1946.

Bibring, E. The mechanism of depression. In P. Greenacre (Ed.), *Affective disorders.* New York: International Universities Press, 1953.

Bibring, E. Psychoanalysis and the dynamic psychotherapies. *Journal of the American Psychoanalytic Association,* 1954, *2,* 745–770.

Binstock, W. A. Purgation through pity and terror. *International Journal of Psychoanalysis,* 1973, 54, 499–504.

Binstock, W. A. Purgation through pity and terror: A reply to the discussion by Clifford Yorke. *International Journal of Psychoanalysis,* 1975, *56,* 225–227.

Brenner, C. Working alliance, therapeutic alliance, and transference. *Journal of the American Psychoanalytic Association,* 1979, *27,* 137–157.

Briggin, C. S., and Zinberg, N. E. Manipulation and its clinical application. *American Journal of Psychotherapy,* 1969, *23,* 198–206.

Bruch, H. *Eating disorders.* New York: Basic Books, 1973.

Buie, D. H., and Adler, G. The uses of confrontation in the psychotherapy of borderline patients. In: G. Adler and P. G. Myerson (Eds.), *Confrontations in psychotherapy.* New York: Science House, 1973.

Devereaux, G. Some criterion for the timing of confrontation and interpretations. *International Journal of Psychoanalysis,* 1951, *32,* 19–24.

Erhard, W. quoted in A. Bry, est. New York: Avon Books, 1976.
Erikson, E. H. Childhood and society. New York: W. W. Norton., 1950.
Fenichel, O. Problems of psychoanalytic technique. Albany, N.Y.: The Psy-
    choanalytic Quarterly, 1941.
Friedman, L. The therapeutic alliance. Int. J. Psycho-Analysis, 1969, 50,
    139–153.
Freud, A. The ego and the mechanisms of defense. London: Hogarth, 1942.
Freud, S. (1895) The project for a scientific psychology. Standard Edition, Vol.
    1. London: Hogarth Press, 1966.
Freud, S. (1912) Recommendations to physicians practicing psychoanalysis.
    Standard Edition, Vol. 12. London: Hogarth Press, 1958.
Freud S. (1913) On beginning the treatment. Standard edition, Vol. 12. London:
    Hogarth Press, 1958.
Freud S. (1915) The unconscious. Standard edition, Vol. 14. London: Hogarth
    Press, 1957.
Freud, S. (1933) New introductory lectures on psychoanalysis. Standard edition,
    Vol. 23, London: Hogarth Press, 1964.
Freud, S. (1940) The technique of psychoanalysis. Standard edition, Vol. 12.
    London: Hogarth Press, 1964.
Gill, M. M. The analysis of the transference. Journal of the American Psychoan-
    alytic Association, 1979 (suppl), 27, 263–288.
Goldberg, A. The psychology of the self: A casebook. New York: International
    Universities Press, 1978.
Greenson, R. R. The working alliance and the transference neurosis. Psychoan-
    alytic Quarterly, 1965, 34, 155–181.
Greenson, R. R. The technique and practice of psychoanalysis, Vol. 1. New
    York: International Universities Press, 1967.
Guest, J. Ordinary people. New York: Ballantine Books, 1976.
Guntrip, H. My experience of analysis with Fairbairn and Winnicott (How com-
    plete a result does psychoanalytic therapy achieve?) International Review
    of Psychoanalysis, 1975, 2, 145–156.
Gutheil, T. G., and Havens, L. L. The therapeutic alliance: Contemporary
    meanings and confusions. International Review of Psychoanalysis, 1979,
    6, 467–481.
Hartmann, H. Ego psychology and the problem of adaptation. New York: In-
    ternational Universities Press, 1958.
Havens, L. L. The existential use of the self. American Journal of Psychiatry,
    1974, 31, 1–10.
Havens, L. L. Approaches to the Mind. Boston: Little & Brown, 1973.
Havens, L. L. The place of confrontation in modern psychotherapy. In: G. Adler
    and P. G. Myerson (Eds.), Confrontation in psychotherapy. New York:
    Science House, 1973.
Havens, L. L. Paper presented at Cambridge Hospital Psychotherapy Sympos-
    ium, 1980.
Kernberg, O. Structural derivatives of object relationshios. International Journal
    of Psychoanalysis, 1966, 47, 236–253.
Kohut, H. The psychoanalytic treatment of narcissistic personality disorders.
    The Psychoanalytic Study of the Child, 1968, 23, 86–113.
Modell, A. H. Does metapsychology still exist? International Journal of Psycho-
    analysis, 1981, 62, 391–402.
Rogers, C. R. Counseling and psychotherapy. Boston: Houghton Mifflin, 1942.
Rogers, C. R. Client-centered therapy. Boston: Houghton Mifflin, 1951.

Schafer, R. *The analytic attitude.* New York: Basic Books, 1983.

Semrad, E. In: S. Rako and H. Mazer (Eds.), *Semrad: The heart of a therapist.* New York: Jason Aronson, 1980.

Shapiro, D. *Neurotic styles.* New York: Basic Books, 1965.

Shapiro, D. *Autonomy and rigid character.* New York: Basic Books, 1981.

Sterba, R. F. The fate of the ego in analytic therapy. *International Journal of Psychoanalysis,* 1934, *15,* 117–126.

Strachey, J. The nature of the therapeutic action of psychoanalysis. *International Journal of Psychoanalysis,* 1934, *15,* 127–159.

Sullivan, H. S. *The psychiatric interview.* New York: W. W. Norton, 1954.

Sullivan, H. S. *Schizophrenia as a human process.* New York: Norton, 1962.

Vaillant, G. E. Theoretical hierarchy of adaptive ego defenses. *Archives of General Psychiatry,* 1971, *24,* 107–118.

Vaillant, G. E. Paper presented at Cambridge Hospital Psychotherapy Symposium, 1980.

Vaillant, G. E. Paper presented at Boston Psychoanalytic Society and Institute 50th Anniversary, 1983.

Wallerstein, R. S. Introduction to panel on psychoanalysis and psychotherapy. *International Journal of Psychoanalysis,* 1969, *50,* 120.

Wesley, J. (1780) *52 standard sermons.* Salem, Ohio: Convention Bookstore, 1967.

Yankelovich, D., and Barret, W. *Ego and instinct.* New York: Random House, 1970.

Zetzel, E.R. Therapeutic alliance in the analysis of hysteria. (1958) In *The capacity for emotional growth.* New York: International Universities Press, 1970.

11
Clarification: Clinical Application

WILLIAM A. BINSTOCK, M.D.

"The unexamined life is not worth living."
Socrates, *Apology*

"To have lived is not enough for them."
"They have to talk about it."
Beckett, *Waiting for Godot*

A DEFINITION OF CLARIFICATION

The following remarks on clarification in relation to better established psychoanalytic concepts are offered in the hope of integrating clarification more completely into the familiar body of theory and technique. In pursuit of brevity, I shall limit the scope of this discussion by structuring it in two ways. First, I confess a strong leaning toward Bibring's (1954, pp. 753–754) setting apart of clarification and interpretation as the only "curative" interventions. In viewing clarification as preparatory to subsequent interpretation, Bibring is part of a broad concensus (Loewenstein, 1957, p. 142; Gitelson, 1962, p. 204), but he stands alone in contrasting these insight-producing, mutative techniques with all other interventions, describing the remainder as merely "technical."

Accepting this distinction as a profoundly important one, I propose as a second step to delimit clarification from interpretation by choosing a definition of interpretation that suits this purpose best. Out of all the words that have been written on the subject of interpretation, and all the valid definitions that have been offered, it is particularly useful for this discussion to state that *interpretation is the making of a connection by the therapist between something unconscious and something conscious* (in the patient's mind at the moment).

This definition is preferred because it allows for both the therapist's participation in the process and the wide variation possible in the outward form of the therapist's intervention.

I now propose to define clarification, by contrast, as *the making of a connection by the therapist between something preconscious and something conscious* (in the patient's mind at the moment). There is nothing new or startling in this, but it does serve to focus attention upon something usually left to the periphery: the momentousness of the distinction between conscious and preconscious.

What is conscious is subject to reality testing; what is preconscious is not. This hair breadth of a difference, which makes *all* the difference, is quite conspicuous when we think about how the day residue got into the dream work or about studies of "subliminal" (i.e., preconscious) perception. In clinical work, by contrast, the spotlight is stolen by the unconscious processes of patient and therapist. The easy, undramatic aspect of the therapist's work lies in the ability to hear the manifest content of the associations far more clearly than the patient does, because the therapist feels free to pay attention to the connections between what is said at different times in the hour and in different hours. As we shall see, Freud (1939, p. 178) remarks in this connection that "we never fail to make a strict distinction between *our* knowledge and *his* knowledge."

There is an old joke to the effect that whereas a psychotic thinks two plus two equals five, a neurotic *knows* that two plus two equals four, but is *bothered* by it. The therapist, by virtue of his or her function as ally to the observing part of the patient's ego and as "auxiliary superego" (Strachey, 1934), can induce the patient to think about what bothers him or her. The emphasis here is placed on the therapist's role in connecting two and two, which the patient has endeavored to keep apart, rather than upon the therapist's role in imparting the information that the sum is four, a fact already known to the patient. The crux of clarification is the calling of attention to a connection, rather than the form of the intervention or the content of what is clarified.

As Adler and Meyerson (1973) have pointed out, clarification may have the outward form of a question, and Olinick's (1954) contributions on questioning are relevant. Clarification may also take the form of the repetition of a single word from the material by the therapist, if this succeeds in connecting for the patient what he or she is talking about now with what he or she was talking about previously. A turning point in one therapy came when the patient declared: "I really think I've explored both of these themes to exhaustion—what is there left for me to do?" The therapist's response, which proved effective, was: "Let both of them receive your attention at the same time." It is the making of the connection that defines the intervention; the form is chosen by "analytic tact" (Loewenstein, 1951).

Special attention must be devoted to differentiating clarification from confrontation (Adler & Meyerson, 1973). I believe, more from the clinical examples offered on this subject than from explicit definitions, that "confrontation" designates interventions that connect something kept from consciousness by reality-distorting defenses (denial, projection, introjection), and that the forcefulness involved arises from the therapist's frustration at the presence or persistence of such defenses. The material is not repressed, but it is also not conscious or even preconscious. If we were perfect therapeutic machines, confrontation would be replaced by interpretation, but fortunately for our patients, we err on the side of optimism (Binstock, 1973a).

There is no concensus that clarification refers to preconscious material, but that appears to be what everyone is talking about—at least if we consider to be conscious that which is receiving attention. Bibring (1954, p. 755) writes of:

> Conscious and/or preconscious processes, of which the patient is not sufficiently aware, which escape his attention but which he recognizes more or less readily when they are clearly presented to him . . . In brief, there is a lack of awareness (recognition) where awareness is possible. Clarification in therapy aims at those vague and obscure factors (frequently below the level of verbalization) that are relevant from the viewpoint of treatment; it refers to those techniques and therapeutic processes that assist the patient to reach a higher degree of self-awareness, clarity, and differentiation of self-observation which makes adequate verbalization possible.

CLARIFICATION AND THE PSYCHIC SURFACE

We are far afield from unconscious mental processes and mechanisms of defense—these thoughts are somewhat alien to the usual perspective of psychodynamic psychotherapy. In truth the topic of clarification appears to drive therapists to talk cognitive psychology! Bibring (1954, p. 755) writes that:

> Many, if not all, patients are often rather vague about certain feelings, attitudes, thoughts, impulses, behavior or reaction patterns, perceptions, etc. They cannot recognize or differentiate adequately what troubles them, they relate matters which are unrelated, or fail to relate what belongs together, or they do not perceive of or evaluate reality properly but in a distorted fashion under the influence of their emotions or neurotic patterns.

This is superficial, of the surface. It is reassuring at this point to recall Freud's admonition that we should approach from the surface and Hartmann's (1939) appeal for the study of the surface. Bibring (1954, pp. 756–77) speaks of "dealing . . . on a phenomenological descriptive level. Consequently clarification as a rule does not encounter resistance, at least not in the proper sense as originating from unconscious defenses . . . as it appears in reaction to interpretation. . . . As a rule patients react to (successful) clarification with surprise and intellectual satisfaction."

Although the forces deployed against a well-timed clarification are of distinctly smaller magnitude than the resistance to an interpretation, they do exist. When the flow of free associations is unimpeded, a seamless fabric is spread before the therapist, whereas it is a patchwork to the patient. The therapist acknowledges himself or herself that the patches are stitched together, but pays attention to the one immediately at hand, and to that one alone. To employ a different metaphor, it is as though each were viewing a map of the same territory, but the patient's is a political map, dramatically divided by artificial boundaries into different entities in contrasting colors, while the therapist has a geographical map showing mountain ranges, valleys, and rivers. The patient is not unconscious of the fact that the territory is continuous, but his or her attention shifts now to the red, now to the blue, now to the yellow. The reason the patient does this is not much different from the reason why, at present, it is more comfortable to look at a map of Egypt or a map of Israel, rather than a map showing both together.

If we assume that this structuring of the surface, this subdivision, is brought about by something more than chance, then the handiest explanatory concept is that of *suppression.* This mental measure is slighted in the psychodynamic literature, but it is well understood by lay people. The advice that "It is better not to think about it!" is the common coin of that folk psychology that rejects Freud's discoveries.

It may be that suppression is not quite a respectable subject for a psychodynamic therapist to discuss—not only is it completely comprehensible to lay people, but it does not even involve unconscious mental processes. As one colleague put it, "Suppression is the ordinary kind of analysis."

In their classic expositions of the mechanisms of defense, the Freuds employed the term as though they expected it to be understood without definition. Sigmund Freud (1894, p. 47) reports that "the patients can recollect as precisely as could be desired their efforts at defense, their intention of 'pushing the thing away,' of not thinking about it, of suppressing it." Anna Freud (1936, p. 126) comments that "the patient herself consciously suppressed some very private material," and mentions in passing (p. 35) "complete supresion of emotion." Fenichel (1945) never mentions it.

Vaillant (1971, p. 118), classifying suppression as a "mature" defense (and perhaps mixing in some minor forms of denial), defines "suppression" as:

> The conscious or semiconscious decision to postpone paying attention to a conscious impulse or conflict. The mechanism includes looking for silver linings, minimizing acknowledged discomfort, employing a stiff upper lip, and deliberately postponing but not avoiding. With suppression one says, "I will think about it tomorrow" and the next day one remembers to think about it.

I would amend this to read, "one thinks about it the next day, when it is no longer relevant." Yet the use of suppression is surely compatible with maturity, even indispensable to normal functioning; it is the means of being able to concentrate on one area by ignoring others. Just as repression and other unconscious mechanisms of defense protect conscious processes from becoming the seething cauldron of acute psychosis, so suppression preserves them from blooming, buzzing confusion. In the psychotherapeutic situation, however, concentration is the antithesis of the attitude of free-floating attention that the therapist cultivates in himself or herself and encourages in the patient.

THE PURPOSE OF CLARIFICATION

The place of these matters in the larger therapeutic context can be approached through a generalization about communication derived from two of Freud's topographic principles. Freud (1900) had observed that for the purpose of reality testing it is necessary that memory traces of objects and their relationships be available to consciousness; subsequently (Freud, 1920), he pointed out that while contents of intrapsychic perception have to pass both the censorship between the *Ucs.* and *Pcs.* and that between the *Pcs.* and *Cs.*, contents of external perception do not run this gamut in becoming conscious. Rapaport (1957) concludes that:

> It is this differential ease in coming to consciousness of external perception that all rational, interpretive therapy exploits. The clarification, integration, and interpretation, by the therapist to the patient, presents to the patient's external perception what he could not quite bring to his consciousness by intrapsychic perception . . . human communication is the most varied, rich, and condensed source of external perceptions, and therefore its role in safeguarding the reality principle, the secondary process, and reality testing cannot be overestimated . . . Thus communication, continuously re-presenting ideas and fitting them into ever-new relationships, militates

against repression. The same goes for most of the other mechanisms of defense also . . .

The argument might be put that we should work horizontally before we work vertically, across the surface before descending into the depths, because the wider the net is spread before it is lowered, the more fish will be in it when it is drawn up. The "patterns" that Bibring advises us to trace are repeated cross-sectionally in the present, and thus they differ from the manifestations of the compulsion to repeat, which is revealed through a succession of actions over a longer historical period. The difference resembles that between observing that the fish arrive in a school and observing that the school recurrently reappears in the same spot through the years.

CLINICAL APPLICATION

Clarification stands always in the shadow of interpretation, so that it is difficult to appreciate the value and limitations of clarification as an intervention in its own right. Yet it is the essential technique of many psychotherapeutic treatments, especially the briefer ones. The early stages of a lengthy psychotherapy may constitute a course of clarification. As a young man put it early in his treatment, "I get it now! Psychotherapy doesn't really *cure* you of anything—it just helps you remember more about yourself before you act."

Both the value and the limitations of clarification alone can be illustrated by presenting some clinical material of a familiar type. (In a technical discussion it seems best to approach psychodynamic therapy as though it were the king's justice, which not only should be done, but should be *seen* to be done.) An obsessional radical female lawyer in her late twenties came to therapy complaining of inhibition and embarrassment during oral argument. Although her courtroom performances were outstanding, she experienced agonies of embarrassment and subjective inhibitions, fantasyzing that the judge, jury, and spectators were looking upon her with pity and contempt as an ugly, inadequate child. Sometimes she would have lapses of memory or stammer, to the real detriment of her case. Following these occasions she would be haunted by an irrational conviction that she had truly been "found out" as unworthy to continue practicing law.

Her feminist beliefs enabled her to slight the subject of her sexual problems at first, but these came to light via her suppressed but enormous overconcern with bathroom functions. It was possible to show her, to her great relief, how worried she was about elimination and about the nether regions of her body. She was inhibited in her marriage by fears that intercourse threatened internal injury to the woman and by feelings of shame and degradation about her body. She could easily accept enlightenment about her pervasive need to be in control, and even the explication of her fantasy of having a cloaca elicited more relief than resistance. The objective lapses in her courtroom performance were quickly cured through a simple expedient: the internal conflict around oral argument was reduced to manageability by spelling out the connections in her mind between speech and elimination, and particularly between vocal sounds and flatulence.

This relief in the courtroom was accompanied by a shift both in what she reported and in the form of her symptomatology. Public performances, it developed, were always associated with attacks of diarrhea and excessive urination. (In fact she now recalled that when she first went to school, she wet her pants every time she was called upon to recite before the class.) The new spotlessness of performance in court was purchased at the price of an intensification of these symptoms. The experience of shame, which was the central aspect of the syndrome from the patient's point of view, merely changed location from courtroom to bathroom.

This adaptive shift from public failure to private distress may appear to be a cure by suggestion, illustrative of Glover's (1931) concept that a new "therapeutic symptom construction" can result from the suggestive action of "inexact interpretation." I wish to stress that the crucial inexactitude in this case lay in the fact that the interventions were not interpretations at all. Their redemption from that questionable category which is suspect of suggestion must come about through subsequent interpretations. These interpretations, in turn, must depend upon the sucess of the clarifications in promoting the movement that Waelder (1960, p. 88) envisaged as the "ultimate technical ideal . . . to transform the neurosis into its earlier stages, and finally into the precipitating conflicts—to roll the process of neurosis back along the path of its development."

The patient responded to these and similar interventions with mild surprise and a sense of recognition, greeting the connections being made as ones she "had known of" all along but had not let herself think about. It was, as she commented, a matter of paying attention to subjects she had ignored. In a way she "hated" the material that was coming to light, as she did any intrusion upon her self-imposed system of thought control, but she also welcomed it as helpful.

Such a series of clinical interaction, viewed in its own right as a course of clarification, could be described as a sophisticated, analytically informed education or counseling. By placing more knowledge of her own intrapsychic patterns at her conscious disposal, she is able to take a more active hand in her own destiny. Yet it falls short of true dynamic depth in exactly the sense that what became conscious was not truly unconscious—it was *preconscious*.

CLARIFICATION AND TRANSFERENCE

The therapeutic course in question did not always proceed so simply, however. The patient began to complain of a growing sense that I possessed an Olympian detachment, was immune to any emotional influence upon my flawless intellectual processes, and was (in fact) always right. The depressing corollary was that she, in consequence, was always wrong. It was easy, and somewhat helpful, to relate this picture to her father, a professor of philosophy who commented on everything that was said in his presence, subjecting it to a seemingly dispassionate intellectual and scholarly analysis that indeed left everyone with the feeling that he, and he alone, was right. Indeed the term "analysis" itself served as a pun of broad significance to us, for it linked together our joint therapeutic enterprise—her father's choice of a school of thought within philosophy, my choice of a discipline within medicine and psychology, and the name she was taught in law school for legal reasoning. "Analysis" was what the men could have and do; she felt extremely guilty for wanting it so much.

Similarly, she later became uncomfortable with my silence in ways that could be linked to her mother's habit of "clamming up" to express disapproval and to her perception of her mother as enraged by her daughter's success in an intellectual pursuit beyond the mother's ability to follow.

The making of these connections cannot comfortably be labeled as "clarification" simply because they involved the explication of transference. Yet they produced neither resolution nor resistance. In fact, they gave rise to other increasingly vivid fantasies and feelings in which she was endlessly compelled to "confess" to me as an inquisitorial figure, culminating in a nightmare of finding the Ten Commandments inscribed on her toilet paper. My making intelligible the transference connections between her expectations of me and her expectations of her parents also led us into elucidating her dilemmas about identifying with these aspects of father and mother.

"If we succeed," wrote Freud (1939, p. 152), "as we usually can, in enlightening the patient on the true nature of the phenomenon of transference, we shall have struck a powerful weapon out of the hand of his resistance and shall have converted dangers into gains . . . This is effected by preparing him in good time for these possibilities and by not overlooking the first signs of them."

These interventions linking fresh conscious perceptions of therapist with old conscious perceptions of parents stand somewhere between clarification and interpretation. They could be discussed as early or preliminary transference interpretations, but their functional role might be better characterized as clarifications of the phenomenon of transference. They were also useful in the more specific sense of that they promoted the preconscious emergence of material for more definitive interpretation, but the same can be said of all correct clarifications and preliminary interpretations.

CLARIFICATION AND MUTATIVE INTERPRETATION

Here the question seems to be how stricly one defines "interpretation." These last examples may appear at first glance to fall far short of Strachey's (1934) concept of a "mutative interpretation." Writing in a day when the menu of recognized interventions was shorter, he boiled down the analytic process to two steps: (1) the consciousness of an impulse and its direction toward the therapist, and (2) the consciousness of a discrepancy between the object and the therapist. Each conjunction of these two steps is mutative because it modifies the patient's superego.

A careful reading of Strachey's monumental contribution reveals, however, his emphasis upon "a series of innumerable small steps" (p. 159), "operations . . . essentially upon a small scale" (p. 144), "minimal doses" (p. 144), "extremely gradual" alterations (p. 144), "the summation of an immense number of minute steps". (p. 144), "the smallness of each step" (p. 144), and even the existence of "implicit mutative interpretations" (p. 149).

Would the interventions I have been discussing as "clarifications" be swallowed up, in this conception, by the category of "small steps" in the process of mutative interpretation? Is the dichotomy of clarification and interpretation simply an artificial view of what is really a continuum? We shall return to this question, and to Strachey, after looking in on a later stage of the lawyer's therapeutic progress.

Toward the end of her second year of treatment, the lawyer began to experience brief episodes of sexual attraction to me. These feelings would immediately plunge her into obsessing about how bizarre it seemed, because it was, for reasons she could not explain, totally irreconcilable with her picture of me. Then one day she reported many recent thoughts and feelings (away from her sessions and excluded from them) about my humanness. She had begun to think of me as having a home, family, habits, and personal emotions. These thoughts evoked contempt and hostility in her—it seemed utterably "awful" that a therapist should not be somehow elevated above the common herd. When I pointed out to her that all of this directly contradicted her attitude throughout the therapy to date, she was surprised, amused, and intrigued. Her associations disclosed that her previous attitude resembled that of her radical friends, and the new one that of some friends whose conservatism troubled her. Subsequently, she saw the new attitude as exactly the one her father would adopt were he the patient.

She began the next session by announcing that she felt as though she had not been helped at all—her problems were just the same and just as severe as when she began. Intellectually she saw it much differently and could reassure me that she knew better, but this was her feeling. She wondered if she were not angry at me, but had no sense of this. She spoke repeatedly of a great need to hear me speak, and of her frustration that this was not being gratified. Her associations invited the interpretation that she was viewing me as constipated and reenacting her previously recalled perceptions of her own toilet training with the roles reversed. Attempts to verbalize this interpretation were met, however, with vigorous interruptions until they were abandoned, and subsequently the patient inquired whether such tactics might be irritating to me. I agreed that they might, and invited her to explain what was going on, which she did quite skillfully, remarking on the "crazy" way she was identifying herself with an image of her father and me with an image of herself as a 2-year-old child. I pointed out the connection between her need to control the situation and the complaint with which she had begun the hour—after all, we well knew how central the need to be in control was to the problems she had brought to therapy. This was helpful and relaxing for a time, but the patient's discomfort reappeared at the end of the hour in the form of a worry that she needed to discuss an important career decision soon, but she felt that she would have to keep talking about her bowel movements instead.

The following session began with an anguished and energetic account of how the intervening hours had been spent in a frenzy of hatred and contempt for me. The discovery of my lowly human status was epitomized by my admission that I could have been irritated by her behavior of demanding a response and then rejecting it when it was offered. Nonsensical as all this seemed, it had become altogether ludicrous to her to find that all these feelings vanished as she approached my office. Upon arriving she experienced an emergent need to have a bowel movement in my bathroom, and this was accomplished with feelings of terror that I might know what she was doing there, that I might go into the bathroom before her appointment and notice the smell.

Recalling in a calmer tone how previous experiences with using the office bathroom had been associated with unacknowledged anger toward her father, she turned to the subject of the recent improvement in her relationship with her parents. The feeling that she had not been helped by therapy seemed connected with her reluctance to give up her anger at her parents, even though their behavior toward her kept improving. It was funny how in her conscious thoughts, before as well as during the therapy, she always experienced herself as angry at her mother but never at her father.

As a matter of fact, her father had written that he would like to visit her, expressing for the first time an interest in seeing her grown-up world—where she worked, her friends, and so on. She welcomed this on the surface and could not account for her determination to prevent the visit. She spoke of her anger at her mother for pussyfooting on the subject of sex and promoting her confusion about her body and its functions. She recalled again a memory from her fifth year that had previously entered the therapy as evidence that her father loved her: Frustrated in her sexual curiosity by her mother's confusing and disapproving replies, she had gone to him and been given some straightforward explanations. She treasured his words: "A woman has a hole down there."

"When your father told you that," I replied, "you thought he was referring to the anus." The patient spoke excitedly of how, upon entering the office for this session, she had looked at my buttocks and found them "incredibly repulsive" and somehow felt them to contain a great and frightening mystery. "You were wondering whether I had an anus," I explained. She recalled excitedly that her father's nude prancing about "with his penis waving" during her early years had been accompanied by his exuberantly slapping his behind. She had focused her attention and resentment all these years on the way he exhibited his penis, but she now could recall that it was the other she had really hated—she had felt he was showing off something about his rear that placed him far above her and humiliated her.

In subsequent sessions many things that had troubled or puzzled the patient were easily elucidated by reference to the fantasy that the lower organs of men were penises, and of women, anuses: her contempt for her mother's body; her fantasy of herself coming into the world as a repellant (fecal) thing; her feelings of both kinship with and contempt toward black women; her jealous rage about her father's and brothers' ability to go into the bathroom together, excluding her; her fantasy that her father went to the bathroom solely for the purpose of masturbating (having no need to eliminate). Above all, she was able to accept the explication that the one thing she "hated" about her husband made him "the right man" for her: he had a grossly exhibitionistic attitude toward his own anus—exhibiting his buttocks a bit too freely, indulging in loud flatulence frequently in all situations, scratching his behind incessantly, and having his bowel movements with the door open and asking her to visit with him in the bathroom during them. It was as though he constantly demonstrated to her that he, at least, did have an anus.

Their sexual relationship improved with dramatic speed, while the patient dreamed in succession that her internist performed the operative removal of a carrot hidden in her body, that she saw her father's genitalia clearly, and that she had anal intercourse and noticed with interest how it was different. She revelled for several weeks in fondling her clitoris, declaring her happy new awareness of it to be a "breakthrough." During this phase she decided to stop taking contraceptive pills and switched for the first time to a diaphragm, exulting in "how the diaphragm makes it so wonderfully clear what the connection is between intercourse and getting pregnant."

A CONTRAST AND A CONTINUUM

This material illustrates the extreme contrast between the time when clarification is the dominant intervention and the time of transference interpretation, the existence of a continuum between them, and the part played by clarification as both the predecessor preparing the way to inter-pretation and also its successor, applied in the wake of transference resolution. I have discussed elsewhere the reciprocal relationship between alliance and transference in the therapeutic relationship, describing it phenomenologically and offering a model of how this works (Binstock, 1973a). It is tempting at this point to relate clarification to alliance and interpretation to transference, but further argument is necessary before this intuitive connection can be considered carefully.

Strachey (1934) approaches this same relationship in his discussion of "nontransference interpretation," a broad category that includes what is now called "clarification." "The fact that the mutative interpretation is the ultimate operative factor in the therapeutic action of psychoanalysis," he concedes, "does not imply the exclusion of many other procedures" (p. 159). And (p. 158):

> A cake cannot be made of nothing but currants: . . . If I may take an analogy from trench warfare, the acceptance of a transference interpretation corresponds to the capture of a key position, while the extra-transference interpretations correspond to the general advance and to the consolidation of a fresh line which are made possible by the capture of the key position. But when this general advance goes beyond a certain point, there will be another check, and the capture of a further key position will be necessary before progress can be resumed. An oscillation of this between transference and extra-transference interpretations will represent the normal course of events in an analysis.

The distinction between clarification and interpretation is a well-defined one both intellectually and phenomenologically, yet they seem to form the extremes of a continuum. The question of interventions transitional between clarification and interpretation, raised in the middle section of the case example, vividly underlines the problem.

THE DEFINITION RECONSIDERED

The clinical material has served to contrast the natural history of clinical events, in which there is a continuous ebb and flow of clarifications and interpretations, with the sharp conceptual distinction between preconscious and unconscious.

The thoughtful student of ego psychology may point out a stumbling block to the progress of this argument. Kris (1952, p. 303) has noted that:

> The reciprocal relationship between the development of ego psychology and therapeutic technique has not only led to an increased concern with the (psychic surface) and many details of behavior, but also to specific advice as to the handling of the relationship of preconscious to unconscious material in therapy, advice that is sometimes too rigidly formulated, and yet eminently important. Briefly stated, this advice is to wait until what you wish to interpret is close to consciousness, until it is preconscious.

If this advice is accepted (and I am inclined to think that it should be), then the distinction I have drawn between clarification and interpretation seems to break down. Yet, again, it would seem that somehow the process of making the *unconscious* conscious has been thrown out the window. The appearances of the argument can be glibly preserved by maintaining that clarification is directed at what is ordinarily preconscious, whereas interpretation is directed at what is ordinarily unconscious.

To escape from this kind of logical hairsplitting, it is helpful to quote from the formulation by Freud (1939, pp. 177–78), which Kris cites as his authority:

> The method by which we strengthen the weakened ego has as a starting-point an extending of its self-knowledge. That is not, of course, the whole story but it is a first step. The loss of such knowledge signifies for the ego a surrender of power and influence; it is the first tangible sign that it is being hemmed in and hampered by the demands of the id and the super-ego. Accordingly, the first part of the help we have to offer is intellectual work on our side and encouragement to the patient to collaborate in it. This first kind of activity, as we know, is intended to pave the way to another, more difficult, task. . . . But in all this we never fail to make a strict distinction between *our* knowledge and *his* knowledge. We avoid telling

him at once things that we have often discovered at an early stage, and we avoid telling him the whole of what we think we have discovered. We reflect carefully over when we shall impart the knowledge of one of our constructions to him and we wait for what seems to us the suitable moment—which it is not always easy to decide. As a rule we put off telling him of a construction or explanation till he himself has so nearly arrived at it that only a single step remains to be taken, though that step is in fact the decisive synthesis.

Although it is comforting to have the support of Freud's authority and eloquence, the paradox remains: therapeutic work comes in two parts, two kinds of work, yet there is a continuous evolution involved. The first, more superficial, more intellectual kind of work clarifies the connection between what is conscious and what is available preconsciously. The second kind of work interprets the connection between what is conscious and what *has now become* available preconsciously, although it *had been* unconscious.

In the final portions of this chapter, I try to elucidate the smooth continuity that unifies these two parts of the work. I pursue this paradox by proceeding further down the path marked out by Strachey. First, however, it will be illuminating to focus upon the topic of affect.

CLARIFICATION AND AFFECT

The rhetorical device I employed in telling the lawyer's story appears to be a fitting one. The "clarification" portion was presented in the third person, the "interpretation" portion in the first person, and the transitional portion in an attenuated first person. The first person relationship in question is the transference neurosis: the unconscious material requiring interpretation is organized around impulses directed at the therapist.

The changes in emotional tone that were conveyed in this way involve something far more important than mere intensity. I have argued elsewhere (Binstock, 1973b) that a therapeutic approach to affects (as opposed to a show-business approach) must be concerned with the particularity of an individual's personal history and the concreteness of specific relationships. Emotions have to do with the concrete and particular; when divorced from these, they function as diversions—always serving the purpose of defense and often serving the purpose of entertainment.

It seems self-evident that the patient must become acquainted with her affects before interpretations can be employed effectively. She must, for example, know that she is angry before mutative interpretation can unburden her of her anger. Yet it would be easy to fall into the error of thinking this means she should be educated about anger, that the nature of anger should be "clarified" for her. Like her therapist, she had been exposed to great works of literature, psychology, and philosophy dealing with anger, and had, in fact, been dealing with angry people all of her life. What did he have to teach her? What she did not know about, because she managed not to notice them, were the innumerable connections between certain feelings and sensations on the one hand, and her body, objects, and history on the other hand. These her therapist was free to notice and to call to her attention.

These concrete, specific particulars are kept from consciousness by suppression, repression, and denial; they are made accessible to consciousness by clarification and interpretation. The initial phase of treatment was impoverished by their absence; it did not involve much of a first person relationship because it was mostly about a generalized patient and a generalized therapist.

(In the termination phase, this patient dreamed that she had had terrible fights with her parents all through childhood, had somehow failed to tell me about this, and must tell me at once. "It was a helpful dream," she observed, "because it reaffirms my determination that we must root out every trace of sadism from those relationships before we finish.")

Had her therapist taken the plausible, yet naive, course of teaching her everything he could about the subject of shame, the result might well have been to produce a suggestion cure by creating a therapeutic substitute neurosis. It would not have changed her. He would simply have been passing along the information that the sum of two and two is four, with the very great likelihood that her unexamined transference would motivate her to embrace this news as a transfiguring revelation.

The making of connections in which he actually engaged led in another direction: the patient's affects came home to roost upon herself, upon her introjects, and upon the person of the therapist. She might have worked up a similar feeling about an abstract archetypal shame—but it would have remained an object of pale contemplation, utterly devoid of *urgency*.

THE POINT OF URGENCY

Strachey's requirement that the mutative interpretation be "concrete," "detailed," and "specific" has already been noted, and a good deal more of what he has to say resonates equally well with these observations about affects. "'Every mutative interpretation must be emotionally 'immediate'; the patient must experience it as something actual" (1934, p. 150). "It can only be applied to an id-impulse which is actually in a state of cathexis: (p. 149) and the object of which is 'actually present' " (p. 154).

This emotional immediacy, which is a necessary precondition to change, involves (1) the establishment of an interaction between what is actual in the patient's inner world and the therapist as an actual object (cf. Binstock, 1973a), and (2) the operation of an "urgent id impulse" in this interaction.

The requirement of emotional immediacy "may be expressed in another way by saying that interpretations must always be directed to the 'point of urgency.' At any given moment some particular id-impulse will be in activity; *this* is the impulse that is susceptible of mutative interpretation at that time, and no other one. It is, no doubt, neither possible nor desirable to be giving mutative interpretations all the time; but, as Melanie Klein has pointed out, it is a most precious quality in a therapist to be able at any moment to pick out the point of urgency" (p. 150).

Yet this is something therapists regularly do; it is difficult to imagine anything more central to therapeutic work. The internal urgencies that the therapist detects in the patient's "material" are contributed by the instinctual drives. Rapaport (1957, p. 5), speaking of id and ego as "concepts . . . abstractions which refer to certain characteristics of behavior," observes that: "In contrast to the id, which refers to peremptory aspects of behavior, the ego refers to aspects of behavior which are delayable, bring about delay, or are themselves products of delay."

It is apparent why "the point of urgency is nearly always to be found in the transference" (Strachey, 1934, p. 154), why it is associated by Strachey with mutative interpretation rather than with other interventions, why it involves the momentary preconsciousness of something previously unconscious, and why it corresponds to "the suitable moment" that Freud associates particularly with the later, "more difficult" kind of analytic activity. In spite of the fluctuating prominence of the transference neurosis, the alternation between the capture of key positions, and the phase of general advance and consolidation (with the consequent oscillation between transference interpretation and clarification), the transference neurosis is nevertheless associated with the later part of the therapy. It arises subsequent to the inception of the therapy, and it grows during its further course. Transference interpretation is the characteristic intervention of this later part of the work; clarification is that of the first.

Zetzel and Meissner (1973, pp. 291–292) have written of the first part of the therapy:

> It should be noted that not all the distortions or misperceptions that the patient brings to the relationship with the analyst—particularly in his initial perception of the analyst—can be attributed to transference. . . . In the initial interaction between analyst and patient, transference elements may play a role, but the patient's responses probably reflect more of his own personality organization than the regressive emergence of previously unconscious infantile fantasies and wishes. . . . The clarifications of the pa-

tient's anxiety, suspicions, fears, and unrealistic hopes and expectations are not to be regarded as transference interpretations.

They go on to say that: "The objective of such interventions on the part of the analyst is to support and reinforce the patient's capacities to enter and establish a meaningful therapeutic relationship." A different view of the purpose of clarification has already been spelled out. I believe that all well-chosen interventions, including transference interpretations, at all stages of the therapy serve to support and reinforce these capacities.

They also offer an explanation for the growing prominence of the transference neurosis during the later part of the therapy: "The capacities which enable the patient to form the therapeutic alliance derive from early pregenital levels. As the transference analysis begins to touch on these levels of pregenital conflicts, transference neurosis and therapeutic alliance tend to merge, often to a degree that they become indistinguishable."

The concept of the point of urgency has directed attention to the later stages of therapy, to moments of intense affect, to interpretation, to transference, and to depth, instead of to the opening stage of analysis with its more intellectual moments, clarification, alliance, and the surface. It is like comparing emergency with routine—the former will always steal the show from the latter. It was, of course, Freud's role as the psychologist of the depths that necessitated his repeated advice to approach from the surface, especially during the period now identified with "id psychology."

But one cannot hold converse with the id of another person; ego addresses ego, even in psychotherapy. The id and its urgencies are not associated in our minds with this interpersonal interface, which is of the surface—they are "deep." "The ambiguity of the term, however, need not bother us. It describes, no doubt, the interpretation of material which is either genetically early and historically distant from the patient's actual experience or which is under an especially heavy weight of repression—material, in any case, which is in the normal course of things exceedingly inaccessible to his ego and remote from it" (Strachey, 1934, p. 150).

At no stage of therapy do we intervene in what is remote from or exceedingly inaccessible to the patient's ego. "One cannot overcome an enemy who is absent or not within range" (Freud, 1914, p. 152). Attempts to do so constitute the "wild analysis," which has no therapeutic effect but does do harm by presenting a caricature of psychotherapy as the real thing. We always approach the patient's urgencies as they are presented at the surface by his or her ego. The surface is of the ego.

Transference is the engine of psychotherapy that brings to the surface, in time, what is in the normal course of things inaccessible and remote. "Transference arises spontaneously in all human relationships . . . psychoanalysis does not create it but merely reveals it to consciousness and gains control of it in order to guide psychical processes toward the desired goal of cure" (Freud, 1910, p. 151).

It is the role of clarification in this process of revealing to consciousness and gaining control that justifies the lengthy exploration of the subject here presented. And clarification, too, is addressed to the point of urgency. The patient's "anxiety, suspicions, fears, and unrealistic hopes and expectations" generate their own urgencies; they too make demands upon the surface.

A RETURN TO THE SURFACE

The point of urgency *is* the surface. The most powerful wellspring of urgency is the transference, yet the surface is structured not only by the past and the legacies of the past in the patient's mind, but also by the real and present relationships with the therapist. It is the immediate impact of the therapeutic situation that arouses impulse, anxiety, and defense. The surface is the site of impulse expression and of defense alike. A more detached and intellectual perspective on the surface is possible only when transference is at a minimum. For this reason, clarification is most relevant to the early period of the therapy and to those periods following the resolution of prominent transference themes by successful interpretation; that is, when impulses directed at the therapist are in relative abeyance.

The lawyer's urgencies were rooted, at bottom, in her exhibitionistic and anal-sadistic impulses. These were neither acknowledged nor openly expressed when we met her, and this had not yet changed when we left her—the case material spans only the investigation of some defenses against these impulses. A sense of progress inheres, nonetheless, in the transition from those initial clarifications that unburden her presenting symptoms of some disguises of content to the later interpretation of (customarily) unconscious fantasies serving the purpose of defense in the transference neurosis and, therefore, of resistance to therapy.

"The exploratory description is aimed . . . mainly at uncovering a defense mechanism and not an id content. The most potent interpretive weapon is naturally the link between this defense and the patient's resistance in analysis . . ." (Kris, 1952, p. 24).

Before she sought treatment, the patient lived with the same impulses and the same defenses against them. Alone with her introjects, or interacting with other people onto whom she might project them, she experienced the intrusion of these urgencies upon the psychic surface as symptoms and other expressions of illness. It was natural for her to encounter both these impulses and the prohibitions against them most intensely when pursuing her ambitions through an adversary proceeding by performing before an audience in a formal public setting complete with judge and jury.

With the onset of treatment, the theater for this drama shifted to her relationship with her therapist. As he became her audience, judge, and jury, the symptoms and illness shifted toward the setting of the therapeutic relationship.

The therapist was by no means an innocent bystander to this development. He did follow Freud's (1914, p. 147) recommendation that "the analyst gives up the attempt to bring a particular moment or problem into focus. He contents himself with studying whatever is present for the time being on the surface of the patient's mind . . ." By doing so he became the first person since her infancy to pay attention to her urgencies instead of his own. His clarifications in the initial stage of the work conveyed this inner stance, as well as his conviction that her illness was an enemy worthy of her mettle, a piece of her personality, which had solid ground for its existence and out of which things of value for her future life had to be derived.

Thus it came about that his explorations of her surface, his elucidation of her patterns, communicated a certain attitude toward both herself and her illness. This, in turn, filled another of Freud's prescriptions (1914, p. 154): "We render the compulsion to repeat harmless, and indeed useful, by giving it the right to assert itself in a definite field. We admit it into the transference as a playground in which it is allowed to expand in almost complete freedom and in which it is expected to display to us everything in the way of pathogenic instincts that is hidden in the patient's mind." The playground is, of course, supervised in the same spirit that attended its opening, the same attitude toward the person and the illness that was contained in the clarification from the beginning.

It remains for me to define "the surface" more carefully. This was an easier task in the years before the structural point of view: it was "Pcpt.-Cs.," the organ of perception and consiousness. When perception became only a function, and consciousness only a quality, the surface was no longer a place: It became a dynamic aspect of ongoing psychic processes.

The surface is that which is conscious at the moment—that is clear enough. The ego defines the surface by selective deployment of attention to the point of urgency. But there is an inescapable quantitative aspect to this that cannot be eliminated by indulging in the currently fashionable disparagement of the psychic energy concept. Only so much can be conscious at a given instant. It does not matter whether one prefers to speak of the sum of hypercathectic energy available or of the capacity for conscious information processing—there is a finite scope of consciousness for which forces compete, gaining relative shares from moment to moment in proportion to their relative strengths.

The competitors within this arena can be subdivided initially into perceptual stimuli and internal demands for attention. In the therapeutic situation, the former would come from the therapist's presence, arrangements, and interventions, plus the patient's ego-alien bodily processes ("'I notice my stomach is growling," as opposed to, "I am hungry"); the latter would come from id and superego.

When all is in harmony, the surface is smooth. At these rare moments, with conflict-free functions in ascendancy, thought content clearly depicts the present relationship of internal and external reality, and affect declares unequivocally the ego's stance with respect to this relationship. It is far more common, however, for the surface to be disturbed to some degree.

The therapist's attention floats freely upon the surface defined by the patient's attention. Its perturbations quicken his or her own inner ear. The therapist's art and science accept a ripple as a microcosm, seeking to infer from it a play of forces, to treat it as the resultant of the patient's urgencies.

The therapist's approach to the patterning of the surface differs from everyone else's in profoundly important ways. Some of these have been touched upon here. Refusing to dismiss the patterns as trivial, random, or ungraspable, the therapist nonetheless bears in mind their superficiality, keeping to the aim of peering into the depths. At first seeing through a glass darkly, the therapist restrains any impatient impulse to clear away the interference, knowing that the structure contemplated at the surface embodies an expression of the depths. He or she watches for his or her own impact, especially when the therapist is a recent arrival on the scene or has intruded either by deliberate intervention or by inadvertence.

Patient and therapist together connect the stirrings of the wind upon the surface with the groundswells and undertows beneath, and ultimately elucidate the tides in their seasons. But they do not bathe in such awe of oceanic majesty that they lose sight of the concrete, specific details to be encountered upon that particular surface, which it is their lot to encounter and to examine.

Trilling (1971, pp. 170–172) has voiced the need for clarification of the concrete and specific particulars of a life in speaking up for "what used to be called seriousness." Addressing himself to the doctrine of R. D. Laing and his followers that: "Madness . . . is a way of seizing *in extremis* the racinating groundwork of the truth that underlies our more specific realization of what we are about," he depicts the contemporary passion for a transcendental "upward psychopathic mobility to the point of divinity, each one of us a Christ—but with none of the inconveniences of undertaking to intercede, of being a sacrifice, of reasoning with rabbis, of making sermons, of having disciples, of going to weddings and to funerals, of beginning something and at a certain point remarking that it is finished."

It is precisely the role of clarification to anchor the truths of interpretation in our more specific realization of what we are about.

REFERENCES

Adler, G., and Meyerson, P. (Eds.), *Confrontation in psychotherapy*. New York: Science House, 1973.

Bibring, E. Psychoanalysis and the dynamic psychotherapies. *Journal of the American Psychoanalytic Association*, 1954, *2*, 745–770.

Binstock, W. A. The therapeutic relationship. *Journal of the American Psychoanalytic Association*, 1973a, *21*, 543–557.

Binstock, W. A. Purgation through pity and terror. *International Journal of Psychoanalysis*, 1973b, *54*, 499–504.

Fenichel, O. *The psychoanalytic theory of neurosis*. New York: Norton, 1945.

Freud, A. (1936) *The ego and the mechanisms of defense*. London: Hogarth Press, 1937.

Freud, S. (1894) The neuro-psychoses of defense. *Standard edition*, Vol. 3, London: Hogarth Press, 1953, pp. 41–62.

Freud, S. (1900) The interpretation of dreams. *Standard Edition*, Vols. 4 and 5. London: Hogarth Press, 1953.

Freud, S. (1910) Five lectures on psycho-analysis. *Standard edition*, Vol. 2. London: Hogarth Press, 1955, pp. 1–56.

Freud S. (1914) Remembering, repeating and working-through. *Standard edition*, Vol. 12, London: Hogarth Press, 1958, pp. 145–157.

Freud, S. (1920) Beyond the pleasure principle. *Standard edition*, Vol. 18, London: Hogarth Press, 1955.

Freud, S. (1939) Moses and monotheism: Three essays. *Standard edition*, Vol. 23. London: Hogarth Press, 1964, pp. 1–139.

Gitelson, M. The curative factors in psychoanalysis, I: The first phase in psychoanalysis. *International Journal of Psycho-Analysis*, 1962, *43*, 194–206.

Glover, E. The therapeutic effect of inexact interpretation: A contribution to the theory of suggestion. *International Journal of Psycho-Analysis*, 1931, *12*, 397–411.

Hartmann, H. (1939) *Ego psychology and the problem of adaptation*. New York: International Universities Press, 1958.

Kris, E. *Psychoanalytic explorations in art*. New York: International Universities Press, 1952.

Loewenstein, R. The problem of interpretation. *Psychoanalytic Quarterly*, 1951, *20*, 1–14.

Loewenstein, R. Some thoughts on interpretation in the theory and practice of psychoanalysis. *The Psychoanalytic Study of the Child*, 1957, *12*, 127–150.

Olinick, S. Some considerations on the use of questions as a psychoanalytic technique. *Journal of the American Psychoanalytic Association*, 1954, *2*, 57–66.

Rapaport, D. Cognitive structures. In: J. S. Bruner (Ed.), *Contemporary approaches to cognition*. Cambridge, Mass.: Harvard University Press, 1957.

Strachey, J. The nature of the therapeutic action of psychoanalysis. *International Journal of Psycho-Analysis*, 1934, *15*, 127–159.

Vaillant, G. E. Theoretical hierarchy of adaptive ego mechanisms. *Archives of General Psychiatry*, 1971, *24*, 107–118.

Waelder, R. *Basic theories of psychoanalysis.* New York: International Universities Press, 1960.

Zetzel, E. R., and Meissner, W. W. Neurotic development and analyzability. In: *Basic concepts of psychoanalytic psychiatry.* New York: Basic Books, 1973.

12
Interpretation: History and Theory

HAROLD N. BORIS

When, in prehistory, something-in-itself was represented by a thought, a sound, a scratching on a cave wall, humankind realized its capacity to form symbols. When that same process of transformation was reversed, and the actual thing or event reconstructed from its symbol, interpretation was born. Thereafter, anyone who wished either to study humankind or extend our humanity—philosophers, poets, mathematicians, linguists, mystics—had to study or enhance the transformational processes.

Still it was for Freud to take up and solve a particular aspect of the matter. Symbols that were contrived to reveal—as these words are—can also be used to conceal. Experience can be as readily encoded to repress meaning as to express it. Experiences too painful to be endured can be transformed, also by rules systematic and lawful, into versions of the actual that at once represent and misrepresent the actual. Such transformations, moreover, must resist interpretation in a way transformations meant to convey the truth of the experience represented in them must not.

By 1895 in *Studies in Hysteria*, Freud (with Breuer) had found a way of intuiting from the bizarre symptoms of his patients the actual experiences that were transfigured in them. The interpretation of the symbolic meaning of symptomatology and the (re)construction of the historical events that were contained and cyphered in them were established.

By 1900 a further development had been made. Ego psychology, or the means by which these special transformations occurred, was in place.

In the famous Chapter 7 of *The Interpretation of Dreams*, Freud (1900) wrote out the transformational rules by which we come no longer to experience what we experience but experience some version of the actual experience instead. From a therapeutic standpoint, it was now possible not only to draw patients' attention to the presence of absences (the gaps in their knowledge of their experience) but also to the means (the so-called mechanisms of defense) by which the counterfeit versions of their experience were substituted for the actual ones.

So remarkable was this advance that only two major additions to the transformational/interpretive processes were left to make. Both were arrived at by seeing that there were other transformations needing interpretation.

The first of these has to do with people's propensity for transforming one experience (e.g., that having to do with a patient and a psychotherapist) into another (e.g., one having to do with a child and its parent) and then acting as if the second were as true as, or more true than, the first. This transformation, of course, is what we call the transference; and it, in turn, represents a kind of field of forces that influence the transformations embedded within it. Not only are different things experienced (e.g., remembered) within the sway of the transference, but things are remembered differently. Unless the transference is interpreted, the experiences that also are represented within it cannot be construed accurately.

Interpretations made within the field of forces that is the transference are also affected. At various times the same intervention—even one so otherwise simple as "What did you feel?"—can be experienced as anything from an accusatory attack through an examination question to a benign benediction. Insofar as the therapist hopes to be understood as simply coveying information, the view the patient takes of the interpretation also has to be subject to interpretation.

The second development follows from the increasing understanding of the force of the transference. This is the prodigious power of the person to whom the transference is made—in psychotherapy, the therapist. Earlier in psychodynamic thinking, the transfer of attributes to and from the therapist could be encapsulated by such placid nouns as indentification, projection, and displacement. But thanks largely to Melanie Klein (1952), attention shifted from the result of these transformative activities (for example, 'he has come to think of his therapist as a father figure') to the activities themselves.

We can now see that to the processes of transformation the patient attaches quite specific fantasies. The so-called projection by which the patient imbues the therapist with certain characteristics is thought of by the patient as perhaps an act of evacuation or of gifting, of impregnation or of soiling. Reciprocally in the therapist's seeming reply to this act—that is, in the silence, movement, or speech that follows the patient's activity—the patient will see acts of menace or seduction. To quote Bion (1970, p. iv) on this subject, we must now "attend not only to the meaning of the patient's communication but the use to which it is being put." The topological and structural expositions of Freud's psychodynamics thus have been enriched by a lively sense of the relation of the "objects." This relationship—who is doing what and with which and to whom—accordingly must occupy the participants. For though the amnesias and paramnesias and the host of defensive maneuvers by which these are achieved are but sleights of mind—experiences contrived simply out of selective attention and inattention—they are imagined to be more than that.

Moreover, they are imagined to transform subject and object alike. Once a little girl and I watched some other children go for a boat ride after supper. "My name," said the little girl who was deemed too young to join the boat party, "is Galen." When the boat turned and headed back to shore, the little girl confided: "My name isn't really Galen. Her name is. But don't tell her I said I was Galen." One person's transformations are supposed by that person to transform others. My young friend might have imagined that the Galen from whom she borrowed her Galen qualities without permission might react as did the gods to Prometheus. Galen too was transformed by the little girl's act. Sullivan (1953) was alert to these matters, as well. He saw that when we cannot bear to know what we experience, we cannot bear to know the truth about others: they too are transfigured and continue to be until we can come once again to know ourselves. Interpretation alters not only our experience of ourselves, but also how we experience others and how we experience others' experiences of us. Let us see this process at work in the course of psychotherapy. I shall begin with the essential *structure* of the therapy, for on it depends the experience of interpretation.

THE PSYCHODYNAMICS OF INTERPRETATION: BACKDROP

Psychodynamic psychotherapy introduces a person to himself or herself. More precisely, it introduces the person at his or her present age to himself or herself at previous ages, and "previous" here can mean a few moments or years and years ago.

At age 5 one cannot know the 15-year-old one will become. A five-year-old can extrapolate from 5 to 15 in imagination, but it is only a small child's vision of 15. Likewise, an adolescent can only know 5 from an adolescent's point of view. The adolescent cannot know 30 and so cannot know that 30 will know 5 differently. If only 5, 15, and 30 could meet and talk things over themselves! But surely an interpreter would be needed.

People think that pain can be reduced and pleasure gained by not knowing certain things about themselves and others. Of course, they have to know what they do not want to know, and this plainly presents certain difficulties. They are rather in the position of one of Kipling's characters who was guaranteed access to a great treasure, provided only that, upon encountering it, he did not think of a white rhinoceros.

Freud likened this dilemma to paragraphs excised from a newspaper by censors. The spaces give away the censor's activities. But what if the spaces were filled with false or innocuous typescript? Repression, not knowing, is not sufficient. One must have something else to know instead: a screen, a cover, a myth, a cypher, a code, a symbol, a dream, or a symptom. Perhaps if Kipling's character thought: Purple elephant, purple elephant, purple. . . .

Interpretation is a two-stage process. It has first to identify the instead of. It has then to identify the instead-of-what.

Fortunately there is a pattern to transfigurations of the actual into the fictive. We say: "In acting (thinking, feeling, perceiving, or remembering) as he or she does, this person is behaving *as if* X were true or had once been true." Binstock illustrates this in Chapter 11 of this book. He imagines: This person is acting as if what we are doing together is not a psychotherapy in which she is a grown woman and a lawyer and I am a grown man and a psychotherapist. Instead she is acting as if this were a toileting experience and she is my mother. He further imagines: For this transfiguration to have taken place, the little girl to whom I must introduce my grown patient must have had the experiences (which he describes), found them unbearable, is afraid that they will still be unbearable, and has changed them by attending to them in a very constricted or selective way. Later still he confides his surmise to his patient—drawing her attention not only to the experiences, but to the system by which she transformed the experiences.

Freud first thought psychotherapy was a matter of making the unconscious conscious: "Where id is, ego shall be." Later he saw that putting his patients in the picture concerning their systems of transfiguration—analysis of the ego—was also important. Since selective inattention (not knowing) combined with selective overattention (creating the instead-of) is so transparent a device, people need not only—as Laing (1969) puts it—to deny, but to deny that they are denying, and to deny that they are denying that they are denying, and so on. This they can do only by creating an "instead-of" for the fact that they actually are merely using selective attention. Thus if, as the Bible has it, one looks to the mote in the other's eye so not to see the beam in one's own, the whole "projection" collapses if one knows one is doing what one is doing. A projection cannot be known to be a projection if it is to survive. What if a projection is instead experienced as if it were a penetrating missile, and not selective attention? Now we have a version of the evil eye. Much better.

But that is what leaves us with the task of identifying not only the substitution of the substantive fiction for the actual one, but also the substitution of the methodological process for the actual one. This is hard work—so much so that therapist and patient often wish there were another avenue to salvation.

This wish, this hope, is at the core of what we term resistance. Normally both therapist and patient experience this, although for understandably self-serving reasons resistance is normally attributed only to the patient. But what therapist does not shrink at the prospect of bringing a patient's attention to aspects of an experience the patient feels unable to bear knowing?

The patient's resistance is better understood perhaps than the therapist's. The patient has predicated his or her life on fictions, such as that time is coextensive with possibility and that neither ebbs, and is not gratified to discover that efforts to realize this illusion are doomed. But the therapist too has wishes for or from the patient. These are evident when the therapist moves beyond displaying to the patient the instead-ofs and the instead-of-whats and starts trying to cure the patient. Any attempt to induce a patient to change reflects the therapist's resistance to interpretation and is, as such, an expression either of countertransference or of an identification that goes beyond empathy.

Interpretations grow out of sympathetic imagination of the sort captured in the phrase, "Nothing human is foreign to me." (Fortunately, as Harry Stack Sullivan remarked, "People are more human than otherwise.") This sympathetic imagination is at its most capacious when its owners (therapists *or* patients) feel receptive to the experience they are having. We can conceive, gestate, nourish, be fruitful and multiply, to the degree we can tolerate without loathing knowing what we and others experience. Insofar as we cannot, we will naturally try to change the experience or, failing that, to know as little as possible about it. At these times the therapist will want to speak to the patient in order to change the patient and get some relief for the intolerable (or about to be intolerable) experience the patient is visiting upon the therapist. Therapists are often unaware of this as a motivating factor in their interventions, interpretive or otherwise. Their own experiences as patients in psychotherapy will often have laid bare the heretofore unconscious elements in their transferences and countertransferences. But as Bion (1966) remarked, the conscious elements are often not subject to analysis for the simple reason that membership in the group—the school or orientation—of therapists makes these intentions appear unexceptional and unremarkable, when often they are anything but. As an example one might consider that psychodynamic psychotherapy deals precisely with that: the dynamics of the patient's psyche. Yet often therapists' ideas about patients' lives may stimulate them to make interventions calculated to affect what their patients do, and how, where, or with whom. To some who read this, the thought that such activities are in any sense a blurring of the line between counseling and interpretive psychotherapy will seem to be of no consequence. In their group that is how psychotherapy is done, and they would protest any implication that they were acting out countertransferences or identifications. To my group, however, that is exactly what it looks like. To return to Bion's point, here it is not what we feel for (or against) any given patient—the unconscious element in the countertransference—but that some of us consciously feel that influencing a patient is within, and others feel it is outside of, the precinct of psychodynamic psychotherapy.

There is a sketch in a Monty Python Show in which a Something-English dictionary is mischievously translated: the poor foreigner laboriously thumbing through it to make a purchase at a tobacconist ends up asking for a kiss and getting belted for his pains. We take it as an article of faith that the interpreter interjects nothing of his or her own into the process, but with the greatest fidelity makes the meaning of one person's communication known to the other. The therapist's job is to be translucent.

This is not a happy point of view to those who wish to be psychoactive. Even capsules and pills are permitted more potency than therapist as translator, therapist as fiberoptic conductor! Indeed, it is not to be wondered at that so many psychotherapists find the work unendurable and wish to go back to being proper physicians, counselors, nurses, and social workers.

All the same, the efficacy of interpretation, as Freud himself counseled, depends more on the position of the therapist vis-à-vis the patient that on the brilliance, or even accuracy, of the interpretation itself. Accordingly, I shall now develop my thinking on this matter.

The patient ordinarily does not note use of interpretations until three conditions are satisfied. First, he or she must be disillusioned about salvation through means other than "systematically understanding his self-deceptions and their motivations" (Hartmann, 1953). Second, he or she has to feel convinced by the data. Third, he or she has to detach the giving of interpretations by the therapist from the belief that the therapist is engaging is lascivious acts in the guise of giving interpretation.

Fulfilling these conditions is at once a matter of technique (to which I will come presently) and a matter having to do with the therapist as a person.

If the therapist does not value interpretive psychotherapy, why should the patient? If the therapist cannot wait for [as Bion (1961) puts it] interpretations to become obvious, and remarkable only in that the patient has not reached them on his/ or her own, how can the patient feel convinced? If the therapist is engaged in changing the patient, how can the patient distinguish the communication of bits of knowledge from expressions of love and hate, lust and yearning? Freud speaks of "sticking coolly to the roles."

Perhaps the single greatest distinction between the psychotherapeutic encounter and other human encounters is the capacity of the therapist to limit (through an act of continuous mourning preceding and during each therapy) what he or she needs from the transaction. As so often happens, this delimitation opens up other possibilities that might otherwise be latent—but of that, more later. People receive information from others all of their lives. Something, after all, has to make the giving of interpretations distinguishable from the welter of other information people are given about themselves. As I have been trying to demonstrate, much of this distinction lies in the patient's experience of the therapist's motives.

Parents, not unnaturally, give information to their children in order to make themselves or the children more lovable. The more urgent this need, the fewer chances the parent (later, perhaps, the lover) can take with a considered, empirical approach; "Because I say so!" is the unspoken, or sometimes spoken, attribution of authority for the information.

The therapist needs to eschew these claims to ominiscience, the more so since many who become our patients have in their helplessness turned to omnipotent thinking as a comfort. Instead, the therapist must allow experience to cumulate and evolve until its interpretation can be assessed by the patient. Patients who complain of being treated as a case out of a book often have a good point. It is understandable that a patient will resist giving out precious or painful material if he or she feels it to be unnecessary to the interpretation. And insofar as the interpretation is based on material the therapist has about the patient (such as the life-history or some rumor, contrived perhaps by the referring agent or a supervisor or a recently read paper), the patient will feel irrelevant and supernumerary. Interpretations have to provide meaning and dimension to what the experience consists *of*. If they do not, the patient can only become more and more like himself or herself; he or she cannot become more and more himself or herself. As a patient of mine once put what I am trying to say, "I have a way of thinking of myself as if I were myself, which is like thinking of today not as Thursday but as if it were Thursday."

How intolerably boring it is when patients go on and on about something we have heard a dozen times if we heard it once! But we may not have heard it once, which is why we are hearing it a dozen times. We may have heard it and interpreted it and in doing so closed it off from

further consideration. Yet for the patient it needs to evolve. And if it
cannot evolve in the patient's mind, the patient needs it to evolve in the
therapist's. Consider a patient who might wish to find out how to go to
Bar Harbor, Maine, but since he cannot bear to know that is where he
wishes to go, asks the directions to Providence, Rhode Island. Given
these, he will know they are wrong without quite knowing what to ask
instead, except directions to Providence, again. Anyone who has hung
around with 4-year-olds who keep asking "But why?" will know what I
mean. Both the patient and the child may have to be asked whether they
are asking what they really want to know.

Much of the information concerning what the patient is being comes
from the impulses being with the patient generates in the therapist. Acting
on those impulses relieves the tension, but loses the information. The
therapists who ask themselves *why* they want to nod or speak or yawn
or look at the clock or remember that the patient lost his or her mother
a year ago have a chance of knowing more of what the patient is experiencing then if they yield to these impulses.*

Between the instant that dice leave the roller's hand and the time they
show their dots on the green baize of the gambling table lies either the
mysterious workings of chance—or a series of activities which, if closely
observed and repeatedly studied, make the outcome understandable, predictable, and controllable. Patients eavesdrop upon themselves; and the
more details they provide the therapist, the more they learn directly from
themselves. What seems mad, random, meaningless, purposeless can be
seen by them to have pattern, design, coherence, intent. The therapist's
patience is the patient's best friend. Provided therapists do not have too
often to give themselves relief from waiting, patients become more and
more obvious to *them*selves.

Now, of course, few if any of us can interpret so well that only
interpretation need serve. Nor does every patient who enters psychotherapy intend to accept a strictly interpretive approach. Preliminary caution
on both sides should be exercised: grandiosity afflicts all who have once
felt impotent to affect their fates. And, as I indicated earlier, there is
bound to be turbulence and upheaval in the course of a psychotherapy
that will be difficult for both parties to stand—and still stick "coolly to
the rules." "Parameters," in Eissler's (1958) phrase, are useful, as the other
chapters in this volume amply illustrate. But, as Eissler indicates, when
these are no longer used as a means to make interpretation possible, they
become the means that make interpretation impossible. Since the object
of the psychotherapy is to enable patients to feel and understand the full
reality of their experiences so that they can recover what they have taken

*This is true particularly in work with patients who devote great energy and skill
to stimulating reactive impulses in the therapist–patients such as anorectics. (See,
in this regard, Boris, 1984a, 1984b.)

pains no longer to experience, the task of the therapist is to become self-effacing. Time and energy are limited and limiting; if the patient's attention is to be drawn to himself or herself, past and present, it is not helpful for the therapist to draw attention to himself or herself. And yet insofar as the therapist wants something for or from the patient (fees perhaps excepted), the patient understandably will become even more preoccupied with influencing his or her therapist than he or she ordinarily would be—and "ordinarily" is. Thus interpretations often are spoiled by the teaching or preaching that surrounds them. Winnicott observed that he could tell when he left off making interpretations: it was when he started saying "moreover." (For his fuller treatment of this, see Winnicott, 1958.)

The introduction of the (at once) deceived and deceiving self to what it experiences requires that experiences evolve. This evolution must take place in both patient and therapist. Neither should "head it off" by analyzing it. Only in so far as the patient and therapist have an experience in common to advert to can either feel convinced. Recognizing the "truth" of an interpretation is only partially mutative. At this stage it is, if shocking, akin to a confrontation, or if intellectually assimilated, akin to a clarification. Only when the "truth" takes on an air of inevitability does an interpretation do its work.

Repression is hard work. It is easier to know what one knows but to detach significance from it. Patients ordinarily know far more about themselves than they ever use. Sometimes they seem to know everything there is to know—except how the proliferation of knowledge mitigates any single insight.

Therapists must, therefore, husband their additions charily. They will need to be careful lest their contributions only add to patients' profligacy of understandings. Only the fullness and intensity of experiencing can truly inform a patient, can help him or her rescue conviction from mere insight.

The dynamic tension in psychotherapy takes place between the patient's need to reveal and need to conceal. Much of this has to do with a wish to influence the therapist's disposition toward the patient in a direction the patient imagines would be favorable. But part of it reflects the fear of certainty. If the patient is the only one who knows what he or she experiences, that knowledge can be forever doubted or be denuded of significance. The same is true so long as the therapist is the only one who knows something. The danger lies in the exponential leap to certainty when something is known to both of them. In this conjunction also lies the immense power of an interpretation.

After some years of work, a patient confided the following.

She wished she could be dressed in a gray pinafore and a white turtleneck and that the therapist would take her onto his lap, put his hand under her skirt, discover she was not wearing anything, and touch and fondle her to orgasm.

She remembered, as a child of 6, standing with her back to a mirror and bending forward peering between her legs to see what she looked like. If her father should chance to pass on the way to his dinner with her mother, he would laugh.

Once, before her menarche, she tried an experiment with her rowdy pal. He tried to put his you know what into her. His sister was present and they were all laughing. Some months later she felt very bad and isolated. She feared she was pregnant but couldn't tell anyone, not even her own dear sister. That winter she had her first menstrual period. She felt awful and didn't tell any of her friends. Two years later her rowdy pal's good friend and her own good friend asked her to show him how she put a tampon in. She showed him with pleasure. The good feelings associated with the experiment and previous times briefly returned. Her pal liked to look at and touch her breasts, but she hated that. She hated her breasts.

With the exception of the fantasy concerning the therapist, the patient had mentioned all of these experiences over a span of months. The incidents were scattered over time as wreckage might be strewn over a landscape. Except for the solace of confiding personal and private pleasures and agonies, the patient, a woman now in her 30s, saw no special reason for telling her therapist of the incidents. They were things that happened.

From time to time the patient allowed herself to have intercourse. She liked the men's excitement, but hated the act itself, though she felt that to be fair she must submit. In response to a question, she said that she did not have orgasms except to her own masturbation. Later she added that as she touched herself she frequently imagined a man and woman discussing her: "How can we make her come? Is there anything we can do? Nothing. There is nothing we can do. Nothing at all."

She did not look at men she found attractive, except when they could not notice she was looking. Ordinarily she fastened her gaze at a point to one or another side of the therapist. She talked falteringly with many stops: "I-uh-uh-so-um . . ." Someone in her therapy group called that manner of talking hostile. Later it was understood to be an enactment of the "nothing" fantasy: "There is nothing we (you) can do to make me go/come. When you have no-thing I will come/go, which will be something!" When she was 6, her parents, who always vacationed with the three girls on Cape Cod, went to Europe, leaving them with the measles and a nurse. Constipation, which may have started as adjunctive to the illness, became, in response to hounding by the nurse, a lifelong misery. Whether she was defying the nurse, or holding on to her parents, or both, of course, matters, as does the question of earlier struggles with ownership and loss. But of no less moment is the series of symbolic transformations: breast = feces = penis = go = stay = come. Quite an achievement, the more so, perhaps, in that her own misery draws her attention from the pain inflicted upon others, on which the member of her therapy group commented (no doubt feelingfully). As do artists with "found" objects, we, all of us, seize upon the adventitious in life to craft and shape our transformations.

This material—both in the way it was communicated, implying at once strewn wreckage and a hostile attack on the therapist's deductive powers, and in itself a content in a life—tells a story of yearning, defect, fury, and a love in danger of being obliterated by envy. The material may be thought to say: Once I discovered I did not have a penis, I soothed my anguish first by believing the condition was temporary, then by forgetting the fact. Finally I had almost to rediscover it. Now all I want is to return to the

days when there were no differences, and to feel alive and all of a piece and
one of the guys.

An interpretation along those lines might (in fact did) produce a flock
of additional memories, further elaboration of the patient's current experience, a sense of the absolute rightness of the construction of the child's
experience to the grown-up patient. But what changes for the patient? The
little pink "moosh" of the six-year-old genital is still the mushy, smushy
"crotch" of the 36-year-old. Both are unconsoled. The 6-year-old is still
heartbroken because her 36-year-old self has done no better for her than
she herself could. What is the use of being 36? The 36-year-old weeps
profusely at her current and her earlier plight. She thinks 6 might do better
than she can at 36—6 has her whole life in front of her. Six had her mother,
which 36 lost. Six could watch her daddy in the bath; 36 doesn't even get
a phone call.

What is happening here? If anything, it has been in whatever 36 had
to endure to make the interpretation possible. The interpretation reflects
the experience back to the experiences. This augments, intensifies, and
amplifies the experience, which, when communicated, makes the interpretation more exact, more vivid, more detailed, more inclusive. Akin to
a laser, the interpretation can now further amplify the experience, which
then further infuses the interpretation, and so on.

There is more to be learned for both parties, having perhaps to do
with earlier disparagements of the mother and the horror of becoming a
mother disparaged. But that too will have to be experienced to be communicated; and it is in the dawning realization that the experience need
not be so cataclysmic now as it was then that the development takes place.
Interpretation is retrospective; before it is mutative, the patient must have
already changed. The adult must be able to stand being 36 and the 6-year-
old must also stand it. If they cannot stand being in the same room
together, there is no way of effecting an introduction. The interpretation
makes them fathomable and comprehensible to one another, but that is
only important if they have already decided to coexist—and to coexist in
the presence of the therapist.

Much, perhaps most, of the work of the therapy lies in providing the
conditions that make such a conjoining seem endurable. The child in
people does not want to know of grown-up limitations. Its helplessness
demands omnipotence of its elders. The elder does not want to know of
its helplessness either, especially in conjunction with the passions of
youth.

Bibring saw this, of course, and knew that while interpretation could
put everyone on speaking terms, much else had to pave the way: abreaction, confrontation, clarification, and the like. But perhaps more than
anything, it is the capacity of the therapist to stand his or her own helplessness, and the patient's, to make do with a good deal less than omnipotence, and to know a lot about passions, that keeps psychotherapy from
being a refined sadomasochistic exercise and interpretation a tutorial.

THE PSYCHOACTIVE INGREDIENT AND THE NATURE OF DEVELOPMENT

Well-being depends on outer options and inner possibilities. To some extent each conditions the other; and to some extent each has a life of its own. Psychotherapy allows people to experience what they experience, bear it, learn from it, and apply what they have learned to their sojourn in the personal and material world. But, as Freud himself knew, "neurotic misery" is all too often replaced by nothing better than "common unhappiness." Outer options do not surrender their constraints to the well-analyzed person.

Still there is something to be said for expanding inner possibility: for understanding that one's experience of past, present, and future are extrapolations from inaccurate appraisals of what is so. These inaccuracies are, of course, not products of faulty cognition. They are the result of wishful thinking. The future is often feared because it is unknown. But there is no special reason the unknown should be feared, or not feared. In fact, when the future is feared (or not), it is because it represents an extrapolation from the past or present. The only unknown thing in this is that it *is* an extrapolation.

Such extrapolations are at once necessary and unreasonable. It is (for most of us) necessary to act as if the sun will rise tomorrow. Some of us can see, however, that the fact that it has risen faithfully in the past holds no inevitable power over the future. Transference is compounded of the same wish-propelled, hopeful extrapolations. The transference, after all, requires a rather optimistic indifference to certain otherwise compelling facts: that time passes, that people differ, that things change. It is a testament to hope that such a thing as the transference exists (Boris, 1976).

Development occurs insofar as one can stand the disillusionment of such wishes and hopes. Why some people can stand disillusionment—can grieve, mourn, and relinquish—and others cannot is not well understood, at least by me. Often we think that as people test reality in the course of psychotherapy, they get on more cordial terms with what is so. But is there any technique or approach in the world that can induce people to take a step that they are convinced will lead to calamity?

Many patients, for example, tell their psychotherapists that they simply cannot "say" something. ("Say" may at other times or in other therapies be "think," "feel," "try," "do," etc.) Their therapists can understand this as a situation needing interpretation ("You are acting as if to say this to me is tantamount to saying X to so and so"), confrontation ("Say it anyway!"), manipulation ("A bright person like you?"), clarification ("Is saying the same as doing?"), catharsis ("What does the thought of saying it *feel* like?"), and so on. The experienced therapists who are coauthors of this book have shown the power of these interventions for nudging patients beyond the impasse and for taking the next step.

But what if the patient does not? What if the helpful nudges contained in the various interventions only frighten the patient more and stiffen resistance? Now there really is an impasse! Experienced therapists have a repertoire; there is more than one arrow in their quivers. They try, as they should, to see what will help when first one interpretation and then another does not.

But as important as trying is the capacity of the therapist to *stop* trying. It is the patient who has to take the plunge—who has to summon the courage to risk calamity—or what is perhaps the greater courage to give up the wish-driven extrapolation that conjured up calamity. For any intervention to be useful, the patient has to use it.

Take the widely known example of Freud and his patient, the Wolf Man (Freud, 1918). For reasons not clear to Freud, at a given point in treatment, the Wolf Man froze progress. Nothing was happening. Interpretation after interpretation failed. The ever-pragmatic Freud finally imposed an ultimatum: six months more of treatment, and termination—no matter what.

The treatment unfroze enough to reveal that the causes of the freezing lay in the patient's observations of and reactions to the primal scene, and the extrapolations of these to the transference. For us there is this question: Was it the ultimatum, or Freud's relinquishment of hope, that freed the patient? Was it the active intervention, or Freud's mourning for his own therapeutic potency, that constituted the psychoactive ingredient?

The answer is probably: Both. But surely the patient simply had finally to take the next step, had to give up the thrall of past and future and attend to the present Freud, the Freud who was primarily Freud. It is the patient who conduces the treatment.

Viewed in this light, the psychoactive ingredient is not the intervention. It is rather the therapist's capacity to be in the treatment in the same way the patient is. Both parties have to develop. Each has to suffer disillusionment. Each has to mourn. Each has to learn from their common experience. When this happens each is as fundamentally necessary to the other as the other is. There is an equality, a jointness, a commensalism. Psychotherapy inevitably imposes a process of mourning upon both therapist and patient. This is not a matter of weaning, with which it is sometimes confused. It means that both therapist and patient must come to stand the limits in their relationship—that they cannot use each other in every kind of way, but must use each other up in the way of work. When, however, longings for different and additional pleasures are renounced and the therapist becomes resigned to the patient as a source of only *some* good experiences, those now delimited experiences become invigorated. For instance, when the therapist is resigned to learning what the patient has to teach, the sessions become less tedious; often the therapist feels bored when listening for things, such as those that make much of him or her, which are all too slow in coming. If the therapist is senior enough to do supervision, the therapists in training may be obliged to hear tales of wonder and woe, as the more senior therapist palliates the wounds to his or her narcissim delivered by his patients.

Insofar as such wishes are taken out of the therapy (even into the supervision), the therapist can treasure what in fact is abundant: One learns a great deal from one's patients—about them individually, about humankind generally, about (by comparison and contrast) oneself, about what helps and what does not, about how things get the way they are and how they change. If one does not have to make the patient help one be good at doing therapy, all this learning feels enriching and unfrightening. People who, as I do, have left over from childhood a certain dread about being inaccurately perceived or wrongly attributed, can have that experience happen again and again, and yet, with time, have it become progressively undone until one is able to feel freely and fully one's self. A lovely instance of this appears in Winnicott's (1977) *The Piggle,* an account of his analysis of a little girl with that nickname. At one point, some years after the analysis began, Winnicott greeted her at his doorstep by her real name, Gabrielle. Somehow, he intuited that he had grown from being Greedy Baby and Bad Mummy into being Dr. Winnicott, who of course greets a young woman by her own grown-up name! (Interpretations do not need to smell of antiseptic!) Szasz (1956) and Winnicott (1977) make helpful additions to the bounty of benefits a therapist may uncoercively draw from a patient.

There is at once much and little to be said for training. Anna Freud was an experienced psychoanalyst of children, a teacher and supervisor to others, when she learned that the person many took to be her rival was proceeding with children in a way Miss Freud had not thought possible. Melanie Klein was not troubling to educate the child's parents, or even the child. Indeed she thought this alliance-making tended to obscure the very transformations she wished to interpret. More to the point, she found a line of interpretation that made the entire prologue unnecessary. Anna Freud (1954) altered her technique.

Such a person, one can imagine, can learn equally well from her patients. In this case she had not. So she learned instead from Klein. But what of those who learn mainly from books, from teachers and supervisors, from tradition? Here is the analog to the extrapolations from the past that earlier we had identified as the impediment to patients' development.

Freud, fortunately, had no such impediment. Once he broke with his tradition, there were few but his patients to teach him. He knew his luck. What he wanted to send on down through time were a spare few discoveries: infantile sexuality, the unconscious, the transference—two more. *"Je suis nes pas un Freudian,"* he said.

We are not quite so fortunate. There are even texts like this to teach us! But, of course, as in the instance of Melanie Klein and Anna Freud, tradition, comprised as it is of the experience of others, can be of great value. But only, I think, if we learn the spirit as well as the letter of it.

The letter is in each word of this and other books. The spirit is what made the letter possible. The letter has to do with finding, the spirit with seeking; the letter with the known, the spirit with the undiscovered; the letter with conveying, the spirit with inquiry; the letter with technique, the spirit with risk.

Above all, the spirit of psychodynamic psychotherapy requires us to remember whose treatment it is. And, in deference to that, to doing only what the patient cannot yet do for himself or herself when he or she is ready to do it. We put the patient back in possession of himself or herself by showing him or her how he or she lost it. We introduce the selves, but do not shape or direct them. Throughout, we efface *ourselves* so that the patient can do what he or she has to do about *him*self or *her*self. When the time comes that we can be entirely self-effacing, we politely withdraw from the process. We will not have completed our development with this patient as he or she will not with us, but there is something in the nature of development that requires the catalysis of the new.

MAKING INTERPRETATIONS

There are several rather useful rules of thumb for offering interpretations to a patient, when (and this is the first) it turns out that the patient's efforts to know what he or she is experiencing absolutely requires offering them.

These are as follows:

Interpret
-patterns before specifics
-anxieties before defenses
-defenses before wishes
-derivatives before deeper material
-there before here
-now before then
and how the patient is interpreting each of the psychotherapist's interpretations.

The "grammar" of transformation is intricate but not really complicated. It is economical in the extreme. It has to be simple and economical because babies and young children need to be able to use it. Thus generalization ("I'm mad at everybody") and specification ("I've only my self to blame") are both "defenses." One, generalization, loses the true target in the crowd. Like Ali Baba, whose hideout was marked with an ineradicable X, and who therefore painted X's on every other door, generalization obscures what is so. But so can simple substitution, as self for other.

Since people come to psychotherapy with most of their transformations intact, their "chief complaint" is often a transformation of their actual complaint. If the complaint is overly specific, the therapist may have to expand it; if overly general, to contract it. The essence of the work here is the effort to display to the patient the role in the countless situtations that cause the patient pain of a constant, repetitive factor that originates with him or her. The patient has to a degree to become alienated from himself or herself. In that measure the patient becomes allied with the psychotherapist. If the world causes the pain (which it well might), there is no cure in psychotherapy. Only insofar as by actual or transformational action the patient contributes to his or her own fate can therapy help. A survey of each situation is necessary so that the patient can see among the variables the constant factor brought by himself or herself. Patterns, then, before specifics.

This display generates anxiety. Transformations are initially effected to avert intolerable frustration and helplessness. The impact of the actual on the fictive threatens to reinvoke that original pain. It is, therefore, frightening and greatly to be resisted. The patient has to know from the therapist that the therapist knows of the anxiety. The patient who does not discover this may believe that the therapist is unaware of the anxiety, and this is as frightening as being with a dentist who does not know that drilling can hurt. Still, no matter how bad the patient feels now, once it was worse.

Reasonable people do not stand around being frightened; they take countermeasures. These are the defenses by which experience is transformed. Perhaps the simplest of these is evasion. As the patient's patterns are being identified, the anxiety that is generated will, in turn, stimulate countermeasures. The patient may feel reluctant to talk, may come late, may forget an appointment. He or she is trying to transform the experience itself. If this cannot be done, the patient will have to resort to transforming what he or she experiences of the experience. As a last resort, the patient will have to direct his or her efforts to transforming the very experiencing apparatus itself—destroying ego to save the self.*

*Increasingly, current research into infants' cognitive, perceptual and memory functions, and skills shows that what Freud called ego functions are well established at an early age (c.f. Gardner, 1983; Miller 1983 for reviews and speculations on these matters). Perhaps Melanie Klein was correct in ascribing to infants and young children the mental sophistication she did. In any case, it is now clear that psychosis involves a systematic and ordered destruction of ego function rather than a developmental failure.

These maneuvers happen so quickly (the patient, after all, has had years of practice) that the psychotherapist needs to link the brief experience of anxiety to the defensive responses that almost instantaneously follow upon it—relieving it, or obscuring it. Since the patient believes the security gained in using his or her defenses is reinforced by severing the connections between experience and transformation (e.g., anxiety and defense), he or she will generally not "know" of the link between, for example, his or her fright in one session and late arrival to the next. A patient who did might remember the anxiety, reexperience the pain of it, and be in danger of experiencing more of the particular experience of which the anxiety was only a foretaste. So, prudently, the patient will not only come late to shorten the session, altering the perturbing experience itself, but will also attribute the lateness to some other cause, some instead-of reason, thus altering the patient's experience of the experience.

"I am sorry I'm late, but the traffic . . ."
"Perhaps there was something in our last meeting."
Oh-oh!

Insofar as the patient discovers that anxiety evaporates when he or she dares to know of what he or she experiences, the patient will less "automatically" use the defensive transfigurations he or she can identify as such. Consequently, more and more of the constituents of the experiencings will become available, though still in the form they took as a result of transformations effected by earlier versions of himself or herself. These constituent elements are, in this sense, derivatives. We may know that the experience the patient is now describing or remembering was not ever thus, but the patient does not. To the patient it is so. And, if the patient's same-self forebears have done their job well, what the patient knows and remembers will have such verisimilitude that the counterfeiting can hardly be spotted—and certainly not by the patient who has so much reason to maintain his or her revisionisms.

Perhaps the most fundamental of the original transformations is this: *"She would if she could"* into *"She could if she would."* With it sorrow transforms into anger; resignation converts to hopefulness, and despair and helplessness blossom into a thousand possibilities concerning what *I* can do to induce her to do what she *can* (now!) do—if *she wants to.* The possibility that she does not do it because/therefore she is bad, leads to one whole branching of the tree (as the twig is bent). Alternatively there is the possibility that she does not do it because/therefore I am bad, leads to another. "Bad" may be in terms of wicked ("I must reform"), size ("I must act big"), gender ("I must change"), and so on; each is fateful. A third transformation is *"She could if she would but will not because (or therefore) someone else is bad and coercive."* This leads toward a 'manic' view, as the previous ("I am bad") leads toward a 'depressive' view and the first ("She is bad") to a 'paranoid' view.

Perceived and remembered experience will be derivatives of this fundamental transformation and the various ones that followed upon it. From them one can infer what the patient cannot and could not bear to experience. These form the basis of working from the derivatives, here and now, to the deeper experiences, then and there. The rules of thumb follow the order in which the transformations were established: the last is first.

In the spirit of dynamic psychotherapy, however, rules are made to be broken. Early in the history of psychoanalysis, people experimented with saying such things as: "You wish to kill your father and lie with your mother, no?" The patient, visualizing the plump, dowdy, middle-aged woman who was his fairly irritating mother, thought it was perhaps his new-found therapist who could do with help of a rather urgent kind. If he confided this thought, it would be "interpreted" as hostile and castrating. "I am the father of whom you are afraid because of your wish to get rid of me and take the mother for yourself, hein?" If, at this, the patient got really angry, the therapist might be heard to give a little grunt of satisfaction. All the same, wild interpretations of this sort did not seem to help much, and the rules of thumb were given respectful development.

Wild "interpretations" of the sort I have parodied did not work, not because they leapfrogged where the patient was in his or her transformations, but because they drew from the books and not from the patient. The assumption behind wild interpretations was that experience is layered, with fictions overlaying the actual experience, but not really replacing them. The recognition that people have to remember what to forget if they are to repress the right bit of knowledge is part of this. We more or less express this when we speak of "at some level . . ." or "somewhere he must have known . . ." or "part of me. . . ." The transformed and the original experience are both present, simultaneously.

Actually, however, experience is not layered vertically or horizontally, but continually, being at once experienced and transformed, with the former in fleeting glimpses of the actual. It can be reached for and found by interpretations that do not follow the rules of thumb.

The breaking of these rules involves interpretations of a rather different sort. The experience to which they allude is what patients are continually doing to, with, and about their therapists: the transformation that is the transference. Everything the patients do has this element in it—what they say, how they say it, what they do not say, why they do not say it. Patients are continually acting upon their therapists—whom they do not know—as if therapists were people or something they know and must deal with in ways designed to avert a catastrophic experience and foment a good one. Accordingly, in Bion's (1970) phrase, the therapist listens not only for the meaning in what the patient is communicating, but for the use to which those communications are being put. No patient simply communicates information regarding his or her experiences—and certainly not for a long time. Patients speak for effect.

Let us say that a patient speaks in such a way as to seek to draw from his or her therapist a kind word. If we are lucky as therapists, we can sense this, intuit it. But even if we cannot intuit it from our responses to what the patient is doing, it will presently become possible to infer it from what the patient is telling us. If we still cannot tell, some patients will lose patience with us and overtly demand "feedback" or "some response." Some patients will even stipulate that warmth and caring are wanted.

In this, as in the figure in the carpet, the therapist may imagine he or she discerns the configurations of the patient's relationship to the therapist as mother or, equally likely as breast, from whom the milk of human kindness is being drawn. What sort of breast is it that the patient conjures when he or she proceeds in this way? Where does goodness lie; where is catastrophic frustration? If the therapist can bear to experience himself or herself as breast being dealt with in a number of quite particular ways, why does not the patient tolerate the experience in such graphically precise terms? What factors has the patient to contend with that the therapist is spared? In whom, breast or mouth, are these factors located by the patient, that he or she proceeds in such a fashion? What early experiences can have accounted for this patient's particular re-creation?

All of the information necessary to answer these questions is available to the therapist whose intuitive, inferential, and imaginative faculties are unimpaired. That information is in both what the patient communicates and in the effects he or she seeks. "Why am I being told this?" joins "What am I being told?" as coequal in the therapist's own interpretive meditations. When the therapist finds something to say, he or she will, of course, be aware that what is said is being experienced as emanating from the breast (or the space where the breast is supposed to be but is not, or the mouth, if the patient imagines that he or she possesses the breast and has been giving the therapist food for thought) and that his or her interpretations are at once being experienced as further information about the breast, feedings, and incitements to envy.

"Do you see what I mean?"
   "Yes, I think so. Your wife didn't understand that . . ." (of the rules-of-thumb procedure becomes perhaps): "The breast needs to be primed, as if one can't be sure it knows it's needed."

All the good rules of thumb are violated, as they should be when the spirit of the enterprise takes precedence over the letter of it. We need the rules because we need to do something while we learn from the patient what his or her plight is and how, with our interpretations, we can help the patient retrace any transformations and be able to experience at 30 what the patient could not endure at 3 months of age.

In a lovely paper, Guntrip (1975) speaks of his first analytic session with Winnicott. Guntrip lies on the couch, and Winnicott sits in a wooden chair behind him, sipping tea. Guntrip has done all the talking and now the session is at its end. The analyst, Winnicott, has nothing helpful to say as yet. All he knows is that he is Guntrip's Mummy and that Guntrip, who is also an analyst, is likely to experience Winnicott's continued silence as if it were a nonfeeding from a bad mother with no-thing to offer him. Since that is the most and the least Winnicott can say, he says: "I have nothing particular to say yet, but if I don't say something, you may begin to feel I'm not here."

In that, one can see references to anxiety, defense, and so forth. The rules of thumb are not wholly absent. But there is the leapfrogging to the heart of the matter—the use to which Guntrip was putting his communication and so the meaning that silence would have. The original and actual are directly culled from the transfigured and fictive. Dr. Guntrip is introduced to himself at an early age. They meet and can stand each other, which is really rather nice, as things go.

SUMMARY

The line "Lady, three white leopards sat under a juniper tree," from Eliot's "Ash Wednesday" can be read as is or as a line intended at once to evoke sensuous images and to convey the beginnings of a prayer to the Virgin concerning the mysteries of death and the intimations of hope and resurrection. Eliot, I believe, intends for the reader to interpret the line in the direction I have suggested; the image contains these meanings; they are not meant to be concealed.

The little boy lying still as can be in his bedroom for fear of disturbing the leopard in the night-shrouded corner has also created an imagaic fragment. Unlike the poet, however, who can interpret his own symbols, the little boy no longer knows what the leopard is meant to represent. The leopard contains meanings that are meant to conceal, not reveal, an aspect of experience. Bad as his fear of disturbing the beast is, worse, we can surmise, would be the opening out of the contained experience: a powerful, lithe leopard, ravenous with desire, unsuspectedly springing, throwing its weight upon a dear soft creature, turning it upon its back and plunging its fangs into the soft underbelly, while other, equally hungry, leopards stalk and skulk, jealous and furious, amid the sweet sickly smell of blood and heat.

Meanings meant to be revealed through interpretation and those meant to be concealed from interpretation require rather different treatment. Accordingly, much of this chapter is devoted to the conditions under which interpretive insights can be transmitted to a patient, who, like the little boy of my example, might rightly believe that his or her cure, the phobia, is better than the therapist's, psychodynamic psychotherapy.

Alone in his rooom, the little boy has only the configuration of his clothes heaped on the chair to sculpt his leopard from and himself to enact the other role in the couple—the victim. In a two-person psychotherapy, there are two people, and if the adult in one's consulting room is to realize what his when 4-year-old forebear was like, he or she has to realize that the leopard in the shadows was to the child the patient once was as his therapist is to the current self—that the dynamics of the transfigurations are the same and that these dynamics are similary motivated. The decrease in the self-deceptions of the adult have to be accompanied by a counterpart decrease in the self-deceptions of the child. Memories from childhood can then give way to memories of childhood.

Interpretation is, as such, an activity within a process. Since interpretations given by leopards differ in intent, and so (one hopes) in effect, from those offered by psychotherapists, the patient's natural wish and lifelong habit of confusing the two needs continual attention. The utterly essential condition is that the psychotherapist not be predatory, at least toward his or her patients. Given that essential, the ways by which the patient transforms the therapist, the purposes these transformations continue to serve, and the dangers averted by containment and concealment can all become subject to interpretation.

The means by which the data are displayed to the patient for affirmation or refutation are considered in the last portion of the chapter. The main thing here, of course, is that two minds are hard at work with equal access to the raw material of expereince, with the entire research project done with great consideration.

REFERENCES

Bion, W. R. *Experiences in groups.* New York: Basic Books, 1961.

Bion, W. R. Book Reiew: Eissler's medical orthodoxy and the future of psychoanalysis. *International Journal of Psychoanalysis,* 1966, *43,* 575–581.

Bion, W. R. *Attention and interpretation.* New York: Basic Books, 1970.

Boris, H. N. On hope: Its nature and psychotherapy. *International Review of Psychoanalysis,* 1976, *3.*

Boris, H. N. The problem of anorexia nervosa. *International Journal of Psychoanalysis,* 1984, *3.*

Boris, H. N. The treatment of anorexia nervosa. *International Journal of Psychoanalysis,* 1984, *4.*

Boris, H. N. *Sleights of mind.* Unpublished manuscript.

Breuer, J., and Freud S. (1895) Studies in hysteria. *Standard edition,* Vol. 2. London: Hogarth Press, 1955.

Eissler, K. R. Notes on problems of technique in the psychoanalytic treatment of adolescents. *The psychoanalytic study of the child*, Vol. XIII. New York: International Universities Press, 1958, pp. 223–254.

Freud, A. Problems of technique in adult analysis. *Bulletin of the Philadelphia Association for Psychoanalysis*, 1954, *4*, 44–46.

Freud, S. (1900) The interpretation of dreams. *Standard edition*, Vols. 4 and 5. London: Hogarth Press, 1953.

Freud, S. (1918) From the history of an infantile neurosis. *Standard edition*, Vol. 17. London: Hogarth Press, 1955.

Gardner, H. *Frames of mind*. New York: Basic Books, 1983.

Guntrip, H. My experience of analysis with Fairbairn and Winnicott. *International Review of Psychoanalysis*, 1975, *2*, 145–156.

Hartmann, H. Psychoanalysis as a scientific theory. In: S. Hook (Ed.), *Psychoanalysis, scientific method and philosophy*. New York: International Universities Press, 1959.

Klein, M. The origins of the transference. *International Journal of Psychoanalysis*, 1952, *33*, 433–438.

Laing, R. D. *Self and others*. New York: Pantheon Press, 1969.

Miller, J. *States of mind*. New York: Basic Books, 1983.

Sullivan, H. S. *The interpersonal theory of psychiatry*. New York: W. W. Norton, 1953.

Szasz, T. On the experience of the analyst in the psychoanalytic situation. *Journal of the American Psychoanalytic Association*, 1956, *4*, 197–223.

Winnicott, D. W. Hate in the counter-transference, Chapter XV. *Collected papers*. New York: Basic Books, 1958.

Winnicott, D. W. *The piggle, an account of the psychoanalytic treatment of a little girl*, Ishak Ramzy, (Ed.). New York: International Universities Press, 1977.

13
Interpretation: Clinical Application

JOSEPH M. NATTERSON, M.D.

An interpretation is a statement that conveys the latent meaning of a patient's thoughts, feelings, or actions. This communication of knowledge from therapist to patient is more than a cognitive event; it is inseparable from the total therapeutic relationship. The purpose of an interpretation is to enhance the self-understanding and self-awareness of the patient, which then leads to conflict resolution. It is offered when the patient is ready and receptive, although this may not always be obvious.

Usually interpretations should be framed as working hypotheses by a friendly, nonauthoritarian therapist. But within this framework, much stylistic variation exists from therapist to therapist, and from patient to patient with the same therapist. Sometimes an interpretation should be conveyed in a categorical and forceful manner if the therapist feels that the patient resists through vagueness. Or a therapist may prefer to be parsimonious with interpretations on the basis that a patient avoids self-confrontation if the therapist too actively constructs and delivers interpretations. Each therapist eventually develops his or her own interpretative style, but this style should be flexible enough to accommodate to changing circumstances.

Interpretations involve the passionate existence, both interior and interpersonal, of the patient. The interpretation is addressed to the life issues of the patient, such as fantasy life, self concept, significant ongoing relationships (especially the patient–therapist relationship), and connections between present and past life experiences.

PAST–PRESENT INTERPRETATION

Interpretations are always made in a psychological context or process. Therefore, interpretations of discrete symptoms, affects, or behaviors without regard for the therapeutic circumstance can be disruptive. They divert attention from the underlying therapeutic process and generate basic confusion while ostensibly providing insight and clarification. On the other hand, if these phenomena can be linked through the patient's associations to some crucial life issue, an interpretation of this kind can be quite valuable. For example, an interpretation of a symptom that connects the symptom to important historical circumstances may be powerfully effective.

C.M., a sensitive, young married woman, suffered from severe, recurrent gastrointestinal cramps. After several years of therapy, and at a time when she was describing her paranoid maternal grandfather who always carried a gun, I told her that, as a family legacy, she suffered "intestinal paranoia." Her mother was an obsessively worrying woman who had been a chronic vomiter during the patient's childhood. So, in fleshing out my interpretation, I proposed that the dynamics of her maternal family had involved the transmission of high levels of anxiety and vigilance from one generation to another, resulting in the spastic colon of the patient reflecting her own chronic inability to relax. She was amused, pleased, and apparently helped by my interpretation because it aided her in recognizing that her surplus anxiety in the present was attributable to conflicts engendered in the past. Interpretation linking past and present was the type most frequently employed with this patient.

Past–present interpretations are especially helpful and satisfying for a patient, such as the one described, for whom the historical dimension is an active part of his or her conscious psychological life. By contrast, patients who suffer from a kind of ahistoricity are in desperate need of openings into the past, yet they tend to be refractory to such interpretations. In these instances the therapist should work on their resistances to the historical perspective, and this sometimes leads to greater receptiveness.

INTELLECTUALIZED INTERPRETATIONS

Certain patients, particularly those who employ denial and manic defenses, require a specific interpretive approach usually eschewed in other cases. These patients do not provide the optimal admixture of shifting emotions and ideas that the therapist can use as the raw materials for the construction of experience-near interpretations. Hence relatively intellectualized interpretations, based on the therapist's understanding of psychodynamics, are necessary. These patients are often very depressed and chaotic beneath a facade of energetic purposefulness. If they have developed a strong bond with the therapist, then such intellectualized interpretations may restore a degree of inner order and coherence in these patients, even though they consciously disbelieve the interpretations.

In one such case, a depressed middle-aged woman came to see me for help in coping with the death of her 20-year-old leukemic daughter several years earlier, and with having been left shortly thereafter by her husband, whom she loved deeply. She was charming and cheerful, and she drove her car in a very unobserving and dangerous manner. While she felt she was recovering from the loss of her daughter, she was far less able to deal with the loss of her husband. There were two other adult children, a daughter and a son. This woman had undergone therapy with another therapist several years earlier with limited success, and immediately before starting with me, she had started with still another experienced therapist, whom she found excessively formal and unavailable. She quickly established a warm relationship with me in which she felt relieved and hopeful. Two factors contributed to the rapid development of strong rapport. First, when she initially telephoned me and told me of her discouragement with her more recent psychiatrist, I immediately inferred a need and responded to her with warm, active interest during this initial call. Second, she told a close woman friend she had called me—a woman who, by chance, had been in treatment with me a number of years earlier when *her* daughter was dying of leukemia. The friend related to the patient how helpful her therapy with me had been, thus reinforcing the patient's positive attitude.

She painted a grim family portrait—in a cheerful manner—of a severely depressed mother who never recovered from the death of an infant son before the patient's birth, and who had made several suicide attempts, and was chronically ill; of a physician father who was invariably cheery but relatively indifferent to the mother; and of two older sisters who were chronically depressed—one severely so and who committed suicide several years before the patient began therapy with me.

Although bright and empathic, the patient was singularly unable to integrate fairly obvious interpretations, such as my pointing out her hostility to her husband. She knew she had been designated the successor to her dead brother and that she was her father's favorite, but it was difficult for her to accept the interpretation that her identification with her father had saved her from the more severe depressions of her sisters who had to rely on identifications with the seriously ill mother. I began interpreting her response to her introjection of her mother's depression—filled with guilt and rage toward the frustrating mother; she listened and understood, but assured me that this made no psychological sense to her. I persevered, and she listened. Later, I extended the interpretation by saying that this profound, mother-linked depression was her basic problem, but that it coexisted with a strong sexualized attachment to her father that engendered guilt and anxiety, and that overlaying these was her peppy, denying surface. I said that these would have to be understood much better in order to liberate her true self. For clarity and emphasis, I presented this to the patient in the following verbal diagram.

1. Cheery, hypomanic, denying surface.
2. Guilty, anxious, eroticized involvement with father—including identification, producing—
3. Pregenital rage, guilt, and symbiotic preoccupation with mother—depression.
4. Patient's true self.

For many months she talked, and we argued over my interpretations, which I derived from basic psychodynamic assumptions buttressed by some of her dream material. Her repudiation of my interpretation was, however, coupled with a profound respect for me that was very sustaining for her. An interpretation she understood, and which made her feel good, consisted of pointing out her exceedingly high development of empathic understanding of other people, coupled with an incongruous inability to use this quality in her approach to her own life. This interpretation of a massive inhibition always made sense to her.

Eventually patience paid off. She began talking of the blighting effect her depressed mother had on her own development, and it was no longer necessary for me continually to introduce the subject. More dramatic was the recall of an event that had occurred about one year prior to the beginning of her work with me. The patient had arranged to be buried next to her dead daughter. But since it was a crowded cemetery, the arrangement was made for the patient to be placed *beneath* her daughter rather than beside her. That same evening, she dreamed her dead daughter was an infant in a crib; when the patient lifted her out, she discovered herself as an infant underneath her daughter in the crib.

She recalled this grim event and the accompanying dream just as she was achieving greater awareness in the therapy of her fateful early relationship to her mother. This meant that the earlier planting of relatively intellectualized interpretations was now bearing experiential fruit: the awareness of submergence of her own crucial needs to those of others (first mother, then husband); the recognition of the powerful depressive impact of her mother; the symbolic portrayal of awareness of a layering of her personality structure; the realization of the necessity for finding and releasing her true self under the layers of neurotic traits.

Intellectualized interpretations tend to be experience-distant, not emotionally felt, by the patient or therapist. They are useful with patients such as the above who have a paucity of useful ideas. Also patients with extreme anxiety and confused thinking may be helped to achieve inner coherence and structure by clearly stated, intellectualized interpretations. The obvious hazard is that patient or therapist may resistively employ intellectualization to impede the emergence of experiential understanding.

EMPATHIC INTERPRETATIONS

In recent years the emphasis on empathy in psychotherapy has been accentuated by the work of Kohut (1977). He noted that many patients feel attacked or criticized by standard interpretations of impulse and defense. If such hurt feelings block rather than facilitate therapeutic progress, he concluded that the nature (or form) of the interpretations should be revised. Instead of emphasizing unconscious drives and defenses, Kohut dealt with patients' desperate longing for loving admiration and their yearning for union with idealized persons. These "empathic" interpretations are intended to search out, define, and validate self needs, and generally they subordinate the issue of aggression. Such interpretations, by the way, need not be regarded as discovered and developed by the Kohutians. Reasonably sensitive therapists have always attempted to avoid being hurtful in their interpretations, knowing that poorly timed and inconsiderately framed interpretations will breed resistance. Empathic interpretations are especially valuable in the early periods of therapy, because many patients are unable to accept responsibility for their assertive, angry, or destructive components until their self-esteem has been raised and stabilized.

T.C. was a young, unmarried actress, sensitive and compassionate, but repeatedly hurt by the men with whom she fell in love. Her parents were not married; and while she lived with her mother, she suffered repeated disruptions of relationships with father figures. Although projected anger seemed quite evident in her dreams and in her fears of being abandoned by men, I postponed interpreting her rage until almost two years of therapy had elapsed. Instead, I focused on her generosity of spirit, her understandable fears of loss, her *guilt* over her sexuality and related desires, and her masochistic tendencies as reflected to some extent in her choice of lovers.

Prior to the more direct interpretations of aggression, I concentrated interpretively for several weeks on transitional phenomena. She spoke of needing to soothe herself at night with an electric heating pad (her version of a security blanket), and she enjoyed stroking a fuzzy stuffed bear. She would experience baffling oscillation of sexual arousal and indifference with her lover, and she began sleeping upside down in her bed, with her head at the foot of the bed. (I regarded both of these as transitional events.) She reported that my comments had become an important resource of comfort, and she talked of clutching my remarks betwen sessions; so I conveyed to her the concept that she was experiencing my words as transitional objects for relief as she was shifting from the symbiotic lack of self-definition and self-esteem to a more autonomous psychological existence. My actual words were to the effect that she clutched my comments as though they were like her security blanket from childhood and that she took home my words until she could see me again, as she attempted to become less dependent on me as a mother and to achieve more autonomy and self-confidence. A gratifying response occurred; the more or less overt transitional phenomena subsided; she became more direct in expressing her full range of affects—including anger; and her desperate, obsessive fantasies over a lost lover diminished.

Empathic interpretations are necessary and helpful for all patients. They are required with particular urgency and regularity in the treatment of patients with low self-confidence and self-esteem, and with patients who are inclined toward intense, defensive, hostile (paranoid-like) projections. One hopes that this extra emphasis can be reduced with successful work, but often this becomes evident only after very long periods of therapy.

TRANSFERENCE INTERPRETATIONS

Transference is, of course, of paramount importance in psychotherapy. All interpretations are influenced to a greater or lesser degree by the nature of the transference. Transference interpretations address the ongoing events and meanings in the therapeutic relationship. Such interpretations deal with the only data in the therapy that are shared by both participants and in that sense are the most direct and reliable resource for understanding the patient's psychological life. Although some value inheres in categorization of various types of transference interpretations, the conditions and characteristics of transference are infinitely varied. Gill's (1982) recent work is an excellent resource for more detailed information. Perhaps the most urgent consideration is: "Do not force such interpretation." Premature transference interpretations, however correct in terms of unconscious processes, invariably breed resistance. It is always better for the therapist to lag a bit behind than to plow ahead too quickly.

A 29-year-old, single, female film producer had been in therapy about ten months. She began this session by announcing that she had had a dream that constituted a true epiphany for her. It was a complex dream that seemed to focus particularly on her growing awareness of *her* contribution to painful hostility between her and her mother. Whereas she had previously regarded herself as the victim of her neurotic mother's aggression, she now recognized, through the dream, her oedipally based wish to kill her mother and replace her mother as her father's mate.

Now she had been pleasantly surprised during a recent holiday visit to her parent's home in that her mother had been unusually warm and affirming of the patient's adult, feminine interests. So the dream converged with this in helping the patient become more aware of the destructive role of her oedipal wishes. The session was lively and, I thought, productive. Yet the patient entered my office next time telling me that she had been hurt and dismayed by my not being impressed by the importance of her "epiphany." Previously in the therapy when I had inquired about thoughts or feelings about me, she always insisted that she needed to perceive me as avuncular, competent, and wise. Only thus could she reveal to me her petty, inconsistent, ambivalent qualities. Although numerous signs of transference had been evident during this early period, I regularly made the judgment that interpreting them would be premature and probably disruptive. Now, however, she was telling me that she had been hurt by me in precisely the mode that she had so often told me her mother hurt her. Furthermore, she was able to report this feeling to me just as she was feeling better toward her mother and able to appreciate how she, herself, wished to hurt her mother. I pointed out that these feelings toward me were obviously derived from her feelings to her mother. She concurred, I added that this was the first occasion when we had been able to mutually recognize feelings toward me that derived from family problems. Again she happily agreed, and added that now she was becoming able to experience me as a real person with variegated traits. I made the further general point that the reappropriation of disowned aggression can be very liberating.

She returned, interestingly enough, to her next session with a dream that I was having an affair, and that she was helping me, but that she was not my lover. She chose to focus on the dream as a reiteration by her of my humanness, and she specifically disclaimed any erotic feelings toward me. I once again decided to be prudent and not to challenge her view—despite the obvious erotic implication for the transference.

While the therapist should continuously monitor the state of the transference during psychotherapy, certain conditions indicate the need for transference interpretation. These conditions include: painful affect of obscure origin, which is blocking therapeutic progress; intensification of the patient's manifest interest in the therapeutic process or the therapist;

direct or thinly veiled reference to the therapist in dreams and fantasies. Stylistic considerations are important. For example, some patients, for lengthy periods, have great difficulty discussing the patient–therapist relationship directly, while other patients do so enthusiastically from the outset of therapy. Skillful therapists obviously adapt their interpretive approach to the patient.

INTERPRETATIONS LINKING THERAPEUTIC REALITY AND TRANSFERENCE

The interpretive use of therapists' idiosyncrasies can be very interesting and useful. A young female patient came for her regular appointment on a chilly, blustery day. She was tired and irritable from overwork, financial worries, and indecision whether to marry. She sadly recalled how, in her love relationships, she would become deeply involved, but the man would avoid complete commitment, and she would feel kept at a distance. The office was exceptionally chilly; my hands were dry and itching. At this point, I applied some hand cream and began to rub my hands together. The patient heard the activity, began to feel very rejected, and said, "You want to wash your hands of me." I pointed out that her lifelong fears of loss and abandonment generated her chronic anxiety, propelled her into relationships with men who would keep her at arm's length (repetition compulsion), and even caused her to have transference distortions of the same nature to the therapist.

Therapists, in my opinion, should not deliberately provoke patients, but for countertransference or other reasons, such provocations may occur. The likely patient response is to feel hurt, misunderstood, rejected, and angry. The therapist's options are basically to interpret the patient's response or acknowledge the reality basis for the patient's reaction, or both. The choice depends upon the basic strength and suppleness of the therapeutic relationship and upon the current defensive state of the patient. In this instance, I chose to interpret the patient's reactions; no reality acknowledgment was necessary. For some patients at some times, however, their sensitivity to rejection by the therapist is so overriding that the therapist must temporize interpretively. To interpret such reactions in terms of their unconscious conflictual meanings only enhances patients' feelings of being criticized and misunderstood.

For instance, a man entered psychotherapy with me after a brief, unsuccessful attempt at therapy with another male therapist whom the patient resented for alleged incompetence and insensitivity. Although the patient hoped that I would be more effective, he soon began to feel annoyed and anxious over my answering the telephone occasionally, my seeming brusqueness in greeting him as he entered my office, and the audible evidence of tension in my voice when I responded to his angry criticisms of my numerous failings. On one occasion, his appointment followed a terrible argument with his rigid father who had always demanded excellence in every way from the patient. The patient in turn harbored strong resentment toward the father. As the patient was recounting this painful encounter with his father, my secretary buzzed me regarding a matter she thought might be an emergency. I took a few minutes to discuss the matter with her. On my return, the patient erupted with fury, despairing that I could ever help him since I was so transparently disorganized and ineffectual.

Although I recognized that the roots of this rage rested in his conflicted relationship with his father, I was also aware that my inattention to therapeutic formalities, plus the unfortunate disruption of this session, had significantly contributed to his acute distress. I felt a guilty concern over this incident. So I concluded that it was necessary to acknowledge my various errors and assure him that henceforth I would be more careful about these significant matters.

It was not timely to interpret the obvious negative father transference inherent in these therapeutic events. From previous experience with this patient, I knew such interpretations could be offered more propitiously at a later, less painful, moment. At this time, however, the necessary therapeutic split in the ego—between the experiencing and the observing parts—was inoperative. The observing faculties of the patient needed to be reactivated in order for an interpretation of negative father transference to be useful.

Errors, acting out, or unavoidable deviations of behavior by the therapist regularly elicit strong reactions in the patient, which may be disruptive, potentially illuminating, or both. Many patients, unlike the two preceding cases, are reticent, and the alert therapist in such instances will raise the issue for discussion in the therapy. Therapists should strive to reduce error, but mistakes frequently occur. If handled skillfully, they may become a valuable therapeutic resource.

INTERPRETATION OF RESISTANCE

The interpretation of resistance is another complex and important issue that obtains in all therapy aimed at self-transformation through insight and enhanced consciousness. Interpretation of resistance does *not* mean telling a patient that he or she is resisting. In fact, therapists should scrupulously avoid using the term "resistance" in their remarks to patients. Any technical jargon is inappropriate because its cultish quality breeds resistance. It has been pointed out that the same behavior, fantasy, association, dream, or other therapeutic event that is seen as resistance at another time (or even simultaneously) may be evidence of progress. As Roy Schafer (1983) has written: "Resisting is not opposing the analysis . . . but rather [is] the analysand's next significant step in the analysis."

My example cannot begin to cover the manifold aspects of resistance interpretation, but I do intend to illustrate an effective interpretive approach with generic implications.

A middle-aged, overweight man came to therapy primarily because of depression, but he also complained of various phobias: flying, strange hotel rooms, and multiple other such fears. He was very unhappy in his third marriage. Although he was extremely successful, he felt burdened by his multitudinous responsibilities, and he anticipated a collapse of his business.

A technical problem confronted me. The patient told me repeatedly that he was feeling increasingly alienated from work, family, and friends. He believed no one else was aware of this, because he was able to maintain a facade of warmth, humor, and charm. Everyone considered him their "best friend," while he felt utterly friendless and alone. He also reported that he did not lose some of his surplus weight because as he began to have mental pictures of himself as a slim, virile man, he became anxious, even panicky. His mother had been a chronic, drug-dependent invalid from the patient's late childhood, and he early became a caretaking, self-sacrificing person. I perceived some pathological unconscious maternal identification in all this, but I was initially unable to mobilize mutative forces. I began to notice, as the months wore on, that a profound discontinuity existed. He often felt relief during a session from some interpretation of mine. However, I never knew from one session to the next what his condition would be. This circumstance coexisted with a striking lack of spontaneous thematic continuity in his associations. That is, even a powerful interpretation in the previous session would not be alluded to in the following session. I constructed a meaning and said to the patient, "Basically, you are struggling against recognition of an unconscious identification with your sick mother. You not only loved her, but you hated her, and you felt very guilty toward her. Yet she and your crucial memories of her are a vital part of you, despite your struggle against this realization. So long as you are unable to recognize that she exists as a part of you, you will be correspondingly crippled in your life. The recognition and acceptance of her in you will be very strengthening." He replied that this was a very important insight, that even though we had previously discussed an identification with her and how her chronic invalidism had damaged his life, he had only now been able consciously to appreciate that an active part of him consisted of her. When he came for his next session, he announced that his depression had greatly subsided, but as usual, he made no effort to connect this session with the last one, even though I felt that the events that had transpired in the session before were the basis for his improvement. This enabled me to extend the preceding interpretation with this follow-up. I suggested that his inability to connect contiguous sessions in our dialogue arose from his prior inability consciously to experience his deep identification with his mother. In fact, I averred, by maintaining a discontinuity of the sessions, he had been able to retard progress toward awareness of the maternal identification. I suggested that the discontinuities of this therapeutic behavior represented his acting out of his identification with his disorganized mother. (Furthermore, I thought, but did not state, that to the extent that his neurotic behavior in the therapy reduced my effectiveness, it might also be intended to make me into the ineffectual mother.) But now, I proposed, since he had become aware of this identification and its disabling consequences, he might be more able to maintain consciousness of the therapeutic process. He understood this, considered it accurate and liberating, and began showing considerably more continuity between sessions.

An interpretation may be regarded as addressing resistance when its emphasis is on the removal of a block in memory, insight, or process. This becomes a matter of degree, since every interpretation is intended to facilitate something. The therapist's awareness of resistance is often retrospective; an effective interpretation enhances therapeutic movement, and the therapist then clearly can perceive the nature of the resistance that preceded the new condition.

AFFECT-LADEN INTERPRETATIONS

In the past, the role of affect in interpretation was not often enough accorded its proper importance. The basic attitude of the therapist to the patient and its inescapable impact on interpretations has already been noted. In addition, colorful language, dramatic gestures, and similar expressions of affect can contribute to interpretive effectiveness. The interpretation that strives to create or evoke an intense emotional experience is particularly useful for a patient who is overintellectualized as a result of some repressive influence, but who appears to the therapist to be now less intensely repressed and needs some assistance in crossing the affective threshold.

A man in his late 50s was a heavy smoker, and he wished for my help in breaking the habit. He had developed a persistent cough and was becoming fearful of serious lung disease. I referred him to a pulmonologist, who found no illness. In the course of his therapy, he had relinquished much of his appeasing, submissive behavior. I graphically told him that he was making himself victim of the hot, searing, charring smoke—an evil, destructive vapor emitted by the same witch or devil parent who had always terrorized him into submission. I grimaced and made writhing, menacing movements with my arms, hands, and fingers as I conveyed these remarks. He was startled and bemused; and he stopped smoking.

A woman patient from New York, who was emotionally quite isolated, always seemed finicky, and behaved as though she feared being messy or attacked. I had two images of her. One was that she and her mother would go regularly to some fashionable Manhattan tearoom for Saturday lunch, and the other was that she always needed to keep her flannel skirt smoothed out while she wore it. I told her that she talked and moved as though she feared she might see, hear, touch, or smell something ugly or offensive. My impressions, conveyed to her in somewhat playful fashion, were part of a broader approach to her massive defenses against emotional contact and freedom, because such concrete, visual images were more difficult for her to isolate by intellectualization.

A 45-year-old man in intensive treatment seemed never to relax. He did not believe in himself as a husband, father, or scholar—all of which he was. His enormous self-doubt was understandable since he had been subjected to extreme psychological abuse by his parents when he was young. For example, his mother told him that his birth had caused her serious later illness. And his father told him later that his mother had developed abdominal cancer because the patient's adolescent mustache had harmed the mother when he kissed her. Both parents had seemed to enjoy the many capriciously motivated beatings they administered to him. In early life he also had a severe case of poliomyelitis. In addition to addressing the more profound issues, I made many comments, also humorously, to the effect that he seemed like a little boy frantically dashing about trying to plug holes in the dike with his finger. These and similar images reflected my experience of him, and it was very important to keep his attention focused on his character defense. This man practiced hypervigilance to deflect the possible penetration of my more profound interpretations. Frequently, he would not let me complete a statement before he would begin to talk of some new hot spot of concern in his life. Or if he did permit me to finish my remarks, he would give me a perfunctory, "You're right," and then urgently divert to some other issue. It was at such moments that I would make the dike plugger or firefighter observations. These colorful comments usually tended to be secondary or auxiliary, in that my intention was to use them to prevent defensive diversionary efforts by the patient and to help keep his attention directed to the central issue of the discussion.

Patients in the course of therapy may require the support of undisguised encouragement by the therapist, the restraint of firm limit setting, or the relief of an amused therapist. The therapist's decision is based on sensitive, empathic appraisal. Since therapists are not immune to narcissistic or exhibitionistic temptations, such affective interventions require continuous self-scrutiny by the therapist.

INTERPRETING INHIBITION

An elaborate neurotic structure may deceive a patient for a lifetime, unless a skillful therapist supervenes. Even such a therapist may be misled for an extended period, until the underlying inhibition is understood and exposed. Clinical manifestations of inhibition are by no means easily discerned. Some people are obviously inhibited. Some, however, appear inhibited and in fact are not. Others suffer from massive inhibition but do not realize it, nor do others in their lives. The crucial facts of a patient's life may not be what they appear. How does the therapist become aware, and help the patient become aware, of the truth? In this case the real fact was the patient's inhibition of a deep and conflicted love that was concealed by complex narcissistic defenses.

The patient was a handsome man in his late 40s, divorced twice, with a child by each marriage. He came for psychotherapy because of anxiety and depression, and a feeling that he was basically a selfish sybarite. Half proudly and half sadly, he announced that he had never been faithful to a woman for more than three months and could only date women who "adored" him. He said he felt guilty but had to confess that he treated women like "dog shit." He attributed all this to the worshipful attitude of his mother and sister in childhood, which coexisted with the absence of the hard-working father. He implied that something was wrong with his relationships with women, and he acknowledged that he avoided relationships with capable women who might be more interesting, if less adoring. As a result of several years of psychoanalysis about ten years earlier, he assured me in so many words that he suffered from an intractable narcissistic personality disorder. I accepted this with a quizzical, frustrated acknowledgment. I could not ignore the evident narcissistic defenses, yet I felt that if I accepted his diagnosis, the therapy might be consigned to futility. I sensed some alternative possibilities that were more hopeful and that hinged on the concept of inhibition. I mention these interior responses of mine, because I believe they are part of the preparatory activity and the grounding of interpretations. My therapeutic responsibility to this man required that I reconceptualize his psychological situation, and not unquestioningly accept his warmed-over version of the conceptual and technical approach employed in his previous therapy.

I soon began to perceive that this patient felt much love, guilt, admiration, and deprecation for his father. And I constructed the notion that his central problem was his feeling that he could not permit himself to enjoy a stable, trusting relationship with a woman of depth and independence because of a certain reparational attitude toward his father. While the father had worked and slaved, the patient had enjoyed the eroticized adoration of his mother and sister. He felt superior to both these women, at least as he grew older, and so his current pattern might continue to reenact an oedipal victory while simultaneously constituting a guilt-based deprivation of fulfillment.

My conscious intent was to convince the patient that he was seriously inhibited and thus to encourage a collaborative search for the reasons for his inhibition. Achieving this primary goal required several corollary interpretive maneuvers. These included noting his frequent, moist-eyed references to his father as a hard worker who sacrificed so much for the family, and my careful pointing out how much love he felt for his father and how much possible guilt he experienced over benefiting so much and moving so far ahead of his father. I also began to express more doubt about the diagnosis of narcissism. I stated that he certainly showed a lot of narcissistic traits, but I told him that the diagnosis of narcissistic personality disorder did not seem to be very helpful. And I averred that, while he certainly behaved selfishly with women, I suspected that the net effect might well be more self-depriving than fulfilling. The last-mentioned point at first seemed especially farfetched, but with repetition and patient explanation of my reasoning, he found it more and more plausible.

After all this careful work, however, when I dared to tell him that I thought he might really be a seriously inhibited man, he just laughed. It seemed almost a matter of pride to him that he be regarded as a self-confident, heartless ladykiller who took his selfish pleasure with women and then abandoned them.

Gradually, he reconsidered even this last outrageous interpretation. This reconsideration was facilitated when I proposed a massive guilt-based inhibition due to his oedipal victory over a beloved father. He began to consider that just as his father had never enjoyed great business success (whereas the patient enjoyed enormous success in his career and was the world's most highly paid person in his field), so the patient had to fail in areas of love and family.

After about six months of such interpretation and intense discussion followed by more interpretation, this concept became consciously paradigmatic for the therapy—in both his mind and mine. Initially my comments were uncertain hypotheses in my mind and in my presentations. Although the transference was not conspicuous in these interpretive transactions, I think that his experience of me as a supportive older brother or father figure tended to elicit tender, confessional feelings, which facilitated the set that enabled me to make the formulations. In his previous therapy, his therapist, also male, but older and European (like his father), had tended to elicit a guilty and defensive therapeutic stance in the patient.

The central issue in this case was a powerful inhibition of important, normal life goals as a result of intense oedipal guilt in a highly sensitive and intelligent man who masked his basic problem with extremely narcissistic defenses.

Inhibitions may not be discernible early in therapy. They may, as in this case, lurk beneath compensatory and concealing characteristics, which initially point away from inhibition. An overtly angry patient may harbor strong inhibited desires to give and receive tenderness, while a patient who appears to be warm and loving ultimately may discover strong latent destructiveness. The importance of initially perceived characteristics is not undermined by the concomitant realization that such traits may help in the inhibition of differing tendencies. Optimally, the therapist should believe what he or she observes but should always be prepared for qualitative and quantitative variations of drastic nature.

WORKING THROUGH

A basic concept in psychotherapy is *working through*. It is implicit in all the material in this chapter. The foregoing case, with its repeated interpretations, both primary and secondary, and over many months, shows the therapist's role in the process of working through. The process, of course, occurs primarily in the patient who responds to relevant interpretations. Initial awe, scorn, outrage, hurt, or cautious acceptance may be followed by forgetting, naive expectation that the interpretation has cured the problem, only to be disillusioned by a hundred new manifestations of the problem or some other defensive stance. Optimally, the patient remembers and gradually extends the range of life meaning of a crucial interpretation, but even this productive tendency may occur in paradoxical form. For example, a reaction of anger to the therapist, as was shown in the case above, was a central aspect of the utilization of the new understanding and resulted in a very important transference interpretation.

Repetition over an extended period of time is the essence of working through. Associations, fantasies, dreams, symptoms, and relationships all reveal that the patient is at work on the particular problem. Thus in a psychological sense the interpretation is being metabolized, and fundamental transformation is occurring. The reiteration of the basic interpretation and its variations does not seem artificial or boring to either patient or therapist. It remains interesting and alive so long as the central problem remains unresolved and in focus.

RAPID-ACTING INTERPRETATIONS

In contrast to the preceding discussion of gradualism, some interpretations seem to work swiftly. When such an event takes place, it may indicate a relatively peripheral life problem, which nevertheless is the source of much psychological pain for the patient. Or a fundamental problem has been gradually covertly eroded by therapy, and the single interpretation now rapidly enables the problem to cross the threshold of consciousness. At times the effects of a correct and rapidly acting interpretation may again become submerged, and the interpretation will be required again at a later time and may once more be consciously felt by the patient to be new. Therapists should be alert to certain patients who are hungry for effective care. Such a patient may be uncritically accepting of an interpretation, which, correct or not, would be less eagerly received by a person in a more self-sufficient state.

A 36-year-old unmarried entertainer had a very sad history of physical and mental abuse by her psychotic father. She had been leading a very isolated life with a few women friends and a total repudiation of any relationships with men that were not safe and normal. As her therapy progressed, she began to experience a renewal of sexual desires, but she was, at that time, adamant in her refusal to date men. She began seriously to contemplate developing a sexual relationship with a woman. One woman friend was pursuing such a goal with the patient, but the patient resisted. She had been heterosexually active, often promiscuously, in her 20s, and she had also been a very heavy drug user. Some additional historical elements persuaded me that she was probably not homosexual, although she did feel some sexual arousal when she thought of women's bodies.

So I asked a question, knowing that it might very well function as an interpretation. I asked, "How do you feel about going down on a woman?" Her instant response was a feeling of intense distaste; she grimaced, expostulated, then laughed and said something to the effect that she got my point and realized that she was not homosexual. From that point, we began to work in a conscious and collaborative mode on the restoration of more satisfying relationships with men.

The same woman enjoyed another acutely powerful change in response to a *single* interpretation. Whenever she began to feel close to me, she would swiftly begin to feel hurt or invaded by some comment that I would make. These reactions produced agony for her, and were also painful for me. At these times she expressed regret over trusting me and felt convinced that I possessed psychological qualities like those of her father that caused me to need to hurt her. After many months of this pattern, I took courage and told her that although I could appreciate how she felt, and that undoubtedly some empathic lapse had occurred in me, nevertheless I thought she should know something else. I explained that, from my standpoint, I felt more like the little child being cruelly attacked and that she seemed like the harsh, relentless, implacable father at these times of crisis in the therapy. I added that one of the cruel ironies of life is that the sadistic aspects of her father were now part of her unconscious identity and contributed greatly to these recurrent episodes of psychological suffering in her relationship to me. This interpretation was immediately experienced as profoundly enlightening and transforming. From that moment she never experienced another episode of hatred and deep distrust of me.

These instances of swift effectiveness of interpretation exemplify a general characteristic of this patient that certainly is also true of other patients. Her therapeutic style requires dramatic, nodal events. Interpretive events similar to these examples, but less dramatic, have been abundant in her psychotherapy. The moments are obviously of the utmost importance, yet they do exist in an experiential context. The therapeutic process goes on quietly, building to these dramatic interpretive moments, followed by a new extended period of apparent quiescence. The cognitive style of the patient determines such a therapeutic pattern. This woman values and practices clarity, precision, and accuracy of verbal communication. Her responses to interpretation are congruent with this communicative tendency.

By contrast, some patients rarely or never respond rapidly to interpretation. Their integrative priorities may not include speed and clarity, or they may be deterred by a devotion to ambiguity, or they may be so burdened with anxiety that they do not yet dare define issues clearly. The therapist should appreciate the possible relevance of these issues as he or she attempts to understand why a patient responds rapidly or slowly to interpretations.

INTERPRETATION OF ABSENT AFFECT AND ASSOCIATIONS

The term "alexithymia" has entered the psychotherapeutic vocabulary. Its meaning is "no words for feelings." Such patients are unable to express themselves emotionally. They do not think emotionally, and they do not speak emotionally. Their mental behavior is characterized by operational thinking that is utterly devoid of manifest or accessible affect. Such patients may desperately need psychotherapy, yet they may be extremely difficult to treat.

A man in his mid-40s, divorced with two children, somewhat alcoholic, and a daredevil motorcyclist who had suffered many serious head injuries, came to therapy for anxiety and depression. In his career he had always been exceptionally successful. He had a history of moderately severe regional ileitis for the preceding several years, which was under good control. He told me that he saw no reason to continue living since he was now entering old age, and he could not stand the thought of becoming like his aged father, whom he described as a quitter. He also revealed that his mother had been a semi-invalid through his childhood because of rheumatic heart disease, and that she had died when he was a young adult. He also pointed out that his mother had emphasized the virtue of silence and the nonexpression of emotion.

This patient not only did not free associate, but he was amused in a disbelieving, scornful way when I offered psychological ideas or explanations to flesh out his scanty verbal productions. He practiced a rigorous mode of speaking only logically and systematically, excluding affect. I perceived him as quite alexithymic, and I explained this to him. It was never clear whether he could consciously understand alexithymia. Yet there were visible signs of anxiety: he looked tense and guarded; he perspired profusely in his chair, and later on the couch; and he complained of unilateral arm and shoulder pain and numbness, which he related to tension. At times he looked haggard and woebegone, but he could not explain such states. I attributed them to profound psychological distress, and he did not contest such speculations. On a few occasions, I asked questions involving confidential aspects of his professional activity or what a women friend thought or said about something. At such times he would become visibly angry and tell me that he resented my invasion of his privacy. The only acknowledgment by him of the value of being emotional with other people was in regard to his two children. He very specifically acknowledged fear that they might become unexpressive like him and that the quality of their lives might suffer thereby.

My interpretations were always directed to relaxing of his stringent defenses against affective communication. Depending on the opportunities and demands of the particular therapeutic instance, I approached him with several types of interpretive intervention.

Early in the therapy, I perceived no evidence for process interpretation or transference interpretation; thus the interpretations tended to be more of a past–present, historical content type. Since he spoke much more of his parents, and more negatively, early in therapy, I interpreted his hostility to his father, his fear of his identification with his father, and an associated deep concern that he would lose his strength as his father did, and that becoming overtly emotional would produce such an effect. I told him that since his mother had imposed such an austere code of expressiveness, he complied with this out of love and loyalty. (He often told me at this time that adopting an emotional way of expressing himself would constitute an act of disloyalty to her.) After about six months or a year of therapy, references to his parents became much fewer. I, however, would continue to tender interpretations about his mother, but now would emphasize guilt in his compliance to her edict and the rage toward her (inferred by me), leading to a withholdingness toward people as a way of passively–aggressively retaliating against his mother.

As I became more familiar with his current life patterns, I focused on his emotional stinginess. For instance, I would say that he would not speak in emotional terms in business relationships or in dealing with women because it would make him feel weak and vulnerable, so it made him feel safe and superior to be noncommunicative. These interpretations gradually became more and more routine, and he became more overtly unreactive to them. However, I always assumed that, in some way, they had meaning and value to him. A counterpart interpretation that gradually became characteristic dealt with him and me. I would say that he withheld his emotions about me for the same reasons as with others. I would insist, however, that I and the therapy meant a lot to him, but that he was one of those people in whom still waters run deep. He rarely would give any more in response to such interpretations other than to voice amazement at such exotic and alien ideas about communication or to say that he did not know how to do this task, but that he hated to stop because that would make him a quitter like his father.

I made numerous suggestions over the years that he should feel free to stop if he chose, but I was careful *always* to couple these remarks with a clear assertion that I felt he needed the therapy and that my opinion was that he should continue. Here the intention was to help him feel free and to reduce an inferred powerful, ambivalent mother transference by indicating respect for his freedom to choose, while at the same time conveying a definite message of nonrejection.

A final category of interpretation concerned dreams and his occasional ungarded associations. These were interpreted largely on the basis of my own associations and were offered in a tentative spirit with an explanation of their derivation.

I believe that my interpretations were effective, but I have no solid evidence to support this in terms of his verbal corroboration. Instead my evidence is indirect, and in one way paradoxical. The paradox is that during the first year of therapy, he gave me considerable developmental information, and he presented dreams fairly often. Over the years his

verbal productions became scantier and scantier, with historical information and dreams becoming quite rare. While this could be regarded as
evidence of therapeutic failure, I believe he made steady gains. His pa-
ternal involvement with his children improved; he became less remote
from co-workers; and, above all, he remarried. His new wife apparently
is a woman who places a high importance on affective communication and
seems to facilitate this in him. He, of course, remains very taciturn, even
secretive, with me about his relationship with her. Also, his sweating and
body odor have diminished, and he appears more relaxed and less anxious.

Cases such as this one tax the therapist's interpretive resources. Above
all the therapist must accept uncertainty and the distinct possibilities of
being unresponded to, ridiculed, harshly criticized, and responded to in
other nongratifying ways. These are themselves affective communications, and, while they are not of the optimal therapeutic variety, they
constitute small elements that over an extended time period build a therapeutic environment.

Chronically silent, unexpressive, severely withholding patients are
invariably challenging, even stressful, for therapists. The task of con-
structing and offering interpretations in a seeming void can be quite vex-
ing. In such circumstances the liberal use of consultation and supervision
is advisable.

IDIOSYNCRATIC INTERPRETATIONS

The variations of interpretive action are endless. In fact, while categorization of interpretation is useful, as the preceding examples demonstrate, it is nevertheless also true that each psychotherapeutic encounter
requires a unique interpretive invention. Usually the nonverbal communication from the patient is crucial. A fantasy is often stimulated in
the therapist that, in effect, defines the nature of the encounter. For
example, the therapist may have a distinct impression of dealing with a
sensitive child, hungry for parental love, or the therapist's fantasy may
consist of some emotion-laden memory of a childhood incident. The interpretation is constructed by weaving the data of the hour in with the
emotion revealed by the therapist's fantasy. It is my experience that most
patients respond to the authenticity of the interpretations with reduction
of anxiety and a renewal of therapeutic progress. Some brief vignettes
will illustrate.

A middle-aged woman had a very distracted and distracting speech
pattern, with unfinished sentences, introduction of new thoughts before
completing preceding ones, frantic gestures of hands, arms, and head,

and anxious and inappropriate giggling. I learned that she had been the youngest child in a large family, and as a little girl was not considered important enough to have her own bedroom. I began to have memories of childhood insecurity, so I repeatedly told her that she seemed to feel very insecure on this planet, that wherever she happened to be—for example, in my office—she felt she did not belong, had no place of her own, felt afraid to make her mark. The interpretations were directed more to her style of speaking than to the content of her remarks.

A young, unmarried man pondered long and hard before selecting a therapist, and then decided to see me. Although very pleased that I was able to find time for him, he immediately began peppering me with criticisms of my therapeutic behavior, and began providing me with lurid confessions of unconventional sexual behavior. I never felt really attacked by him; instead he seemed to be pleading for kindness. I insisted on interpreting his search for love (he had a psychotic mother, and his parents divorced during his puberty) and his hopes for understanding versus his fears of being misunderstood and rejected. He continued to mock and deride me, while simultaneously soaking up insight and acceptance. He demanded that I attack him but was regularly relieved and pleased that I continued to make the correct, empathic interpretations.

An artist in his mid-40s had a dream with a thinly veiled homosexual meaning. This man's effect upon me was very charming, almost erotic, so I sensed a probable underlying feminine urge in him. He was ultra-sophisticated and seemed impervious to shock regarding any unusual sexual interests. Nevertheless, I decided to make a straightforward interpretation of the homosexual wish, which had the effect of putting him off balance. He defensively assured me that he could hardly have any conflict over sexual feelings toward men because he had sampled homosexuality and found it only mildly diverting. I insisted that "the bigger they are, the harder they fall." I assured him I was not deceived by his defense of blasé sophistication. His quickmindedness then enabled him to penetrate his own self-deception. This was followed by an outpouring of dreams and associations revealing a strong unconscious feminine identification that had crucial linkage to early aspects of his relations with both his mother and his father.

It has become a virtual truism among psychotherapists that the countertransference is important—for good or ill. The idiosyncratic ingredients of interpretation derive from the unique fantasy and feeling of the patient interacting with the subjective response elicited in the therapist. Together these establish the vitally important intersubjective field from which and within which the interpretation is conceived, developed, delivered, and responded to.

CONCLUSIONS

Therapeutic action obviously involves change resulting from insight, which is the formal goal of interpretation. But change also takes place through the enhanced conscious experiencing of repressed aspects of the patient's life, which occurs through the nonverbal therapeutic holding environment and the empathic aspects of the therapist's interventions.

Interpretations have always been the primary instrument of psychodynamic psychotherapy. They basically address unconscious, and conflicted, aspects of the patient's psychological life. The clinical examples in this chapter are intended to demonstrate this.

Interpretations must be experiential as well as cognitive. The therapist's construction and conveyance of an interpretation are much more than a contribution to the intellectual understanding of the patient and his or her problems. In fact, it is an act of love, of faith, of hope. It implicitly assures the doubt-laden patient of the possibility of change through sharing with another caring person, based on the essential commonality of the human experience. It is useful to develop theories and categories of interpretation on the basis of their formal properties and indications. However, an essential quality of an interpretation is the passionate impingement and involvement of the therapist. Without this an interpretation is rote and lifeless, an insincere interpretation. An interpretation with conviction is necessary. Patients readily discern the difference.

REFERENCES

Gill, M. *Analysis of transference.* New York: International Universities Press, 1982.
Kohut, H. *Restoration of the self.* New York: International Universities Press, 1977.
Schafer, R. *The analytic attitude.* New York: Basic Books, 1983.

Index